Westward
the Course!

Westward the Course!

THE NEW WORLD OF OCEANIA

by

Paul McGuire

NEW YORK · 1942
WILLIAM MORROW & CO.

Published, February, 1942
Second printing, February, 1942
Third printing, April, 1942

PRINTED IN THE UNITED STATES OF AMERICA

Note

WESTWARD THE COURSE! was written during 1941, finished last September, and went to press two days after the Japanese bombed Pearl Harbor. Because this is a book about the southwestern Pacific, our editors naturally considered carefully whether or not the outbreak of war called for revisions or additions to the pages. Since Mr. McGuire's book concerns places and people—ideas and beliefs and history, rather than strictly contemporary events—the answer was "no."

Westward the Course! may be called a modern man's rediscovery of the great world in the southwestern Pacific. We use the word "rediscovery" because until very recently we in America have known little or nothing of the lands of Oceania. Interest has been developing slowly, and it took the Japanese attack on Honolulu to shock us into the general realization that Australia, New Zealand, the Dutch East Indies and British Malaya are in one sense very close and in every sense very vital.

Westward the Course! appears at a moment when, in the author's own words, "From New York to Sydney and from Sydney to Singapore, there is now one common character. It is in the American, the Dutch, and the British, it appears in the Indian, the Chinese, the Malay: it is that which struck off the ancient shackles and gives his final dignity to man. . . . This, in a sense, is a book about Empire. Political and material domination, if you like, but

v

also that Empire which is of the mind and spirit. . . .
The book is most concerned with the expansion of Western man and the Western mind in the lands under Asia,
beyond the Pacific, where our people, perhaps, recover
faith in themselves and in their work. . . . For here is
realized that which sounded in the soul of Europe when
first it heard the crashing doctrine of Free Will: that has
never ceased to echo there, never let us rest, never let us
become again fellaheen and slaves. . . . It appears as we
struggle for it, it exists in our effort. It is within us, and
we call it liberty."

THE PUBLISHERS

New York,
December 9, 1941

Contents

viii   *Contents*

Illustrations

MAPS

Westward
the Course!

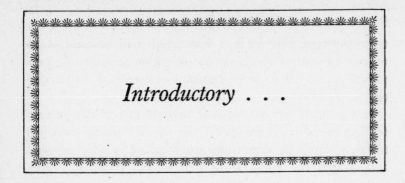

Introductory . . .

NEW YORK

THIS BOOK really begins on an autumn afternoon in 1940 when I had just returned from South America and sat talking to Thayer Hobson at The Players in New York. The world was very much with us that afternoon, our world and what Mrs. Lindbergh has prettily called the Wave of the Future. In South America I had seen its tide running in unexpected channels. Now, here in the North, was that same strange irresolution which has everywhere preceded the flood.

We were dismal that day, for it seemed then that our generation was fallen fatally into moral and intellectual confusion. Its breath was soured and its stomach revolted against strong doctrine, such doctrine as America once spoke: "We hold these truths to be self-evident, that all men are created equal, that they are endowed by their Creator with certain unalienable Rights. . . ."

That is fighting talk in a world which savagely disputes it. It represents the sense of a faith and a culture far older than Independence, a faith which gave us strength to slough our slavery and to reveal the Human Person, to make discovery of lands and knowledge, to open the waste places, to people the Americas, to command the islands of the sea, to enlarge the life of men in the West and to the East, to define and to defend liberty. We still had the doc-

3

trine perhaps, but what, I wondered, had become of its moral? Yet there had been an old persuasion of our peoples that it is the peculiar business of men and their societies to promote good and to resist evil.

It has been our virtue that through all our dark centuries of cruelty and stupidity we saw a light as on a hill towards which we sometimes stumbled. The only progress conceivable has come from that effort. When it ceases, then we are returned to our vomit, and upon us again is the darkness of the understanding and the weakness of the will.

We had been given a vision of a kingdom, a kingdom of man. But great things are realized in sweat and labor, in tribulations and fastings, and in a sense of what is real and necessary. Such kingdoms also are within us.

Or so it seemed to me (and perhaps to Hobson, though I would not wish it on him) that afternoon in New York, when we conceived this book. Nor do I recant. We have still to know whether the fire will melt or purify our world. But, if we are not "changed, changed utterly," yet "a terrible beauty is born."

This, in a sense, is a book about Empire: political and material dominion if you like, but also that Empire which is of the mind and spirit, and of what we call a way of life: the dominion which Western man has put out in the world. It belongs to our civilization as the history of some individual's life belongs to him. We may like it as little as we like ourselves, but it is all that we have, except the future. It belongs to us, with our sins upon it, but also with what was ours of greatness and of goodness.

The book is most concerned with the expansion of Western man and the Western mind in the lands under Asia, beyond the Pacific, where our people, perhaps, recover faith in themselves and in their work. But I do not think it out of place that the book should begin in the greatest of all imperial cities and at the heart of Western man's new dominion. For America is an Empire too.

EMPIRE AND CULTURE

Empire, amongst the British stocks, has been an affair of their two dominant characters, their pragmatism and their poetry: the characters in which Englishmen and Americans are most alike.

The English went to India and Africa and Oceania for the reasons that set the wagon wheels rolling to the Mississippi and beyond. There was profit in Asia, but there was also poetry in the passage: and along the Oregon Trail men were thinking of the pastures and the pinelands at the end of trail, but they were thinking too of the vision that is over the hills and far away. The restlessness of the frontiersman was like the restlessness of a poet. He created but he was not content with his creation. As humanity settled behind him, he up-staked and moved on, from frontier to frontier until the last frontier, breaking the earth, cutting the roads, breeding the herds, in what is justly called an epic. The Australians had the same restlessness as they drove their sheep and cattle into the wilderness. They had the same disquiet: there was always better country further out.

The British were born to the sea, and their islands had been peopled from the sea, from Celts, Phoenicians, Romans, Saxons, Danes, and Normans. They had adventure and salt in their veins: and phantasy. From their narrow lands they expanded necessarily across the oceans, but the men of Connecticut and Virginia and Massachusetts had a continent before them, and their Empire followed the wheelruts over mountains and prairies. The American colonist fought his little wars with his Indians as Britain fought little wars from Kabul to Coromandel.

California, Texas and the Lone Star prefigured Jameson and Rhodes. Both British and American Governments lagged behind their traders, settlers, whalers and gold-diggers.

The United States has knit into a nation partly because her empire was a geographic unit, partly because she was able to colonize her spaces with her own civilization, partly because the aborigines were too weak to retain their separate culture and armed strength, but mostly because her people finally accepted, after 1865, a single system of government and one philosophy of politics. Britain has not attempted that unity over all her realms. Canada, Australia, New Zealand, South Africa have grown their national structures and polities, India has preserved her own life. They remain an association of nations rather than one nation. In both, freedom was enlarged upon the earth.

QUIRÓS, MENDAÑA, TORRES

I was, that afternoon, much in mind of a man whose curious adventures in life had in part prompted my visit to South America; and he has constantly recurred to me in the course which this book takes, for he is something of a symptom and a symbol; and he belongs eternally to the westward passage of the Pacific, which this book makes.

His name was Pedro Fernandez de Quirós, and he was one of the last of the great Portuguese pilots. He comes out of the shadow of history as a competent, working pilot on the coast of Peru, chosen (perhaps because the Portuguese were said to have special, secret knowledge of the South Seas) as navigator by Alvaro Mendaña de Neyra for his voyage of 1595. It was Mendaña's second effort to find the Great South Land, the Terra Australis premised by the ancient geographers as a necessary counter-weight in this uncertain world to the vast land-masses of the northern hemisphere. Mendaña had sought it long before when he was a young man, and saw the islands that he thought Ophir and so named for King Solomon. All his life afterwards, Mendaña dreamed of renewing and extending his discoveries, but he waited thirty years for approval and resources.

His ambitions, as men's usually are, were mixed. Like most of his fellows, he sought gold and spices, El Dorado and Cipango. He sought too dominion, new territories for the Royalty of Spain and a Vice-royalty *in perpetuum* for the house of Mendaña. With these ambitions was interwoven another theme, the old sense of apostolate which is at the root of European dynamics. The Christian then still remembered that he had been given a mission to the world. He did not believe with us that one truth is as good as another because both are probably wrong. He still had faith in his creed and his culture.

Mendaña's lustier ambitions were probably those of his clay: royalty, riches, and a loud name in the world. But on this voyage with Quirós he was an old man, travelling to his death in the Marquesas, and during those last months his mind must have been more on God than on the bubble reputation. His wife was with him and people of his family, concerned for the Vice-royalty to come: but she was a strange, hard woman who carried the expedition off to the Philippines after his death and there married, out of hand, a young caballero. The Portuguese pilot may have been easier company for the dying man; but, however it was, in the course of that voyage Quirós suddenly saw through old Mendaña's eyes and further. He caught a sudden vision of the City of God.

It rose before him like a mirage out of the blue waters and the green islands of Oceania, and it took possession of him. When the expedition ended at Manila, and he somehow worked back to Mexico, he was already its passionate instrument. He would return to the south and he would raise up the Christian City in the still undiscovered Antipodes.

He sailed to Spain. Through years of grinding poverty he walked and talked his way to Rome and from Rome back to Spain, to the Pope and to the King. Somehow, with his strange fever on him, he made himself heard in the two greatest courts of his world: and his stubborn solicitude at last moved wheels in the slow machinery of the Vatican and Madrid. Quirós, ten years after his parting with Mendaña, sailed out of Lima with a squadron of ships and a commission to discover, to colonize, and to convert the fifth part of the world.

Early in 1606, he reached an island of the New Hebrides which he took to be some out-thrust of the Unknown Continent. He called it Espiritu Santo, the land of the Holy Spirit. There, with every solemnity, spiritual and temporal, and with all the offices of a European state, he set up his kingdom of God. It endured for several months.

His was the first of such utopian colonies with their strange philanthropy: though perhaps he loved God more than men, for if he had loved men more he might have known them better.

His pattern was a sort of communitarian hierarchy, with a new Order of Knighthood, half military and half missionary, designed to protect and to convert the pagan. Its failure was quite inevitable. As soon as his people found themselves at ease in Zion, they reverted to the familiar habits of mankind, swearing, fighting, whoring. A colony of saints could not have succeeded on Quirós' principles. But a saint would not have made Quirós' mistake. The narrator of More's *Utopia* was called Hythlodaeus, Nonsense, for More knew that such things would always be but the noblest jests of man's wit. He would have known that such a representative human assembly as the sailors, soldiers, settlers from Quirós' fleet was very raw recruitment for a community of moralists. Saints are realistic men, for it is a first condition of sanctity to know yourself, and whoever knows himself has learnt to expect little of his kind, and expecting little still to cherish more. Your saint is most uncomfortably aware that each man has his own problem of moral revolution, and that each generation starts at pretty much the same old point of potential turpitude. It is the pantisocrats, progressivists and theorists of revolution who expect too much of man; and who, when he fails them, lose their silly tempers, as we have seen so often in contemporary letters. Yet Quirós was a man not of the study but of the full air. He should have known better than Mr. Wells.

In that first chill of failure the temper of Quirós, which had carried him through the long painful years of poverty and supplication and of hope deferred, suddenly snapped. Appalled by the revelation of man, he broke. Mutiny perhaps and sickness had weakened him, but mutiny and sickness do not destroy a man still resolute. Quirós threw in his hand. He let his seamen turn back his ship to New Spain. His Admiral, Torres, in another ship, returned by what we know as Torres Straits to the Moluccan Seas and Manila, and his discoveries were all that came of the great enterprise.

Quirós was compounded of Don Quixote and of Hamlet and of the art of navigation. His end still seems sicklied o'er with the pale cast of thought. He introduces to Empire the theme which has haunted our own minds: whether 'tis nobler in the mind to suffer the slings and arrows of outrageous fortune or to take arms against a sea of troubles: even against that wave upon which Mrs. Lindbergh so blithely rides, skilfully surfing.

XAVIER

North and west of Quirós, the islands met another
European man and this a saint. He would have known
the answer to Hamlet's question and to ours. Xavier per-
mitted himself no Mexico or New Spain of retreat. He
worked and strove and sweated, not with visions, but
with people: Hindus, Portuguese, Malays, Ambonese,
Japanese. He had caught the true key to the City of God,
and he knew that what it turned was in the hearts of
sweating, stinking humanity, in Pedro and Ahmad, Yagiro
and Chang Sin Chong. He knew that the City of God was
within: and that if you want to make any real change in
the world then you had better start with people, who are
the world. He also knew, we may take it, that you cannot
make an omelette without eggs. Perhaps he learnt it at
the University of Paris, that rational place: but it does
not seem acceptable in every institute of higher learning.

Xavier, anyhow, did not believe that the business of
reform was with the trappings and the tools of society.
He believed it was with people, so he worked at people.
But he was not oblivious to social forces, and especially
not to that notorious adversary who goes about roaring,
seeking whom he may devour. When Xavier met that
unmitigated lion, he believed that it should be hit
squarely and where a hit might be useful. He was not
willing that the sprigs of virtue should make meals for
an uproarious beast. Xavier might go himself, alone, unarmed, towards the Forbidden Kingdom. He could love
the sinner's soul, though not his sin. But he could also
rise terribly in the pulpit of Malacca and cry upon the
Lord and the Lord's local soldiery to scatter utterly and
destroy those who came raging against the little Christian
city. He knew a great deal about evil or the ways of the

devil (call it as you like, it visibly appears). He knew too
the way the world wags and what manner of thing man
is. He also remembered his moral theology. He was a refreshing person, and I recommend him to the reader, if
the reader is still with us.

Xavier too I have had much in mind as I travelled with
this book.

RIDING THROUGH GEORGIA

There were twelve British seamen on that Louisville
and Nashville train, bound for Galveston to take a ship
to sea.

One was a Cockney with London's swift, edged humour,
and tiny wrinkles that gave his face the texture of a brick.
He made considerable play with the local passengers, from
Atlanta and thereabouts, and put a strong case for Abraham Lincoln: though he confided to me privately that his
sympathies in the Civil War were really with Rhett But-
ler. I imagine that London saw a good deal of his ancestors in the days when its apprentices shook thrones.

Two of the seamen were from Devon with the Devon
speech which always sounds to me nearer to the old English of the Virginias and the Carolinas than to modern
English. A couple more were men of Hull, which has
brought its fish to market from the cold wastes of the
sea through all the vicissitudes of English history. Three
were Bristol men, faces that would have been familiar on
the *Mayflower* and emigrant ships through three centuries. If one knows English letters and English painting
and English prints, one knows how little these basic
stocks of England change. You can still hear in any Somerset bar the sort of wry, broad, parochial joke that is
carved in the stones and on the bench-ends of Wells Cathedral.

Four of the sailors had lately drifted seven days in an open boat. One had survived three torpedoings in the last disturbance. None of them thought the wild wet water pleasant. They had seen men drown in the Wave of the Future. But they were going back to sea as their fathers had steadily gone, and one may forgive them if they seemed to think of it as the English sea.

They were shabby men, but for the Cockney, and he was flashy as a pearly coster. But each wore in his lapel a little badge that was not shabby: a crown and two letters, M.N., the Merchant Navy. I remembered then the look of Drake's crew and Lancaster's, out of Bristol and Bideford, Plymouth and Portsmouth, the North Sea fishing smacks and the Yorkshire colliers: each unquestionably equipped with a bow-legged little Cockney, flashy as a Poplar pearly.

The seamen and the saints are too much forgotten in the growing business of Empire, for they rarely acquire any tangible assets in it; without them, however, the thing would never have been done. And seamen seldom make saints in the official and canonical order. Even Quirós bungled his attempt to double. I take it, though, that most seamen get to heaven, for God must like their company. Certainly Xavier preferred it to his surfeit of civil and ecclesiastical politicians, for he went to sea at every opportunity. It was some Ordinary Seaman or perhaps A.B. who, with a Chinese boy, buried him in his lonely grave on the salt marshes outside the Customs barriers of Canton at the border of the Forbidden Kingdom.

AND THE DUTCH

By odd chance (unless I was being prepared for things to come or the trains nowadays are filled with overlanding sailors), I travelled my next stage westward with a crew-load of Dutchmen whose ship was at San Francisco. They steadily ate their way from meal to meal and across the States of Texas, New Mexico, Arizona and up through California, confounding the diner service of the *Sunset* which is more used to the appetites of Hollywood producers and Texas cattlemen. I have since been up and down and across a large part of the Dutch Empire, but I have not shaken off the awe and admiration I then shared with the dining-car staff.

But theirs is another theme for the legend of Empire: the Dutch shipmen who first made a steady proposition of the thing.

Behind those fellows in the dining car was the long line of Dutch schippers, going down to Lisbon in the days before Alva, to fill their holds with spices: and then, when Lisbon was shut against them, pushing their stubborn prows past Africa and about the Cape and up by Cocos and across the Indian seas, to batter down monopoly and at last to wreck the Empire which Portugal had spread from Good Hope to Japan in her magnificent hour.

Behind the schippers, Houtman, Hartog, Cartensz and the rest, were the merchants of Amsterdam, broad-faced and solemn men with shrewd eyes and mouths, whom Rembrandt knew. They sat about their tables calculating their accounts, and sometimes they carefully put money on the board for charters, victuals, seamen, for the spices of the Moluccas and the silks of Deshima.

PEOPLE OF THE DRAMA

One begins to people the drama of Europe in the Orient: Mendaña and the Dons, Quirós, Torres, the Portuguese seamen and Spain's soldiers of the sea: Xavier and his Jesuits, the brown Franciscans, and the London

Missionary Society to come: the English captains and the Dutch schippers and their men from Combe Martin, Southwark, Lyme and the fishing hamlets of the Zuyder Zee: the City merchants, capon-lined, and the solemn, black-suited, narrow-ruffed burghers of Dordrecht and Amsterdam who now occupy the walls of Dutch galleries, looking oddly like Directors of the K.P.M.: the Governors with their banners, the soldiers in red and steel, and presently the clerks, factors, harbour masters, nuns, buccaneers, convicts, colonists and Scottish engineers. Amongst them all they solved the last mysteries of geography and loosed in the unchanging East incalculable processes of change. At their impact, cultures static through millennia felt the first shock of dissolution which precedes God knows what new syntheses. They changed the whole economy of the earth. They brought down thrones and dominations and powers and principalities. Out of their earnings and to fill the maws of their imperial commerce came the Industrial Revolution, the machine, and megalopolitan civilization. They carried splendour and misery in their train, at home and abroad. They have made the world one small room, and they have set the moral intelligence of man problems that he hardly begins to solve. Some went forth with the sword and some remembered the Cross. Some were buried in marble and some rotted on the alien beaches. Some fed on turtle and some were articles of diet in the Cannibal Isles.

We cannot weigh and judge the whole phenomenon of that expansion, because it represents the fiercest energies of a civilization, and it had in it every mean and noble thing that is in us, the people of what was Christendom. Only the Angel of the Records will see it whole, as the Dons and the friars and the merchants and the shipmasters, the clerks, compradores, coolies, slaves, abo-

rigines, and Chinese boys come up for general judgment. But however it all balances, it was life and life
abounding: and better than the quiet where faith is dead
and men are mute and the springs of hope and passion
are all spent.

CHAPTER ONE

Westward Ho!

MEDITATION IN VANCOUVER

IN WARTIME you mostly sit about and wait. We waited at Vancouver while the grey afternoon slid into dusk and mists curled in from the Sound, condensing in dismal drops along the railings and on the glass of the promenade forward. Across the dock a Canadian Pacific liner, after some adventures seaward, was putting on camouflage. The town, going up from the end of the wharf, looked drear and deserted. Towards teatime a few pale, diffused lights suggested that the new towerlike hotel still stood where it had stood at lunch. I shall always prefer the Belgravian comforts of the old pub, which has as much history in its brown bones as any building in western Canada. It has joined the Army now.

I was thinking, while I watched a broken crate bump by, of Vancouver: Vancouver the man who gave his name to the city and seems very like it in his sober, respectable competence. He came and went, in his days, over most of the route I was to take; and he curiously ties together much Pacific history. He came out as one of Cook's officers. He was at Hawaii when Cook died. He returned with his own command by the Indian Ocean and the northwest of Australia to deal for Britain with Spain along the coasts that Drake had called New Albion and the Spaniards California. Hereabouts, in what is now British

17

Columbia, he took over, under treaty, fur-posts from
Spain. He met the Russians northward. He was a friend
to the Polynesians and particularly of Kamehameha I in
Hawaii. He was Sea Power in the North Pacific, but he
was also Pax. His negotiations, surveys and patrols
brought a peace amongst the Pacific Powers not broken
until now outside the coastal waters of Asia. He was that
much-abused phenomenon: British imperialism in brass
buttons.

Canada belongs both to North America and to what we
call the British Empire (or, if we feel prim, the British
Commonwealth; the thing actually is new, and needs a
new name), and so bridges the two major political achieve-
ments of man since the Roman Empire.

America's achievement was to resolve the conflicts of
blood and race within a single society and by the power
of a great dogma. Americans often neglect their Jeffer-
sonian creed as men neglect their religion, but it feeds the
roots and fills the fruit of America's life.

As America made a community of peoples, the British
Commonwealth makes a community of sovereign states
scattered across the world but associated for their common
good. And the two efforts are complementary. In a world
bogged down in national and racial enmities, they represent a great human advance. If we ever make sense in the
world at large we must draw on the strength and experience of the American Union and the British Concert of
Sovereign States.

Through history men have struggled for the balance
between social order and personal freedom which makes
governance tolerable. It is a problem of law, but also a
problem of assent. Rome solved the problem of law. She
disciplined her Empire in one vast, majestic frame imposed by Caesar. Her incomparable system of Law compelled men and their customs to its rational pattern. But

England went otherwise. Obscurely, slowly, *libertas* informed her law. "No free man shall be taken, or imprisoned, or dispossessed, or outlawed, or in any way destroyed . . . save through the lawful judgements of his equals and the law of the land." [1] Then the figure of Christ the Worker appeared amongst the carved mediaeval saints. Through centuries of much bitterness and oppression, that sense has slowly worked to produce the jury, representative government, responsible government, the Bill of Rights, and the Common Law sprung from the instinct of common man for natural justice. Imperfectly, with many backslidings, it changed the moral and intellectual climate of the Western world. It produced communities of free men. Now the Commonwealth produces a community of free nations. "What touches all must be approved by all," cried Edward I, defining the liberties of Englishmen. More prosily, a modern Minister echoes him to declare the liberties of British nations: "It is not a possible arrangement that one set of men should contribute the lives and treasures of their people and should have no voice in the way in which those lives and that treasure are expended." [2]

EMPIRE PAST AND PRESENT

An English Empire rose with the Angevins and died, as dominion lacking assent from men and history must die, at Mary's loss of Calais. New Empire came with the Stuarts' union of two crowns, with plantations, charters, mercantilism, Pilgrims, Proprietors, and East Indiamen. It broke at the American Revolution because it forgot

[1] *Magna Charta,* the 39th Clause.
[2] Mr. Bonar Law. Quoted by Sir John A. R. Marriott, *The Evolution of the British Empire and Commonwealth.* London, 1939.

Edward's tremendous principle and was tangled in archaic formulae. A third Empire grew through the old colonial system: and from within it develops (now fully in the Dominions) a fourth, striking off every fetter that might chafe and cramp the growing life of young nations. It is the great exemplar of assent. Its people speak of it as of a family. Its one formal bond is its common kingship whose values now belong more to the mystical and moral than the material life.

It is not a product of the planning so fashionable of late. It is more of the heart than the head. There is some truth in the saying that it was achieved in successive fits of absence of mind. It is not a piece of political machinery, like the League of Nations to which it has been compared. It belongs to life, not to mechanics.

It inherited some of the sins of its fathers, even its remote Angevin fathers, who left the trouble of Ireland. Its maturity still has to solve the problems of India and Africa. But there are new humours in the body to heal these sores. In 1941, the Prime Minister of Canada was a grandson of the rebel, Mackenzie; and a man who once brilliantly bore arms against the British Crown was Prime Minister of South Africa and long the Elder Statesman of the Empire. These are interesting symptoms if we look for reason in a haunted world.

England now is one equal partner in a fellowship.[3]

[3] ". . . the group of self-governing communities composed of Great Britain and the Dominions . . . are autonomous Communities within the British Empire, equal in status, in no way subordinate one to another in any aspect of their domestic or external affairs, though united by a common allegiance to the Crown and freely associated as members of the British Commonwealth of Nations." From *Report of the Committee on Inter-Imperial Relations of the Imperial Conference of 1926*. The sense finds expression in the Statute of Westminster.

Towards partnership or independence move the rest of the old colonial system, and the Empire of India. The principle of their progress is clearly fixed. Its pace chiefly depends upon varying local circumstances.

The new Empire can be seen across the border; not a dangerous excursion, even if the Union Jack does flaunt the breeze and you meet the brutal British discipline of tea. In some matters, the Canadians are more British than the colonels' widows perched in their feudal fastnesses of Bournemouth, Cheltenham, and Tooting Bec.

The deck was deserted as I leaned against the rails and remembered these things. The policeman below, symbol of *imperium* and *magisterium,* was very Irish. His brogue drifted up as he talked at the foot of the gangway with three people from the Empire Air Scheme. One was in the dark-blue Australian uniform, and two in the familiar blue-grey: a New Zealander, and a Canadian who had come to see the others sail.

I thought of Mr. Chesterton who celebrated in his young enthusiasm an Empire which existed

> . . . *that Lancashire merchants whenever they like*
> *Can water the beer of a man in Klondike.*

Neither watered beer nor any brand of merchandise could have assembled the group at the gangway.

WHY AND HOW PACIFIC

We did sail, but don't mention it. The enemy is listening. Every one in Vancouver shut his eyes and stuffed his ears against guilty knowledge of us. A full month before in the United States I had been given all the details I wanted by telephone from a travel-agency. The ship I remembered from the Australia-New Zealand trade, where she used to streak across the rough, tough twelve hundred

miles between Sydney and Wellington. She was now replacing the Canadian-Australian Line's old *Niagara,* which
had more mileage than any liner afloat when she bumped
a mine outside Auckland on June 19, 1940. When the
Niagara's boats pulled in to Auckland, authority was at
first sceptical about the mine. Perhaps it believed that the
Niagara had been bitten by a whale. But the sweepers
found evidence enough, and presently mines began to
drift ashore on Australian beaches.

What with mines and raiders there had been plenty of
casualties in Western waters. For just a few, the *Haxby,* the
Tropic Sea, the French *Notou,* the American motorship
City of Rayville, the *Holmwood,* the liner *Rangitane* (a
dirty business, with passengers including women killed in
their cabins), and the most gallant *Turakina,* a smallish
steamer mounting one gun that sustained an action against
a heavily armed German raider for nearly three hours
until she was a smoking, reeking shambles, with two-thirds
of her complement dead. The survivors were taken only
when their feet were in the sea.

So we were blacked-out from our first evening in the
Sound: no lights on deck, lights uncompromisingly out
in all cabins at midnight. I find it difficult to like blackouts. In the Atlantic, a dismal ditch at any time, they in-
duce colds and sniffles: in the Pacific, blackouts are
grossly at odds with such blue sky and palms as may be
and the effects of tourist literature generally. More, the
Pacific swings abominably, and if I have to roll between
the washbasin and the bed, I do it better with the lights
on. Since I first met the Pacific I suspect the people who
named it of ironic intent; though they have support from
the sober Dutch who call it the Stille Ocean.

The Pacific may have seemed, to the old navigators,
comparatively restrained when they came about Cape
Horn; but for us it began to kick that night while the

SINGAPORE

" 'What Malta is in the West . . .' "

NORTHERN SHORE, AUSTRALIA

"There the tide of Empire, and of effort, seems to have halted."

TRANSCONTINENTAL ROAD, CENTRAL AUSTRALIA

"Seven hundred miles remain between the railheads."

Australian Dept. of Informa

lights of what must have been Victoria (that tidy little city which has made an amiable career of being more English than England) were north of east, and Seattle and Bremerton Navy Yard were somewhere over the port bow.

During the week, I had seen the huge new training centre of the Royal Canadian Navy near Victoria, where some of its 30,000 sailors are being trained for the 413 ships it will presently have; and off Seattle, I had watched United States battleships headed for Honolulu and perhaps history. On both shores I had listened to a whole crop of new stories about Japanese fishing-boats. The rise and fall of Japanese fishermen in longshore talk is a political thermometer on all the Pacific coasts, from the Aleutians down to Chile and across to Sydney and around Australia to Perth and up to Singapore. There is probably truth in the legend but it grows by what it feeds upon: the alarm which Japan has evoked in all her neighbours. I personally doubt that all Japanese fishing-smacks are commanded by rear-admirals. But in May, 1941, the Customs at Hawaii seized ten alien craft on the charge of fraudulent registration, and were proposing, when I last heard, to arrest seventy more.

There is a great deal of activity about Victoria, though fewer tourists now drop in for tweeds. It is the eastern anchor of the British system of Pacific patrol. But Britain lacks, in the eastern and central Pacific, bases comparable to the great naval forts which guard her other lines of communication. Britain assumed that she did not need strength where America was strong; while America, with great industrial centres on her eastern seaboard, was content to leave their ocean approaches largely to the British Watch. America has needed until now no Pearl Harbours in the Atlantic while Britain stood at Gibraltar, at Portsmouth and at Plymouth. It is curious evidence of the long, almost unacknowledged co-operation between the two great naval Powers, and of their confidence in one another.

In the peace they kept upon the seas came the nineteenth century's vast expansion of peoples and commerce. Thirty-five million migrants crossed to the United States and tens of millions more went to South America, Canada, Australia, New Zealand, Africa. Whole continents were peopled. With it grew America's gigantic export, spurring her western march and the opening of her great wheat-belts, meat-belts, corn-belts to feed industrializing Europe. Masses of mankind found new homes, new fortune, new loyalties. New nations rose, in freedom. Life was unbelievably enriched, and chiefly because of one neglected fact: that through it all there was peace upon the seas. Emerson noticed that "the stability of England is the security of the modern world." He might have been echoed in Melbourne and San Francisco, Buenos Aires, Dunedin, Soerabaja, Cape Town, Portland and Papeete, in the steerages of emigrant-ships and in Conestoga wagons toiling across Iowa, Nebraska, and Kansas.

Until now sea power in the Pacific has served its proper end, to keep the seas for peaceful merchantmen. Singapore and Sydney, Pearl Harbour and Cavite are precinct stations of the Pacific, designed in two great systems. America's reaches from San Diego and Pearl Harbour north to the Alaskan stations, west to the Philippines via Wake and Guam, and southwest to Pago-Pago. It meets, west and southwest, the British system, Hong Kong, Singapore, Darwin, Moresby, Sydney, Auckland, Suva. The two systems could comfortably interlock. At their extremities only a few hundred miles divide Hongkong from Manila, and Pago-Pago from Suva. Together, they provide an extraordinary range of operations for sea and air fleets based on them. Modern ships now have a much smaller range than the sailing squadrons of Nelson's day, which could stay at sea while they still had biscuit, water and powder; and sometimes cruised for months at a time.

A modern battle fleet, with its necessary auxiliaries and ancillaries, has an operating range of perhaps five days: certainly less than three days outward if it has to return on its tracks for supply. But fleets operating on the Anglo-American frame could leapfrog from San Francisco to Suez and from Alaska to the Antarctic, command every pass into the Pacific, from the Straits of Sunda and of Malacca to the Horn and Panama and Behring Straits. British and United States ships already have access in crisis to that vast double structure. British warships now are docked in American shipyards. Singapore will serve, if occasion comes, America's Pacific fleet; and the great new dock building at Sydney is a contribution, when needed, to America's power at sea.

Draw lines between the bases and you have a kind of frame. It has been a frame of order, of peace, of civilization. From those stations British and American ships have patrolled the long ocean beats. From them the reign of law in the Pacific has come; and, as order once established will, has grown.

This is what some people call bloody imperialism. I prefer Aquinas' phrase, "the tranquillity of order."

TRIBUTARIES TO SINGAPORE

Things might have gone otherwise in the Pacific. But Britain and America damped down the struggle for power which was impending there in the first half of the nineteenth century, when Hawaii and Australia armed against the Muscovite. Britain and America smashed piracy, which within the last hundred years came near to strangling the China trade and all traffic east of the Malaccan Straits. We forget too easily that our recent maritime peace was almost unique in history, that through most of our deplorable story the sea was a constant battleground for its users. Anarchy will come walking again upon the waters if the great instruments which gave them peace pass. British and American sea power are conditions of the civilization which has grown from Halifax to Melbourne and Pretoria to the Plate.

We move, for good and ill, towards an unprecedented economic, political and cultural complex. The world has become a small place when salmon caught off Alaska is eaten in Nigeria, and graduates of Harvard are in office at Chungking, when Goodyear tires are grown about Siantar, and California oranges are sucked at Wembley Stadium, when Australian wool is sold in Boston to buy machine tools in Cincinnati, and an experiment begun at Cape Town may be concluded at Carnegie Tech, when Japanese bicycles are ridden in Brazil, and the wild native of the Amazon goes to work for Mr. Henry Ford. In such a world there can be no real isolationist even in the igloos of the Esquimaux. The last hermit-kingdom returned to public life at the loud suggestion of Commodore Perry speaking, if ever man spoke, an inevitable decision of history.

The Pacific becomes the meeting and perhaps melting place of the world's major cultures. There they will clash in violence still inconceivable or they will work out new relations and syntheses. They may manage both, for man is a versatile creature; but if humanity is to escape long, terrible strains and conflicts, racial and national rivalries must be subordinated to the general interest. The job is up to Britain and America.

"All Empire is no more than power in trust," said Dryden, a sound man. Britain and America may shed much of their power if they mislike it: but much belongs inevitably to their existence as it is, and to their place in contemporary history. That cannot be shed: nor indeed has a nation the right to bury its talents.

The moral obligation, it seems to me, is perfectly clear. The nations have responsibilities, like men, to their neighbours. There was, of course, a Levite who has had spiritual heirs: but he is not commonly regarded as a model or a mentor as he goes eternally to Jericho.

But if moral arguments lack weight (and sometimes they do), look at material aspects of our growing interdependence. Look, for example, at one instance: at Singapore, not Singapore the naval base but Singapore the merchant city. Singapore ships two-thirds of the world's rubber, most of the world's tin, and has developed the world's chief copra supply. Without copra, we would go largely unwashed, and so would our friends if we retained them. Copra provides part of our food supply, char for gasmasks, and the lipstick now necessary to half the creation's bold face upon the world. Without rubber, we moderns could hardly ride or walk or talk. We use rubber for automobiles, for telephones, and for almost every variety of electrical equipment, for heels, and for rubbing out heels. We are tributaries to Singapore when we wash, shave, shampoo, ride in motor cars, trains, buses, trolleys, perambulators, airplanes or even horse buggies: when we buy iceboxes, washing machines, fountain pens, candy, radio, tinned peaches, films, or baby's napkins, when we play golf or have an operation or wear garters or have our teeth drilled. From the cradle with its rubber-nippled bottle to the grave in a rubber-tired hearse, we draw on Singapore. In short, whether we live at Sioux City or Seringapatam or stops between, we all have immediate, personal interest in the future of the Pacific. Its peace rests upon the intelligent collaboration of its peoples jointly to solve tremendous social, ethnic, economic and political problems now plainly pending. The American and British peoples about its shores have lately got together. That is a beginning.

Those not moved by the moral obligations involved may well be concerned for their canned goods and galoshes.

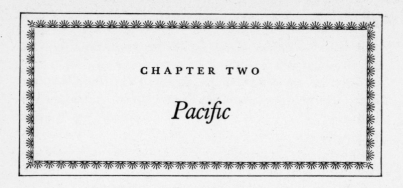

PACIFIC DISCOVERY

THE PACIFIC, oddly, went unnoticed in Europe until Balboa mounted his well-known peak in Darien, although it occupies almost half of the globe's surface, and Europeans had already sailed seas westward which are, for all but geographic purists, part of its general content.

There was Odoric, for example, who in 1318 left Padua to reinforce three of his Franciscan brethren who had gone fifty or sixty years before to evangelize Central Asia, and might, even in the Franciscan discipline, be presumed to have earned a relief. Odoric took a roundabout way to Central Asia. Perhaps he was not sure of its locality, perhaps he was of an inquiring mind, but he went out by Trebizond, Tauris and the Archbishopric which John XIII had erected at Sultaniah in Persia, by Farsistan, Hormuz, to Tana in the island of Salsette, north of Bombay. (We miss a great deal of fun, I think, since the world became a small, familiar place at the disposition of American Express.) There, or at Surat, he gathered and took to bury in China relics of brother Franciscans, martyred in 1321. He went on, with their bones (and in some part of the way, with an Irishman, Friar James) to Malabar, and Flandrina near Calicut, along the Coromandel Coast, by ship from Madras to Ceylon and the Nicobars, to Sumatra, Java, Borneo; thence north to China where he found one

friar he sought still reigning as Archbishop of Peking.
Odoric remained in Peking for three years and was properly astonished by the Imperial postal services. He came
home overland, to vary the monotony, being the first
European to visit Tibet, and, had he not been put upon
his obedience, would never have thought to record his
memoirs, there being more useful things to do while the
brief candle burns.

Marco Polo is better known to a world less interested
in preachers than profits. He travelled in the South China
seas and about Malaya and Sumatra on his romantic journey with the Lady Kukachin to the Court of Persia, and
he acquired a considerable knowledge, factual and fabu-
lous. And God now only knows how many others there
were, friars, adventurers and merchants' spies, captured
seamen and Christian slaves.

Japanese and Chinese junks must have sometimes gone
in the Kuro Siwo current to northwestern America, and
touched at times in Polynesia and Micronesia. Arabs
traded in Java, Sumatra, and as far as Canton; and told
tales of marsupials. Junks met dhows in the East Indian
ports and Burma and Siam. Arabs met Europeans at the
ports of Syria and Palestine, Egypt and Constantinople,
where the trade routes came to the gates of the Mediterranean. Hindu influences appear in the Philippines from
the early centuries of the Christian era. The Chinese were
regular visitors there from the tenth century. In all the
ages of traffic between China, Malayu, Java, Sumatra, India, Persia, the Caspian and Mediterranean coasts, rumour
of the Pacific must have spread where seamen trans-
shipped cargoes; and from junk to dhow, dhow to galley,
galley to caravel and galleon; from beach to beach, doss-
house to doss-house. If the classicists held that the world
still ended where it had ended for Alexander and Aris-
totle, some of the map makers had other notions, gleaned

in the waterside bagnios and wineshops of the Mediterranean ports. Seamen still live oddly detached from the life ashore, and many then doubtless had strange stuff in their heads which never caught the ears of respectable burghers. When Columbus sailed westward, I can believe that he had heard of seaways east from Cathay, and of men who had reached Cipango from the west. Magellan certainly was not sailing utterly uninstructed when he held northwestward from his Straits. Discussions on the rotundity of earth were one thing; the talk of old salts on the quays of Venice and Genoa was another, though an ambitious navigator might air it less in academic circles and political salons.

But through their thousands of years, the empires of Asia made no remembered effort at Pacific expansion. China's centre of gravity was always in its ancestral graves and the familiar places of its fathers. The Chinese gone abroad were like souls lost. And the enormous drag of that great society held the minds and imaginations of men East and South. Moreover, the European dynamic is a thing almost peculiar to the European tribes, which perhaps is just as well. The cultures of Asia seek quiet, rest, and fixed forms. They tend, except when population pressure becomes intolerable, to turn in on themselves, as Japan did after its first experience of Europeans. Japan might then have laid hands on all the Pacific and its hinterlands, from the Rocky Mountains to the Australian deserts, but the ambition probably did not occur to one solitary Samurai. The restless energy of the European is not native to Japan. Japan imitates the gestures, and the effort imposes appalling strain on its character and culture. If his excursion in the world goes badly the Japanese may, with a sudden sense of almost overwhelming relief, return to what he was: a highly civilized being chiefly con-

cerned to cultivate his garden and his sensibilities. It is
unfortunate that his garden is so cramped. Something
should be arranged.

SAILS FROM EAST AND WEST

However, these are only generalizations, with perhaps
some bias towards the truth. But this remains, that the
Pacific enters world history first with the little tubs of
ships which followed Magellan or crept out on the vast
waters from the ports of Peru and Panama and Mexico.
And except for the annual galleon trudging between Panama and Manila, there was little traffic and no regular
route of trade until the eighteenth century.

At intervals a little lonely ship appears, moving slowly
across the immense scene; gilded prow, carved poop, and
painted sails, her bright reflection on the purple sea. Magellan and del Cano, Diego de Rocha, de Loaisa, de
Saavedra, de Villalobos, Lopez de Legazpi, Mendaña,
Drake, Cavendish (who made England again with sails of
damask, his masts flagged with cloth of gold, his sailors
all in silk), Van Noort, Quirós, Torres, Lemaire, Schou-
ten, Tasman, Lazeano: the *Vittoria, Trinidad, San Gero-
nino, Pelican, Desire, Almiranta, Hoorn, Eendracht,
Heemskirk, Cygnet, Roebuck.*

No one knows the full tally. Many sailed secretly and
on unlawful occasions, for the Pacific route was chiefly
used by buccaneers, and by merchants who, being unli-
censed for the great royal or chartered monopolies,
slipped in through Cape Horn's back door. Some foun-
dered in the sea, some broke on reefs, and some went
home to Bantam, Lisbon, Lima, Plymouth and Torbay.

But the Pacific kept most of its secrets until the eighteenth century's systematic explorations reached their climax (if that is not too loud a word for his steady, careful

work) with the three voyages of Cook, the incomparable
model and mirror of pilots. Roggeveen, Bouvet, Byron,
Carteret, Wallis, de Bougainville, Gilbert, Marshall, Vancouver, Edwards, d'Entrecasteaux with long traverses and
patient quarterings blocked in the charts. While they
worked, the fishermen and traders blew in.

Russia reached the Pacific in its fast drive across Siberia
in the middle of the seventeenth century. Presently came,
in the wilderness east and west of Behring Straits, a traffic
in furs, and to share it British, French, Spanish and American ships. Fur traders, sealers, and whalers break the
Pacific quiet, violently. In the northern winters, they
debouched on Hawaiian beaches. They ranged across
Polynesia and Melanesia, from the Marquesas to the Solomons and Fiji. They fought the Maoris and traded with
them for human heads. They went after sandalwood, they
recruited convicts escaped from Norfolk Island and Port
Jackson, they dealt with the natives in nails, axes, rum,
and women. When bargaining got to quarrelling, the
beaches ran red. Hundreds, perhaps thousands of white
seamen died in the shallows and under the palms, for the
Melanesians and Polynesians were not designed for slaves.

Ships from Nantucket and New London were familiar
with remote inlets on the furthest coasts of Australia by
the first decades of the nineteenth century. There is still
an American River on Kangaroo Island; and the survey
ships of His Majesty's Navy found Americans melting
blubber under the headlands of King George's Sound and
about Tasmania. Sydney first became a port of consequence when the whalers careened on its beaches and
the northern bays of its harbour reeked with the render-
ing fires.

All across the Pacific appalling holocausts of whales and
seals worked out the fisheries in a few decades. Whaling
is only lately much revived and chiefly along the Antarctic

ice. The modern whaler with his factory ships makes enormously larger killings, but he is under some measure of
control. The old sea hunters left a smear of blood across
the islands and the ocean, which is not yet washed out.

THE IRRESISTIBLE FORCE

Into the maelstrom of this early, furious life Chinese,
Japanese, and Malays were sucked. For a generation or
two, the Pacific belonged to the heaviest fists and the wildest heads. Then things began to shake down. Civilization
spread on shores that had been no-man's lands. With the
substantial settlement of the Australian colonies, with
naval patrols, the development of California, the building
of the Pacific railroad, the growth of sober trading, and
the missionaries, order and law appeared and grew.

But the hurricane left wrack and wreck behind it.
Within half a century great populations in Melanesia and
Polynesia had been decimated, their traditional cultures
and the structure of their societies weakened beyond re-
pair. The impact of the European had been cataclysmic.

Without discounting the part that lust, cupidity, and
sheer damnable brutality had in the tragedy, it was largely
inevitable unless the men who came had been saints (when
they might mostly have become martyrs) or the men who
were there could have been sealed off and quarantined
from the world.

The first strong wash of this European tide in the Pacific
carried the toughest of contemporary human material,
much of it swirling from the stews and sewers of the Western world. The convicts who escaped from Botany or
Norfolk were men whose fierce temper had survived a system designed to crush it. They had been uprooted and
cast half the earth away from whatever homes and human
kindness they had known. They had nothing to expect

from life but what they could desperately win in that world beyond the law. The sealers and the whalers too were pretty grim stuff, men hammered in the roughest trade humanity ever designed for its discomfort. They lived, years at a stretch, in constant danger and incredible hardships, toiling in small boats and on decks reeking with blood and blubber. The New England whalemen may have feared God on Sunday mornings at home: but they feared nothing else unless their wives and they seldom saw their wives.

The peoples with whom they clashed were not weaklings. Maoris and Fijians were fierce and resolute, with tricks that still chill in the reading. Quarter was not given or expected when parleys grew to quarrels and sorties.

The actual killings were not the worst of it. Two subtler evils overtook the Pacific peoples: disease and the dissolution of their cultures.

Some diseases might have been checked if medical skill and knowledge had been available from the first. Others were inevitable when the European appeared. Measles and influenza are an inconvenience to peoples long exposed to them, but they swept the Pacific as plagues and still in remote places may decimate whole districts.

Equally inevitable and pathetic was the destruction of native cultures. The beliefs, forms, and habits which had given values, meaning, discipline, character and perhaps joy to Polynesian life dissolved and ran away like water. Only a very gradual process of education, development and slow change could have avoided that disaster.

The native, a profound conservative, lived by ancient custom and convention, by a pattern revealed in the mists beyond time when men's first fathers walked and talked with gods, sometimes as gods. Personal habit and social behaviour were shaped within rigid rules; the smallest act and event had spiritual and moral significance. The codes were necessary to a proper life here and to a good end.

Then men came who utterly disregarded the sacred traditions and the tabus and to whom the gods, devils, and daemons of the woods and waters were jests. These people got away with unspeakable blasphemies and not only with blasphemy but with almost everything in sight: and yet had gifts and talents, like gunboats, rum, pistols, and canoes as high as forests, unrevealed to the faithful. Faith got a hefty shock; and remember that the whole structure of society, its organization, disciplines, arts, crafts rested upon faith. A man bred in such a culture hardly knew how to marry and beget, to plant crops and take his fruits, to speak to his brother, to recognize his mother, to live out his life, if his faith failed. The European has departmentalized his life, and he can shed his beliefs without even noticing that they are gone. Many a man would be shocked to discover that his pious professions have no attachment whatsoever to the conduct of his life. But the will of primitive peoples (if these are what we call primitive) has no such independence. It is guided in faith, and if faith fails him, the man is blind and lost.

The break began from such simple things as the natives' wonder and admiration at the European marvels. It is unhappily true that most other peoples admire our skills more than our character or morals. The Japanese and the Malay have little respect for our arts and letters or even for our political competence: but they think we are damnably good at bridges, roads, and making use and fat fortunes out of such unlikely stuff as oil, coal, and rubber trees.

The missionaries not only rejected the customs (and indeed many of them were revolting enough), but they took to the gods with axes. The native eyed the shattered fragments of his unresisting idol and then the gunboat in the bay. He put one thing with another, and it added up. The god of these newcomers was plainly a very superior god indeed. Which, on the whole, was so far and so good.

But the missionaries were seldom trained to the patience now necessary. The native's soul was still held in the fast coils of his custom. Slowly these should have been unwound, and new belief carefully fastened to bind the puling, naked thing that is the unsupported soul of man. The missionaries mostly hacked away beliefs and traditions as you might hack a poisonous parasite from a tree. They had excuse enough, for much of that inheritance was vicious and debased, profoundly shocking even to men who knew the secrets of European confessionals. But with it were inextricably tangled the supports of life.

Consider a broad example. The Fijians were given to constant and bloody war, conducted chiefly because it produced captives and corpses for their cannibal pots. Good Methodists of the Missionary Societies properly threw all their eloquence into pleas for pacifism. They did with their immediate contacts what they believed a good day's work for the Lord, until they discovered that their demilitarized flocks were being rapidly eaten by unregenerate warriors. The lambs had been led to the slaughter. It is curious to observe the growing militancy in the minds of the faithful shepherds from Exeter Hall. They discovered what pacifists must too often learn: man has not two fists that he should deliver himself utterly up.

In more subtle things, the damage was more subtle, but evident. When some vicious custom was torn out, the sinner was not being recalled to a narrow path which he had lately missed. His social life was ripped apart, and his personal life left without compass or reference. He had been cast naked out of his only Eden. If a Christian culture and a Christian social structure had come with the formulae of Christian belief, all might have been well.

Certainly, all would have been better than it was before. But a culture and a way of life are the slow, the very slow, effect of beliefs working through generations.

The missionaries themselves, in their real humanity, saw what was happening. They made almost fantastic efforts to produce a new structure. But the most devoted missionaries had, like us all, the limitations of their time, mentalities, imaginations, and education. Those staunch nineteenth-century Liberal Nonconformists usually produced some imitation of the institutions they had themselves known. So, here and there across the Pacific, under the palm trees and on the white coral beaches, appeared Houses of Parliament: for was not the parliamentary system, after all, the crowning achievement and final end of political man? In each native chief they saw a village Gladstone: and about his evening fires sat potential Cobdens, Brights, and radical young Chamberlains. While, aloof but not too far aloof, a darker Disraeli counted not heads (an embarrassing memory here) but the voters of the loyal Opposition.

We may laugh at what was really tragedy; but until reluctant Colonial Offices moved in, the missionaries toiled and sweated blood to produce some workable machinery in place of what had gone.

They were often ignorant and sometimes harshly intolerant: but most learnt wisdom and charity in the long, bitter experiences of harvest. They brought their dogmatic schisms with them to confuse the native mind, but they also brought medicine and hygiene and some image of the Christian virtues: the best of what was ours to bring.

There were knaves and fools amongst them as there are in any selection of men, and indeed in each one man. They have been complained against and made butts; but chiefly by men whose ambitions for the natives were something quite else than that they should be raised from their dark-

VOLCANIC THERMAL POOL, NORTH ISLAND, N. Z.

"There has been . . . a real renaissance for the Maoris."—Page 90

Publicity Dept. K.P.M., Batavia-Centrum (Java)

SUMATRA

"A country of wide fields and golden palms, of cliffs torn by seismic
shocks, ravines and terraced sawahs."

ness, educated, healed. The missions helped to break the native cultures, but the native cultures were doomed, anyhow, from our first appearance. And the missions did give much in return. One remembers the scene which Kotzebue saw at Hawaii, of the royal palace crowded to the doors and up the staircases with children and adults and old people learning to write upon their slates. It was not the traders or the planters who went out to found schools, to create written language, to check abortion, to keep the aged, to nurse the sick, to die amongst the lepers. The missionaries and the Navy captains were, whatever their deficiencies, our best ambassadors to the Pacific peoples and to many another, perhaps because both belong to Services which keep the ancient superstitions of vocation and responsibility. Even Bligh of the *Bounty* was not at all Charles Laughton's monster. The eighteenth century was almost as brutal as our own, but its great seamen, its Cook, Vancouver, Phillip were also great gentlemen, in Polynesia as in Kensington or St. James'.

But from it all this fact emerges: what had been Polynesia, what had been Melanesia, were Polynesia and Melanesia no more. What they were to become only now is shadowed out, in most parts of the Pacific. But at one point it begins to take substantial form.

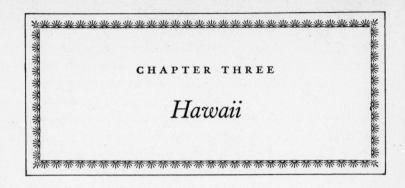

CHAPTER THREE

Hawaii

THE MAN OF TOMORROW

WHENEVER I walk up a street in Honolulu, I feel that I am walking into the future. The future was with me the other day, perhaps in part because I had just exchanged farewell howdys with several husky Navy babies, fellow-travellers to Hawaii (the Navy is very good at babies, and one, ten months old, already had the bearing and voice of a Sergeant of Marines), but chiefly because of the person of the clerk walking uptown with me. He had come to help in some item of business, which he managed pleasantly and with much intelligence. He is a Chinese-Japanese-Scandinavian compound with flecks of Polynesian, and he is, I suspect, the man of tomorrow.

Hawaii, much more than New York, is the type of the melting pot. It is also the prototype of things to come in the Pacific. Someone has calculated [1] that the future Hawaiian will be something like ten per cent Polynesian, twenty per cent Caucasian, forty per cent Japanese, ten per cent Chinese, fifteen per cent Filipino, and two per cent Puerto Rican. I do not suppose that we shall actually see a man with these nicely adjusted proportions, but he suggests what is happening and will increasingly happen in the world between Singapore and San Diego. He seems

[1] In *Mixing the Races in Hawaii,* Sidney L. Gulick. Honolulu, 1937.

to qualify as a citizen of the World State, when it comes. Certainly a new and significant figure has moved on to the stage of history: the human product of forces loosed when Europe turned the capes of Africa and America.

In Hawaii, the economic and social status of natives and immigrant Asiatics is nearer the whites' than in most tropical colonies. A large proportion of the European population has made Hawaii its home, expects to live out its life and die there; and, more important perhaps, it is working at all sorts of jobs: as barbers, mechanics, soda clerks and small farmers. Its everyday relations with other Hawaiians are consequently freer and more intimate than in most such places: and with the way thus opened, the immigrant, the native, and the various hybrids have preferred the Americo-European culture and habit of life to their own. The new Pacific man will have, it seems, a preponderance of Asiatic blood, but an Americo-European civilization, unless we and our ways are discredited and defeated.

The American, in spite of his dislike for the trappings of Empire, makes a very good colonist. He may have the talent in his blood, or it may be just the winters back home, but he is now firmly planted in the Pacific. And the structure of the new Pacific life is largely his. Honolulu looks like any small big city of the mainland, as it already did when Froude was there in 1885. Neither native nor Asiatic culture has withstood the American's energy.

I have a Polynesian friend who does things with surfboards on the beach at Waikiki and sometimes in the water. We chatted while I drank the last planter's punch a man should risk on the westward passage. I remembered a famous film star to whom I had once listened at length on that terrace. The two conversations ran to much the same matter and style, except that the Hawaiian's grammar was rather better. I asked what he thought of his

people's prospects. He put on a minor air of melancholy
and complaint, but I do not think he was much interested.
The grandeur that was Kamehameha's is dead, and so are
his ambitions. My surfboard rider wants to be a beach-
guard in Miami.

When Cook discovered Hawaii in 1778, it was a Polynesian preserve. Possibly it had been visited by Spaniards
and perhaps by Portuguese. From one corner of the Pacific to another you find rumours of Portuguese and Spaniards who escape the history books, whether because their
doings are buried in the dead archives of Seville and Lisbon or because they themselves nevermore reported home,
no man knoweth. But I have heard people argue for hours
about Spanish galleons in the mud of lonely Australian
coasts. A Spanish helmet was once fished up at Wellington,
and the last warm exchanges I had in Sydney concerned
some local carvings said to be a Spanish text.

But when Cook arrived at the Sandwich Islands,[2] the
inhabitants were so little visited that they mistook him
for the distinguished divinity, Lono. Discovering their
error, they rose in outraged piety and killed him: a queer
end for so kind a man amongst a people on the whole so
pleasant. A god should never disappoint his public.

POLYNESIANS OUT OF ASIA

The Polynesians are as fascinating a human problem as
the Malays, though we know much less about them. They
carry some mixture of bloods, but they are basically Euro-

[2] It is strange what things will recommend a man to the
future. Here was a noble lord who would now be dust but
that Cook owed him a courtesy; and that his Lordship had
a knack which we all practise at the icebox of spreading between two slices of bread a fragment of broken meats or what
have you there.

poids. They came at some incalculable period from the West, and to the West at death they all return, their souls taking off from appointed places on their islands to follow the declining sun. All their traditions from New Zealand to Hawaii look back to the West; all their genealogies go back to an Arrival: like Chaucer's Knight, at many a noble Aryve had they been. Throughout the Pacific they had much the same conception of the beginnings of things: Nothingness, the Abyss, Darkness, Sunrise, Light, Thought and the Thought Made Flesh. Somewhere behind them was a notable culture or a revelation. But they first appear to history on the sea.

Through ages men have slowly moved south and east from continental Asia. One wave leisurely follows another, sometimes driving the predecessor on, sometimes submerging it, sometimes leaving small pockets, backwaters, of the race before. The Australian aborigines and the Tasmanians, the Negritoes and the Melanesian-Papuan peoples, the primitive forest dwellers of Malaya and Sumatra, the races of Java, and the Malays all came down by the southeastern peninsula of Asia and the islands of Indonesia. Their course was from somewhere in Thailand, Burma, Cambodia, and heaven knows where beyond. The last great wave, in progress now for centuries, is Chinese: and to it, possibly, the future of Indonesia belongs.

As one of several of such waves came the Polynesians.[3] What set those great migrations marching? Perhaps the pressure of populations or more vigorous peoples behind. But who in Asia thrust out a people capable of the Polynesians' discovery of the Pacific? One thinks inevitably of

[3] A course which might have taken them along the narrow Seas of Java and of Sunda seems to have been diverted, perhaps by the resistance of peoples gone ahead. They turned north and east, by Pelew, Yap, the Carolines, the Marshalls, and the Gilberts.

the fantastic spirit of adventure which marks man from the beasts. The tiger timelessly paces his familiar fifteen miles of grass and brakes, but men are called from over the hills and far away. There is a constant itch in our imaginations, as if, looking before and after, we had some faint perception of lands and life unseen.

MEN ON THE OCEAN

The Polynesians-to-be were the first oceanic navigators. While other seamen still crept cautiously from cape to cape, these struck out into the vast open seas; perhaps first from the Gilberts in three prongs, like the sticks of a fan. One line went northeastwards to become the dwarf Menehunes of later Hawaiian myth, a faery people like the familiars of the Irish countryside. Another went east to Phoenix and then southeast to become the primitive Menehunes of the Society Islands. Another edged Melanesia to reach Samoa, where their successors thought them locally generated from the worms of rotting vines. These advance guards were old inhabitants of the Pacific when the main Polynesian migrations followed them.

These too went through Micronesia to by-pass the Melanesian bloc from New Guinea to the Fijis, and any one who has contemplated the Papuan or Fijian in war array will not blame them.

They travelled in great canoes, developed from the original dugouts to outriggers and then to double canoes: two canoes joined by a deck between, on which, for long voyages, you could pile wives, children, cooking pots, mats, tools, plants, pigs, dogs, and a popular god or two. Some, it seems, were built by faeries and launched down the rainbow's arch. But most were shaped in more pedestrian fashion, with fast-flying adzes of basalt. They had triangular tall sails of plaited pandanus on one, two, or three masts: and when the wind fell, they were paddled. For long voyages, canoes of fifty, sixty, and seventy feet were built. On a decked double canoe, half a village might set out for foreign parts. They made tremendous voyages, those great canoes, *Mahina-i-te-pua*, the Crescent-Wave-at-the-Bow that-bursts-into Foam-like-a-Flower, *Te Manu-ka-rere*, Flight-of-Birds, and the rest: [4] from Tahiti to New Zealand, from the Marquesas to Hawaii, and perhaps from the Marquesas to Peru, for they ate the Peruvian sweet potato in Hawaii by the thirteenth century, in New Zealand during the fourteenth. From the Marquesas to northern Peru is about 4000 miles, more if the passage goes by Easter, which Polynesians had already colonized,[5] but which itself lacked timber for ocean-going canoes.

For their long passages, the Polynesians prepared, like Hitler's parachutists, with rigorous exercises and regulated diets.

Their advance from the Gilberts took them in the fifth century to the Society Islands, about Havai'a and Tahiti. Thence, as populations or the urge for adventure rose once more, they spread, led probably, as in other Empires, by

[4] From Dr. Peter H. Buck's *Vikings of the Sunrise*, New York, 1938. Whoever writes of the Polynesians now must be in debt to Dr. Buck. I acknowledge mine without hope of repayment unless to send more readers to his remarkable book. Dr. Buck (Te Rangi Hiroa) himself is privileged to be half-Maori. He has made the most of his two worlds and done them both great service.

[5] Easter Island's stone images, by the way, seem to me very like antique items turned up in Sumatra, if one must go hunting likenesses between these things. I sometimes think that if you give men at equivalent levels of culture good hefty rocks and means to chip them with they will probably turn you out much the same sort of article. But it is easily conceivable that the Polynesians in their long migrations carried some recollections or models of things they had made or seen in the countries whence they came or where they passed.

the Younger Sons. The Marquesas became a new centre
for expansion eastward, and perhaps served as a stage on
the route to Hawaii. The distribution of plants and beasts
throughout the Polynesian area suggests systematic colonization after preliminary scoutings and surveys. Somewhere
about the twelfth century, hundreds of years behind their
Menehune vanguard, the families of historic Hawaii arrived:

> *Behold Hawai'i, an island, a people!*
> *The people of Hawai'i are the offspring of Tahiti.*[6]

Hawai'i, Of-the-Green-Back (the bard, it will be noticed,
is everywhere a prophet) was, according to one school of
historians, fathered by Wakea, Space, on the fruitful Papa
Who Gave Birth to Islands. But, as David Malo, the
Hawaiian historian, has pointed out, "if the women in that
ancient time gave birth to countries then indeed they
would do so in these days; and if at that time they were
made by the hands of Wakea, doubtless the same thing
would be done now," [7] an argument so unanswerable that
Wakea and Papa are reluctantly surrendered.

HAWAII ÜBER ALLES

The Polynesians now have been followed to Hawaii by
colonists from Kobe and Canton, Kyushu, Yokohama,
Moppa, Kunsan, Lansing, Pittsburgh and Salt Lake City.

Cook estimated the population at 400,000 in 1788, but
his opportunities were limited and abruptly ended. Vancouver, who had been with Cook, made the count lower
when he returned in 1792. Kamehameha I had been busily
reducing the four old kingdoms of the Territory to one:

[6] Quoted from *Vikings of the Sunrise,* Peter H. Buck. New
York, 1938.
[7] *Ibid.*

and a great many people who objected to his New Order were reduced too by the length of their heads. In 1823, the missionaries estimated 142,000. Internecine war and local bad habits (infanticide and abortion, for example) contributed to the decline. There was a pestilence in Vancouver's time that held up the wars; and cholera swept the islands in 1804.

The Hawaiians, however, were what we would call adjusting themselves to civilization. Between Vancouver's first and second visits, numbers of natives had left home to see the world, and King Kamehameha went to work to modernize his realm. He acquired a merchant marine by killing the crew of an American schooner: and he employed Europeans as artillery instructors and on fortifications. The chiefs adopted odd articles of European costume and sufficient vocabulary from visiting sailors to compete with any sea-going parrot from Rotherhithe to Canton. The population at large discovered (as many travellers ruefully remarked) that Spanish silver dollars were of greater value than old nails and soleless shoes and rusty cutlasses when trading for pigs, cane, taro, coconuts, melons, wood and water.

Kamehameha took up civilization with energy and zeal. He dished the Russians, quashed the Spanish pirates, played off one European Power against another, achieved a fortune in dollars (Spanish), and built 800 war canoes. He cut sandalwood as a royal monopoly and kept his people at it until they began to die of starvation in the neglected fields. But he sometimes took good advice, especially from Vancouver, who brought him cattle and sheep, reconciled him with his wife, and built him a naval ship.

But neither Kamehameha nor the missionaries who began to flow from New England in 1820 could check the racial decline. The kingdom of Hawaii was less pathetic than the parliaments in Samoa and in Tonga; but it is sadly symbolized by the fate of Kamehameha II and his Queen. In 1794, Kamehameha I had recognized British sovereignty in the islands (somewhat, it seems, to the embarrassment of Vancouver) and he and his people had declared themselves *Tanta no Britannee,* people of Britain. His son may have had some curiosity to see the patria: and, as a rising king with problems of protocol, to inspect that model of regal proprieties, the court of George IV. So it happened that on May 22 of 1824 he and his Queen were guests for a gala at the Theatre Royal in Covent Garden, where they saw Mr. Young and Miss Lacy and Mrs. Ogilvie perform the Tragick Play *Pizarro* (surely a title which might have given a King of the Sandwich Islands furiously to think) and the New Grand Melo-Dramatick Egyptian Romantick called . . . but what does it matter how it was called? A few days later both the King and his Queen were dead, of measles.

Lord Byron, a cousin of the poet, brought their bodies home in one of King George's ships: and that was pretty much the pathetic end of Hawaiian royalty's ambition to hobnob with its crowned cousins of Europe.

Power went to a succession of royal matriarchs who gave Hawaii something (not all, but something) of a mid-Victorian air. The ladies supported missions. The increasing white population opposed them, especially when the missionaries wanted laws controlling the supply of labour, liquor and girls. Difficulties rose between Protestants and Catholics, and with consuls, beachcombers, and all the general wash and débris of human stuff flowing in on the new tides. Whaling began in 1820, sugar in 1835. In 1843, the British Government disowned Lord George Paulet, who had taken Kamehameha's old gesture seriously and run up the Union Jack. When his government was restored to him the king uttered a phrase worthy of Mr. Gladstone and of the moral and political instructors that New England had given him: "The life of the land is continued by righteousness—*Ua mau ke ea o ka aina i ka pono.*"

OUTPOST AND MELTING POT

Hawaii signed with the United States its first foreign treaty as a sovereign Power in 1826. The United States neglected to ratify the treaty, but a seed was planted. By the middle of the century, America had reached her last frontier, in Oregon and at the Pacific Ocean. From then on, the future of Hawaii was sealed, though it was not until 1898 that the last frontier moved west again and over a lot of water.

With its population on the skids, Hawaii went in for organized immigration from 1859 on, first from other Pacific islands, then from the United States and northern Europe, then from Portugal and Spain and Puerto Rico. The Chinese were encouraged in the third quarter of the century and restricted from 1883. The Japanese, at first assisted migrants, began to tumble in from 1885, to the tune of 65,000 before the century was out. They had increased to 140,000 three decades later.

By 1890, the islands could show nearly every major breed of humanity with permutations and combinations. In 1894, the clash of what we may politely call circumstance ejected the Royal House, and a republic appeared, to be tossed on its own dilemmas. The place was a seething racial hotchpotch. Until it could settle into its own stability, a strong hand was necessary to order. Congress moved at last.

The United States annexed Hawaii for much the same reasons as other governments have often annexed other places. Asia was, as they used to say at the time, stirring from its age-old sleep, which meant that it was buying guns, training officers, and building ironclads. Russia was interested once more in Pacific ports and traffic, and there were still people alive who could remember a Russian fort on the coast just above the Golden Gate. The more prescient were looking towards Japan with thoughtful eyes. There was trouble with Spain. And there was talk of "our manifest destiny." In other words, an offshore base for the Pacific Fleet seemed more than merely desirable.

There was the problem too of protecting commerce. Traffic with Asia was constantly increasing, but the line was long and exposed. There were the interests and investments of American citizens in the islands, and the distressing precedent which Hawaiian anarchy might set. All these are the sort of solid and weighty reasons that can never be ignored by responsible statesmanship, whatever capital may subsequently be made in Union Square and such places. One is reminded of both British and Dutch experience further west. Traders and merchants move in to do business. Business is their ambition, not politics or power. But local government is tyrannical or anarchic. There is no enduring security for agreements, for property or for persons. Inevitably, and first entirely as a matter of business, the merchants begin to deal in local politics. The East India Companies could not stay in business and neglect the machinations of a Mogul Emperor or a Sultan of Bantam any more than the automobile industry can function in blithe indifference to affairs at Washington. If American citizens were to do business in Hawaii or with Hawaii, America could not be utterly indifferent to happenings in Hawaii.

This is not a defence of what is called economic imperialism, but a statement of the human facts as they appear in a world admittedly imperfect. The British East India Company had but two possible courses in India: to go into Indian politics or to get out of India. Perhaps it should have got out, for conscience's sake, leaving India

to its own tyrannies, to anarchy, or to the French. The
British preferred to impose order and to take large profits
for benefits bestowed. When all is said and done, that was
very much America's decision in Hawaii. I don't know
who is prepared to sit in final judgement. For my part, I
leave it to the Recording Angel, who has access to more
consciences and information generally than I have, and
the experience of all time to inform his judgement. The
best the general citizenry can do is to be honest about
such rights and wrongs as appear, and to kick on government's door when the record is too bad.

Materially, Hawaii is vastly better off for American
control and protection. Whether it likes being better off is
another question, which echoes throughout the great
colonial domains. America is trying to develop in its peoples political and social competence and responsibility.
The British and Dutch are doing much the same in Malaya and the East Indies. The pace of the advance must
always vary with local conditions. In Hawaii, the United
States can work with and through a comparatively high
proportion of literate and progressive people.[8]

Remember my friend the clerk, that man of omen. East
and West are no longer where Mr. Kipling put them. In
the Pacific Basin and Indonesia they have already met,
however long it takes for the decision to appear. So far the

[8] Every one knows that there are still sharp and serious
racial difficulties; but the difficulties are less impressive than
the degree of order achieved in what once appeared an impossible situation. The 1930 census breaks down the Hawaiian
population thus: 22,635 Hawaiians, 15,632 Caucasian Hawaiians, 12,592 Asiatic Hawaiians. At the census of 1940, out of a
total of 423,330, there were 64,310 Hawaiians and part Hawaiians, 103,791 Caucasians, 28,774 Chinese, 52,569 Filipinos,
157,905 Japanese, 6851 Koreans, 8296 Puerto Ricans, 834
others, each of these groups including the hybrids which it
dominates.

bias of influence comes from the European contribution, but the weight of blood is Asia's. Pidgin English is the common language east of the Malayan sphere, and Pacific dialects are loaded with English words. Education and such morals as may be take a European-American character, and so do social habits and social organization. Trousers, cinemas, ice-cream sodas, labour legislation, fraternal societies, bowling alleys, monogamy (if monogamy is still a character of Western civilization), bacon and eggs, petting parties, the novels of Mr. Hemingway, the Red Cross, neon signs, steak dinners, Mrs. Eddy, baseball diamonds, bank accounts, secondhand cars, and a steady eight-hour day are all benefits of Western culture. It has been a one-sided exchange. Not many of our people do the *hula* with native suppleness, and we wear *leis* awkwardly. Nor do many of us read the Chinese poets and philosophers or follow the delicate ceremonies of Japan. The culture of the new man, in outward habit at least, is more Americo-European than anything else and will probably continue so. The European is strategically placed in the Pacific for political, economic and cultural influence. If the white peoples of the Americas, of Australia and New Zealand follow their interests, as people frequently do, some measure of politico-economic union amongst them will appear in the early future: and their variety of civilization will control the cultural and social formation of the new races.

As the world grows smaller and the contacts of peoples increase, there will be much more interbreeding, unless some world-empire comes with master-races and subject-races and exclusive castes of blood.

These are matters to which internationalists might give more consideration. But then, we are less concerned nowadays for life than for the machinery of life.

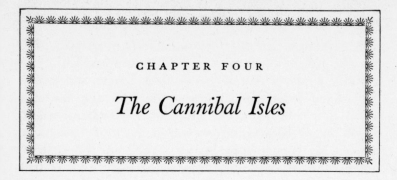

CHAPTER FOUR

The Cannibal Isles

RED SABBATH

THE port Suva, capital of the Fijis, is 2736 miles south-southeast of Honolulu. On a Sunday of my last passage down, we were under the Equator and approaching the Date Line. Somewhere north of east, beyond a lot of flying scud and darksome cloud, was the little phosphate island of Nauru.[1] It was sharing our dirty weather and our lazy Sunday. Offshore, ships were drifting as they waited for the westerly to move before they entered the difficult harbour. Early in the day a patch of horizon momentarily cleared, and some one along the beach saw smoke rising from a vessel far out. He thought of fire, but nothing extraordinary had been heard, no signals of distress, and there were two other ships approaching, apparently in company. Then the clouds and the Sunday calm descended.

The weather was distinctly dirty. A hurricane was brewing, and if sounds were heard from the sea they were mistaken in the noisy wind and water that thereabouts gets

[1] Nauru has an area of about eight square miles; and a population of about 190 Europeans and 3000 natives and others. Its product is phosphate, of which it ships up to 900,000 tons a year, and it is administered jointly by Great Britain, Australia, and New Zealand, under a C Class of Mandate of the League of Nations which forbids the military training or equipment of the population.

up. We were ploughing pretty heavily that afternoon ourselves, away to eastward.

Sometime before dusk, the clouds were blown apart: and then a burst of flame was seen rising with huge smoke from a fourth steamer, which was being shelled by one of two others, the two seen in company at dawn. Now, as the weather lifted, the pair streaked away to sea. But during that dank, dark day they had sent five ships to the bottom off Nauru.

Our first news of it came from our engines, suddenly accelerating. We made a very smart run for Suva. Eighteen days later Nauru was attacked again, this time its harbour works and plants ashore being heavily shelled by a raider which appeared under Japanese colours and only hoisted her own as she opened fire.

MELANESIA—THE FIJIS

At Suva you pass from Polynesia into Melanesia and into the Australasian sphere of influence. The Fijis are ruled from London, but one begins to be aware of Sydney and Wellington west and south.

The 250 islands of the Fijis are scattered through nearly six degrees of latitude and across the Date Line. Only about eighty of the islands are inhabited, so there is an opening still for Mr. Compton Mackenzie. Suva is on Viti Levu, which is eighty-two miles long and fifty-seven miles from north to south sea by the *Fijian Handbook*.[2]

Suva and Honolulu are the chief crossroad ports of all the islands, and the Fijis have been a meeting place of commerce and cultures since Melanesians and Polynesians

[2] Ninety-seven miles long and sixty-seven miles wide if you prefer the *Encyclopaedia Britannica:* both authorities, with considerable ingenuity, agree on its area as 4053 square miles.

first met upon these seas.³ The Melanesian, as his name
suggests, is darker than the Polynesian and is basically
negroid. Negroid man, somewhere in the remote Asiatic
home of humanity, split into two main branches. One
moved on Africa, another swung away east, probably
fighting clear of the outskirts of the Mongoloids then
fastening their hold on continental East Asia, and took to
the sea. They thrust ahead of them the Negritos, a distinc-
tive branch of their own stock, and moved on steadily
eastwards by islands and waterways to New Guinea,
whence they spilled over in time on the Solomons and
Fijis. The Fijis are a Melanesian out-thrust in the Polynesian world. Polynesia, in effect, is on three sides of the
Fijis, the Gilberts are north, New Zealand south, and
Hawaii, the Samoans, the Societies and the Marquesas in
something like an irregular arc eastward. The Fijians have
a tradition that their progenitors came from the west in
the great canoe *Kaunitoni* and landed first on Viti Levu,
as the incoming traveller still does. Perhaps there were
enemies on their heels, for they took to the mountains,
which are wild and woody, and there founded village settlements, only slowly and after a long interval creeping
down the riverways again to occupy the coasts and to cross
the channels to the larger island of Vanua Levu and the
smaller islands between and about. Various village groups
developed federations, and the Fijian, whose intelligence
is high, displayed considerable political agility. But his
federations found their principal pleasures in war and the
long pig which battle provided. His talent for battle and
slaughter rivals the European's. But its local exercise has
been restricted of late: the Fijian fights now only as a free
citizen of the British Empire.

As far as we know, Tasman was the first European to

³ In the Fijis Melanesian and Polynesian traded tools, root-
vegetables, ideas and genes.

sight the Fijis. His great swing during 1642-'43, from Batavia to Batavia, encompassed most of the Indian Ocean and half the Pacific. The inevitable Cook (known hereabouts as Toote) was there in 1774, and left four fowls on Vatoa, the locals say: and as Vatoa means four fowls and as Cook went around discreetly doing good, perhaps they are right. Bligh passed through the archipelago in his open-boat excursion from the *Bounty* to Koepang. Mr. Fletcher Christian had given him no firearms and the Fijians were after him in war canoes, so he did not land: but, thirsty and half-dazed by heat, with crude instruments and tossing in an open boat, Bligh made and recorded his bearings so accurately that his charts will still serve for the ticklish passages that he took.

A good many ships saw the islands before many of their boat-crews landed. Navigation throughout the archipelago is touchy, with isolated reefs and submergent coral patches, but one Captain Barber was ashore in 1794, and presently there was traffic in sandalwood and *bêche-de-mer*. As the merchants and seamen arrived, they began to join in the local battles, such being their disposition. In 1808, for example, when the American brig *Eliza* broke on a reef off Nairai, one of the crew, Charles Savage, set himself up as a sort of Grand Vizier in Mbau, where he trained the local guard to firearms and conducted a series of successful campaigns until he was, happily or unhappily, killed and eaten in 1814, and his bones made into needles for mementos. His activities produced in rival states a brisk demand for soldiers of fortune, and Paddy Connell achieved reputation and forty-nine children at the court of Rewa.[4] He was a teller of tales, which pleased others besides the Chief of Rewa. His countrymen, sensitive for the national dignity,

[4] *The natives there*
They liked his hair
They liked his Irish smile.

will gratefully hear that he was neither cooked nor eaten raw. But he was a less successful master in arms (the arms of war, at least) than the *Eliza's* Savage: and by the eighteen-fifties Savage's educated Mbauns had won for Thakombau the style of King of the Fijis. He is really the King of the Cannibal Isles famous in music-hall song and story, and a very notable figure of a man, even if he did not have rings on his fingers and bells on his toes, and elephants to ride upon, or a little Irish rose.

FIRECRACKERS

It was Thakombau who first invited British rule: and oddly enough, the remote impetus was connected with America's Declaration of Independence. On the 4th of July, 1849, the American Consul was piously celebrating, according to the rubrics, with fireworks and cannon. In the course of the solemnities his house was burnt down. The American residents were naturally very indignant with King Thakombau, presumably for lacking a fire brigade. They made claim for compensation, to which various other claims were presently added, with such noise that the United States sent a Navy officer to adjudicate. His verdict was for £9000, to be found by Thakombau for United States citizens. Thakombau had no local prospects of raising the cash, so he and his chiefs offered to trade the islands to Britain if Britain would foot the bill and leave to Thakombau his title of *Tui Viti*, King of Fiji, and 200,000 acres of selected land as his private domain. The Australian and New Zealand governments, always sensitive to Pacific proprietorships, were all for it, and so were a number of people who had discovered that the Fijis had gold and could grow cotton. But Downing Street, which sometimes achieved Empire but often has had Empire thrust upon it, refused, stubbornly and with such pointed comment that Thakombau reacted and offered his kingdom to the offended Americans. But, by the time things had come to this pass (there was leisure in the old world), the United States were at war amongst themselves, and Mr. Lincoln had little opportunity to consider the case of the Cannibal Isles. Thakombau was left to his own responsibilities. One cannot help feeling sympathy for him: there are few more bothersome situations than that of a king who cannot even give his kingdom away.

But in 1874 Britain finally agreed to take up what she certainly considered a thankless task. The islands were in a profound depression, the troubles of government had grown, the traffic in Polynesian labour had become a scandal that only strong authority based in the Central Pacific could hope to check. Things had fallen into much the mess that was later to make America take over in Hawaii. Britain moved in, after King and chiefs had solemnly ceded sovereignty to the little, middle-aged lady of Windsor.

ROUSSEAU NOTWITHSTANDING

Some of the spadework of civilization had been done. The missionaries, after enough of their earlier converts had been eaten, struck a more militant note; and when in 1854 the good Methodist tribes smote the heathen hip and thigh, they propounded a convincing apologetic. Cannibalism too was on the way out, with the practise of strangling widows, long regarded as something like a necessary life insurance for husbands. When a chief ran to forty or fifty wives, he had to take precautions against poison in his soup: but what wife, however legitimate her complaints, would care to walk the difficult long pathway of the dead with a lately assassinated husband? The missionaries had difficulty in checking the custom of strangling widows, for the widows themselves insisted upon it as their right. Grandmothers too could demand that their grandchildren club them or bury them alive, and it was difficult for a delicately bred Fijian to refuse these filial duties. The Fijians were an advanced people. Some of their notions only now make progress amongst us. When a boy's leg was mauled by a shark, his solicitous friends would kill him off rather than see him hobble through the years. But I doubt whether it would chime even yet with euthanasian doctrine to tear off the leg of an unpopular acquaintance and then to make him eat it.[5]

Dampier once declared that he had never met a confirmed cannibal, but I fear there is little doubt about the Fijians. Canoes came back from battle heavily laden with long pig, which was dismembered for the feast with skilful butchery. If occasion for feasting developed (as when some neighbour chieftain dropped in) and the larder lacked supply to grace an adequate bill, then women and children fishing on the reefs might legitimately be stalked. Women and children anyhow were preferred to stringy warriors; and were commonly considered much superior to turtle, fish, or fowl. Ritual sanctioned cannibalism and the ancestral god always received his piece of thigh or bicep, the choicest cuts: but Fijian ate Fijian because he liked the taste and not merely to fulfil his spiritual obligations.[6]

[5] There is what some may consider a more than adequate account of these matters in *Fiji and the Fijians,* by Professor G. C. Henderson (Sydney, 1931); *sapiens homo cum primus nostrae civitatis,* to whom I much listened in my youth *pro meâ sapientia.*

[6] Their diet, of course, was not restricted to the human sort. One of the early missionaries mentions a feast where was provided a wall of fish five feet high and sixty feet in length, with

Human carcases were also used for rollers when a new canoe took the water, and the canoe itself was encouraged at launching by a splash of human blood. An architect might properly hope to rest his house-tree on a foundation of flesh. The Bataks of Sumatra kept until lately this custom, and thought no house well founded unless it had a corpse or two beneath its posts.

We have had, since Rousseau, a good deal of silly thinking about the Natural Man in his arboreal innocence. People who protest at imperial rule or missionary influences might have protested less if they had arrived in time for the cannibal feasts, even if only as academic observers. Yet there is an oddity about cannibalism which would have pleased Rousseau and may still gratify the misanthropist. Cannibalism seems to be a trick of comparatively advanced peoples. I have some acquaintance amongst both Bataks and Fijians, eminent above most rivals for their flair in this direction: and both are notably superior in general intelligence, manners, dignity and physical habit to many of their neighbours, and my own.

Captain Cook, a most discerning man (it is difficult to mention him without some tribute), noticed in Tonga that Fijians were respected for their power and ferocity, but also for their ingenuity. They made excellent pottery, cloths, mats, and shrewdly carved woodwork, superb canoes, good dyes, and mosquito nets. They are a race of

side dishes ten feet by four and three feet deep spread with green leaves, turtles and roast pigs. Fijians have a curious seasonal dish, the *mbalolo,* a thing like a small green worm which is actually the egg sac of an annelid and rises from the underwater reefs in October and November. The Fijians gather and eat it with tremendous gusto, though I have met only one European who professed to like the stuff. That was on my first visit to Fiji, and I imagine he must since have succumbed to one or another of the curious enterprises which charged his conversation with romance.

extroverts, with a language extraordinarily rich in words of action, making, doing, but lending itself less to the subtler intellectual and moral distinctions. But it has a notable vein of metaphor as Professor Henderson suggests: *tui* for king and for hawk, *senembia,* flower on the wave, for racing foam, and the word for modesty suggests the softening, exquisite light after sunset. They still have a passion for *meke,* their traditional songs and dances.[7] In their brief moments of peace, they went in strenuously for athletics, and they play now a furious game of football. They were and are a magnificent-looking people, especially those of the blood of chieftains, commonly less negroid than the minor orders. Thakombau himself was a gigantic man.

This other day when we were in Fiji, we saw something of the native defence force, considerably enlarged since the war began. I record my belief that their aspect would frighten tanks off their tractors. The New Zealanders were there in strength, and the New Zealanders with the Australians are, over all, just about the heftiest white stuff there is, if one excepts a brand of Dutchmen: but half the Fijians hung head and shoulders above them. I mention shoulders because one could be deceived by the enormous head of hair which is a peculiarity of the oceanic negroids and rather resembles a mass of clotted mops, bleached with lime to a fearful gingeriness.

[7] Some Polynesian poetry now strikes a vigorous contemporary note, with that concrete imagery so admired by the modern. I have heard, and I hope that somebody can confirm it (these confounded steamers don't stay long enough at Pago-Pago), that the contemporary love lyric in Samoa has substituted for such figures of affection as "my flower" or "my love, my dove, my beautiful one" comparisons much more evocative, with canned tomatoes and pork-and-beans.

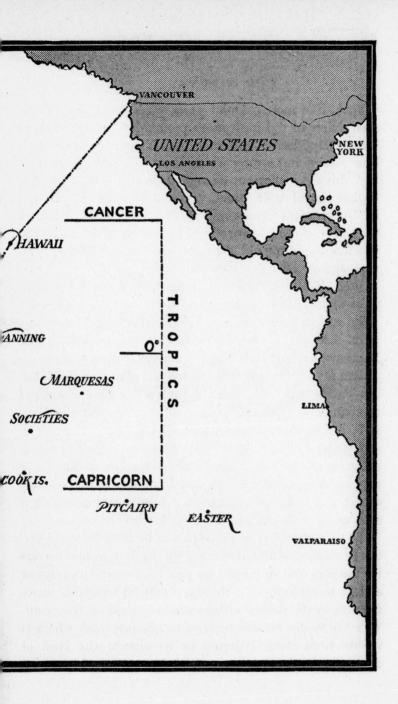

SUVA

Suva, like most colonial ports, gives you a very inadequate view of the indigenous population, except perhaps
for the superlative policemen by the gangway in the neat
blue tunics and strong white *lavas* wrapped about their
legs. Suva is a pleasant enough little place, with its Australian sort of main street, verandahed pubs and all, and
its Government House and gardens, and a hotel out on
the beach where you are served by Indian servants and can
watch a dog of my old acquaintance fishing below the terrace, and a native boy or two spearing amongst the rocks.
It used, like most crossroad ports with no or low tariffs,
to be a good place to buy shirts, shorts, and slops, but even
Aden and Colombo are now for years no longer what they
were. But here, on the westward ride, you meet your first
Bombay merchants, and here is a general store of the Australian firm of Burns-Philp, which has played in the Western Pacific much the rôle of the earlier great chartered
companies in India, Africa, and the Netherlands East.
B.-P. has steamship routes across a quarter of the world,
and trades in pretty well everything that is grown, made,
eaten, worn, used or wasted from Singapore to Samoa. It
may be short on elephants, but I am sure it can manage
everything from an anchor to a needle and probably a
ship to go with one and a haystack with the other.

To see something of the Fijian as he is, one should certainly avoid that tour favoured by the Indian taxi-drivers
for the innocent in transit, up past the hospital and by the
asylum to the cemetery, though it may be a suitable introduction to the dismal village which rounds off the jaunt.
The Fijian deserves to be seen in his own land, which is
visible from Suva, hanging in its clouds: the land of
mountains and fierce torrents, of dense forests hung with

orchids, the land where Dengei burns logs thirty miles in circumference at the door of his cave on Kauvaundra. When Dengei rolls in his cups, the island trembles and seismographs record in Los Angeles and Sydney. Viti Levu is less than his club: one day perhaps he will pick it up and smite the tourists with it, for he is a jealous god and tourists are not always tactful, but that is a chance worth taking to see his territory. Or one may go down from the mountains to the further beaches and take ship with the Fijian boatmen to islands but a few feet above the sea, where palms are mirrored in water above gardens whose bright seaplants climb over coral like ramblers in a rockery.

From the western waters of Viti Levu or travelling between Lautoka and Nandi, you see the mountain of Tuleita, whence all good Fijians return to their fathers, following like the Polynesians the path of the sun, to the land of Yavatu, the divine ancestor, whence came the great canoe *Kaunitoni*.

THE FIJIAN TO-DAY

The Fijian now is purged of his savage doctrine and practices: what remains is a man hospitable and courteous. He has a pleasant, swift humour; and respect without subservience for authority, a quality of dignity which we somehow have lately missed. He is distinctly a person.

The British Colonial Office has built its structure of administration upon the native traditions of government. Before the British came, the Fijians themselves had evolved a Great Council of Chiefs to make general provision for control of game and fisheries and such matters. Its established custom became at annexation the basis for the Code of Native Regulations under which the Fijian lives. The Great Council continues to consult with the

Governor and his executive officers, who compose, with
nominated and elected representatives of the European,
Fijian and Indian populations, a Legislative Council.[8]

The Fijians are a politically active people, and most of
the population attends the assemblies to keep an eye on
the politicians and to do its share of the eating and junket-
ings proper to solemn occasions: in this sense at least the
Fijian demands his share of political gravy.

The Fijian, in brief, has a vigorous system of local government which gives almost any citizen opportunity to
make the noises he thinks appropriate at the times he
thinks fitting: which is more than can be said for a good
many governmental structures.

To throw as much responsibility as possible back upon
the people themselves is a favourite British method, where
it can be done. It provokes some criticism, because it admittedly slows the social progress of natives less apt than
ourselves at catching modern meanings and devices. But
it provides for political education and for a steady evolution. The British themselves have never had much faith
in sudden leaps. They notoriously broaden down from
precedent to precedent. They like things to work out

[8] The Great Council is also the apex of a pyramid of native administration. Beneath it are Provincial Councils, which
consist of the Provincial Commissioner, the native Assistant
Commissioner, the headmen of districts, the native magis-
trates and native medical officers, elected chiefs and representatives of the various social divisions which have persisted
in Fiji since the gods designed them: chiefs, priests, and those
counsellors, envoys and courtiers who are the "eyes of the
land," soldiers and freemen. Every Fijian has his elected representative in the Provincial Councils and in the District
Councils of headmen and the like at the next rung of administration. The Resolutions of the various Councils become,
upon the Governor's assent, Native Regulations for the area
concerned, with the force of law.

gradually according to circumstances, character, and talents. They have never been good at planning, because they remain, at bottom, unconvinced that you can blueprint the course of that curious creature, man. Consequently, the reformer in a hurry is often very annoyed with them, both at home and abroad. The Fijian, certainly, has not progressed as rapidly as some others in hygiene, education or towards extinction.[9] But like the Maori, he now has a good chance of survival and of becoming an important figure in the strange medley of peoples which makes the British Commonwealth. His future will much depend upon himself. In large numbers, he still likes to sit beneath his palms or to take every day off for fishing, to draw some rent from his Indian farmer-tenants, and to chat in the sun: which seems to me in my more lucid moments a rather better sort of life than riding the subway at 8.30 every morning. But if you talk to a Fijian medical officer now or to a District Headman, you begin to glimpse other possibilities. The example of the Maoris, with their Ministers in New Zealand Governments, is before the peoples of the British Pacific.

The Fijians, like the Hawaiians, have suffered perhaps from immigration in the sense that they might have tackled jobs which now they leave to others. I suppose these Pacific peoples must learn our trick of working if they are to make much moral and social progress from within themselves. Work was not, I imagine, the curse laid upon Adam: it was the antidote to the darkened understanding and the weakened will.

[9] The Fijian is still in the majority at home, but only just. There are about 100,000 of him, but more than 80,000 British Indians, with about 5000 Europeans (in peacetime), 3700 half-castes, 1500 Chinese, 1900 Polynesians, and a handful of others. Both Fijians and Indians are increasing.

INDIA IN FIJI

The Indians came on the heels of British rule. When the British took over, the islands were in the dismal depths of depression. The sandalwood was mostly cut out, copra was down, gold was unworked, and the few plantations could not find labourers either at the first or the eleventh hour. The Fijian had other ways to pass his time. But if you are going to run a community on anything approaching modern lines, you need revenue. And to get revenue, you need a revenue-producing economy. Those who complain of exploitation by planters and the like sometimes forget that the planters' taxes provide schools, medicine, and social services. The simple native economies alone would not produce the surpluses necessary for such things. In spite of much modern persuasion to the contrary, it is still true that you cannot have your cake and eat it. If you want doctors and teachers, you have to pay them. If you have to pay them, you must earn the money.

Anyhow, the new British régime in 1874 looked about for sources of revenue. The planters were the answer. But the planters were making little headway because they could not get sufficient labour. They had tried Solomon Islanders and New Hebrideans, but Solomon Islanders and New Hebrideans shared the Fijian's general attitude to work. The new administration decided to go after two birds with one proposition.

In British India, the hard-working peasant was living a life of penury, underfed and miserable, because he could not get land. In Fiji, there was land but a lack of labour. The British introduced the Indian. In the first ten years something over 6000 came: and after ten years, each was entitled to his passage home. A two-way traffic was built up of Indians coming and going. A great many went home on leave, so to speak, and returned again: but more settled in the colony and propagated in the lush Indian habit. They made excellent colonists. Fiji sugar boomed; and presently, as peasants will, Indians began to acquire holdings for themselves, developing field crops, vegetables, fruits, and export plantation products. Some became rich men, many continue as working farmers: but they have given Fiji rice, cotton, maize, lentils, kava, pineapples, bananas, poultry, and dairy cattle: and they farm about 85,000 of the 90,000 acres under sugar for the Colonial Refining Company.

The Fijian was protected in his ownership of land, so most of the holdings are leased from him. The two races live comfortably together, considering their relations and circumstances, although a Fiji-bred Indian often inclines to share the Fijian's distaste for digging and delving. There has been less interbreeding than one might expect, but here again new syntheses, human and cultural, appear. Empire is a much more complicated affair than your simple jingo and anti-jingo suspect.

To British dominion Fiji provides a useful port and base for the protection of commerce: it pays a few people some dividends: it maintains a few officers who draw, amongst them all, a few thousand pounds a year (two or three may get over a thousand each). But the really important consequences are in the future of the two races now established in the Islands, the Indian peasants who have found relief from the poverty of India, the Fijians who have found, for good and ill, a whole new way of life.

THE USE OF EMPIRE

If the patterns of history are shaped by some presiding genius, then Empire would seem in part a device for encouraging the flow and interflow of peoples and cultures within a frame of order. The conscious motives of expansion are one thing: the divinity which shapes their ends another. An overseas jail becomes the Commonwealth of Australia; a trading company is chartered to send ships to India; and who could now give a fair reading of the Pilgrims' doctrine?

If you look at a map of the Pacific (and it is an exercise I urgently recommend) Fiji appears the natural hub of the south-central Pacific, as Hawaii is of the north-central. Their cogs sooner or later will mesh or clash. The Fijis lie under the flank of the Japanese mandates in Micronesia. That is why they now house a force of New Zealanders: a very considerable force.

From Micronesia, the Fijis would offer the next decisive foothold to command of the Pacific. The United States has a minor counter a few hundreds of miles eastward at Pago-Pago, in Tutuila of Samoa: but with the Fijis in hostile hands, Pago-Pago too might easily be made untenable, and the way opened to the East by the stepping-stones of Tonga and Tahiti, the Tuamotus and Marquesas. A strong Power established along that line might comfortably command the western approaches of Panama, the Pacific routes between North and South America, and exert a powerful political pressure upon the whole western coast line of the South American countries and upon Australia and New Zealand. Japan is busy in Peru, and not unmindful of the route thither. Tahiti is about the same distance from California as California is from the Canal, by sea: and closer to both than is Buenos Aires to New York. It may not have the immediate interest to "hemisphere defence" that Dakar and the West Indies have; yet if I were trying to define the difficult word "hemisphere" I should stretch a point to include the archipelagos of the south-central Pacific.

But the effective command of all this area will be largely determined by the future of Australia and New Zealand. These, as we should not forget, are the only considerable white communities in all the vast sweep of the world between Chile and Natal, Suez and Panama, the tip of Kamchatka and the South Pole. They underprop the frame of order in two-thirds of the world. If they should lose their status as free white powers, their catastrophe will mark the turn of the great tide which flowed out of Europe to people the Americas, to command Africa, to quicken the life of Asia: it will sound retreat for European man. Rome, it is true, did not fall in a day, but the Goth was girded for the long march when forts were first abandoned on the far frontiers. If we think only of our dominion in the world as of territories, armies and such, we may be prepared to yield the outer marches. But is it not also a dominion of the mind and spirit and has it not yet benefits for the whole race of men? If we abandon it, we abandon what is essentially ourselves, and our end will be the fate of fellaheen.

POLYNESIAN PROMETHEUS

A THOROUGHLY irritating individual named Maui once hobbled the sun to give us all a longer working-day and start incalculable bothers for the Trades Unions. He pulled at the nose and coccyx of his brother-in-law until his brother-in-law barked and turned into the first dog, a dachshund of sorts, presumably. He visited the underworld and brought back fire for men to play with: and in Tahiti he grew eight heads, a questionable accomplishment, even for a collectivist. In Tonga he pushed up the sky, which had, until then, a ceiling brushing tree-tops; for which the twentieth century need not thank him. His one redeeming feat was that he caught New Zealand.

The North Island, as you may notice while you are there, is a fish. Maui's hook still clings as what we call Hawke's Bay, but

> *Within the circle of the sea,*
> *It holds a fish of note.*[1]

Dr. Buck insists that it is a sting-ray, with its long tail curving in the North Auckland Peninsula, and Wellington, the capital of government, shrewdly placed right in

[1] Aitutaki Chant. Quoted from Dr. Peter H. Buck's *Vikings of the Sunrise*. New York, 1938.

the centre of the head: which perhaps flatters some administrators who have reigned there.

But Maui's fish was long untenanted. Civilizations rose and fell on the Nile and Euphrates and the sand again blew over the sites of cities; China grew great and Socrates talked Greek and the Ancient Britons ceased to paint with woad. Rajputs governed India and Rome marched out along her superlative highways and then marched back again. Wild Saxons took to raiding across the North Sea. An English king saved Christendom, won a prize for reading and burnt some cakes. All those objectionable people came over with William the Conqueror. The Norsemen reached America. The Incas founded kingdoms, and then, at about the time when the Abbot of Muchelney was building a house where I have lived in Somerset, men first walked in New Zealand. They called it the Land of Birds: for Kupe, who discovered it, said that he saw no people other than a fantail flitting and a bellbird singing in the forest.

The South Pacific is still a lonely ocean, lonelier since the days of sail when ships went round the world in the roaring forties south. New Zealand hangs upon the end of the old world of man, though a good many people think it may be the beginning of a new. It is perhaps fitting and in a way encouraging that the latest of humanity's habitations should set a pace for the rest.

Trudging down the eleven hundred miles of windy water from Suva to North Cape, you have time and occasion to contemplate the queer restlessness of our kind which sent them in open canoes and small bouncing boats to inherit the ultimate parts of the earth. *I will make nations of thee and kings shall come out of thee.*

The ages are dimmed since men began to coil on the long treks from Babel or Baluchistan or wherever it may have been. But here in New Zealand you can glimpse, within historical times, the aboriginal trek.

MAORI

The Maoris came, in the last of the Polynesian migrations, from the Havai'a, which is in the Society Islands, the distributing centre of Polynesian expansion. Their main tide reached New Zealand about the fourteenth century, though the route had been known and pioneers possibly went to settle for three hundred years before.[2]

They found a country which after six centuries of man is still beautiful: a place of mountains, where white peaks are seen through tangles of blossom and swift rivers leap in deep green forests; where lakes reflect wild crags above banks smooth and domestic as a cloistered lawn; where rolling savannahs beckoned for their cows, and whitebait ran in the tidal waters and oysters grew fat in soft estuarial muds; where trout, once brought, would fill to ten and even fifteen pounds; where superb timbers, kauri and totara, rimu, matai, were a heritage to man which he wasted with axe and fire. It was a country of fiords which wound like rivers under mountains and forests, of tussocky headlands, of plateaux with thick woods of treeferns; of cool, curving bays, and every climate in the world except extremes: though even these you find in the hanging glaciers of the south or in the fantastic region of boiling mud and thermal geysers which the Maoris, with a

[2] The Maoris found a handful of people on the east coast whom they called Morioros, inferiors. They were of the same racial stock, and the Maoris absorbed them or drove them to the extremities of the South Island and to the Chathams, which are extremities indeed. The last of the Morioros died in 1933. They represent probably the first thin trickles of the Polynesians in the centuries before the main immigration.

fine indifference to natural drama, use for cooking eggs, New Zealand has more variety than any country near its size: and, until man came, was singularly free from pests.

It has toheroa, the noble shellfish rivalling turtle for the crown of soups, and bluebells, gentians, mountain daisies and silver fern, grasses for butter (unquestionably the *best* butter), and landscapes designed for rosy milk-maids in print bonnets. Its great birds had never learned to fly perhaps because they had known nothing to fear; but the Maoris ran down the giant twelve-foot moa, and the takahe has not been seen since 1898.

When Cook first met the Maoris they numbered per-haps 90,000 to 100,000 in a land almost as large as the sum of all the New England States, New York, and New Jersey. When British colonists took a first census in 1856, there were 56,000 Maoris. Before the British settled in, the Maoris, by constant inter-tribal wars, had reduced their numbers much. War was the Maori's sport and he conducted it with the rigid etiquette of all military aris-tocracies. He developed its art and auxiliary crafts much more than the other Polynesians, perhaps to keep warm in his new brisk air. He was expert at fortification and his *pa* one day gave British artillerymen some trouble. The first visitors, excepting the admirable Cook, had vigorous reception on the beaches; but when the Maori discovered the use and source of muskets, he traded even the skulls above his doorpost for the means to bag more skulls. Muskets gave new gusto to forays and campaigns, and the Maoris began to pop one another off with the utmost enthusiasm. When the great chief Hongi went with a mis-sionary to England in 1819, he brought a cargo of firearms home, converting the gifts of the pious and the profane into shooting-iron. He did keep, however, a suit of armour presented by his fellow Majesty of England, and wore it in battle to the admiration of foes and friends. Hongi sug-

gests the Maori soldier who declined to evacuate Crete.
While others were marching towards the beach, he was
making towards the Germans, girdled with ammunition
and carrying three machine-guns, two taken from captured
parachutists. Against all remonstrance, he shook his head
gleefully. When a man has just acquired three good
machine-guns, that, of all times, is not the time to stop
a fight.

Once the Maori found his feet in the new order and
understood that he might be, as he is, the first citizen in
the nation, he began to increase again, now at a rate faster
than white New Zealanders. In 1936, there were 82,326
Maoris, sixty-eight per cent of the full blood, fourteen per
cent three-quarter caste, eighteen per cent half-caste. In
New Zealand it is honourable to have Maori blood, and
the half-caste may prefer to be known as a Maori. Some
12,000 other New Zealanders are quarter-caste.

Maoris are grouped in tribes, each tracing its descent to
the people of one of the great canoes which brought them
in the fourteenth century: *Tokomaru*,[3] the Southwest
Wind; *Tainui*, which gave its name to the shrub grown
in New Zealand from the wood of its skids; *Te Arawa*, the
Shark; *Aotea*, the Daybreak; *Takitumu*, which drives before the wind; and the rest, much as if the Americans had
split up into Mayflowers, Phoenixes, Arks, and Doves.

When the Pan-Pacific Clipper drops into Auckland she
is in the wake of the *Tainui*, which made her landfall
here and was drawn across the narrow neck where Auckland now stands to the western sea at Manakau. In Auckland's excellent little museum you may still see such a
canoe: *Te Toka-a-Tapiri*, more than eighty feet long. It
was captured during the Maori Wars by an officer who
was subsequently captured in his turn and whose head,

---

[3] *Tokomaru* is Dr. Buck's Canoe. He has place in it, no
doubt, near Kakeiora, its navigator.

neatly shrunk, plastered and feathered, was sent amongst the tribes as a sort of fiery cross.

The Maoris kept some traffic across the 1700 miles of stormy sea with Rarotonga, where they had paused on their way, and which became, with the other Cook Islands, a part of New Zealand in 1901. They brought with them or sent back for sweet potato, yam, taro, each accompanied by its appropriate divinity; and in their new cold climate they learnt to make clothes of native flax. The change in climate quickened the culture generally. The Maoris built more substantial houses, and the houses prompted new developments in crafts and arts. Their natural skill as carvers flourished and found new forms about the roof-posts and the lintels. But their best work always went, as was fitting, into the canoes.

Within the fortified villages were the sacred groves and shrines and oracles, and the meeting houses upon which skill was lavished and which remain a feature of Maori life and landscape, for the Maori farmer still returns to the communal *marae* to meet with his people. It is his social and political centre, much as the old parish was for Englishmen.

The Maoris are mostly in the North Island, where the climate is more or less Californian, with a semi-tropic touch to the long thin peninsula north of Auckland, the tail of the fish. They amount to about four per cent of the population, and they possess as groups or individuals about one-fourteenth of the land of New Zealand.

Nearly a quarter of New Zealand is public reserve, and about three-fifths is held by white people in 85,000 holdings across which graze four and one-half million cattle and over thirty million sheep. There are about 1,600,000 white New Zealanders, so they come closer than most pavement-thumping moderns to three acres and a cow.

LAND UPLIFTED

Tasman was the first European, it seems, to look at New Zealand. He did little more, for the Maoris killed a boat's crew of his men to discourage the others: but it was his Dutch employers who gave Nieuw Zeeland its name, now misspelled in British fashion. Tasman called it "a great land much uplifted," and I doubt whether any one has described it better since, for its rugged Scotch moralists have vied with Mount Cook itself. I don't suppose there was ever such a place as New Zealand for earnest reformers.

From Tasman to Cook was 147 years. Cook was a sort of season-ticket holder amongst discoverers and he was in New Zealand in 1769, 1773, 1774, and 1777, a record which suggests the persistent industry of the man. He found it, as they like to remind you in New Zealand, a line on the map and left it an archipelago. It is now considerably more, for New Zealand's influence extends from the mandates of Nauru and Samoa just below the Line to the Ross Dependency at the bottom of the world, and it owns a packet of little islands which together make a few hundred square miles.

De Surville was there also in 1769, and du Fresne in 1772, Vancouver and Hanson in the nineties and a Spaniard with the splendid name of José de Bustamente y Guerra: but the first to linger were sealers from Raven's ship *Britannia,* who spent twelve uncomfortable months in the South Island about 1792. Then ships began to come for spars as they discovered the fine timbers; but the Maoris regularly stole their axes. By 1805 you might have seen seven or eight whalers at a time in local waters.

It was in one of those whalers that a Maori chief decided one happy day to ship for Sydney, perhaps to push the trade in tattooed heads and muskets. There he chanced to meet an astonishing old gentleman named Samuel Marsden, probably the most muscular Christian since St. Paul. He certainly fought, and not as one beating the air; and he would have made short work of wild beasts at Ephesus.

Marsden had come to Australia as chaplain of the First Fleet with a Cure of convicts and very salt marines. He combined, in the fashion of his century, preaching with the local magistracy, and the convicts had a holy terror of him. But he was a stalwart, Bullish short of Christian, and now, when he resolved to convert the Maoris, it was bad news for devils. Marsden landed in 1814 with cattle, sheep, and people to teach the natives handicrafts, for he believed that Christianity was a way of life to which the virtues of industry should contribute. Satan should find no idle hands when Samuel Marsden was playing tackle.

Marsden made the first of many trades to be made for Maori land, buying a couple of hundred acres for a dozen axes: and I like best to remember him, the thick Englishman in his black coat and white clerical stock and three-cornered hat, his dozen axes neatly spread, making treaty with Hongi (he of the chain mail) and Ruatara at the Bay of Islands, which is just at your right as you come in. Marsden was backward and forward between Sydney and New Zealand seven times before his death, for he believed as much in journeys and less in epistles than did St. Paul: and it must be confessed that the Church Missionary Society was then a trifle short of aides like Timothy and Titus. Marsden's grim zeal first struck the note characteristic of New Zealand life: and doubtless God has discreetly given him, as the Church of England did, some distant colony of the difficult blessed to command. If St. Paul is ever shipwrecked on the New Zealand coast (for his Lord must still allow that great adventurer adventures), one trusts that he is sound on the Thirty-Nine Articles.

DOMESTIC LION AND ROVING QUAKER

While Marsden's missionaries taught the Gospel and carpentry, and patiently reduced the Maori tongue to "a rational orthography" (Marsden's orthography would be rational or nothing), whalers and traffickers in wood, flax, and human parts were raising hell at other points about. After some particularly devilish business in the late eighteen-twenties, a British Resident was sent from New South Wales to keep an eye on the Europeans. But the Home Government was oddly reluctant to annex New Zealand. It is my considered opinion that if the Home Government had always had its comfortable way there would now be no British Empire at all except perhaps in Scilly and the Isle of Man. The notion of a predatory power going about seeking what it might gobble up is comically untrue of such people as Goderich and Gladstone. Though, admittedly, the left hand was often up to tricks while the right hand was not looking.

Cook had taken New Zealand for George III, with solemn proclamation. The Government of George III had promptly disavowed him. American colonists were trouble enough without more problems of the sort; and no Whiggish prophet rose to foretell the countless cheeses and lamb cutlets yet to come from Taranaki and Otago, Wellington and Canterbury. That prospect needed a visionary like Wakefield.

The British Empire, as Mr. Chesterton once said, is not an empire at all but a series of adventures, and chiefly of personal adventures. New Zealand was one adventure of Mr. Edward Gibbon Wakefield. He had others with heiresses, judges and jailers, but New Zealand was his particular triumph.

Mr. Wakefield derived maternally from the Barclays of

Barclay's Bank, one of those solid Quaker banking families which helped to found the material greatness of England; and of America, for that matter. He had from his Quakers their heavenly practicality; the sober capacity for detail that the Lord may be served; the strong Quaker philanthropy which is all the stronger because it is hardheaded. Quaker charity succeeds because Quakers insist that those they help must also help themselves. Wakefield's grandmother prompted the first savings bank in England: a very typical Quaker device. I know men working in Quaker relief organizations who have dropped their own affairs at a moment's notice to work sixteen hours a day without payment. And Quaker business is not a light matter to drop, for quiet habits of virtue have been long rewarded. The Quaker does not forget that charity begins at home: but unlike most of us he thinks that it should also go abroad. He sought the kingdom of heaven, and other things were certainly added unto him.

Wakefield belonged in that tradition, even if he had aberrations that the Quiet People could not approve.[4] He was not a success at school, even at Westminster School, which has had some strange successes: but, like a hero headed for romance, he became a King's Messenger (prophecy again here missed an opportunity) and spent rather more time in Paris than his family liked. At twenty he eloped with a ward in Chancery, the daughter of an East India merchant, owning a pleasantly mercantilish sort of name, Eliza Susan Pattle. He satisfied the Lord Chancellor and the lady's mother about the affair, which suggests that his verbal agility was already developed. The marriage was extremely happy and kept Wakefield at home until Eliza Susan died.

[4] Mr. A. J. Harrop, a New Zealander appropriately, has made a conscientious study of the man in *The Amazing Career of Edward Gibbon Wakefield*. London, 1928.

He then became a secretary to the Embassy in Paris, and there presumably hatched his second elopement, to the village smithy at Gretna Green, with the daughter of a wealthy manufacturer (as one suggested, his romantic temperament did not blind him to useful detail). But this second affair landed him in jail, and for three years he contemplated the lot of Newgate Man. His Quaker heart was moved and so, as is the way of that admirable persuasion, was his Quaker head. He evolved a New Deal for England's forgotten men. Colonies were the Wakefield answer, colonies self-supported by the sale of land; the profits paying passage for necessary hired help, which might, by industry and thrift, in time buy land for itself. Colonies, in Wakefield's view, should be founded not by a collection of individual oddities but by systematically transplanting a section of the mother community, capitalists and artisans, agriculturists and white-collars. With Wakefield's provisions for control, the scheme, ideally at least, solved the two chief problems of colonization, encouraging capital and supplying a flow of skilled and honest labour. In practice, it worked very well with modifications and might have worked better without them, both in South Australia, its first exemplar, and in New Zealand. It had troubles, to which all flesh and its devices are heir, but it set up two stable, solid colonies: both of which still have the air of conscious rectitude which should belong to philosophic experiments.

But Wakefield had a devilish hard job to get the thing going and to keep it on the straight and narrow path of Wakefieldian theory. The South Australian Company went into heresy if not into open schism.[5] Wakefield sighed and looked for new worlds to colonize. His eye dropped on

[5] Though it revered him in the names of South Australian streets and towns. I have always thought it very characteristic of the staunch Liberal Nonconformists whom Wakefield

New Zealand, and not any eye of gods who get their names into mythologies could glow with more creative zest than the eye of Edward Gibbon Wakefield.

Very fortunately, considering Mr. Wakefield's ambitions, just at that time de Thierry, a curious dear Frenchman, about whom ladies in New Zealand still like to write poems, was considering himself for King or possibly Emperor of the place.

The English always think of themselves as just making a little quiet fortune out of pigs or cotton goods, which is perhaps why they seem to get on at the business of Empire better than most imperialists. And indeed, as you think of it, there may be something much more poetical in their vision of quiet pastures and little homes than ever there was in the trappings of Empire and the inchoate phantasies of Napoleons and such (whom we could name if we liked): for in the English view there has always been room for that antique English figure, the free man on his acres, amongst his byres and fallow fields, with his hearth and his home his castle, and such simple things in it as the love of his wife and the breechclouts of his children.

That was what Wakefield saw, and when one looks at the queer world that England has made, whether in Maryland or Massachusetts or Western Australia or even in the little original island, that is what England essentially is. Shakespeare, who knew it and perhaps loved it as no man else save all its generations of peasants and ostlers, barmen and squires, caught its real majesty: *this earth of majesty;* and then, to hammer the thing home, *this blessed plot, this earth, this realm, this England.* New Zealand was to be England's earth, too, and Scotland's and Ireland's, in that queer inseparable trinity which belongs to-

mostly attracted that they printed their first South Australian newspaper before ever they left London, and founded a university when the colony was barely a generation old.

gether forever, whatever each member may think of the others.

In 1837, Wakefield and his friends had formed an association to promote a colony. But Government was opposed because a colony might sooner or later mean British sovereignty. The Church Missionary Society was equally hostile because it believed colonisation would ruin the Maori. *The Times* was ponderously satirical. It discussed "rapacious radicals and their dupes" and "the gorgeous fancy of Mr. Edward Gibbon Wakefield" and "a radical Utopia in the Great Pacific, wherein, in pure honour of Queen Victoria, and in pure spite of home institutions, the doctrines of Jeremy Bentham and Robert Owen are to realize such unheard-of triumphs as shall utterly shame and outstrip the laggard progress of more antiquated nations." [6]

When the Baron de Thierry appeared with a French bishop in his wake, opinions wavered. Maori independence was one thing; but the Maori Frenchified and given over to Papistry was another. The Lords Spiritual looked at the Lords Temporal and nodded each to each.

While debate continued, Mr. Wakefield went to Canada with Lord Durham, where he helped to father Durham's famous Report, one of the great turning points of change from old Empire to new Commonwealth. Wakefield's curious thread thus weaves its way through the major destinies of three great Dominions. [7] He returned from Canada to learn that the Government had at last decided, what with French ambitions and urgent colonists, to treat with the

[6] Quoted in *My New Zealand*, A. J. Harrop. London, 1939.
[7] Neither Lord Durham nor any one else seemed much to mind that he had been in stir; but the English, as possibly some one has noticed before, are an odd sort of people, and after all the misdemeanor had been a very sporting event. The marriage needed a special Act of Parliament to undo it, which was impressive in itself.

Maoris for sovereignty: and he and his Company hurried
their preparations. In fact they took the bit between their
teeth. While Lord Palmerston, that uproarious imperialist,
was still sniffing that a colony would be disastrous for the
Maoris, the New Zealand Company's first ship, ironically
the *Tory,* was already off Fort Nicholson and the site of
Wellington.

A NATION IS BORN

The Colony had the customary difficulties of colonies,
and notably with the British Consul, Colonel Hobson.
But it was he who dealt with the Maori Chiefs at Waitangi
for the cession of sovereignty to the Queen, then a young
lady girlishly thrilled by her Prime Minister, Lord Melbourne, whose name was just being given to what was then
"the place for a village," and is now the seventh city
of the British Empire. On May 21, 1840, New Zealand
entered, a good, hefty jewel, the crown of Empire: and
the skittish young lady who wore it all perhaps looked
again in her schoolroom atlas. She was to live until New
Zealand Premiers came with Jubilee gifts and New Zealanders died in her khaki on the veldts of Africa.

The Maoris had, from that first treaty, full status and
rights as British subjects.

With the Jack flying, New Zealand colonization boomed.
An association formed in Plymouth to settle New Plym-
outh. The Company sent a second fleet to found Nelson.
A Scottish settlement, sternly Presbyterian, appeared in
the South Island at Dunedin. Not to be outdone, the
Anglicans launched another Canterbury. It lacked a St.
Augustine, but two Archbishops, seven Bishops, and half
the rectories in England were modest shareholders.
Christchurch is its city, where streets are named for the
English Sees, and virtue fills the air like bells. It is excep-

tionally nice of Providence that Canterbury has flourished and grown famous for its lambs.

The Queen's Representative, scorning the irritating colonists at Wellington, set up his own establishment at Auckland. So, with the five colonies, New Zealand has grown, like Australia, from six several pieces, which became its Provinces until Provinces were done away with in the seventies. But by then the country had been, for twenty years, in possession of its own Parliament and Government and the worries which come with them. It marked its liberties by shifting its headquarters back to Wellington, which remains the capital: though Auckland long ago outgrew it. Each vied with the other in what you might call respectability. There were no convicts in New Zealand as in a place which one could mention across the Tasman. Here sons of peers dropped in to tea, and working men united in Self-Improvement Associations, and native flora were found most suitable for trim English hedges. A newly landed working man might have thirty shillings a week, pigs, and a garden for his vegetables, and hope to be a yeoman before he died. There were no snakes and even the Maoris seemed mild, pleasant creatures, though somewhat given to picking up unconsidered trifles left lying about or even locked away. In short, a man was much better off here than at home. The water was excellent for beer.

It was as near an idyll as life can much hope to be: a sane, sober idyll that might have issued from the Epworth Press.

It was rudely interrupted.

THE MAORI WARS

The Maoris had been guaranteed in the ownership of "their lands and estates, forests, fisheries, and other prop-

ANTIPODEAN VISTAS—ABOVE, WELLINGTON FROM
TINAKORI HILL

"New Zealand has more variety than any country near its size; and,
until man came, was singularly free from pests."—Page 75

DAIRY FACTORY, TARANAKI

"The New Zealander is an ardent co-operator."—Page 103

MAORI CARVER, ROTORUA

"The Maoris . . . possess as groups or individuals about one-four-teenth of the land of New Zealand."—Page 77

New Zealand

erties which they may collectively or individually possess, so long as it is their wish and desire to retain the same in their possession." [8] But, when they were offered axes, shoes, bullets, blankets and such items they found them objects of greater desire and heartily swapped. Sometimes tribes traded their own lands, forests, or fisheries, sometimes other people's. In a society pretty much communist or communal, one was not always certain what belonged to whom, if anybody: and in such circumstances it was perhaps best to sell what was clearly not one's own. Furthermore, they were as entangled, tribe with tribe, over claims to various territories as the European nations have been over Alsace or Polish Silesia. A tribe which had lately lost a strip of soil in battle would cheerfully dispose of its claims to the innocent European and let him argue it with the recent enemy while the vendor gathered strength to swipe them both. For a time, at least, the Maoris thought they had discovered a way to grow rich without working. But presently they noticed that these newcomers wanted not only to ride over the land, to grow sheep on it good for both white and brown, but to clear it, to fence it, to sit down on it, and to keep the Maori off it. The Maori brooded over the problem: and then he rose and made noises which sounded ominously like war cries. The settlers began to remember their muskets and to take them down and look for an oil-rag. Then it needed only some nervous finger on a trigger, and of course there was a nervous finger on a trigger, as somehow there always is.

In April, 1843, Captain Wakefield (E. G.'s brother) took police officers to cover a party of surveyors who had been threatened. The Maoris gathered round them, a shot was fired, and the battle began. Wakefield called on the Europeans to cease fire. They dropped their arms, and were

[8] The Treaty of Waitangi.

promptly slaughtered. Brisk actions followed. Several
Maori villages were carried by storm, but the Maoris had
their share of successes and they had matched themselves
against redcoats. The country quietened down when
Captain George Grey came to govern the colony, but the
seeds of the future were sown.

Grey had already, as an incredibly young man, pulled
the new colony of South Australia out of a financial quag-
mire; he was to make a reputation in South Africa; he
was to come again as Governor to New Zealand; and
through it all to jump on the toes of the Colonial Office
until every corn in that Department of State cried out
against him. Towards the end, he returned once more to
New Zealand and became its Premier. He was a tough,
intelligent, integrated person; and even as Vice-royalty
represented, in effect, the development of local responsibility and the shift of power to the man on the spot. That
movement has produced the local independence and responsibility which we now see worked out in Dominion
Status: the end of colonialism and the rise of free association. Grey was one of the makers of the British Commonwealth.

The Maori trouble simmered, with occasional flashes,
until the sixties. The Maoris now understood that the
white man was come to stay, and they attempted amongst
themselves a measure of union to protect their interests.
It took shape as a movement for a Maori kingship, subject to the British Crown but only to the British Crown.
Government declined to recognize two suns in the sky,
and it may have been right. But British colonial policy
has often, with great success, left a measure of sovereignty
and a centre of traditional allegiance to native peoples. In
Malaya, for example, several native States like Johore retain formal independence and are bound only by treaty to

the British structure. Others are components of a federation of native states. A Maori kingship might have been a centre of discipline and authority through which Government could have conveniently dealt in reasonable harmony. Perhaps so, perhaps not. There were ancient rivalries amongst the Maoris themselves, and through the troubles a large proportion of the Maori peoples supported the British. In many ways, their situation resembled that of the Indians in North America; but the Maori has survived to play a full human part in the life of New Zealand.

By 1860 the King movement, in spite of the prohibitions of Government, was making head.[9] Skirmishing began along the hinterland of the North Island's west coast and developed into a campaign against roving Maori war parties who burnt and slashed through the lonelier settlements and cut at outposts and communications. Interspersed were occasional stubborn assaults and stubborn defences of the fortified Maori villages. At home in England, Parliament disliked the war and Government wavered between policies of reinforcing and withdrawing troops. Grey, successful before, was sent again from South Africa, and conducted uproarious controversies with the military command, which had a miserable time enough, what with British reluctance and Maori enthusiasm. It was a curious campaign, which might have ended sooner if there had been more mind and will for it. At times it was utterly ruthless, yet conducted on both sides with considerable social polish. The British regulars developed a confirmed admiration for the Maori warrior and in mo-

[9] Among the tribes in the north, about Taranaki, under Mount Egmont, and with the Waikato south of Auckland. You pass through the Waikato country when you ride down to Rotorua from the ship.

ments of emotion set up memorials to him. The Maori, on his side, decided that the *pakeha* Army was one in which a man might serve without loss of reputation, and his presence in a column has comforted many British commanders since.

DECLINE AND RISE

The war gradually died out, but it left one nasty scar: as a measure partly protective, partly punitive, excessively large areas of native lands were confiscated. The Maoris involved withdrew into country recognized as theirs, and for a few years a dull despair seemed to invest them. Their *mana,* the aura which belongs to the dignity of a man, had suffered. Their numbers fell sharply, and it seemed as if the old fears of the Church Missionary Society would be fulfilled and an heroic race decay.

Confiscation set a precedent for subsequent alienations of land which should have been preserved to the Maori, even when he was ready to sell it. Now, as the Maori numbers increase, some part of that old wrong should be righted. The Maori remains a large landholder, but if he is the only New Zealander prepared to propagate the population that New Zealand needs, he should be given more land to people.

There has been, nevertheless, a real renaissance for the Maoris. It has come from two chief causes: the revival of their own magnificent spirit, and the fond respect which every decent white New Zealander has for the Maoris. The first was their own achievement, stimulated by a group of men, some full-bloods, some half-caste: Sir Apirana Ngata, himself a Minister for Native Affairs, Sir Maui Pomare, Sir James Carroll, and Peter Buck,[10] a doctor of medicine

[10] Buck and Carroll had Irish fathers, Maori mothers, apparently a superlative combination.

and a brilliant ethnologist, now Director of the Bishop Museum at Honolulu. The Maoris have their own Members of Parliament, four in a House of eighty Representatives.[11]

The Maoris have had notable women. Several Rotorua guides have been famous: those large Maori ladies, with neat dresses and thick, sensible shoes, woven baskets and fat umbrellas, who skip lightly amongst the geysers. Maggie Papakura died at Oxford while completing her studies on Maori life and custom. But visitors hear less of women like Te Puea Herangi, one of the great women of our times, whose life is given to magnificent labours for her people, inspiring, educating, strengthening their resolution for their new part in the world. She is a daughter of the second Maori king and Maori royalty takes a new *mana* from her.

For the Maoris, in spite of the debate, have their king, Koroki, fifth of the line, reigning with the hearty approval of King George. Loyalty to him, as the Maoris repeatedly prove, is wholly consistent with loyalty to the British Crown.[12]

So the Maori returns to his greatness, a whole man once more. When we at last join Ecclesiasticus to praise famous men, Maoris will have their meed: *such as have borne rule in their dominions . . . and by the strength of wisdom instructed the people.*

[11] In this latest Parliament Sir Apirana Ngata, Paruire Karaka Paikea, Haami Tokouro Ratana, and Eruera Tihema Tirikatene.

[12] "King" is a misnomer, but the Maoris had the word from the Bible. Koroki's status is social, almost religious (because of his *mana* and blood), rather than political. His strength is greatest amongst the Waikato, who kept their tradition, faith, and allegiance through years of proud poverty.

GOLD AND DIGGERS

While hostilities dragged on in the North Island, the South took a sudden leap with gold. Gold provided a special leaven in the lump of the Australasian colonies. Both in Australia and New Zealand the course had seemed towards large, landed estates with a renewal in the Antipodes of pastoral squires, with slow-growing populations built about the great acreages of sheep. Sheep made the first substantial plank of the new economies. Countless sheep in both remain a major industry. But gold brought the populations, tough and vigorous. The diggers were to turn the current and character of history in the South Lands; and it is not without pride that the Australian soldier still likes to call himself a Digger.

Gold drew the diggers, but when the more accessible lodes had been worked, gold-mining became an affair of corporate companies and large capital. The digger took a job with them or he went on as some did all their restless lives seeking new El Dorados; or he settled down, as he mostly did in California, Victoria, New South Wales and New Zealand. With gold in his pocket he bought land or opened a store. Without gold, he usually started with a grievance, which may on apt occasion be quite as useful. In either case, he bumped up against the monopolists of land; and before any one really knew what had happened, you had a radical party in politics. Radical, anyhow, in the sense that it wanted access to land and opportunity.

In both Australia and New Zealand, gold and the business that follows gold more than doubled populations. In 1858, New Zealand had 59,000 people; in 1864, 171,000. In 1850, Australia had 405,000; in 1860, 1,145,000. Astonishingly, those huge increases were absorbed without violent shock, if one excepts a small flurry of insurrection on the Victorian fields, the nearest approach to a battle that Australian soil has known. But they could not be absorbed without great adjustments of the polity and economy.

In New Zealand the digger usually turned small farmer, and the yeoman, not the squire, became the characteristic figure on the rural scene. Some fringe of the digger population provided the first labour force for other industry. And together the small proprietor and the industrial worker launched New Zealand on its famous social legislation.

The great figures of the first phases are Vogel and Seddon. Julius Vogel was a journalist from Australia, and a man with an idea which has had tremendous consequences in both countries. In 1869 he became Colonial Treasurer in the Government of New Zealand; and he proposed that the future should be evoked to redress the balance (which was in the red) of the present, and that the children who would inherit the greatness and wealth of an advancing nation should also pay for it. In other words, he started the country off on a career of borrowing for development. In 1870, New Zealand owed less than £8,000,000. In 1880, it owed £28,000,000. In 1939, it owed £300,000,000. With the war two years on, one does not like to think of what it owes now.

Vogel's idea was that debts should be secured on the public estate, Crown lands and the like; but that suggestion was set aside, and the Public Revenues are pledge for the Public Debt.

Vast borrowings immeasurably quickened the life of both Australia and New Zealand, but with various consequences. Central government became enormously strong in the economic field. Politics in these countries has controlled the economies much more than in most, which is in itself proper. Popular political control opens the way to economic reforms. But it also intensifies the struggle for political power amongst the economic interests. One party becomes identified more or less with the interests of capital, another party becomes, in effect, the instrument of the trades unions. Political labour movements came early in Australia and New Zealand because political power was a prize worth fighting for, as perhaps it should be.

SHORT CUT TO . . . ?

But the huge waves of borrowed money had another consequence: on their tide both countries floated upwards to a level of prosperity that would otherwise have come very, very gradually. The pump was not merely primed, but the well was flooded. Up bounced prices, wages, and the standard of living. But a large proportion of the money spent was not earned money but money borrowed, which came not out of the antipodean earth by the sweat of antipodean toil, but from the pockets of London moneylenders, the profits of British business, the purses of little old ladies in Brighton and Balham.

The conventional colonial story took a new twist. Instead of the long painful process by which the frontiersman slowly ploughed and hacked his way to his own social security, which he did not think of as social at all, there gradually formed the faith that the State not only could but should foot whatever bill was necessary to ensure a general competence, either directly, in its expanding public works, or indirectly by the stimulation which borrowed money gave to private industry. New Zealand borrowed in London much as a business man with cheerful prospects may borrow from a bank. The whole process of national development was hastened. But the national development rested now not only on the labour of the pioneer and the harvested fruits of the earth, but largely on a structure of debt. The moral effects upon the com-

munity could be debated but it is yet another of those
verdicts more discreetly left to the end of time when
doubtless we shall be judged not according to the sight
of the eyes, nor be reproved according to the hearing of
the ears. There are some earthly consequences we may
notice, however.

One is a sharp development of secondary industries,
especially in Australia where agriculture was often a much
tougher proposition for the small man than in New Zealand. In itself, again, the development of secondary industries was useful to both countries. It has made them
more self-reliant in a world where they may have to depend very much upon themselves; and it strengthened
in mechanical terms their potential for defence.

But it also produced a drain from country to town
which in Australia reached grotesque and ridiculous and
unhealthy proportions and which is certainly excessive
even in New Zealand. It produced too a huge class of
wage-earners, what the jargon to which we submit calls
proletarians. Industry inflated by the flow of borrowed
money could afford high wages. Labour in politics kept
the State up to the mark. And that in itself was good, for
industry should pay its people a living wage. Unless it
does, it loses its first claim to consideration from the community. But if high wages are being paid to wage-earners,
young men are less inclined to the slow, laborious effort
of developing the land, especially new land, with its tardy
and uncertain returns. In Australia, for more than a generation rural development has almost entirely waited on
Government subsidies and new boodles of borrowed
money. The rugged individualist with his covered wagon
is replaced by the worried settler with his mortgage. Admittedly, the country is hard and difficult and there has
been much ill-considered exploitation of its thin soils.
The frontiers of agriculture are retreating and the sand

blows where wheat once grew. But the decline is chargeable largely to the attractions of the cities, to the comparatively high wages of city-dwellers, and to the capital which provides the wages and thus, in turn, to the London moneylender, the great insurance houses, and the little old lady in Brighton or Balham. No doubt she divides her time between the two, while the interest cheques keep coming regularly. And they do. Australia and New Zealand pay their reckonings. (New Zealand, by the way, is one of its 1914-'18 Associates which does not owe America any war debt.) At least they pay their interest. No one has much discussed, in public, whether they will ever get round to paying the enormous debt itself. These things are better left to time, which has its own way of answering such problems.[13]

I would not be misunderstood. In the distressing situation of an investor, I should as much prefer to buy New Zealand or Australian stocks as anything I can think of except a cow or two and a patch of earth to put them on. Both countries have an admirable record for public honesty and it will doubtless continue while their world stands. Their honest reputation is of tremendous importance to them. Loan money is not exactly the skeleton of their economies, but it is a large part of the arterial system; and if its flow was suddenly checked, the economies would develop anaemia or sag flaccidly from malnutrition.

To meet the charges of their overseas debts, both countries must maintain huge export business. New Zealand

[13] Only thrice in its history has the gargantuan growth of New Zealand's debt been in any measure checked: once in 1891-'92, when it was reduced by £117,282; once in 1922-'23, when it came down £101,061, and on one astonishing occasion in 1934-'35, when the floating debt of £22,856,981 was entirely wiped out.

actually does more overseas business per capita than any
other country in the world. While this, of course, is in
many senses admirable, both countries are unusually dependent upon the state of other people's markets. Moreover, the great rural industries have consequently been
dominated by the markets-and-profits motive as against
the subsistence motive. Both Australia and New Zealand
have many happy farms, but the farmers' ambitions are
commonly for money crops rather than for what Dr. S. J.
Ingwersen happily calls "the homestead." The land is exploited rather than cultivated; it is given over less to an
agriculture than to an agricapitalism. The effects of exploitation are already only too evident in wasted forests
and denuded fields, and (throughout Australia especially)
in declining countrysides. The war has accelerated the
movement from rural to urban areas, for most of the
armaments and munitions plants have been established
about the already overcrowded cities. When I made these
notes, it was difficult to rent any sort of decent house in
Sydney or Melbourne for less than two pounds a week.
But in scores of country townships you could have rented
a good solid house for a few shillings.

The Australians and New Zealanders apparently lack
that attachment to the soil which is the true basis of a
rural culture. Of New Zealand's 85,000 holdings, about
one in sixteen changed hands in 1938-'39, a rate which
hardly suggests the appearance of a stable rural population attached, generation by generation, to ancestral acres.
Both Australians and New Zealanders have a high contempt for the notion of a peasantry, but one could hope
that the yeoman would not seem beneath them. Both
countries certainly have need of yeomen's virtues and of
yeomen families. But I have no serious hope that more
than a handful of Australians or New Zealanders will
agree with me in this. The farmer will still yearn for

suburban villas, and his son will still be educated for some dull white-collar job, and his daughter will still prefer a typewriter to a cow, and the slick city fellow will still sniff at Dad and Dave. All the fruits, sweet and sour, of urbanism, industrialism, and a finance culture will continue to flourish while the tree stands. But how long stands a tree without deep roots in earth and strong natural sap?

UTOPIA, LTD.

New Zealand's social legislation is, in its circumstances, admirable. If that is the way the world must go, then New Zealand advances with decency and decorum. Post Office savings banks date from the sixties, and so does state control of telegraphs. State railroads were built from Vogel's time and, as in Australia, the railroads are owned and managed by the state. State hospitals appeared in the seventies, on the heels of state insurance and a public trustee office. National education, free, secular and compulsory, dates from 1877, and Sir George Grey, returned to the colony and his governorships done, led the Radical Party to power in 1879. He was succeeded by the Conservatives for a dozen years and then the Liberals began, in 1891, their long reign.

The Liberals were the party both of the small farmer and the working man, and their rise marks the final defeat of squirearchy. Richard Seddon, their second Premier and greatest figure, was significantly a digger on Australian and New Zealand fields before he turned storekeeper and local panjandrum. His reign lasted from 1893 until 1906 and New Zealand finally gave him his due and dubbed him King Dick. He left his party entrenched in office, and its governments survived for half a dozen years more. That long period of sustained progressive rule was important, for reforms were developed by men with the experience of office and the responsibility of applying their own measures. It is a merit of the British type of government that the legislator has had or has or hopes to have executive responsibility: and that the executive itself works in daily membership of the legislature, advancing and defending, in personal contact and debate, its propositions. The man who frames the laws is consequently sensitive to their practical application. The man who administers the laws is equally aware of the legislative problem.[14]

The Liberal Party in New Zealand left a tradition of peaceful progress because, unlike some reformers, it was necessarily concerned with practice as well as preaching. It was working in human facts as well as in theory, and human facts are sometimes very salutary for theorists.

Under Seddon came Votes for Women and Old Age Pensions; Superannuation for Public Servants; compulsory resumption of land for closer settlement; the Advances to Settlers Act under which Government financed farmers and which has been profitable for both; state coal mining; state fire and accident assurance; control of water power; and a whole series of enactments governing working conditions, wages, hours, employers' liability

[14] There is much to say for the division of powers in the United States Constitution; but a man may be all his active life a great figure in Congress without ever knowing the care of office. Office is an effective discipline and a proper experience for the law-maker, just as it is good for the man who holds office to understand the gestation and the growth of the law. A great politician like Borah goes eternally into opposition because (one believes) his political abilities were never fully exercised, and had consequently something of the fury of frustration. If he had better understood, from his own experience, the nature and needs of responsible policy his course and the course of history might well have taken another and happier way.

and trades unions. Industrial Conciliation and Arbitration Acts set up courts to determine wages and working-conditions, and prohibited or attempted to prohibit strikes and lockouts, compulsorily haling all disputes before the state tribunals. The state opened maternity hospitals, and New Zealand began the magnificent effort which has made its infant-mortality rate the lowest in the world, thirty-two in 1000 births as against forty in Australia, fifty-six in the United States, seventy in Canada.[15]

Sir Joseph Ward was Prime Minister from 1906 to 1912, and in his time came widows' pensions, housing schemes, and provident funds.

The more conservative Reform Party was in power from 1912. Its strength came chiefly from the farmers, now become men of substance, and less inclined to general political co-operation with industrial labour, which in 1910 had dropped the Liberals to form its own party designed on the Australian model. The war produced a Coalition of Reformers and Liberals which survived until 1919. Reform continued in office alone until 1928, another curiously long passage for the party in power and evidence of the political stability of the country. Ward returned as Prime Minister in 1928 with the United Party, heir to the Liberals: but in 1931 his successor was forced by the depression, which hit New Zealand heavily, into a coalition with Reform that was decisively beaten by Labour at the elections of 1935. Labour is still in office and looks like repeating the long-term performances of earlier parties.

The state continued in what some people call socialism under the several sorts of government, but the Labour Cabinet under the late Mr. Savage, and latterly under

[15] In 1934-'38.

Peter Fraser, has made the longest strides since Seddon. The Reserve Bank has become completely a state institution. School-children have free medical and dental care, ride to school in government buses, drink government milk. Exports, imports and the movement of money have been controlled since 1938. The government guarantees farm prices, a measure which has made farming less like a gamble and more like a public service. A high-wage public-works programme is reminiscent of W.P.A. and P.W.A. in the United States; but Labour's most dramatic performance has been its social security legislation. The Social Security Act gets rid of the familiar civil pensions, old age, widows', invalids' and so on, and substitutes a general contributory scheme on the lines of national insurance; and it introduces a whole series of medical, hospital and related benefits. Pensions of thirty shillings a week are paid from the age of sixty, and free medical and hospital service and medicines are provided to the sick, with unemployment benefits graded according to the number of dependents and rising to a maximum of four pounds a week. The general provision is for all the urgent necessities of life; and where the social structure permits few people to provide adequately for themselves against all the contingencies of health and fortune, the measure seems just and necessary.

New Zealand was living in 358,000 dwellings, pretty well one to a family. The typical house of five rooms with a sun-porch was possibly state-built and its rent was £1.10.6 a week.

THE CITIZEN AND HIS LIVING

The New Zealander who emerges from all this is materially a fortunate man, as men go in a vale of tears. He can expect to live longer than any other citizen of the world. His death rate is 8.6 in the 1000 against 11.1 in the U. S. A. and 11.9 in England. He kept the peace with 1440 policemen in 1939, but as he only had 808 people in jail on the day of reckoning, they were not overwhelmingly busy. He shipped five-sixths of his exports to Great Britain, and of its constituents he was the most loyal to the British economic Empire, for he bought 73.5 per cent of his imports from British countries, against Australia's 59.1 per cent, India's 54.8 per cent, South Africa's 53 per cent, Britain's 40.4 per cent and Canada's 29.2 per cent. The United States was his best connection outside the Empire and a very profitable one for the Americans, because New Zealand spent with them five times as much as it sold them. More than ninety per cent of his export was from his pastoral industries: butter, wool, cheese, lamb, mutton and pork. He bought heavily motor cars, machinery and manufactures. He had more telephones per head than any country except the United States. He owned 32,000,000 sheep and 4,500,000 cattle and produced 376,000,000 pounds of butter and 196,000,000 pounds of cheese, which is a lot of butter and cheese for 1,600,000 people. Only Denmark exported more butter and cheese, but did every Dane possess two and a half hens? (Recalling the Denmark that was, he probably did.)

More than 100,000 New Zealanders were working in factories with a capital investment of £53,000,000. The war has lifted both figures. In 1939, New Zealand paid an average of £23.8.9 in taxes, direct and indirect. He owed on his national debt £186.17.0 a head. He had much reduced his debt for the last war, but he still was in the red for it to the tune of £37.13.4. The capital value of his land and improvements was over £400 a head, or £636,000,000 in all. Three in five of his relatives, friends, and acquaintances had Post Office savings accounts with average deposits of about thirty pounds. He had £65,000,-

ooo on deposit in trading banks, and £14,000,000 in Trustee Savings Bank. His average life assurance was for £105. His private wealth in all stood at £710,000,000, his public wealth at £360,000,000.

He can afford to take himself out to dinner, but he has to dine early because everybody, including cooks and waiters, have shortened their working hours by a quarter or more since 1914. He probably made a good meal, for he eats more bread, flour and sugar than an American, nearly twice as much butter, more than twice as much beef, twelve times as much lamb and mutton and only loses his appetite with pig, where the American out-eats him two and a half pigs to one. The American drinks more wine and smokes almost twice as much tobacco, but the Englishmen leave them both innocents in the matter of beer. The New Zealander's tea balances the American's coffee, but the American gets down three times as much hard liquor.

The New Zealander is an ardent co-operator. He is also professedly a solid Christian. The two characteristics may not be wholly unrelated. At the census of 1936, only 1499 people of 1,491,484 would declare themselves agnostic, while Rationalists [16] ran to 2066 and Freethinkers to 778, against 600,000 Anglicans, 368,000 Presbyterians, 195,000 Catholics, 121,000 Methodists.

The New Zealander is, taken all round, a large, hearty fellow and the healthiest in the world, so it is odd that he is barely reproducing himself. He may have inadequate resources but he is at least as well off as his father was and most people in the world. It can't be that he dislikes New Zealanders, but he (and she) evidently think them rather more trouble than they are worth. Yet,

[16] It may have some significance in a calendar of culture that Rationalist Associations remain active in Australia and New Zealand, as though we were still in good Victoria's reign.

watching young New Zealanders lately, both at home and abroad, I cannot agree. I think we need a lot more of the breed. There would now have been several hundreds of thousands more to meet New Zealand's great crisis if the present generation of parents had done as well as their parents. Now, nearly two-thirds of the population is past twenty-one years of age and getting older: and presently it will be possible to close down schools; which will, of course, make more tax money available to feed the aged and bury the dead who will have no children of their own to attend filially their passing.

THE FIGHTER

One might have argued that comfort and security had weakened New Zealand's stomach for the strong realities of life, if it were not for the sort of soldier the New Zealander still makes. Though, like the people of other Dominions, he has much taken his own way, he has also been a vigorous imperialist. This is natural enough; for his stock, like Australia's, is more British than Britain's own.

New Zealand sent 6500 men to the Boer War, almost the same proportion of population as Britain herself dispatched. At the outbreak of the War of 1914-'18, New Zealand immediately occupied German Samoa. Before the war ended, a population of 1,100,000 had sent more than 100,000 men overseas. The war cost New Zealand £82,-245,672 and 16,697 lives. There were 50,000 casualties in all, *but precisely 341 were captured by the enemy.* The Maoris put 2200 volunteers in the field and lost 336. Anzac became the symbol of New Zealand's effort and of its surely imperishable union with the other great Dominion across the Tasman: for Anzac was first stamped on the transport and packing-cases of the original Australian New Zealand Army Corps. New Zealand, as the war lengthened, introduced a draft, but so heavy was the volunteering that draftees never made more than a quarter of her enlistment.

In this war, we go shyly with figures, but up to July, 1940, when conscription was introduced, 80,000 volunteers, 4000 of them Maoris, had offered for service, 14,000 in the Air Force (the Air Force had been able to absorb 5000 by the end of the year). The Royal Air Force (as distinct from the R.N.Z.A.F.) had 1000 New Zealanders, the Empire Air Scheme was taking 3700 a year. In June, 1940, the Labour Government took authority to call up all men and to control all property and finances.

By November, 1940, more than 20,000 men were overseas, including a Maori battalion that did imperishable things in Crete. The Royal Navy and its New Zealand Division had 3000 New Zealanders. A standing army of 30,000 was established in New Zealand: a large home guard had been formed. New Zealand was spending $160,000,000 (U. S.) a year, five times above the annual charge of the last war. It was selling all its wool, butter, cheese and meat to Great Britain for the duration.

Population, recall, 1,600,000.

New Zealand defence has been dovetailed with general imperial strategy since the Russian scare of 1878, when she mounted twenty-two guns in coastal batteries, and began to contribute towards the upkeep of a Royal Navy Squadron in Australasian waters. Since 1921 she has developed the New Zealand Division of the Royal Navy.[17] One of its ships, *Achilles*, helped to deal with the *Graf Spee*. Imperial sentiment grew through the eighties and the nineties, and Mr. Seddon cheerfully forecast, like a

[17] Which since September, 1941, has been known as the Royal New Zealand Navy.

good many other people, a Parliament and Council of Empire. Australia and New Zealand each adopted compulsory training for home defence in 1910, and though both countries suspended its operation during the pre-Hitler years, the militias have been useful feeders to the wartime forces.

COMMONWEALTH

New Zealand and Australia gave assent to the Statute of Westminster but have never troubled to embody it in their own legislation. They have not thought it necessary to underline their freedom even when they exercise it. Both New Zealand and Canada supported strongly the Covenant of the League during the Abyssinian affair. Each Dominion develops and exercises its own foreign policy, is free to make what engagements it likes, may enter or stay out of Britain's wars. An attempt has been made to form a common mind on all the major lines of foreign policy, but the practical difficulties of information and consultation have not yet been wholly met. Nevertheless, in every crisis of magnitude, Britain and the Dominions produce an almost startling unanimity of view. Though New Zealand and Australia are ten thousand miles further from Berlin, their popular verdict in 1939 went unhesitatingly with Britain's.

They had no more obligation to enter the war than had the United States; and they could reasonably expect to profit nothing from it and to pay a heavy price of blood and treasure.

The decision was in the long view probably to their own interest; but many peoples lately have only seen their interest in a brief unhappy ride upon the tiger. When the tiger is loose, perhaps men and nations do better, both in reason and morals, boldly to take a gun.

CHAPTER SIX

Australia

DISCOVERIES

THE Australian coastline came up like a thin blue line
on the horizon with a shadowy suggestion of distant
mountains. The Pacific rolls heavily here to crash on its
last, lazy beaches; and the great harbour of Sydney opens
like a crack in the coast. Cook was the first man to record
Australia's eastern face. Australia was born of a transit of
Venus. Cook was on his homeward swing after observing
from Otaheite that astronomical performance.

The year was 1769. Cook perhaps knew of a map of
1555 which hints at Australia; and that Wytfliet's Lou-
vain book of 1598 noticed a land below New Guinea
likely to prove a fifth part of the earth. He remembered
Quirós, and the rational, eighteenth-century Cook probably understood him well enough: they were both great
pilots and had seen wonders. Cook knew charts and narra-
tives of the Dutchmen who first sketched in the west and
northern outlines.

The Dutch were solid seamen with their minds on
practical matters and pre-eminently on the annual balance of the merchants of Amsterdam. When a Dutch ship
went to sea, she went on business. She carried no phantasies about the City of God. Tahitian eclipses are all very
well, but what porridge had John Keats or even the scientific Galileo? The Dutch were the true prototypes of the

modern capitalist. They invented many of capitalism's most interesting devices, and Dutch names are long in the roll of great capitalist fortunes.

When the pinnace *Duyfken* in 1605 made the first known landfall on the Australian coast, she was out of Bantam to investigate the chances of trade with the dim island of New Guinea. Dirk Hartog cruised up the western Australian coast in 1616 while seeking a route to clip long profitless months off the passage between the Indies and the Scheldt. Through the century Dutchmen at intervals touched here and there in the north and west. Tasman discovered Tasmania, but the Dutch had little luck, for most of the mainland coasts they saw were miserable stretches of sand and swamp that are still much as they were when Hartog and Houtman passed.

The English, as you might expect, appeared in the person of an extremely odd character, the buccaneer and scientist William Dampier, native of the sweet county of Somerset. Some paradox in the English genius makes its oddest people its most representative: Dampier has the English tang and flavour which is in Chaucer, Shakespeare, More, G. K. Chesterton, a Dorset ploughman or the Elephant and Castle.

The English defeat generalizations—except perhaps this one itself. You have all the tags, for instance, about the English ruling classes: but the British Empire is chiefly the product of poor clerks like Clive and Raffles; of people like Nelson and Rhodes, sons of little country parsonages; like Phillip, a half-pay seaman, and Cook, the son of an agricultural labourer. Cook was apprenticed to a grocer and taught himself navigation as a North Sea fisherman before he joined the Navy to chart the St. Lawrence for Wolfe's campaign of Canada. There is a good deal of England in Cook's career and in Dampier's.

Dampier came first to Australia in the *Cygnet,* Captain

Swan, a merchant ship turned buccaneer. Dampier was not devoted to the Skull and Crossbones, but pirates and privateers then got about the world more than most, and William Dampier wanted to get about the world. There never was such a man for going about, unless one of whom young Dampier must often have heard the Somerset neighbours gossip: Tom Coryat of Odcombe, who walked over half Europe and Asia until at Surat, crying, "Sack, Sack, is there such a thing as Sack? I pray give me some Sack," he drank overmuch (though moderately, being a temperate man) for his flux and died. His shoes hung two hundred years in Odcombe Church until they went, like a Cardinal's Hat, to dust. Dampier may have seen them before they were quite rotted, admired them perhaps with youthful piety; for Dampier and Coryat were of the same stuff. Dampier lacked Coryat's romantic interest in nunneries, but he shared his Elizabethan sort of gusto. He began the scientific perambulation which Wallace, Huxley, and Darwin continued, making the world their laboratory.

Dampier's second voyage, like Cook's, was instigated by the Royal Society; but he had as little luck with Australia as the Dutchmen, and he thought its native inhabitants the miserablest people in the world, not excepting even the Hodmadods of Monomatapa.

Cook was the first man to give Australia a good name, so Australians properly incline to view him as their only true discoverer. At Botany Bay, a suburban bus-ride now from Sydney, he landed and took possession for the King's Majesty, then busily losing his original set of colonies.

Neither King's Majesty nor King's Ministers were excited at the news. Britain seldom shows marked enthusiasm for empire-building, and empire-builders, the Clives and Hastingses and Raffleses, commonly get into trouble at home. Her ambition has been to rule the waves, and her deliberated annexations were most often designed to launch her on her favourite element. She likes best some hefty rock above a sheltered bay. It was American colonists who insisted that the French gates to their hinterland should be forced. It was a commercial company, hopelessly embarrassed, which thrust the Eastern Empire into her lap. The Home Government has often (surprisingly often, if one regards the general practice of the Powers) returned the pickings of its wars to previous owners: as when Holland got back in 1817 her vast East Indian Empire, the choicest of all colonial estates.

This is no defence of Britain's brand of imperialism. In fact, by tidy-minded people it might be made an accusation. But Britain seldom seems interested in Empire for Empire's sake, as Hohenzollerns, Hapsburgs or a Hitler would understand it. I sometimes think that she is more interested in a quiet life, when she can get it.

THE UNITED STATES AGAIN

A quiet life certainly had something to do with the Australian settlement, when at last it came, for Australia was Government's answer to the noisy problem of the hulks and jails. America was in part responsible for the problem. American colonies had long taken for their plantations a large proportion of British convicts; and the loss of the Colonies jammed British jails. Jammed jails usually meant epidemics and epidemics had been known to carry off even Cabinet Ministers!

Prudence and Benevolence went to work. Benevolence suggested that convicts would be happier in the healthy climate of Botany Bay than rotting in the hulks. Prudence considered the distance and noted that a convict so far removed was unlikely to come again as a charge upon the rates. Reports were consulted, from Banks and Matra, who had been with Cook: and Australia was conceived by one of the dullest of all English Ministries, and born into the world during January, 1788, rather a momentous year for young nations. The place of her nativity was just where Sydney ferries now run into Circular Quay.

Ironic Providence had a field day in the matter of Australia. Britain, losing one empire, had little inclination for another. If Ministers had suspected Australian responsibilities to come, they might have quietly dispatched the lugs to Sierra Leone or some such unfruitful place. But they were rational men, and it was against all reason that a minor answer to a minor problem should evoke a new empire destined to spread across a continent and half the Pacific and to bear, in time, two great Dominions and a flock of vigorous dependencies. The wildest philanthropist could not expect that a little convict colony would be delivered of a major democracy, and that from a jail should come such grandeur.

Yet the possibilities were present to the mind of Phillip, a Navy captain resurrected from his farm to the command. He was a remarkable manager of men, although no one seems much to have noticed his quality before. He brought his fleet of convicts and their warders with an astonishingly small mortality for the times. He had Cook's concern and methods for the health of his people on long voyages: limejuice (whence the American seaman's tag of "limey" for the Englishman) against scurvy, and such tricks. He tried, with kindness and patience, to civilize the aborigines he met; and he saw in his convicts potential citizens of a new nation.

CONVICT AND FREE

The Convict System lasted only half a century, except in Western Australia, where it was later introduced at the request of free settlers who had neglected Mr. Wakefield's shrewd provision for a supply of labour. When transportation to New South Wales ceased in 1840 at the demand of the colonists, only a quarter of the population was convict. Few Australians have convict blood, because the great immigrations came after the thing was ended. But convicts made their contribution. Some became merchants and landowners, some established industries. Simeon Lord dealt in New Zealand flax, opening commerce there and with Peru. Francis Greenway designed for Governor Macquarie what are still the most delightful buildings in the country. Men were transported for offences that we should now think trivial. Many were political prisoners from Ireland, Scotland, and the trades unions. (In later years Boyle O'Reilly was to escape in an American whaler from Western Australia to become a famous editor in Boston.) And many, of course, were the savage scourings of society.

The first years were desperately hard. Trade was restricted by the East India Company's monopoly of traffic from Good Hope to the Horn and China. The Government at home, in holts with Napoleon, was inclined to forget the Colony until colonial belts were tightly drawn. The place was on rations for years: once an American brigantine just staved off famine in salt beef and rum.

Rum became the basis of the first economy. The officers of the New South Wales Regiment acquired monopoly of it and made it the colonial currency. The fact that they were army officers did not prevent them from extending their grip to trade. With their profits they bought land. One of them, John Macarthur, first bred in Australia the merino sheep which were to be Australia's great staple. When the Regiment arrested Governor Bligh (that unfortunate man destined to mutinies and much more

sinned against than sinning), they seized the political
power, and it took Governor Macquarie, a grim Scot with
grim troops at his back, to break their control.

Sydney soon became a smuggling centre, for the new
century saw two and three thousand whaling ships a year
in Australasian waters, and Nantucket and Providence
had no obligations to the Governor and Court of Directors of the Honourable Company in Leadenhall Street,
where Charles Lamb was then a clerk and probably acquainted with a junior named Thomas Stamford Raffles.
But the colonials had a dour struggle before they broke
the bonds of mercantilism. No regulations could confine
the fierce energies coming into play as officers, merchants,
and emancipated convicts began to gather the harvests of
new lands and seas.

The Emancipists were favoured by Macquarie during
a reign (1809-'21) which set the colony on its forward
march. He found Sydney a dirty hamlet and he left it on
its way to becoming the metropolis of a continent and of
the Western Pacific. In his time the mountain barrier
westward was crossed, and growing flocks moved out to
the great plains.

The crossing of the mountains, once thought impass-
able, opened a continent, and was appropriately adven-
tured by sheep-farmers and a young man named Wentworth, who was to become Australia's first statesman and
who was to win full self-government for her in 1856.

Rum and monopoly, wool, and gold. Wool brought the
shepherds and the graziers, at first just squatters on the
new lands beyond the mountains, but to become something like an incipient feudal aristocracy. Gold and population broke their control, and swirled away the pool of
convict blood into a great stream of national life.

AUSTRALIAN

The convict system had less social consequence in Australia than slavery has had in America. But that early experience did influence the Australian spirit, which prizes freedom with a strong, positive passion. Its temper is adult, dry, ironic, hard, and not given to illusions. But it recognizes human quality, as people do who have sweated and suffered together. The Australian is a rugged personalist rather than a rugged individualist. He has social virtues, but the words "comrade" and "brother" do not suit his sentiment. "Mate" is his word: as of two men who will stand and stick together, drive a saw or build a union, but never submerge their personal being in a collectivity. He has a sense of social responsibility. He has organized the strongest trades unions in the world, built up the largest body of social legislation. But he also prizes his personal liberty and initiatives. The combination makes him a superb soldier, and if it remains will make him a great citizen of the world.

These virtues come more from other sources than convictism: from the democracy of the gold fields, from the Irish political exiles and the angry Irish peasants dispossessed at home, from the emigrant who had spirit enough to wrench himself from the industrial slums of England, from the Scottish shepherds and school-teachers and lawyers; and above all perhaps from the strange, hard country itself, no land of milk and honey but a wide, sunbeaten world that could be subdued to human use only by men stronger than itself. But to these the convict memory left an edge of iron.

All this is in the Australian. He is the least sentimental of people, the least given to utopianism. His glaring landscape has enough of mirages. But he has learnt that if you sweat, hang on, and try your damnedest, you can make something of deserts and of life. He is suspicious of mystics and even of his own pre-selected politicians. He is not much caught up in clouds of glory or oratory. It is characteristic of his shrewd tough sense that long and often bitter industrial struggles have hardly ever produced physical violence. He is a pragmatist. His only real Utopians took their New Australia off to Paraguay, sufficiently remote from cool stares and crooked grins at home. "Where the hell does that get you?" is the great Australian question: and the answer had better be pat and pertinent.

An economy of rum, convicts, and monopoly produced capital for its successor, the wool economy, which opened the interior. (Cattle were grown in Australia on country where a Red Indian would die of thirst and loneliness.) Wool, an export industry, gave the Australian economy a characteristic bias: the authentic peasant has never appeared. The rural Australian is producing mainly for overseas markets upon which he is consequently much dependent. The Australian wheat farmer buys his vegetables from the grocer. I have seen Australian sheep properties where thousands of gallons of water each day were running from bores but the people never bothered to grow a single cabbage. The Australian bushman (not the wild aborigines, but the people of the interior, the outback) is an iron man. He survives his duodenal ulcers and even his patent pills.

Gold doubled the population in ten years, 1851-'61. There is never enough gold for all who seek it; and by the late sixties, diggers were clamouring for land or industrial employment. A long tussle came between the large land-holders and the multitude in whom anxieties evoked a vigorous political consciousness. The "selection" system gave the small man some privilege of selecting holdings from the vast estates, but much rural poverty persisted, to produce the "bushrangers," whose significance in Australian history is far greater than their numbers. They were usually small farmers driven by poverty to the roads, much in the style of the Daltons and Jesse James. They provide a dash of romance in the monotonously respectable pattern of Australian life and until they shot a few people they had a good deal of public sympathy as symbols of resistance to the landed interests who sat broad-bottomed across the countryside and in the ample seats of power. Ned Kelly still rides in the hearts of Australian youth, or used to, and doubtless will again when Hollywood gets round to Australia in its progress through the higher history. But the bushranger and the worst of rural poverty disappeared as estates in the more settled parts were forced to sub-divide, and the "cocky" farmer could work towards substantial prosperity.

LABOUR PAINS

In the towns, the new populations became industrial workers, and Protection appeared to foster industries.

The industrial workers began to form unions for their protection. The organized gold-miners led the national protest against Chinese labour, which was pouring into the country during the sixties and seventies. They won the first major political victory of labour, for New South Wales presently forbade Chinese immigration, and Australia was launched upon its "White Australia" programme, the most consequential of her national policies. "White Australia" has been a good deal misunderstood. It is essentially a domestic programme, though its external implications are formidable, how formidable we perhaps do not yet know. It shuts the Asiatic out, but it also implies that the Australian will tackle the development of tropical Australia. He actually is the only man of full European blood who really does work "like a nigger" in tropical country. His sugar industry has been protected and bolstered to sustain him there and to give opportunity for the breeding of a tropically born and nurtured white population. The proportion of Australians living above Capricorn is minute, and mostly in Queensland; but significantly it is the healthiest and most procreative section; and the tropical Australian baby is born, in the average, heavier and bigger than any other Caucasian child. But he is not born often enough. Australia has striven to justify her sovereign exclusiveness: history will tell us whether the effort was sufficient.

Chinese Exclusion was the first considerable occasion when an Australian Government in a matter involving foreign relations departed from the expressed views of the British Government.

In the seventies and eighties, the country boomed, with wool and gold; and with money pouring in from English investors. State Governments went on spending sprees with borrowed money. One is reminded of Mr. Coolidge's America. And of its sad dénouement.

The crash began in the late eighties. Gold production was declining, interest increasing on larger and larger debts. Drought hit the pastoralists and so did their creditors. By 1893 nearly half the banks in the country were rocking and men with paper fortunes were starting life again. And labour had lost the great strike of 1890. It began, surprisingly, with the Marine Officers Union, and spread, in a wave of sympathy strikes, to wharf labourers, miners, shearers, carters, labourers: and too far, for the strike funds could not feed them all. It broke in catastrophic failure. But this was one of those defeats which breed victories. It convinced labour that the economic weapon was not enough. It sent the unions into politics. Labour Leagues elected a quarter of the New South Wales Parliament in 1891. They formed a Labour Party. It used its power, at first mostly a balance of power between older parties, to achieve wage and factory legislation, old-age pensions, and industrial arbitration. From its beginnings it demonstrated the vigorous economic nationalism which has since made such noise in the world at large.

In the rural areas, where drought and debt had broken up many large estates, small farms multiplied (the Australian version of small farm might run to a thousand acres). New methods of dry farming in lands of low rainfall, and new drought-resistant wheats were developed, and by the middle nineties Australia had added to her major exports wheat, meat and dairy produce.

The farmer still largely went with labour, and both were going more and more nationalist. Every one read the Sydney *Bulletin*, then and now the most vigorous weekly in the country: and the *Bulletin* was preaching Australianism from its initial letter to its tail-piece, in political leaders, contributors' paragraphs, verse, short stories and literary criticism. It had more influence on Australia in those years than any other newspaper, even the London *Times*, has ever had upon a people. It was a vehicle of a new Australian literature, of an Australian art, its first great black-and-white man was the brilliant American, Hopkins; it employed Phil May, and it was to nurture Norman Lindsay and Low. Above all it presented an Australian Programme: Australian, as against the provincialisms of New South Wales, Victoria, Queensland, Tasmania, South Australia, and Western Australia.

FEDERATION OF THE SIX

New South Wales was founded in 1788. Tasmania was an off-shoot convict colony of 1803 which set up in business as a separate province in 1825. From it, sheepmen crossed Bass Strait to "squat" along the south coast and about Port Phillip Bay. In 1851 the southern settlements, below the Murray, were constituted the State of Victoria. Six and seven hundred miles north of Sydney, convicts, cattlemen and shepherds settled in new rich pastures during the twenties and thirties. In 1859 their first settlement became the capital of the new State of Queensland, stretching away to the remoteness of the Gulf of Carpentaria and to the northernmost tip of the eastern coast: a vast domain that is still largely to-morrow's. An English company separately colonized the Swan River on the opposite side of the continent in 1827 and 1829, and the hamlets of Perth and Fremantle, with the little military post of Albany on King George's Sound, long familiar to American whalemen, were the nucleus of the enormous State of Western Australia which, superimposed on North America, would run pretty well from New Orleans to Hudson Bay. South Australia was a Wakefieldian experiment independent of the other colonies from the first, and very conscious of its stainless scutcheon. It has rather a Bostonian flavour, with a drop or two of Bath or Salisbury.

Federation of the Six was argued for more than a generation before it came. Each was developing its own character and to some extent its own economy; and rivalries were rank. Australia still suffers from breaks of railway gauge resulting from an I'll-be-damned-if-I-do-what-you-do attitude.[1] The more conservative politicians were

[1] Federal Departments are still divided between Canberra, the little Capital, and the two grasping giants, Melbourne

on the whole opposed to local union. Imperial Federation was in the air, and many Australians believed in an imperial rather than an Australian union only. The growth of imperial sentiment was more rapid in the colonies than at home in Britain. British statesmen remained cool to the whole idea of Empire. In a frequent metaphor, they regarded the colonies as fruits which would, in their season, drop from the parent tree. Colonies were an expense and frequently a mild nuisance. Since Free Trade had been established as a final law of nature, colonial markets would be worth as much or little in or out of the Empire. "The thing is done," said one Colonial Secretary. "The great colonies are gone. It is but a question of a year or two." And breathed perhaps or not the softest sigh. Palmerston, forming a Ministry, could find no one to take the Colonial Office. He turned to one of his people and said, "I suppose I must take the thing myself. Come upstairs with me, Helps, when the Council is over. We will look at the maps and you shall show me where these places are." [2] A colonial governorship, it is said, was declined by a certain duke on the grounds that he was still solvent. One is irresistibly reminded of Mr. Belloc's Lord Lundy:

> . . . *My language fails!*
> *Go out and govern New South Wales.*

In the Colonies themselves, such pillars of New South Wales' society as the Presbyterian divine, Dr. John Dunmore Lang, could be Republican, and people often dis-

and Sydney, much as if the Army and Navy chiefs were housed in Boston, the Congress at Washington and the President and his Secretaries spent most of their time in Chicago. Australian Federal Ministers frequently travel two nights a week between one and another of their offices: and are not as fresh as the lark when they come off morning trains.

[2] Quoted from J. A. Froude, *Oceana*. London, 1886.

cussed whether it might not be amiable to provide one or other of Queen Victoria's numerous progeny with an independent throne in latitudes south. The Australians were brooding over a Monroe Doctrine for their quarter of the world, and bitterly resented the casual attitude of the Home Government to German intrusions in the Pacific and New Guinea. Queensland almost declared war against Germany on her own account in the eighties.

But the mood suddenly changed, both in the Mother Country and the Daughters' Houses. Perhaps the turning point was the federation of the Canadian Provinces in 1867. Most people in England cheerfully assumed that Dominion was but the prelude to full independence. When the Canadians declined to depart, imagination was suddenly stirred, and presently a new possibility appeared, a new conception of a new sort of Empire. The roots of the Commonwealth are further back, in the Durham Report, in Wentworth's claim for New South Wales of complete self-government within the frame of Empire; and beyond. They sucked nourishment from the lesson taught by the American colonists. Now they were slowly pushing through the ground. Mr. Disraeli with his rather Oriental imagination had something to do with it. The Queen had more. The Jubilees, in the fiftieth and sixtieth years of her reign, brought Colonial troops and Colonial politicians to parade before admiring London crowds. The music-halls, with their songs about the "thin red line" and "We don't want to fight, but by Jingo if we do," contributed a lyric note. Mr. Disraeli, the imperialist, had rejected Bismarck's hints for a drive down the Nile Valley. Mr. Gladstone, the anti-imperialist, quite unexpectedly found himself sub-dividing Africa. And Mr. Kipling roused suburbia. From his pages marched into every villa parlour the heroic figures of Empire: the private soldiers and the Scottish engineers, the Indian Civil Servants, the schoolboys gone to battle, the master mariners and the Sikhs: elephants, camels, marine engines, and long post-roads. The clerk, the stock-broker, the English school-teacher were caught up. They shared vicariously the fortunes of their countrymen in Mr. Kipling's projection: more, Mr. Kipling's attention to detail gave them, too, a place in the picture. The little shipping clerk in a Liverpool office suddenly understood what all his laboured manifests meant: Bombay, Sydney, Penang, Lagos unrolled, became real places to him.

But it was a now almost forgotten gesture from New South Wales which gave this sentiment a point hard enough to draw a straight, strong line in imperial history. In 1885 Mr. Dalley, the Acting Premier of New South Wales, significantly an Irish Catholic, offered an expeditionary force for the Sudan. It was a gesture towards imperial unity: and England responded. The enthusiasm in Sydney revealed an underlying well of emotion. Volunteers rolled in and so did money: and the Catholic Archbishop who was to become Australia's first Cardinal headed the subscription list.

Since then, the old religious bigotries have declined in Australia and Catholics have led governments of both major parties in the Federation.

In this temper, the Colonials went to the first Imperial Conference in 1887, where the Australian Deakin demanded a colonial part in framing foreign policy. Australia and New Zealand offered in return contributions to the Pacific squadron of the Royal Navy. The Home Government could then have had an Imperial Federation if it had cared to, but perhaps the statesmen were wise to be cautious. Adequate machinery is still needed for general control of such common concerns as imperial foreign policy; but an elaborated structure might then have weighed too heavily on the growing child.[3]

But its failure to make head encouraged local federation in Australia. The Czar first and then Count Bismarck helped. The Australian colonies had old memories of Russian scares, and now German gunboats and German colonists were thrusting into what Australians had once thought their private world: and the young German Kaiser was rattling such a sword as Europe had not heard since Napoleon went to St. Helena. Common defence became a convincing motive for federation. It was backed by the new nationalism and by the new industries which looked to a national market and national protection, and by the common sense of the people at large. Australia appeared as a united nation in 1901: and found a war on its hands.

The Boer War was as popular and unpopular in Australia as in England, where its opponents ranged from Mr. Chesterton to Mr. Lloyd George. The war was hard on the Boers, but it shocked the British out of their more rabid Jingoism, in spite of Mafeking, and within seven years of its miserable end, Boers were again in power in South Africa with a Boer General as Prime Minister of the Union. In five more years Botha and Smuts led British armies in the field.

Australia sent 16,314 men to South Africa. One could have wished them a better cause, but the campaign nevertheless revealed the principle of voluntary co-operation and joint responsibility which is the essential of the Commonwealth Idea. It proved that this new thing in the

[3] Imperial Federation continued a popular air until the World War. Since 1918 less has been heard of it, perhaps because the Commonwealth functioned in war and peace without it. The British seldom fool with constitutional machinery for the sake of the machinery.

world would really work. Dalley's case had been made. And perhaps the blood of Australian soldiers sealed the bond of the Six States and their Federal Union of 1901.

COLONIAL ADMINISTRATION

The Australian has shown, in spite of his White Australian Faith, capacity to understand and to work with peoples of other bloods. His administration in New Guinea and Papua is admirably distinguished for its sense and sensibilities.

Papua came under Australian administration in 1906. It is a territory of about 90,000 square miles, a tortuous, tangled and difficult terrain where even exploration has been slow. It has about 300,000 natives and their rights have been scrupulously protected. For instance, only about 272,000 of the 58,000,000 acres have been alienated to white settlers. Petroleum exists, but one reason for its non-exploitation is concern for the native interest. The economy of copra, beans, hemp, coir, sago, vanilla, bamboo, rattan, spices, kapok is being developed slowly as something of a school and a field-laboratory. Australia carries most of the costs of services including native health and education. It collects insignificant taxes, chiefly as an exercise in citizenship, but the natives are exempt from taxation if they form communal plantations, with aid from agricultural experts. The white man who fools with native women is made to provide for his offspring. The Papuan is being trained to administration. He already polices the villages, and takes a citizen's part in his defence. He has confidence in his government and, more important, the government shows confidence in him.

Australia occupied what was German New Guinea in September, 1914, and in 1919 received a League of Nations Mandate for it. The native population is estimated at 666,000, a sharp rise on German figures, by natural increase and by more systematic census. Some Germans and some Asiatics whom they introduced as indentured labourers remain. The natives are peasant proprietors and ownership of land is individual, not communal. The Australians have pushed education and medical services into the jungles and mountains, with travelling doctors, native medical orderlies, plantation hospitals and the like. The native agriculturist is trained by demonstration plantations to cultivate the general range of tropical products.

In New Guinea, Australians have worked with and for other peoples: demonstrating qualities which, educated, should fit them for their rendezvous with history and their neighbours.

POLITICAL AND SOCIAL ECONOMY

The years between the Boer War and 1914 saw growth in every phase of the national life. Agriculture and secondary industries advanced, immigrants poured in, and the social conscience was active. It found expression in Deakin's new mercantilism: protection for industries and a family wage for workers.

The Federal Arbitration Court promulgated the "basic wage" in 1907. The basic wage is the lowest wage that may lawfully be paid to an unskilled labourer and it is based upon the "normal needs of an average employee regarded as a human being living in a civilized country." [4] To this

---

[4] It is regulated by tribunals operating under State and federal laws, and it varies from time to time according to the cost of living. (The normal employee is assumed to be responsible for a family of five.) The 1907 figure was reached by a survey of prices: the basic wage subsequently was automatically adjusted to retail prices, rising when they rose, and intended to fall if they ever fell. Various "loadings" were added

level of wages industry is expected to conform. The country clearly declared that industry existed for men, not men for industry: and on the whole it has clung tenaciously to that belief.

State intervention to control wages and working conditions was developed before federation. Both the states and the Federation now have their system of Conciliation, Arbitration, and Industrial Courts. The huge body of labour legislation and judgements has produced lawyers specializing in such matters; and the trades union secretary is an expert in court-work.

The Australian effort, in the broadest interpretation, puts the general interest of the political community before the interests of particular economic groups. In practice, the community interest is served by the give-and-take, the pendulum-swing between the sectional interests. These are roughly represented in politics by three parties, reading from Right to Left (but only half Right and half Left): the Country Party, the United Australia Party, the Labour Party. Detached labour groups have a Communist bent, but the great party machine has not. The Country Party was first formed to protest the rising tariffs and costs which largely benefited labour and industry at the expense of rural industries. It is now chiefly concerned to obtain a share in aid, relief, and subsidy for the primary producer. The U.A.P. represents the industrialist, the *rentier*, the business man, but neither it nor labour rests exclu-

to the wage from time to time, and in 1934 a new basic wage was declared. It varies according to the local price index, but in December, 1939, the average for the six capital cities was seventy-nine shillings a week. In 1941 it was about eighty-one shillings, with a prosperity "loading" of six shillings more. "Secondary" wages are added to "basic" wages for skills; and in particular industries a "minimum" wage is declared, usually exceeding the "basic" wage.

sively on class-support. There is a large floating vote amongst the mass of workers and the white-collars. Labour has been little influenced, however, by bourgeois and sub-bourgeois intellectuals: it has always been much a working man's show and often also the party of the small farmer, the shopkeeper and the Civil Servant. It shares the mentality of the industrialists in that its aims are mostly fixed on material ends: on the practical, the possible, and the immediate benefit, on matters like housing, wages, health, working conditions, holidays. I doubt if Australians will ever sacrifice existing social gains for an experiment, however distinguished, unless they are completely convinced of its practical usefulness.

Trades unions have a membership of nearly 900,000: of all adult wage and salary earners nearly a half are unionists, an unusually high proportion. Employers are organized almost as strongly: 175,690 of them in 506 associations, when last checked.

The industrial unions are powerfully disciplined, and campaign with the grim skill of old soldiers, using every hump and tussock of the industrial terrain to advance their interest. Public opinion is friendly enough, but if a strain appears the unions calculate its tolerance with almost uncanny shrewdness.

The Australian believes in the constant play of social forces. Progress is by trial-and-error. Rivalries and oppositions are symptoms of energetic life. But a civilized society must learn to resolve its conflicts without violence to the State and the community. The tone of the Australian's industrial and sometimes of his political debate is often severe and highly provocative, but he always seems to keep his head. He may blood a nose for pleasure but he has yet to blood the body politic; just as he may punch a policeman on festive occasions but seldom in the interests of social reform. Australian troops have been said to lack discipline, and they are certainly not enamoured of military punctilio and convention. The great Australian armies of volunteers never forget that they are citizens, and of no mean city. But if discipline means the capacity to control yourself for the job in hand, then I rate the Australian as its pre-eminent possessor. D. H. Lawrence long ago noticed the Australian capacity for self-discipline, and he has the country's history to support him. It comes, again, from a harsh common sense, but also from a hard, gem-like flame of loyalty to Australia and the Australian Thing.

In 1914 the Labour Party came to power in the Federation and in five of the Six States. It set up the Commonwealth Bank to control the nation's credit, to finance homes, farms, industries, and perhaps to provide the groundwork of a socialist order. The community's canny caution accepted the Bank but has preserved a private banking system.

Labour launched the Royal Australian Navy, a Service now already rich in tradition. Labour introduced compulsory military training for home-defence and thus laid the foundations for glory in Gallipoli, Palestine, and France. Labour in 1914 pledged Australia to the Imperial cause "to the last man and the last shilling." The promise was met to the tune of 226,073 casualties, 59,258 lives, and an immediate bill of £270,000,000 (none of it owing to America, incidentally), which pensions, repatriation and interest have almost doubled. It was a high and terrible endeavour for 5,000,000 people.

I think it true that Australia felt more than most countries the loss of that manhood. She was young and needed its young energies to break her soils, to build her towns, to father her children. Her voluntary system (she rejected compulsion for overseas service and labour split on the issue) swept the cream of her life, as voluntary systems do. One may exaggerate a single cause, but I believe that her public life and social effort have not recovered the temper of 1901-'14.

PROBLEMS UNRESOLVED

Her constant emphasis on the immediate, the practical, has the defects of its virtue. The Australian is often indifferent to long views and larger problems. He lacks, for instance, sufficient instructed opinion on such urgent matters as population and land conservation. The population is near standstill and decline. Vast stretches of the countryside are deteriorating from denudation, often the result of reckless exploitation. I suppose that if there are to be fewer and fewer babies, Australia can manage with less and less topsoil: until the two processes reach their conclusion in a desert peopled chiefly by the memories of a nation that once was and the even less tangible suggestions of a nation that might have been.[5]

[5] The Federal Government has lately introduced a scheme for Child Endowment. Families are to receive five shillings a week for every child after the first until its sixteenth year.

It will be a useful supplement to the basic and minimum wages, lifting them nearer to the level of a proper family wage which is, of course, the first and essential criterion of a healthy economic order.

But this matter of children is not an economic matter only. Standards of living are not lower than they were in the 1890s: although people now have a variety of new uses for their earnings. Beauty parlours, lipstick, cigarettes, automobiles, cinemas, fancy panties, canned goods, druggists' supplies, radio equipment, and tourism are apparently now necessities of life. But people eat less; and if their beer costs more they also drink less. Clothes are cheaper, though they wear out

It is difficult to absolve politicians and those whose
function is to inform and educate opinion. Politicians and
publicists should instruct as well as express the public
mind. The sun does not shine only that we may all make
hay and roll logs. It may also be used to observe the landscape and what moves upon it. Even the log-roller is
sometimes wise to look at the wood and not mistake it for
his vendable trees.

The Australian community represents, more than most
in this disappointing world, liberty and equality and
fraternity, with perhaps overmuch emphasis on equality,
for public figures tend to be of fair average quality rather
than a shade above it. Merit must not shine too brilliantly,
a politician must not see too clearly, a success must not
be too great. This is provincialism, of course, yet I do not
think that it should be unrestrainedly damned. We have
seen rather overmuch of brilliant people and city slickers
lately, and it is still better to be good, sweet maid, than
clever. So one commends to the Australian statesman renewed exercises in virtue, and trusts with Winchester that
maneres makyth man.

sooner. We no longer sustain respectability with aspidistras.
We buy fewer fiddles and pianos, corsets and long woollen
underpants.

We can afford children much as our parents could afford
us. Maybe Child Endowment is necessary, but it meets only
one need. People will not propagate for bread alone.

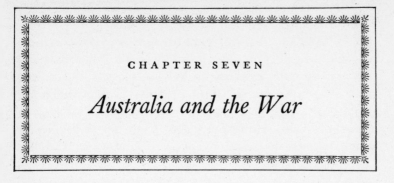

CHAPTER SEVEN

Australia and the War

TO-DAY

THE year 1939 found the Australian in a comparatively happy situation amongst the world's peoples. There were 7,000,000 of him in a continent of 2,974,581 square miles, approximately the size of the United States and four-fifths the size of Canada, with a coastline of 12,210 miles (suggesting a very blockish piece of land) and a legislator for each two hundred miles. His largest city has, in 150 years, outgrown Rome, Warsaw, Bombay and Glasgow: it is a fantastic symbol of our megalopolitanomania. His second city is bigger than Nanking, Montreal, Kobe or Cleveland. Obviously, he lives too much in cities. His birth rate is a trifle better than America's, 17.46 per 1000 of the population. In 1901, before he took to automobiles, it was 27.16. In 1939 he had more motor vehicles than all Africa or all Asia, and many more than he had babies. In spite of his automobility, his six states and the nation as a whole provided seven of the nine lowest death rates in the world. He marries late, which may have something to do with the lack of babies and the presence of motor cars.

Like the New Zealander, the Australian remains a Christian. At the last census, eighty-six per cent of the population declared themselves church members.

He lives in about 1,700,000 houses (but only 40,000 apartments) averaging 5.03 rooms each, so now he is bet-

ter housed than man has ever been since he dropped from
the tree or emerged from the cave. The average rental of
houses is about seventeen shillings or $2.60 a week. But
more than half the houses are occupied by owners, not
tenants; and in Queensland, where what some people call
a Socialist Government has long reigned, seventy per cent
of the houses are owner-occupied.

Wage and salary workers numbered, before the war,
1,909,000, of whom the seven governments employed 365,-
000: evidence of the extent of government ownership and
intervention in the economic province and of huge expenditure from revenues and loans. Civil Services breed
Civil Services. If they also breed a preference for security
and stability to the chances and adventures of private enterprise, the Australian character should presently reveal
it. I am inclined to believe that it already does appear in
the slowing temper of social advance.

The proportion of rural workers declines, the proportion of industrial workers sharply rises. But the Australian, like Abraham, has great pastoral wealth. He grows
more wool by far than any other country. He is one of
the chief producers of wheat, hay, oats, forage, barley,
sugar-cane, maize (corn, popped or unpopped, to you),
and fruit. He eats nearly twice as much meat as an American but drinks less liquor, though the visitor or repatriate
may not believe it, for he will see more drunks on the
Australian streets than in any other country that I know,
probably because Australia has a ridiculous habit of taking most of its liquor in crowded bars between 5 and 6
P.M. and on an empty stomach.

The Australian was heavily hit by the depression of the
early thirties, which battered at his export industries,
threw a huge proportion of his people out of work, and
emphasized the monstrous shadow of his public debt. But
he set his teeth, tightened his belt, and pulled through

without serious social dislocation. Labour, in Federal power for the first time since its wartime split, piled up tariffs, encouraged new industries, cut salaries and pensions.

Another party split upset its Government in 1931, and some Labour Members joined with the Opposition to form the United Australia Party which, in coalition with the Country Party, survived until the death of the Prime Minister, Joseph A. Lyons, in 1939. The Government's strength was largely in the personal qualities of the Prime Minister. He was father of an enormous family and Australia could still admire where it would not emulate.

In 1934 20.5 per cent of trades unionists were out of work: in 1938 8.8 per cent, bettering the pre-depression years. Outside mining, 1938 had only sixty-two strikes, involving loss in wages of £400,000 (roughly $1,200,000). But Lyons' death threw the parties of his coalition into a confusion from which they have not yet entirely recovered. With considerable agility, however, this United Australia Party Ministry clung to office until the war was six months old, when the Country Party joined a new Coalition, under Robert G. Menzies.[1]

The Australian economy was undergoing a startling change in the course of the war effort; and there was use for criticism by His Majesty's Loyal Opposition of the hasty and often improvised measures to which His Majesty's Government was often compelled. An Opposition in being makes a useful safety valve in a society under a heavy head of steam. But the wartime play of party tried both people and politicians. The public mind was on the urgent job, and party politics seemed recklessly wasteful of time and energy.

[1] The Coalition, led first by Mr. Menzies and then by Arthur W. Fadden, was replaced in October of 1941 by a Labour Government, headed by John Curtin.

War has brought a sweeping reorganization of the whole national economy. Exports, imports, marketing, foreign exchange, investments and prices were all made subject to rigid controls. New Departments popped up right and left and Departments to Co-ordinate Departments: all necessary, but a maze even to initiates. For example, exports became the tender charge of the Shipping Control Board, the Advisory Committee on Sea-borne Trade, the Overseas Shipping Committee, the Wool Committee, the Wheat Board, the Barley Board, the Hides and Leather Board, the Apple and Pear Board.

In effect, the whole economy has come under political direction. Many Australians believe and some hope that it will not again free itself from many or any of the restrictions imposed. But popular dislike for much of the machinery and the methods suggests that every one is not yet ready for the strait-jacket of collectivism.

Labour, with the unions' consent, was organized and subjected to certain restrictions and dilutions of the skilled trades. The war industries pulled in to engineering shops agricultural labourers, retired craftsmen, business men, barmen, bookmakers' clerks, town councillors, pensioners, waiters, saxophone players, and a vast regiment of women which was chiefly engaged with light metal work and ammunition. The strain on established labour conditions and organizations was very great, while the tension of wartime production with its calls for overtime and its ceaseless drive inevitably produced local disputes. To meet these, Conciliation Commissions were established, working under Arbitration Court judges, to investigate and parley as disputes arose. From the viewpoint of the public, with its mind bent on the war, labour difficulties, especially in the coal industry, have seemed excessive and irritating. From the workers' viewpoint, especially the engineering worker subject to unprecedented develop-

THE AUSSIE OVERSEAS

". . . Was serving from Yorkshire to the Solomon Islands."—Page 137

Australian Dept. of Information

THE AUSSIE OVERSEAS

"Within one year t
A.I.F. had foug
campaigns in Lib
Greece, Crete, Syri
—Page 137

Australian Dept. of Informat

ments in his trade, occasional protests have been necessary to preserve conditions. Against local difficulties must be set Labour's mighty contribution to Australia's mighty programme of defence: and that must warm the bowels and stiffen the spine of any man who believes in the democratic way.

WAR INDUSTRY

In 1940, Australia spent eighteen times as much on munitions as she had in 1938. From three government munitions plants had grown a system to cover the whole engineering industry and nearly every machine-shop, however small, in the country. Some plants were producing three times the quantity of material for which they were designed. Before the war, five plants had some acquaintance with machine-tool making. By 1941, eighty-five firms were making machine tools. Australian lathes and gauging machines are better than German models. Something like 70,000 tools, parts and gauges are needed for the Bren gun alone. Models and blueprints were sunk at sea or held in England. Australians who had never had such problems before drew their own blueprints and designed their own models and had the gun in production six months ahead of the original schedule.

The general plan has provided for the multiplication of war production sixty times over between December, 1939, and December, 1941.

Three years ago there was a very second-rate golf-course near Melbourne. By 1941 it was covered with great aircraft plants which had already put hundreds of machines in the sky. A country which had never built its own automobile engines was building fighters, bombers, reconnaissance and training planes, with every item of their equipment: guns, instruments, engines, and the tools to make them. It had created a National Standards Labora-

tory, the fifth only in the world; an optical industry producing its own optical glass for gun-sights, predictors; an
instrument industry for radio compasses, direction-finders,
altimeters and indicators; an aluminum industry. It was
making uniforms, steel helmets, gas masks, transports,
wheeled workshops, medical supplies, roller mills, steel
presses, stamping machines, mines, depth charges, shells,
howitzers, field guns, naval guns, machine guns, rifles and
ammunition, anti-aircraft guns, parachutes, searchlights,
pontoons, boots, tanks, gun-carriers, cotton cord, abrasives,
stainless steel, and ships. A little town in South Australia,
which had perhaps 3000 people three years before, was
building 15,000-ton steamers. The Royal Australian Navy
began the war with five cruisers and a handful of destroyers and escort vessels, and some converted auxiliary cruisers. In two years it built six or seven times as many ships.
Ships laid down since the war began have already met the
enemy from East Africa to the Western Ocean. To catch
the immensity of the achievement, one must think in
terms of men to be trained, plants to be built: like that
series of aircraft factories on a Melbourne golf-course,
like the barmen and the farm labourers turned mechanics.

In 1940 the Eastern Group Supply Conference met at
Delhi, representing India, South Africa, Australia, New
Zealand, to provide for them all and for Northern and
Southern Rhodesia, the East African territories, Palestine,
Ceylon, Burma, British Malaya and Hong Kong: an in-
teresting demonstration of the strength of the Empire
under and east of Suez. Australia, during 1941, became a
major arsenal for all that area.

When the Australian delegation proposed what it could
do, experts from Britain flatly refused to believe it, on the
simple ground that any sane man knows an impossibility
when he sees one. But the Australians already had the

impossible in their pockets. They are an enterprising people, and now completely equip whole armies, from bottled
beer to ack-ack batteries. Australian ammunition blazed
at Messerschmitts over Cologne: Australian pants were
on Punjabis in Syria; Australia designed and made the
Wirraway planes I saw over Singapore. In 1901 her population spent less than a million pounds on defence. In
the four years to the end of June, 1942, she conservatively
estimated her war expenditure at £453,750,000, or a trifle
of £65 for each man, woman and child in the country. So
the world progresses. And intrudes upon a people whose
whole ambition was to get on with the task of building up
a new nation, if they ever thought of it that way: people
on the whole very like and normally as militant as farmers in Iowa or stenographers on Madison Avenue.

ARMY, AIR FORCE, NAVY

When the war began, Australia had a regular army of
about 4000 men, chiefly of staff and instructional details;
and a volunteer militia of about 70,000, drilling in its
spare time. Ten months later she had 90,000 volunteers
for overseas in the Australian Imperial Force; and had
organized her militia to provide a Home Army of 250,000.
The Australian Imperial Force went on growing. A mechanized Division, whose equipment alone cost £30,000,000,
was formed. Within one year, the A.I.F. had fought campaigns in Libya, Greece, Crete, Syria. It had provided
a powerful force to Malaya. The A.I.F. was serving from
Yorkshire to the Solomon Islands. The voluntary principle has been much criticized at home, but it is, wisely
or not, a proud tradition of the Australian democracy
clung to through the most desperate passages of the last
war: and in this war it was producing a larger quota than

before. By the middle of 1941, 162,000 men of the A.I.F. were serving overseas.

The Royal Australian Air Force began the war with about 3000 officers and men. Within a year its strength was 38,000. Six months later it was probably twice as great. But pilots, air crews, and ground staffs take a long time to train. Two hundred thousand had offered for the R.A.A.F. by the middle of 1941, and it called them up as it could use them. Australia's provision for the Empire Air Scheme was 30,000 air crews. Seven in nine of R.A.A.F. personnel were being completely trained in Australia, the remainer finishing for the Empire Scheme in Canada or Rhodesia. Australia was completely ringed with aerodromes and operating stations. She manned Sunderland Flying Boats in the Atlantic from the beginning of the war. The R.A.A.F. has served over England, Africa, southeastern Asia, and the Western Pacific.

The Royal Australian Navy is now a generation old, with a brilliant record from the last war. It works in close liaison with the Royal Navy but it is, of course, an independent Service, though Australia in wartime usually places it under the operational dispositions of the London Admiralty. The First Sea Member and some of the senior officers are still borrowed from the Royal Navy, because the R.A.N. is not yet old enough to have produced full admirals. At the beginning of the war, it mustered 850 officers and 8648 men. Its figures since are secret, but the First Sea Member spoke to me early in 1941 of 20,000 men in training and of no difficulties in recruiting, even though the R.A.A.F. was a dashing competitor for manpower since the last war. Australia was providing crews for at least fifty new naval vessels she was building. She had sent crews to the Royal Navy. In the first few months of the war she had put gun-crews on 200 merchant ships.

One of her cruisers had been in action more than eighty times up to the middle of 1941. The *Sydney* had emulated the first *Sydney's* dispatch of the *Emden* in 1914 (an engagement which baptized the R.A.N.), sinking in a single-ship action the Italian *Bartolomeo Colleoni*.

CHAPTER EIGHT

Australia and the Future

PROBLEMS OF PEACE

AUSTRALIA has met the challenge of war. The problems of peace will provide other tests.

Now the Australian nationalist economy has been an interesting experiment in lifting yourself by your own bootstraps. The strain has been eased by a constant flow of borrowed money, but the experiment so far has certainly not been proven a failure.

But consider one phase of the economic problem. Australia is largely dependent on her exports of primary products to Great Britain. Britain pays by her own exports of goods and by "invisible exports": shipping and financial services and the interest on her loans and investments. But even before the war, Britain's visible exports were away below her visible imports, and she was living partly on the returns from services and investments.

The war compelled her to realize much of her overseas investment.[1] Dwindling capital means dwindling income: and consequently dwindling purchases of American wheat and meat that Britain has bought for generations. The money spent in America is also, if the last war is a precedent, strengthening future competitors.

[1] In the United States, for instance, her assets before the war were $4,483,000,000. By December, 1940, she had spent $4,360,000,000 on American shells, ships, aircraft and the rest.

With variations, Australia presents a corresponding theme. Australia is producing (war has given great impetus) its own machines, textiles, chemicals, instruments, paper, and most of the things formerly bought from or through Britain. Australia is not likely to put its economy in reverse, discharge skilled tradesmen, dismantle factories, let the machines rust. But again, if its purchases from Britain fall, so must Britain's buying. What then happens to both economies? Where Britain cannot sell her manufactured wares, she cannot buy food or raw materials. She will begin to grow every pound she can of her own butter, meat, cheese, as she should in her own interest have done long ago. But as she grows more, she will need less from America, Australia, New Zealand. Nor can Nebraska or New South Wales fairly complain if they force her to buy from Argentina because Argentina buys from her.

This puts only one phase of the economic difficulty and in very broad terms: but here is an elementary problem for those people who keep talking, usually with a remarkable indifference to the simplest and most brutal facts, about New Orders.

Australia's living standards must fall if Britain's loans and purchases fall, unless Australia finds other markets and creditors. Australian producers may learn to farm more for subsistence and less for markets: to seek, as one of their economists puts it, a standard of contentment rather than a standard of living in its Australian sense. Even if the purchasing power of the Australian consumer was much increased, he cannot, with the best appetite in the world, eat all the meat, wheat, fruit, butter, eggs, or wear all the wool he produces. He still needs large markets, wheat cheques and wool cheques. Moreover, something is owing to the workers of Britain who have known the blood, the sweat and the tears. If professions of ad-

miration for the Commons of England mean more than
a twitter of sentiment, we shall want to help the English
worker [2] earn his daily bread.

This is one phase only of a problem immensely more
complex which will clearly demand an heroic effort at
co-operation, first among the British people themselves
and then with others concerned, the Americans especially;
for American bread-and-butter as well as America's higher
interests are involved in this. All talk about a good time
coming is treacherous stuff if by it is meant a good time
only in the material sense. It is going to be a time of work
and sacrifice. A doctrine once held by our peoples would
make a time of work and sacrifice the best of all good
times, producing mind and will and guts and man's salva-
tion. It is not a very popular doctrine nowadays, perhaps
because few of its professors practise it.

The post-war problems cannot be solved by economic
means only: unless economic interests are subdued to
larger conceptions of good, the conflict of nations, classes
and individuals will persist.

So the economic problem leads back, as it always will
(for man is a whole being) to the moral and intellectual
problem. I confess myself dismayed. Morals and mind are
everywhere at low ebb. They are hardly thought relevant
any more to practical problems, for we are fallen into a
sottish cynicism which will destroy us and ours if it persists. The mess we are in is evidence of our state. Nor do
the shepherds of the flock seem much inspired. Those
whose charge it was to teach all nations now do not teach
their own: and our education and our arts are designed
as easy escapes from the difficult affair of living.

Those who have light lack fire. Those who have fire
lack light. When sound doctrine is silent, fools fill the air.

---

[2] And not only Englishmen, of course; one restricts the
argument for patience's sake.

When the shepherd will not lead, the flock follows the most random, silly sheep. It is all very dismal.

Australia has already drawn largely upon what you might call its social credit, raising huge loans to bolster its living standards. A good many Australians now have a notion that economic goods appear by a sort of spontaneous generation or sleight of hand. But white rabbits— or white elephants, for that matter—do not really come out of thin air. National wealth, wheat in ear, cattle on the hoof, cars on the road, mean work. You cannot eat a social dole or dividend until you convert it into the product of sweat and toil. You cannot either have your cake or eat it unless somebody makes the cake.

When you make shells instead of cakes there will be a shortage of cakes. When your steel and skill are in tanks instead of cars there will be a shortage of cars. When national wealth is in cannon and national income is exploded, you will have less national wealth for other projects and less national income for your daily needs.

By the end of the war, Australian public debts may be nearer £2,000,000,000 than to the £1,000,000,000 already long passed. The interest burden, apart from the other costs of Government (now normally over £20 per head of population annually), will become a terrific strain on the economy and on the economically active elements of the community. Internal repudiation would be ruinous to the half of the Australian population which carries life insurance policies to an average of about $500, and the two-thirds of the population which has savings bank accounts to an average of about $1000. To repudiate external debts would choke off loans and wreck the export industries. There are also, let me tediously repeat, the ethics of the matter.

THE COMING TEST OF DEMOCRACY

Australians on the whole have been slow to understand these simple matters. They have been befuddled by much loose talk: and, of course, by the constant flow until now of borrowed capital which has made them mildly intoxicated, and has seemed like manna from heaven. It must cease upon some midnight, and I dread the morning's hangover.

The crisis has so far been staved off by Britain's purchase of the wartime wool clips, and of meat and butter, sugar, fruits.[3] Britain in 1941 was spending in Australia more than usual: but her buying may drop sharply at that very moment when an economy geared for war is suddenly at war no longer, when arms factories are closing or retooling, and the 600,000 war-workers have no war to work for.

What happens then will depend upon the Australian's ability still to solve his problems, however appalling, in quiet and good order. The social economy will not spring prettily back into shape when it is released from war's iron grip. The readjustment of a war economy to peace is more difficult than the adjustment of a peace economy to war. War tightens social bonds, loyalties, and disciplines. But peace releases these tensions. Differences subdued and grievances suppressed light up. Every narrow ambition and self-interest revives, all the stronger for its hibernation. The social organism is tired, jaded, jumpy. The social machinery jars out of joint. Every political,

[3] Because of shipping shortages (*e.g.*, forty per cent of the ships carrying New Zealand produce via Panama have been reported sunk), much durable produce will necessarily be stored. Under an Anglo-American Agreement, 250,000,000 pounds of Australian wool was to go for storage in the U. S., as shipping space was available.

social and economic difficulty is aggravated in our time by the ideological quarrels, which range over every field of values, and concern not only the means and machinery of life but the end and nature of life itself. Were we agreed spiritually, morally and intellectually upon essentials and ends, we might better unite our strengths to solve the problems of means. But there can be no real co-operation and peace in the world while there is no peace in the soul and mind of man.

The great test for democracy is coming: whether it can resolve the quarrel in peace and by reason achieve again the "tranquillity of order" necessary to the good life of men and their societies. Peace is not the absence of strife, but a positive creation of the will and mind of man. Like redemption, it is bought with a great price and must be pursued with perseverence until the end.

I do not know if the Australian or any one of us is ready, morally and intellectually, for the labours and sacrifices of peace. Mr. Brian Penton, the Australian publicist, shakes a grim head: "For the stockbroker in his castle and the trades unionist in his cot, for the worker in a tariff-protected factory, and the yeoman on a bounty-protected farm, for boodler and bozo, social justice begins at home and stays there." [4] Perhaps I could find heart to disagree with him if I had spent more time lately with the armies in the field and less in the lush atmosphere where war means wages and dividends, not wounds and death: where jackasses are loud in the land, and social reformers are ready to reform everybody but themselves. It is curious that social reformers so often miss that immediate field of endeavour.

[4] In *The Daily Telegraph,* Sydney, June 18, 1941.

EXTERNAL RELATIONS

Australia's external relations fall into three principal divisions, each interlocked: her membership in the British Commonwealth, her situation as a sub-Asiatic country, and her relations with the United States. Through her imperial associations, political and economic, she is concerned with Europe and the Near East. Within the British Empire itself, her relations are chiefly with the Mother Country, Overseas Ministers meet together at Imperial Conferences more or less chaired by Great Britain and at occasional parleys like the Ottawa Conference, but until now the younger partners have not much developed acquaintance amongst themselves. The Australian view of Indian problems, for instance, is pretty much as detached and as uninstructed as the popular American view. Australia trades with Canada, South Africa and much with New Zealand, but Canada unhappily does not play international cricket and sends abroad no Rugby teams, which leaves her rather out of the great system of Empire. Lately, after some radio talks, I had a note from a Canadian which sums up the matter neatly: "I have always thought it a great pity that the members of the family regularly write home to Mother but seldom to one another." But the Empire Air Scheme and the Eastern Supply Conference are instances of co-operation that may encourage more. Mr. Menzies has talked to the Canadian Parliament. It would be a good thing if Mr. Mackenzie King could talk to the Australian.

The Dominions have not much exerted themselves in the conduct of Imperial foreign policy. British Governments may constantly consult Dominion Governments, but in practice the Dominions consider British policy and co-operate or not as they feel inclined. Loyalty sometimes prompts co-operation when the head does not cheerfully follow the heart. The Dominions have had a sort of sublime trust in the talent available at Westminster. This loyalty is a precious thing. But it is more likely to endure if it is accompanied by a proper measure of responsibility and co-operation. No British interest requires that British statesmen should be the only scapegoats when scapegoats are sought. The loyalty of the Dominions and the share they bear of Imperial burdens earn them responsibility: they themselves should accept responsibility as an obligation accompanying the privilege of criticism which they employ very readily, especially in the tuppenny press.

Britain's experience and equipment must give her the larger responsibility, and she must always have the chief influence in the Empire's European policies. But Canada is entitled to a special influence in the American sphere, and Australia in the Pacific-Indonesian world where she resides. In theory the principle is already accepted. In practice it waits upon adequate machinery. Perhaps the machinery waits on sufficient concern in the Dominions themselves. For, truth to tell, the Dominions have not been at much trouble to equip themselves for an intelligent approach to foreign problems.

The conduct of foreign policy requires a measure of education: knowledge of other peoples, acquaintance with their characters, constitutions, traditions and habits of thought, historical purposes and ambitions, economics, needs, beliefs, manners and so on.

Australian newspapers carry a high proportion of overseas news, and most cultivate some sense of public responsibility. Much space goes to snippets of London and New York opinion but the bias, perhaps because of cable rates, is not to what you might call documentation. There are more interpretations than texts. The Australian library-subscriber has much the same acquaintance with European affairs as the easy readers of Illinois and Texas. They take in books like Mr. Gunther's, Mr. Sheean's, and Mr. Douglas Reed's. They share the modern taste for predigested opinion, and they like it spiced with personalities and a tart knowingness, actual or assumed. Books now must compete with ten-minute radio pundits and are designed, I imagine, chiefly to lend brightness to conversation; which sadly needs it. So Australians are as well informed as most Uitlanders on the exciting highlights of Europe's queer career.

Of problems Asiatic and its northern neighbours, it is hardly informed at all. Particular instances are seldom satisfying: but if you remind Australians that they have a land frontier with a European power they are inclined to blink and wonder where. I have been privileged to see a not unimportant packet of documents addressed from Australia to *Singapore, Batavia.* You may now lunch in Australia and take afternoon tea in Koepang, yet I have heard a heavyweight in Australian officialdom ask a Dutchman: "Now, how many people have you got up there? Seven millions?" These are trivialities, no doubt, but like Sherlock Holmes one may draw conclusions. Her northern seas are strategically to Australia what the Caribbean is to the United States, but I doubt whether two in ten Australians could name in order of approach the lands that lie across them or would have very much notion of the distances between, even in terms of battle fleets or bombers. Except for a Trade Commissioner and a small office in Batavia, Australia has had no representation in the Indies until just now, except via London and the British Consulates. Her view of Asia has been dominated by two considerations: the White Australia policy and her recurrent anxiety about Japan. In general, she favoured the old Japanese alliance, but agreed with Britain to surrender it at America's request during the Washington Conference. In 1940 she appointed for the first time a Minister to Tokyo. In 1941, tardily, she sent one to Chungking. Both appointments suggest a slow awakening. There is now talk of "definite responsibilities, concrete activities" in "our own region": one can only trust that they will be guided by adequate information intelligently used. The significance of Singapore and the dispatch of Australian troops to Malaya have caught the public mind and imagination.

But Australia still needs education for the task that geography has set her.

Much of her innocence derives from long seclusion and easy security. While Britain ruled the waves, the Australian has wrapt himself in his local life. Even the war of 1914-'18, despite the cost to him and his effort, did not disturb his feeling of local security much more than it disturbed, say, California's. His courtship of a virgin continent has been an exciting affair, and his domestic preoccupations have blurred his sense of the rougher, ruder world outside. But now the honeymoon is over.

The Australian thinks of his as a Pacific country when only one and the briefest of his coasts overlooks that ocean. His troubles will not come from the scattered archipelagos and the deep sea-bottoms off Sydney: they will come down the channels and stepping-stones of Malaya, Indonesia, and New Guinea, which hang above Australia like a great curved sword, three thousand miles in length.

The Australians and New Zealanders are the only considerable white communities between Panama and Suez. Their future must be lived out in that area, not in isolation from it. Asia is moving and not only in the somewhat mechanical gestures of Japan. Incalculable forces are working in China, India, and Indonesia: forces which

cannot be checked but with which we might co-operate
for the general good and decency of the world.

This war has revealed that Malaya, the Indies and Aus-
tralasia form an inevitable bloc designed geographically
and historically for social, political, and economic co-
operation: the new world of Oceania.

There is not one serious local obstacle to an intense
development of something like the "good-neighbour"
programme: which happens, by the way, to be an innova-
tion and a revolution in diplomatic method. Australia is
the most formidable resident partner in that bloc and
unless she grossly misplays her hand she will from now
on swing much more weight than her own in the world.

The Indo-Australasian bloc interlocks northwestward
with the Indo-Burmese system, north with the Chinese,
northeast with the American. The possibilities for creative statesmanship are dazzling. Strong, liberal, generous
policies in the coming generation might bring enduring
stability and order in two-thirds of the world. This is
emphatically Australia's business, and London, Lanca-
shire and Canberra will all be wise to see it so.

It is also Washington's business, unless America is to
retreat from the Western Pacific and abandon her interests in China, Malaya, and the Indies at large. I do not
see how she could if she wanted to, and I do not think
that she will want to. Apart from rubber, tin, copra and
quinine, considerations of world peace and world commerce, the matters we call high policy are involved: and
clearly the peace and security of the world are necessary
to the peace and security of its constituents. None of us,
unfortunately, can step on and off the planet as we please.
Australian-American co-operation exists and will in-

Publicity Dept. K.P.M., Batavia-Centrum (Java)

IRRIGATION PROJECT

"The Javanese have immemorially adopted all streams and waterways as baths and public conveniences."·

JAVA ROAD
"The volcanic soil is rich and red, with . . . exact tidy farming."

TOWARDS BUITENZORG
"The irrigation channels cross the hillsides, and naked bathers lie in the long grass."

crease in war and peace. The advantage is not all Australia's.

Australia, as Professor Alexander has emphasized, is the "central land mass and core" of the rich region between Samoa and Singapore. "The direction of the whole of this region lay in the hands of people whose political ideas correspond closely with those of the democracy which dominates the Ocean on its north-eastern shores." [5] No one in a world split by ideologies will underrate the importance of this. Australia and the United States share the same philosophy and want the same sort of world. They fight for the same basic beliefs, they would use the same language to express them: "the unalienable rights . . . life, liberty, the pursuit of happiness . . . government of the people, by the people . . . shall not perish from the earth." From the earth. Lincoln meant a universal freedom. "Men are endowed by their Creator": not some little local happy sect of men. So Mr. Roosevelt can speak of "four essential human freedoms . . . everywhere in the world," and be at one with Jefferson and Lincoln.

Australians and Americans resemble one another in many ways: in none more than this profound political sense. The Australian Federation, framing its Constitution, drew largely on United States experience, not in imitation but because the political principles and circumstances of the two peoples were so much alike. The likeness runs too through common life. Thousands of English, Irish, Scottish families divided their emigrants between Australia and America. Moreover, there has been much migration between the two continents themselves. Many California "diggers" came from Australia: many Australian "diggers" from California. Herbert Hoover was for a time a mining engineer in Australia. Mr. King

[5] *Australia and the United States.* Professor F. Alexander. No. 1 in *America Looks Ahead* Series. Boston, 1941.

O'Malley, an Australian Federal Minister who had much to do with the foundation of Canberra, was an American. The first town-plan of Canberra was drafted in a Chicago office. Some of the first Americans sent to France in 1917 were brigaded with Australians; not all brass hats were idiots. Americans were Australia's first frequent visitors. Many an old whaler knew Australian beaches as he knew Martha's Vineyard or Buzzards' Bay.

The United States has invested $500,000,000 in Australia. The Australian buys from the United States four times as much per head as the South American and more in total than any South American country except sometimes Argentina. The Australian is normally a better customer than a Frenchman, a German, an Italian, and a Japanese all lumped together. The United States has sold Australia about $1,000,000,000 worth of stuff in the last dozen years. Australia has sold her about $300,000,000 worth.

The intercourse of peoples, however, is largely a matter of their arts. For every American who sees England a hundred read English books. The arts, after all, are only the ways in which we communicate (unless we are the sort of modern artist who communicates only with himself, as people do in padded cells). American cinema now conditions the world, Christian, Hindu, Moslem, Animist, old Tom Cobleigh and all. These things too are a phase of Empire, for they inform the mind of man and his behaviour.

Our peoples now, if they heed it, have such an opportunity as has not come before to any people. But one remembers the servant who went away and buried his talent. It might be salutary to look him up and reflect upon his fate.

AUSTRALIAN LANDSCAPE

FLYING from Sydney to Darwin, you see the proportion of things in Australia: the overgrown urbanism on the edge of the southern seas, the rich coast, the arc of eastern mountains, the undulating wheat lands, the sheep lands, the cattle country and the emptiness, the desolating, overwhelming emptiness receding towards the west, to the Red Centre, the deserts of stone, and the plateau stretching on and on to the Indian Ocean. It is a continent incredibly old, weathered and worn westward to a tableland which is broken only by sudden sharp monuments of towering rock, memorials of highlands long eroded, great splinters, ridges, and ranges of granite and quartzite. When you are moving down there across the plains, you notice the earth no more than the floor of a room: the sky is not only above you but all about you, as it is in a dead-calm sea, when no wave moves to catch the eye. The plains' dry wind from across thousands of miles whips at you, and the stars are yellow flames at night. Nature is stripped to its Archaean and Precambrian bones.

I have travelled a great deal in Australia, but I did not have the proportions right until I flew across it. You may take plane at Darwin and not see a town beneath until Sydney is sprawled out thirty or forty miles each way. Towns are there, but few and scattered and small. Population is mostly in the southeastern corner, between the sea and the Murray-Darling river system; and southward in Victoria; in the patch about Adelaide; another patch in the deep southwest; and up along the eastern shore of Queensland. As you strike inland it thins rapidly, until there are only a few nomads, brown and white. A third of the continent has less than a ten-inch rainfall, and most of the lowlands which cross the continent to divide the western plateau from the eastern highlands are sterile. About the huge saltpan of Lake Eyre and its companions, the rainfall is almost nil. I once met a desert northeast of Eyre which has been only once crossed by man.

You fly northwest from the Dividing Range over the blacksoil plains (where during the wet a car bogs more stubbornly than in any other mud I know except Argentina's), and then over the red soils, with low trees and scrub, and winding watercourses like the wrinkles on an old face. I always think of this Australia as a country of dull reds and brown-green: but I have flown over it in March, when it shimmered for hundreds of leagues with the swamps, streams and slush of autumn rains. A sharp eye, with luck and a clear day, may catch some lonely house where two or three cattlemen and perhaps a few native stockmen work a station [1] half the size of Britain.

Though Australia, with extensive irrigation and water conservation, might carry eight or ten times its present population, enormous stretches of it will remain for ever a dominion of the wind and sun but not of man.

You may travel for thousands of miles amongst the quiet valleys and wooded hills and rich savannahs of the east and south and never sense the deserts except on summer days when the hot wind blows from the far inland with a breath of sand. On the Queensland coasts, amongst

[1] Station: Australian for ranch; cattle or sheep, but not dude.

rain-forests and by swift rivers, you might be in Sumatran jungle: but its coastal pastures can look as lush as English summer meadows. The hardwoods of the southeast, where trees grow a hundred yards high in the Victorian ranges, and the superb karri of the Cape Leeuwin corner were a heritage, now largely wasted, of forest splendour. The Australian landscape has a special character from its eucalypts (gum-trees, in Australian), with their blue-grey and green-grey sheen of leaves, and from its acacias, the wattles, mulga, brigalow, myall. But the Australians, owning a smaller proportion of timbered lands than any other nation in the world, take to trees remorselessly with fire and axe. The once richly wooded east is now a cemetery of dead trees. Timber is sacrificed for grass and for one or two generations' brief profits before erosion ruins the land. The natural economy of Australia was spare and balanced: men and rabbits have worked havoc with it.

There were coils of smoke from forest fires in the Blue Mountains as we flew out from Sydney. You look down and imagine the sequence: the ring-barked trees, the dried grass, the fires, the crumbling creek banks, the seepages in catchment areas, the trickles growing to harsh scars, the topsoils washing down to silt the streams; floods and then drought, the rocks exposed to split with sun and frost, the wasting land. But no one seems much concerned in Sydney or in Melbourne, where they are busy about many things: horses, dogs, tin hares, votes, building allotments, taxes, strikes, wages, social reform, the price of silk stockings, and their cramped, sour brick houses and pathetic garden flowers.

Sydney, beneath you, is one of the most exciting things to see in the world. Its harbour, a mile wide at the entrance, has two hundred miles of coastline inside with blue arms spread like branches from the trunk. Outside is the ocean, and north and south of the entrance the Pacific ends in golden bays between headland after headland. The streets run eccentrically from the harbour's winding little capes and coves. The bridge, which is not the world's greatest but looks it, jumps from the city to the North Shore where the harbour narrows near Governor Phillip's first settlement, now the packed business centre of the place. From it spreads the old town, the tight little streets of brick, grossly overbuilt and shadowed by towering apartment houses which will presently be tenements. Sydney is a siren sort of place, lively and seductive, and has quite another air than the grim purposefulness of Melbourne: but she is now, I fear, rather a bloated siren with a hard glint in her eye. I was once very much in love with her, but now I have misgivings. Her metropolitan extravagances suck at the life of the land. She dominates New South Wales and the Western Pacific more than New York City dominates New York State: and the quality of her living nowadays sets my teeth on edge. But only a Cobbett could deal sufficiently with that.

Perhaps I am a straggler from my times, but I think you must go to the smaller cities, to the country towns and to the wide brown land itself to see the best of Australia. They raise complaints, but the world has no happier cities for common men than Adelaide, Brisbane, Perth, and Hobart, with their hills, their seas, their vegetable patches, and their domestic quiet and decencies: and they are less clamorous with factious cliques.

As we went out over Sydney, an American naval squadron was lying in the harbour. It arrived within the octave of Lend-and-Lease, and the city celebrated with even more zeal and zest than it had for the *Sydney* itself, lately home from battle with *Bartolomeo Colleoni*. I was at dinner with several officers of the U. S. squadron the night before I left. They were rather astonished at things.

From the air you see why the first crossing of the tangled mumps of mountains which rise slowly from Sydney's back gate was late and long. And when you cross, you understand why the rich downs westward moved the discoverer Wentworth to solemn verse. A few hundred miles on, with the country dropping towards the great flat, you appreciate the Australian vocabulary. We listened to it at Charleville in Queensland, where we came down for lunch, as people plucked their feet out of the glue. We also used it. There had been eight inches of rain in the previous forty-eight hours, and it was still drizzling from the bulging clouds that drift in circular motion about Australia and sometimes condescend to break. Our particular weather system for this trip was tied in with storms over Asia and much the same heavy cloud persisted from Sydney to Soerabaja. It seemed symbolic.

THE DAUGHTER TONGUE

The Australian cities now talk in the language of cinema, badly; but the Australian lingo still runs up-country. There you do hard yakka for your tucker, and the swagman on the wallaby may steal a jumbuck by the billabong unless the jack or dog gets after him. You learn to count your change in thrums and treys, zacks, deeners, notes and fiddleys. If the beer is good, that's bonzer. If the barman is slick, he's a dab. If the barmaid is pretty, she's a purler. If she is honest (and what barmaid is not?), she's dinkum, dink, or dinkie-di. On the other hand, if she is the unpleasantly gossiping sort (and what barmaid ever was?) she pokes mullock, and you'll probably go crook and lob somewhere else, even if only as a lurk. In the backblocks bar you meet your cobbers or the push, squatters, rouseabouts, jackeroos, in from the never-never and looking for a change of diet from damper and billy tea before they go bush again.[2] (I limit myself to the more delicate usages.)

Charleville is 502 miles from Sydney, northwest, over the Queensland border, and much like most Australian country towns. I always think of wide dusty roads, a trickle of bitumen on either side of the "reserve" in the main street, where a few straggly trees look on the usually brown, dry grass. Pubs are generally two-storied with balconies. The shops hang verandahs over a broad sidewalk of beaten earth, sometimes paved for a few hundred yards. The houses are one-storied with galvanized-iron roofs (to catch rainwater for washing) and tired-looking fences, and each with a half-acre or two or three or a hundred acres of ground. Long grass grows by wire fences. People have fruit trees about the house and perhaps their own windmill and well. The churches commonly look like Nonconformist chapels, and the town halls are splashed with cinema posters. The gnarled pepper trees droop thin,

[2] You still work hard for your keep, and the hobo (but how much more than a hobo) on the track may steal a sheep by the river lagoon (backwater) unless the policeman or the policeman gets after him. You learn to count your change in threepences or threepences, sixpences, shillings, pounds and pounds. If the beer is good, that's very good. If the barman is slick, he's an expert. If the barmaid is pretty, she's champion, as they say in Yorkshire. If she is honest, she is . . . well, dinkum. But she may, as we remark, have a nasty tongue, and you'll probably protest and go away, even if only as a gag. The inland bar will offer friends or the gang, pastoralists, men of all work, new hands, in from the further out, who are tired of their flour-and-water cakes and tea brewed in tin cans (though that, unquestionably, is the best of all ways to brew it, over a fire of gum leaves and twigs). The New York *Herald Tribune,* in an account of the folksong *Waltzing Matilda* which Australian soldiers sing and which has nothing to do with Matilda at all, lately described the jumbuck as "a strange Australian animal." Tut, tut!

bright leaves and crisp little nutty berries at corners over grey palings or dusty hedges of boxthorn, bluebush, or lucerne-tree.

It is a country of half-tones, blue-greys and green-greys, browns and red-browns. The sky is always immense. The air is thin and clear except when there is heat haze or dust. The first settlers often hated it and called it harsh and ironic names: Dismal Swamp and Rosewater. Others let humour play across the map: Howlong and Nevertire, Quartpot, and Jerry Bailey. Some were dull and perhaps a little homesick for Aberdeen and Dublin, Swansea, Richmond, Tottenham. But they left some native names: Manoora and Bundanoon, Gundagai and Kurrajong, Wallerawang, Quandialla, Canowindra, Illawarra. Your eye must grow used to long views and strong lights, your face brown and wrinkle in fierce suns, before you suddenly one day find that you belong to the monotonies of sky and plain. Then, wherever you are, your nostrils will sometimes twitch nostalgically for that air, for the smell of gums beside the creeks, of hot dry grass, baked earth and desert winds.

OVER CAPRICORN

We put down at Cloncurry for the night, 1372 miles out of Sydney, in the cattle and mining country under the Gulf of Carpentaria, within the Australian tropics, which look much like the rest of the sprawling country, except for more rain and rivers. Many Australian rivers are dry most of the year and sometimes for years at a stretch; and run, when they run, into the sands and salt-pans of the Centre. But here is a network of waters going north to the great Gulf. Queensland has half a million square miles of pastoral country (all Texas is 265,000 square miles), and the Gulf country is one of the cattle domains. Roads run miles wide to carry the slow herds travelling for months to markets: and the drover, with his long stirrup leathers and his easy seat, his old, punched hat and its fly net, living out his life with herds on the track, is still the classic figure of the landscape. Over beyond, at Mount Isa, is a brash new mining town with modern architecture and company-run hospital and all the polish of joint-stock collectivism. But Cloncurry is the old Australia of iron-bound individualists, slow, drawling blokes in slacks and shirts and tugged felt hats; of battered trucks bumping over the potholes of the broad streets, and a big, verandahed pub on each corner, with beds along the balconies and old-timers on the wooden seats or propped against the verandah posts. Two or three thousand people live in the fifty miles about Cloncurry, so it opens, as Australian towns usually do, with an imperial flourish of pubs: the Royal, His Majesty's, the Queen (familiarly known as Sweeney's), the Prince of Wales, the inevitable Central, the (with a bold stroke of imagination) Oasis, the Post Office, the Selwyn and the Leichhardt.

This is Leichhardt country. He made the first journey in the north, from Brisbane to Cape York, under Carpentaria and on up to Port Essington. He walked three thousand miles, and arrived naked, his naturalist murdered by the aborigines, his stores done, but an immortal journey behind him. Three years later, in 1884, he went into the Queensland wilderness again in an attempt to cross the continent east to west. He disappeared, and his fate is one of those mysteries that tantalize the imagination. Rumours of him and supposed relics have since continued to come in from a million square miles of country.

This way also Burke and Wills, the first to cross from south to north, went to the Gulf in 1860. They died of

starvation before they could get through again to civilization in the south. Australian exploration was a desperate
business. Sturt was once penned for six months in a terrible valley, prisoner of the sun. Men died of thirst, of
hunger, were speared or clubbed. Again and again Mc-
Douall Stuart was driven back by the deserts before he
broke through from Adelaide to the Timor Sea in 1862.
You cross his track as you approach Darwin from the east.
Nearly all that northern country remains as the explorers
knew it. The wild, the very wild aborigine, still wanders
naked across Arnhem Land, which takes its name from Jan
Cartensz's ship of 1623. Japanese trepangers and fishermen
foolishly wandering on the beaches are sometimes speared;
though policemen make lonely patrols, and missions work
from islands of the Gulf.

RACE-WEEK, GOATS, AND MEN

But nobody, unless myself, was thinking much of Burke
or Wills or Leichhardt this night in Cloncurry. It was
race-night, and the days and nights of a race-meeting in
the outback are the big time of the year. I do not know
how far people travel to Cloncurry track, but away southwest in country that I know better they will come in for
three, four, and five hundred miles. The races were off,
as it happened, because the course was flooded, but the
dance was on. At the hotel before dinner, every girl in the
place (and it was crowded with girls from the stations)
was hunting round to iron her frock, while huge bush-
men worked their necks into stiff collars. In the old days,
a country dance went to such airs as the babbling brook [3]
might get from his accordion and some old-timer from his

[3] Cook: but if you are going that way, you may as well
learn the language.

flute or fiddle. Now you truck to a piano, cornet, sax, and drums. Time marches on, as Mr. Luce insists.

But Australians still manage without a good many creature comforts. Australian pubs run to the dirtiest w.c.'s outside France, and there are always holes in the mosquitonets and often doubt in the beds. They say labour is the problem. I don't know. Perhaps the money is in beer and the guests are just bloody nuisances. That is the impression you are given, certainly, by 97 of the 101 Australian country pubs to which I, for my sins, have paid twelve or fourteen shillings a day. At Cloncurry, the pub was better than most. Drinks, for instance, were cold. But it reminded me.

To and from the dance hall, we more or less pushed through goats, which are a characteristic feature of the northern street scene. They eat tins and old boots when they have gone through the local sales announcements and cinema posters. They are partial, I am informed, to billposters' gum. We also became acquainted, cautiously, with several cattlemen's dogs that sat about the door trying to decide what the heck the boss was up to in there. If I ever possess enough ground to give him exercise (say a couple of hundred square miles) I shall have an Australian cattle dog. A country like that makes or breaks dogs and men. Loneliness, grim, unending work, sun, floods, then years of grinding drought. I have seen a good piece of the world, but I have not met anything tougher in it than the gaunt, big-boned men who keep the Australian herds and ride the long fences. They belong to what is great in Australia, and I wish to God there were more of them.

You can sleep now on three successive nights in Sydney, Cloncurry, and Bali. Sydney is the twentieth century: urbanism, industrialism, headlines, cheap excitements, milk bars, labour politics, rush hours, trolley-buses, bargain counters, white-collar girls, sports stadia, and loudspeakers. Cloncurry is the nineteenth century on the frontiers: cattle, slag heaps, wandering dirt tracks. It is a Wild West set, though the inhabitants do not wear hair on their pants or carry Colts. It is still older. It is Abraham and Chaldea, the mines of Ophir, pastoral man. But Bali is Asia of the immemorial peasant, of the rice fields, of Vishnu and Ganesha, of Animists, Moslems, and Hindus, of exquisite, intricate arts and meanings that the European in all his life cannot piece together, of strange sacrifices and hidden things, of light and of darknesses abysmal.

We were in the air above Queensland before it was light. The dawn came slowly because we were flying from it, and we ate breakfast out of thermos flasks as we crossed over into North Australia, somewhere north of Camooweal and the headwaters of the Gregory.

N. T.

This is the Northern Territory, once of South Australia but since 1911 of the whole Australian Commonwealth: and Australia's unanswered problem. It is a large problem: 523,620 square miles of it, with only, apart from aborigines, 5645 people in 1938, two thousand less than in 1888. That is the problem, because this is the land nearest Asia, only three or four hundred miles from the outer islands of Indonesia.

Few Australians have seen it. Few more have any real knowledge of it. Darwin was a village beyond their consciousness until the airplanes began to come in from Europe. Now it appears as one of the vital strategic points in the world. The United States Navy has thought it worthwhile to post, since 1941, an observer there. More Australians will know about the north in the future, because Darwin now is packed with troops. But Darwin is only one tiny point in the Territory, and the Overland Telegraph and the new Overland Road from the south are one thin line drawn across an almost empty map. The city of any consequence nearest to Darwin is Adelaide, seventeen hundred miles across some of the most desperate country in the world. Yet it was from Adelaide and around six thousand miles of coast that the first sustained effort was made to develop the northern land.

Both Flinders and King, two great naval surveyors who charted it in the "earlies" of the nineteenth century, believed that the north must soon grow populous and great. King thought Port Essington the finest harbour in the world and certain to become "at no very distant date a place of great trade and of very considerable importance." You will have difficulty now in finding Port Essington on a map. In 1824, a detachment of soldiers, marines, convicts and a surgeon, with cattle and stores, were put ashore near there on Melville Island. Their fort and graves are now in tangled jungle. In 1827, a second start was made at Raffles Bay, near Essington. For a moment it seemed to succeed. Malay traders came, but so did fever and prowling natives with long spears. In 1830 Raffles Bay was abandoned for the new settlement of Perth, two thousand miles southwest.

In 1837, when there were rumours of French occupation, the British Government tried again, at Essington itself. The Navy commander enthusiastically surveyed the site for a dockyard, built a little town, envisioned the harbour filled with ships of the line and hundreds of merchantmen. He was hardly installed when the French arrived and ran up their flag over abandoned Raffles Bay. They were ushered out with great politeness. The French were always too late in Australia. Phillip raced them to Botany Bay, and Wakefield's Company to New Zealand. But every one was always polite to every one else, except when Napoleon's governor kept Flinders cooped in Mauritius seven years to suppress his discoveries on the southern Australian coasts which Baudin, coming after, had called Terre Napoléon.

The English bitterly (and properly, according to the higher standards of those times) resented that detention, though both countries were at war and Flinders a Navy captain in a Navy ship. But Baudin and his French expedition had been handsomely entertained and supplied at Sydney a little earlier. War has developed new savageries. It might be depressing but profitable to enquire just why. Perhaps because in 1839 an officer could write from Port Essington as he would never think of writing from anywhere now: "Among other buildings in progress was the church which planted as it was on the northern shores of the Australian Continent was expected to form a nucleus from which offshoots might by degrees draw within its influence the islands in the Arafura Sea and thus widely spread the pure blessings of Christianity." [4] People still believed in the things that had made Western civilization, still respected if they did not always observe substantial codes. The real difficulties about spreading "pure Christianity" were not as apparent as they are now, when the lack of pure Christians is become more evident. Curiously, that officer of simple faith was the first lieutenant of *H.M.S. Beagle:* and upon the *Beagle* he had for years travelled as friend and shipmate of one who was to make some impact upon simple faith. Port Darwin has its name to commemorate the *Beagle's* naturalist: upon the *Beagle* he gathered his notes towards *The Origin of Species.*

Another naturalist, who also had his influence on the public mind, visited Essington a few years later: Thomas

[4] John Lort Stokes: quoted by C. Price Conigrave in his *North Australia.* London, 1936.

Huxley, Assistant Surgeon of *H.M.S. Rattlesnake*. He
thought Port Essington "the most useless, miserable, ill-
managed hole in Her Majesty's dominions."

It was sad but true. In 1840 Essington was presently to
rival Singapore. Why not? The garrison was already playing cricket. In 1850 there were neither cricketers nor garrison; only a few more lonely graves on the Arafura shore.
Somehow, the thing would not go.

Then came other explorers: Gregory from the west,
accompanied by Ferdinand von Mueller (North Australia
did not lack illustrious visitors), working across the territory and deep into Queensland much along the line which
we now fly over. Next, Stuart, breaking a trail from Adelaide to the Timor that the Overland Telegraph followed.

Stuart's was a South Australian expedition. In 1863 it
bore fruit, something of a Dead Sea fruit. The Colonial
Office granted the north to South Australia.

South Australia, the painstaking reader will recall, was
of Mr. Wakefield's inspiration. It was settled by gentlemen in long black coats and stovepipe hats and by their
ladies in crinolines, who brought pianos with them. They
were magnificent colonists, and had a longer view of Australia's needs than Australians generally have since acquired. They saw that there must be an effort to colonize
the north. South Australia itself was only twenty-six years
old; but they set to, much in Wakefield's fashion, buying
town sites and country farms before any one had even
settled where the city should be. In 1864 the first parties
from Adelaide established themselves at Escape Cliffs:
ominously named, for they all had lost their tempers and
much of their substance before South Australia's Surveyor-
General, G. W. Goyder, pegged out another site at Darwin in 1869.

HAULING IN A THRESHER SHARK, NORTHERN AUSTRALIA

"The Australoids are everywhere food gatherers."—Page 174

CORROBOREE: NATIVE CEREMONIAL NEAR DARWIN, AUSTRALIA

THE OODNADATTA EXPRESS

South Australia, with small resources and few men, made an heroic effort. It drove the world's longest land-line across the continent to give Australia a cable service with Europe. The Overland Telegraph is comparable in national significance to the building of America's transcontinental railway. Sir Charles Todd, South Australia's Postmaster-General, did the job. His men died of scurvy and fever. He built through blistering deserts, through swamps, through the terrible rains of the tropical summer. Men and materials were shipped north by sea, carried up rivers, transported across wastes. Even poles had to be hauled in by camels for hundreds of miles. Stations were built as blockhouses against native attack: bushfires fought. Savage scrub had to be hacked through. Bullocks bogged and men drowned in flooded waterways, wandered off into unknown country. Camels died amongst the sands. But Todd carried the line across seventeen hundred miles in less than two years, 1870-'72.

I met lately in Sydney a man interested in Australian films. "The trouble with this country," he said, stretching in a fat armchair, "is that it really hasn't any themes. Nothing, for instance, like that Western Union story or the Pony Express."

After the O. T., South Australia began to build a transcontinental railway. It actually reached Oodnadatta, seven hundred miles north, towards the heart of the continent and across some of the cruelest stretches of the earth: and from the north it reached Pine Creek, although men and materials again had to come by thousands of sea-miles. There the little colony had to stop. The job was too big and too costly for it. But all the resources of the Australian Federation, which took over the Territory in 1909, have not sufficed to bridge the whole gap, and seven hundred miles remain between the railheads. Only in 1940, with the emergency of war and threat of invasion in the north, were they linked by a made road.

Even that has been justly regarded in Australia as a colossal job, requiring the Army engineers and the resources of Roads Departments in three states. There was again the race against the rains, the fight against deserts, sickness, sand, and iron scrub. It followed the line of Todd's O. T. stations. For they and the little places along the railroads are still the only settlements through the Australian Centre, save for a few scattered pastoral homesteads.

South Australia used some Chinese on construction of the Territory section of its railroad. The White Australia sentiment and legislation of the railway eighties and nineties ended Asiatic immigration. But White Australia has done little for the Territory since, except to bury there some minor political reputations and a host of political promises.

PROMISSORY LAND

If the Territory and the north of Western Australia had been freed from the high-tariff economy of the industrializing south, their primary industries might have developed markets in adjacent Asia. Australia has not been very bright about Asiatic markets. It spends in the Dutch Indies about seven times as much as it earns there. Australian business men will tell you that there is no real market for Australia amongst the native populations northward. But in any kampong of Sumatra or Malaya you find shelves stacked with American canned and manufactured goods, fruits, fish, jam. Millions of natives cannot afford meat, cheese, butter from the distant, expensive Australian south: millions could afford to buy from the neighbouring north if the north had stuff to sell. But tariffs, labour and transport costs have overwhelmed the infant economies of the north. All could and should have been eased, but the south did not know, the south did not care, and there has never been the glimmer of a real national concern for the urgent national problem of the north. The Territory is voteless even in the Federal Parliament, and its inhabitants have less political responsibility than Fijians. The place is governed from Canberra and under an Administrator. I have never yet talked to any resident of the Territory without hearing new stories, some amusing enough, of business and labour rackets.

The Territory may be an omen, for there the tide of Empire, and of effort, seems to have halted. If the ebb begins, where will it end?

It is not a country to rejoice the scouts of Joshua. It is a hard, hot land, but it would do a lot better than it does if people with the stomach to work were given opportunities to work profitably, and if some of the money spent on suburban roads in the inflated southern cities had been spent for basic economic services in the north.

Its occupied country is mostly split into eight or nine hundred holdings averaging 160 square miles each. Herds overlanded in South Australian days have grown to a million head. But the meatworks opened by Vestey's in 1917 closed in 1921, and remain a symbol of the Territory's history. Rice, coconuts, cotton, tobacco, bananas, fodder are all potential staples. Peanuts are now the principal crop, which seems very apt. Twelve hundred acres in the half-million square miles are under peanuts. Peanuts are one of the principal exports. I repeat, peanuts.

There are extensive mineral fields, mostly unworked. Tennant's Creek, the nearest thing to a town from Darwin down to the Centre, produces gold. Its population in 1938 was 457 men, 80 women, 27 children. Wolfram is mined, and mica, a little tin, silver, copper, tantalite. Pearlers and bêche-de-mer luggers out of Darwin earn £70,000 a year.

The railway has gone on to Birdum, 316 miles from Darwin. It characteristically ended, when last reported, on an unfinished bridge half-way across a creek. It and the new military road may help to open more country. The presence of considerable bodies of troops and the development, in consequence, of water supplies and services about Darwin may help too. The Army has planted vegetable gardens. Perhaps some one else may try cabbages or a carrot or two. Perhaps some of the soldiers will go back after the war to break, as their fathers broke, new soils. Perhaps some day the handful of people who have stuck the place out through the years waiting for their countrymen to remember their country's needs may be rewarded. Or perhaps the epitaph of the north and of the Australia which neglected it will be written in three words: *Blind, blind, blind.*

Darwin's greatest fillip since the railway (whose rolling stock is reminiscent of the brave beginnings in eighteen-seventy-something) and until 1940 came from the air.

On December 10, 1919, four young men of the original Australian Flying Corps came home from the wars in a Vickers-Vimy. They were twenty-eight days out from England. They had flown across deserts, jungles, and seas which no man had before seen from on high. They had discovered everything there was to discover about landing and lifting planes in unprepared places. Their names were Ross Smith and Keith Smith, Bennet and Shiers: and some one will yet "write them out in a verse." [5]

[5] Mr. Day Lewis, in the best poem so far made about flying, has already done that for Lieutenant Parer and Lieutenant McIntosh who came to Darwin on August 3, 1920, seven months from England, in an old crate held together

Now Qantas-Empire, the British-Australian service, and K.N.I.L.M., the Dutch line, flit to and fro across the Timor several times a week, and most of Australia's overseas air traffic comes in or out at Darwin. So the place has polished up a bit. It has a new hotel designed for the tropics in Dutch-Malayan style, and an impressive airport.[6] Air routes branch off the main stem for points in Queensland, Western Australia, South Australia.

A good part of the Darwin population drinks beer for a week or two after a ship arrives from the south and then thinks about beer until the next ship arrives. This is done most comfortably out in the long grass amongst the empties. But ships are normally few, and Darwin's chief excitement is football. Darwin plays football with a fury that refutes every generalization you have ever heard about white men in the tropics. The aborigines play too, and lacking jerseys paint their appropriate colours in stripes from neck to rump.

The Australian Army has produced a characteristic item on Darwin. Like all the best folk poetry it is anonymous and probably communal. It found print lately on the Sydney *Bulletin's* "Red Page."

more or less by bootlaces, safety-pins and will-power; and with not enough petrol in its tank to taxi up the Darwin paddock. Parer, when I last heard of him, was still flying planes over mountains in New Guinea. Some say that he is the greatest flier of them all. But he had little talent for self-promotion.

[6] It seemed very Darwinian, however, that, when we passed the other day, the mirrors in the women's room were (I was informed by one who has access to such places) missing. There was a redundancy in the men's room. It appeared that some of the lads had wanted more mirrors for shaving. The airport and the pubs have septic tanks: but, as one of His Majesty's more learned judges has remarked, most things in Darwin, including sanitation, are à la carte.

This bloody town's a bloody cuss;
No bloody trams, no bloody bus,
No one cares for bloody us,
So bloody, bloody, bloody.

The bloody roads are bloody bad,
The bloody folks are bloody mad,
They even say "You bloody cad!"
So bloody, bloody, bloody.

No bloody clouds, no bloody rains;
All bloody stones, no bloody drains;
The council's got no bloody brains,
So bloody, bloody, bloody.

And everything's so bloody dear,
Two-and-nine for bloody beer—
And is it good? No bloody fear!
So bloody, bloody, bloody.

The bloody flicks are bloody old,
The bloody seats are always sold,
You can't get in for bloody gold,
So bloody, bloody, bloody.

The bloody dances make me smile,
The bloody bands are bloody vile,
They only cramp your bloody style,
So bloody, bloody, bloody.

The best bloody place is bloody bed,
With bloody ice on bloody head,
And then they think you're bloody dead,
So bloody, bloody, bloody.

Since the war and the arrival of the soldiers and the contractors both beer and football have reached all-time highs: the soldiers are formidable opponents at football but the locals still head the major leagues in beer. Darwin in 1941 was Boomtown. Anybody with a truck and him-

self to hire on Army contracts was living like a cattle-king.
And Darwin was in the world's news. Old-timers were
disturbed because they are kindly people and you could
not toss idly away an empty bottle without fear of hitting
some migratory journalist. Even the aborigines were inter-
viewed.

THE OLDEST INHABITANT

Darwin is the only Australian port of entry where the
general tourist is likely to see aborigines. Few of the Darwin Binghis do their people justice. The aborigine is
primitive man, and primitive man does not look his best
huddling in squalor on the edge of town.

About fifty thousand full-blooded aborigines survive in
Australia. Half are still nomad, mostly in the centre, west
and north. Perhaps ten thousand are employed, and the
rest are in supervised camps. Sixty-seven thousand square
miles have been made aborigine reservations, in fifteen
sectors, for now some effort is made to preserve his own
tribal lands for the native. Each tribe wanders over its
own defined territories; and within the tribe, clans and
families keep their hunting grounds. Tribes fight but
never to conquer another's territory. They lack possessive-
ness. Yet a tribe uprooted or ousted dies within a generation or two, for the aborigine's landscape is associated
with his culture heroes and with his spiritual and moral
life. Every hillock and twist of a creek has profound meanings for the aborigine. His soul abides in his local places
in the Dream Time before and after life; and if he dies
away from his country, he wanders, lost. A dying man
will crawl hundreds of miles to reach, before his end, the
land where his spirit is at home. It is much as if the soul
of a New Yorker had lodged, before it entered flesh, in
some rocky edifice along Park Avenue, to which it must

return when its poor player has ceased to strut and fret. The Australian clan derives its title and social psyche from a feature of its scenery: much as we use Eastern Shore or Back Bay to describe a way of life and state of soul, but even more so.

The aborigine is not Europoid, Negroid or Mongoloid. He has his own distinction as an Australoid and very few relatives in the world except the Sakai of Malaya (who now ask a dollar a time if you want to photograph them) and the Veddas of Ceylon, both perhaps stragglers from the Australoid migration which moved down the immemorial eastern highway two thousand or two hundred thousand years ago. The Australoids are everywhere food-gatherers, hunters without thought for the morrow either of herds or of granaries: parasites and wanderers on the earth. This apparently makes them the most primitive of peoples known.[7] The aborigine is chocolate-brown, when scraped and scrubbed, hairy, broad-nosed, heavy-browed, lean-legged and a good deal amused by the oddities of white Australians which he sometimes imitates with gusto. Hence, amongst other things, football.

He is an amazing hunter. He can make a living off a salt claypan. His boomerang is the most ingenious weapon man ever made before guns. He is skilful with snares, traps, spears, and along the northern coast and rivers with canoes. There were originally perhaps four or five hundred tribes scattered about the continent, each with its own language or dialect: the aborigine commonly spoke two or three tongues, which is more than his successor in

---

[7] Several of my aboriginal acquaintances are rather tickled about that. When I was young an old gentleman who had an astonishing resemblance to the Emperor Franz Joseph sometimes came out of the neighbouring scrub: and F. J. himself could not have borne with higher air the dignity of an Anthropological Survival.

Australia does. It has always seemed to me ridiculous to talk of one or other race as superior or inferior. The aborigine had never learnt to build himself a house and he still dislikes clothes, very sensibly, because they harbour fleas and disease for him. His mind took another direction than ours. His economic environment compelled a tremendous concentration of mental energy on the affairs of the chase, in which he excels all other men. But he has an elaborated ritual and moral life. His are not our morals, but in some aspects they better our contemporary habits. His social and family life is intensely organized. It is true that a wife may sometimes be sociably lent round but only according to the strictest conventions: not the sort perhaps that Queen Victoria would have approved but none the less formidable, in their time and place.

The aborigine has had a tough deal in Australia, most often perhaps because he was not understood. Now that his habits and needs and beliefs are better known, it will be unforgivable if ignorance and neglect confirm the threatened end of all his tribes. The white Australian has too smugly assumed that his native predecessors were inevitably doomed. The aborigine need not die if Australia does what is necessary for his survival.

So far, our record in the matter stinks.

ENVOI

It drops away beneath you: the little town, the wide bay, the distant river, the sandy beaches, the mangroves and the flats, the old gums beside the creeks, the brown hawk lifting. A big seaplane comes drumming up the coast from a long patrol. You know that a distant blur of dust is rising from a column of mechanized gun-carriers. You think maybe it is going to be all right.

There is a second British Power in the world beside and beyond the little island itself and its dependencies, protectorates and colonial régimes. The group of self-governing Dominions have grown great almost unobserved. Together they control vast areas of land and seas, with ports, forts, and routes on every ocean. They have immense resources, human and material. The stuff of their fathers, English, Irish, Scottish, Welsh, French, Dutch has been toughened and hardened by the labours of new lands. They are a new force in history. But more, they are a new way of life.

Look back over the wide land, twenty-two hundred miles to Sydney, two thousand miles to Perth. There, in the dusty paddocks, the dingy factories, even in the sourest streets is the true Cipango and treasure of the East which set European man on his long, slow beat about Good Hope and the Horn: for here is realized that which sounded in the soul of Europe when first it heard the crashing doctrine of Free Will: which has never ceased to echo there, never let us rest, never let us become again fellaheen and slaves. It is not perfected here because it will be perfected nowhere. It is not an object of art, but a quality of ourselves. It appears as we struggle for it, it exists in our effort. It is within us, and we call it liberty.

This is the real significance of the new dominions of man from Cape Race to the Leeuwin. They have stupidities, crimes, oppressions like all of Adam's sort. But they have enlarged the achievement of the European spirit. They have carried its fire on the earth.

Men exploit, and men are exploited, most are poor and some are angry: but here, nevertheless, men do walk, if not as kings, yet as heirs and joint-heirs also. . . .

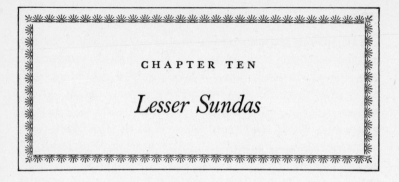

TIMOR CROSSING

SYDNEY to Darwin is twelve or fourteen hours' flying for most passenger ships. Darwin to Timor is three. Darwin is nearer to Singapore than to Melbourne; and the whole northwestern segment of Australia to the Dutchmen's capital at Batavia than to its own at Canberra. I labour the point because its implications are barely grasped even in Australia.[1] A sea power based on the Indies anywhere could seize Darwin much more easily than Australia could recover it. The destiny of Australia is as inextricably bound with the waters and islands northwards as the destiny of England has been bound with the Channel and the opposite Flanders coast.

The Timor Sea is like a sheath of opal: shallows of bronze and malachite-green, purple shadows of rolling cumuli, streams of drifting golden weed; and, if you could see them from upstairs, sea snakes, turtles, pearl oysters and rich fisheries. It is a very entertaining sea to fly over. In the unlikely event of my becoming an angel, I shall

[1] This statement needed no qualification when it was written a few months ago. To-day it does. There was a rude awakening on the 15th of October, 1941, when it was announced in Sydney that the Japanese had extended their "commercial" air line with daily service from Palau Island to Portuguese Dilli at the east end of Timor.

cruise there regularly. If eternity is long enough and our talents sufficiently magnified, I shall practise painting it, drifting about with aerial easel. One difficulty now is to hold the point of view. Especially as you approach the Timor beaches where the draughts might bump even great Gabriel about.

Timor appears suddenly under the wings as a strip of beach and foam overhung by colossal hills: then you are skimming scrubby ranges and looking deep into valleys where patches of cultivation and groups of little round huts hang on the hillsides.

Timor is the largest of the Lesser Sunda Islands, which come down in a chain from Java towards Australia and New Guinea; Timor itself is about three hundred miles long, sixty across and goes up to nearly ten thousand feet. The whole arc of islands from Sumatra to New Guinea actually belongs to a mountain-complex, part submerged and excessively volcanic. Tradition has it that Timor Peak was once visible for three hundred miles and so to Australia: but it blew its mighty head off in 1638. Timor now mildly bubbles mud, and leaves more explosive displays to its neighbours westward. We came down at Koepang which is the capital of Dutch Timor and at the western tip: a rather melancholy place that may yet be a hub of history. A generation earlier and we might have seen an annual virgin presented to the crocodiles in the bay who are related to the local sultans.

A Portuguese plane of the Servicos Aeros da Colonia Portuguesa da Timor stood there, bought or borrowed from the second-hand stock of the Koninklijke Nederlandsch-Indische Luchtvaart Maatschappij, and flown by a Dutch pilot to and from Dilli. Dilli is the capital of Portuguese Timor, which occupies the eastern half of the island and an enclave nearer Koepang. As things warm up in the neighbouring seas, keep an eye on Dilli. Since 1937 the Japanese have had certain definite commercial interests in Portuguese Timor, but nothing that could justify the new daily air service from Palau 1200 miles away. Here is the obvious stepping-stone towards Australia.

The old town is a museum-piece, for the Portuguese have been there since early in the sixteenth century, and they are a conservative people. Portuguese Timor, with Macao in China and Goa, Damao and Diu in India are all that is left of Portugal's Eastern Empire. She still remembers her colony, for every now and again a new governor comes out to Timor. It has also several automobiles and occasionally electric light. Dr. Salazar's *Estado Novo* has revived the colonial energies and interest of Portugal: but Timor is a long way from home.

Timor is less lush than the Indies at large; it withers seasonally under Australia's hot winds, and its soils are thin. It has little to attract the more lavishly endowed, and while the Dutch and British hegemony survives, so presumably will the Portuguese reign in eastern Timor. Britain, it is worth recalling, has been singuarly amiable to other small empire-holders. During the British supremacy in the world, Portugal and Belgium and Holland, tiny countries, have remained in possession of their vast colonial estates. If the British power declines, a good many titles will rapidly change hands. Britain actually is a guarantor of Portuguese Timor.

THE GREAT EXPLORERS

In the waters of Timor, under and about the Philippines, the great eastern march of Portugal met the Spaniards' westward drive. The adventure of Portugal in the East is the most fantastic story in the whole history of expansion: and we have too readily forgotten its tremendous importance for all mankind.

Portugal grew to be a kingdom during its struggle with the Moors in the eleventh century.

Expansion overseas began with John I. In 1387, he married a daughter of John of Gaunt, to seal an alliance with England maintained for five and a half centuries since. In 1415 he captured Ceuta, and started Portugal for the Cape of Good Hope.

Portugal opens towards the seas, by her river mouth. Behind her is a tangle of arid hills. Her people find much of their living on the seas. Sometimes at night off the Portuguese coast I have seen the whole sea flecked with little lights where the Portuguese boats and net-buoys were drifting. The sardine fishermen of the Tagus and the Douro estuaries launched Europe on the oceans.

Prince Henry the Navigator was the brain behind them. He was John of Gaunt's grandson, and half an Englishman. He diverted the resources of the Knightly Order of Christ to exploration and discovery. He trained pilots, collected instruments and maps, outfitted ships. In 1433 Cape Bojador was passed, belowed the Canaries and in 1445 Cape Verde, the westernmost point of Africa. In 1482 Portugal reached the Congo, and in 1488 Diaz doubled Good Hope and looked upon the Indian Ocean four years before Columbus led out the march of Spain.

In 1494 Spain and Portugal signed the treaty of Tordesillas, defining their spheres of influence: a piece of statesmanship much misrepresented in English texts, its foresight (remember, America was just discovered, Africa just turned) as remarkable as the giant ambitions of the two little kingdoms, and the energy with which they encompassed the world. The energy came from centuries of poverty and battle in which they had held the frontiers of Europe against the enemies of Europe. Hardship and

valour make peoples great: riches and large estate seem
to rot them.

Tordesillas drew a line which in effect went round the
world giving yet undiscovered Brazil to Portugal because
it lay eastward of the mark, and the Moluccas here above
Timor to Spain if she could get them. Timor itself is the
eastern extremity of Portugal's hemisphere.

In 1497 Vasco da Gama reached India. In 1500, King
Emanuel of Portugal became "Lord of the Conquest,
Navigation, and Commerce of India, Ethiopia, Arabia,
and Persia." It was the year of Brazil. In the next five
years, the Portuguese Empire was grown up the African
coasts: Madagascar, Mauritius, Socotra, Sofala, Mozambique, Mombasa, and Malindi in Kenya, whence da Gama
had struck across to Calicut, which is on the western coast
of India in Malabar.

Da Gama had two major ambitions, for souls and for
trade; and we mistake the whole character of his era if
we forget the first. Empire has always been an affair of
ideas as well as of politics and economics. In the long run,
the ideas are vastly more formidable than the emeralds,
spices, bicycles and Manchester goods. The new syntheses
of culture which follow the discoverers, the missionaries,
the soldiers, the merchants and the governors are the matters of lasting consequence, and we do not yet see the end
of the moral and intellectual change which began when
da Gama's caravel dropped sails off Calicut.

He believed that he had come to a Christian country.
The Portuguese, through their history, had known no
paynims other than the Moors, and the Moors were icono-
clasts, haters and wreckers of images. But the first Indians
da Gama saw, in African ports, bowed to the Virgin and
Saints set under his poop deck. Now, in Malabar, he saw
temples carven with coloured images that could remind
a man of the painted west fronts of the Christian Gothic.

Some of the Indian images must have shocked a Christian soul, but the Gothic carvers too had been free enough with devils and anatomy: and there were figures in the Hindu pantheon of great spirituality whose shapes still move the religious sense. Moreover, the Christian world still believed that St. Thomas had evangelized the Indies. Only the Moors were in deadly heresy, and all heretics were long just Moors to the Portuguese, who said their Aves before Hindu goddesses, until in time they learnt more about the manners and morals of those ladies.

Portugal sought not territory but treaties. When da Gama went to visit the Zamorin at Pandarana, he told his people to attempt no reprisals if he was taken but to go peacefully home and report the world unveiled. He did get a treaty with the Zamorin, though his gifts seemed poor stuff to a magnificent Eastern monarch: a box of sugar, two barrels of oil, a pot of honey and six Lisbon hats. But they marked the most consequential trade any man has ever made.

THE MERCHANTMEN'S CRUSADE

Before da Gama's six felt hats were quite worn out, the commercial power of Islam was broken, and its political power fallen into decline. For a thousand years Islam's commercial strength lay in its command of traffic between East and West, along the camel routes from the Mediterranean and in its flat-bottomed ships that sailed from the Red Sea to the coasts of China. The Prophet himself was of a merchant family and Islam was a trading as well as a spiritual empire. It had its superintendents and its controllers, its agents, its factors, its converts all the way to Malacca and beyond. Da Gama's treaty was the final turning point of Portugal's long wars with the Moslems, and the most decisive blow she ever struck.

DUTCH TOWN HALL, 1712: BATAVIA

"They built it like Amsterdam and Rotterdam."—Page 216

DILLI, CAPITAL OF PORTUGUESE TIMOR

It was also a signal of defeat for the great Mediterranean Powers of Venice and Genoa.[2] And it evoked the
empires of the oceanic peoples, of Portugal itself, of England, of Holland. A pot of honey, a barrel of oil: Lord of
the Conquest, Navigation and Commerce: the ships of
Amsterdam, the East India Companies, English cotton
manufactures, Southern cotton plantations, Negro slaves,
Clive, Hastings, Empress of India, Abe Lincoln and the
War between the States, Japan, the struggle for markets,
Sun Yat Sen, and God knows what yet to come. It was
quite a day's business that Dom Vasco da Gama did in
1498 with the Zamorin at Pandarana in Malabar.

The Portuguese pushed on: to Massawa in Ethiopia
whence they shortly went to call on Prester John, to
Suez and to Hormuz in the Persian Gulf, to Cochin, Goa,
Ceylon, Sumatra, Malacca, and Siam. By 1513, fifteen
years after da Gama came about the Cape, they were in
the Moluccas. By 1517 they were trading in China. In
1520 Franciscan missionaries reached Timor. There they
have been during four centuries since Henry VIII sat on
the English throne and Australia was less than a rumour
in the world. Portugal, in one generation, reached the
ends of the earth, from Greenland to the Banda Sea, via
the coasts of Brazil, Africa, Persia, India, Malaya and Indonesia. She was nearly three generations ahead in Asia
of any other European Power. Her population was then
rather less than a million.

Their impress is still deep. There were never many of
them, and they often intermarried with the natives. But
you find, through the East as here in Timor, Portuguese
culture and Portuguese language in little enclaves

[2] The Portuguese understood all this very well: thus Albuquerque pointed out in the first years of the sixteenth century
that if the Portuguese took Malacca "out of the hands of the
Moors, Cairo and Mecca would be utterly ruined. . . ."

amongst many races. The "black Portuguese" of Timor still in the western part of the island sometimes make things lively for the Dutch patrols.

DUTCH, BRITISH, JAPANESE

The Dutch reached Timor early in the seventeenth century. They established relations with the Sultan at Koepang and seized the Portuguese post there. Then, for two centuries, there were borderland skirmishes between the Portuguese and Dutch and their various native allies, fairly bloody on occasion with a good deal of cattle and pony duffing, in the style of other borders. During the Napoleonic Wars, when the French overran the Netherlands, the British moved in and occupied Dutch Timor (with the rest of the Indies) from the Portuguese base at Dilli. The Portuguese Government was itself then gone abroad to Rio de Janeiro (curious how the pattern of the times is repeated) and Britain was taking her precautions all round the world. But when Napoleon was done with, she retired from the scene. It is officially denied that in 1934, when the skies were darkening again, she offered to purchase Timor. The Japanese were already busy thereabouts.

In 1937, the Nanyo Kahatsu Kaisha, the South Seas Development Company, formed a special branch with a capital of about five million yen for trade with Timor. It began at once to buy into local trading firms and plantations, and in 1940 it took almost the entire coffee crop, Portuguese Timor's principal export. With Macao in China at her mercy, Japan could wield a big stick. She also opened her purse and Timor urgently needed customers and capital. The Australians were foolish not to have offered both.

The Japanese line of approach is from the Palaus or

Pelews, east of the Carolines, squarely off the middle Philippines, and another future hub if the wheel of Japanese imperialism yet revolves heavily over these parts. Palau commands routes between Manila and Hawaii. It offers access to the Moluccas and New Guinea. It is a well-established base of Dai Nippon Airways, which have been flying into Dilli occasionally since 1940 and in October, 1941, established a base there and regular service.

The early Japanese "survey" flights reminded some Australians that Dilli was less than an hour by modern bomber from their beaches, and in January, 1941, Qantas-Empire made it a regular stop on their service from Sydney to Singapore. In these days the Governor, Manuel d'Abreu Ferreira de Carvalho, is finding unexpected and perhaps conflicting demands on his diplomacy and his hospitality.

The potential resources of Timor have never been fully developed. They will be, if the Japanese have a free hand there. Portugal has lacked the cash and perhaps much inclination: for the Portuguese have long developed a discreet quietism in their colonial properties. But any one aware of the ways of the wicked world must be astonished that Australia has not established substantial interests in Portuguese Timor. An Australian official was established in Dilli in 1941, to make the second Briton present, but I doubt whether ten Australians in a thousand knew until very recently where Dilli was. Which is much as if the United States lacked acquaintance with Mexico or Cuba. Yet here we were lunching in Timor after morning tea at Darwin.

The Portuguese Army in Timor, when last reported, numbered seven officers and 368 men, seventy of them Europeans. Give both Palau and Dilli little red circles on the map of to-morrow.

KOEPANG

Lunch was that Dutch colonial dish curiously called "nassi goring," a reduced version of a primitive "rijst-tafel": a mess of rice, shredded chicken, chopped beef, yellowish beans, small potatoes, and anonymous herbs. The Dutch tricolour floated over us, the posters warned us not to talk of ships, and gave heartening assurances that the Dictators were Doomed. In token, perhaps, items of the Dutch colonial army sat about on their haunches, little brown men buckled with formidable swords and in cheap green uniforms and large straw hats turned up at the side in the fashion of the Australian Army. Some, we hoped, might have been the ferocious local Meo who used to bury the heads of their enemies a while and then dig them up and gnaw them as proof of military virtue. But these soldiers were mostly men of Ambon and Ternate, whom the Dutch use for police and military services. They were Christianized by the Portuguese and early given European status in the Indies. They are grim fighting men, and aboundingly loyal to a régime in which they have been privileged.

There was considerable activity about the aerodrome, which may presently serve martial purposes. One Timorese was at intervals applying oil to unlikely points of a small steam-roller, while six or seven of his countrymen admired him. They might have discussed his technique if the weather had been cooler. Several scores more loitered beyond the barbed wire which now girds most airfields. Here and there a pagan investigated another pagan's hair. Timorese Christians wear their hair short and lack this gentle occupation. I suppose that if one slept in the little hive-like huts ("kopans," whence Koepang) of lontar leaves things would be inclined to drop into your hair grown greasy and thick. Lontar is a useful palm for making houses and guitars; and its sap washes down the local diet of Indian corn.

The Timorese are a darker and more primitive people than their neighbours to the west. They appear to be a Polynesian-Papuan mixture diluted with Malay blood, and their principal possessions are ponies, palm-leaf umbrellas, long shawls, ghosts, fetishes and taboos.

To Koepang, Bligh came at the end of his famous open-boat excursion in 1791: and in a cluster of little stone graves by the beach some of his men are buried.

Matthew Flinders was there in 1803, when the Governor at Dilli was the one white Portuguese on the island, and the Dutch régime extended nearly five miles in every direction. A British garrison during the first of two occupations in the Napoleonic Wars had half its numbers massacred before its survivors evacuated the island. There were only four Europeans then resident at Koepang, one the surgeon who had tended Bligh. One thinks curiously of the life that a graduate of Leiden or Utrecht must have lived during long, lonely years in such a miserable and danger-ridden outpost. Empire during the sixteenth, seventeenth and eighteenth centuries mostly meant such places where two or three or four men might live (if they lasted) ten, fifteen, twenty years, infested by fevers, surrounded by peoples with talents for torture, surviving largely on the sufferance of temperamental native rajahs. They had no home leaves. The handful who lived might return, yellowed by agues and low diets and raw spirits, in their late thirties or forties, to shiver a winter or two in Haarlem or some English village before they gratefully filled an early grave. Sometimes they bred families and sometimes they (the Portuguese especially) took their own women out to Asia with them. Even from such records as exist for a place like Malacca, it is still impossible to sense again the experience of those people. I think they may have been made of some different stuff than their heirs.

Flinders, though he had worked for years to and fro along the desolate Australian coasts, thought Koepang a dismal place. He noticed a little trade chiefly carried on by Chinese: sandalwood, beeswax, honey and slaves outward; rice, arrack, sugar, tea, coffee, and betel-nut inward. He met the American ship *Hunter,* buying beeswax and sandalwood with prospect of three hundred per cent profit at Canton. The *Hunter* had lately purchased slaves in neighbouring Solor for two muskets apiece and expected to sell them for eighty or a hundred dollars in Batavia. "If such advantages," reflected the good Flinders, "attend this traffic, humanity must expect no weak struggle to accomplish its suppression." But sometimes other Authority took a hand. The *Hunter's* captain and nearly all of his crew were dead of fever before their ship reached Batavia.

Pirates haunted the narrow straits between the islands where we now fly. Flinders was at Koepang again late in 1803, to patch his ship which he made watertight "as long as she remained at anchor." His was a naval vessel, but he hung out boarding nets lest the Malays attack; and he steered off for Mauritius rather than through the island passages to Batavia, though he had "no chart of Mauritius, nor other description than what is contained in the third edition of the *Encyclopaedia Britannica.*" Unhappily, the *Britannica* had not included an account of local French manners, and in Mauritius poor Flinders was seized and lodged in squalor.

As you ride out of Keopang on the air you may see little bright ships below which are (plank for plank and sail for sail and rope for rope) the pirates of the other year: and, if the strong Dutch patrols relaxed, might be the pirates of this year or next.

A MAZE OF ISLANDS

The waters now were green marble, and cumuli streamed across the sky like sailing towers, thousands of feet high above the Sawoe Zee. Flores, named for its orchids, rose up on the right, hundreds of miles long, with ragged heights and valleys still unexplored. Its forests have saponwood and the yellow dye, "kajoe-koening," that the Malays use. On Mount Gelimoetoe, which comes up first as you fly from Timor, are three lakes adjoining: one dark red, one a jade-green, one night-blue.

Under the port wing is Soemba in its shallow seas, where the Bugis still trade for tortoiseshell and sandalwood. In Flores and Soemba the people have a Papuan strain, though there is a race in Flores part Portuguese and still Christian. Here are the frontiers of the Malayan world, where Mongoloid meets Melanesian. Between Lombok and Bali is Wallace's Line, frontier between Asiatic and Australasian fauna and flora. Monkeys reach Timor, but the tiger ends in Bali. The wild ox, banteng, is not east of Borneo and Java; but marsupials reach westward to Timor and the Celebes, in the person of that entertaining little cuss, cuscus, whom I have also met in the North Queensland tropics. The bird of paradise belongs to Australia and New Guinea and the North Moluccas, and disputes no ground with elephant or rhinoceros which keep to Borneo and Sumatra, though Java has a rhino of its own.

At Soemba and Soembawa which succeed Flores over the right there, you meet the eastern vestiges of the Hindu civilization once grown from Java and still a major theme in Bali. The peoples of Soemba [3] and Soembawa are

[3] The Soemba people, like white Australians, worship varieties of the horse.

mostly reverted to Animism (which indeed is the core of native culture through all southwestern Asia), with some tatters surviving of Hinduism and some acquired of Islam. Once the Portuguese had Christian schools along here, but the old Dutch encouraged any god of darkness rather than the priests of Christian Rome. But Portuguese remained a *lingua franca* in these remote places and even in Dutch Batavia itself until the Dutchmen assiduously encouraged the wide use of Malay.

Soembawa is an island of deep bays under giant hills, and in its heart is the Gulf of Saleh, almost landlocked. Beyond Saleh, soaring from the water, you can see the head of Tambora, nine thousand feet up amongst its ragged clouds. Tambora has a sullen air, perhaps remembering 1815 when it erupted from April until July and made itself heard to the English at Benkoolen, eleven hundred miles away in Sumatra, and darkened skies to Brunei, nine hundred miles northward, where the natives subsequently reckoned dates from the event. The sea here was covered with ashes two feet thick. Somewhere in the Bay of Saleh, where you see it bluely across the hills as you pass, is sunk the town of Tambora and most of the old province where twelve thousand people died.

All this course is over a maze of islands, some large as Connecticut or Scotland, some of coral just thrusting their first palms from the sea. Between Soembawa and Flores, amongst a hundred others, is Komodo, distinguished for dragons. Sadly, Alfred Wallace, who gave so much attention to all these parts, missed the dragons. No man would have enjoyed them more, unless my amiable acquaintance, G. E. P. Collins, who was a shipping clerk at Mansfield's in Singapore, until he went off to make a ship of his own (and to write a very good book about it, called *Makassar Sailing*), in a remote village of the Celebes. He used to cruise about the islands until he went down with beri-

beri and things of the sort, when he put up in Komodo, and to while away his convalescence there taught dragons to jump through hoops. When I met him the other day he was Information Officer at the British Consulate in Batavia. Putting dragons through hoops seems an apt noviciate for a job in Information.

Beyond Soembawa, across the Straits of Alas, comes Lombok, as exciting a line in islands as any that exists. I have seen it at morning like a cloud of rose and blue and gold filling a third of the sky: and at evening when it was a purple pyramid in a sea of fire. The Peak of Lombok is twelve thousand feet above waters whitening in breakers along a coast of cliffs draped in green forest and silver beaches under drooping palms: while rivers fall like threads down the hills and the rice fields go up in terraced steps. The author of Genesis wisely failed to report the outward shape of Eden. Lombok is fifty-five miles long, forty-five miles wide; and there I too rest.

The people are Sasaks and nominally Moslems. During the eighteenth century they were conquered by the Balinese and thus by Hinduism: an uncommon experience for Moslems. The Balinese, for all their gentle arts and airs, are a tough breed. Their régime in Lombok was extremely harsh. The Dutch knew both islands by the early seventeenth century and traded there from 1674, but only established control after a smart campaign in 1894.[4]

The Straits between Lombok and Bali are very narrow, but they divide the continental shelves of Asia and Australia. From Bali the sea-floor rises sharply north and east.

[4] Even then, they were kept busy hereabouts for two decades more. Punitive measures were needed in Flores in 1890 and 1908. In 1904 pirates gave trouble in Bali. In 1906 a brisk action was fought at Den Pasar. In 1914 the soldiers were busy in Soemba.

If you lift it forty, fifty, two hundred, three hundred feet, you join Java, Sumatra, Borneo in one land mass with Malaya, Siam, Indo-China and all Asia. I rather suspect the Dutch. The first public office I noticed in Batavia was the Land Reclamation Bureau, and after what has happened to the Zuyder Zee, we may find the South China Seas drained off one of these days.

Towards the Indian Ocean Bali has a long, hooked finger of alluvial plain dropping gently from the mountains northward whose curves seem almost maternal: an introduction perhaps to the most publicized features of the Bali scene.

But it was not ladies without shifts that caught our eye as we dropped across the beach of surf and the shallow lagoon with its fishermen and their nets to land on the wide airport by the sandy beach at Djimbaran. Drawn up across the field were fighters of the Netherlands Indies Air Force. They looked very stubby and sinister as the sun went down over the Last Paradise.

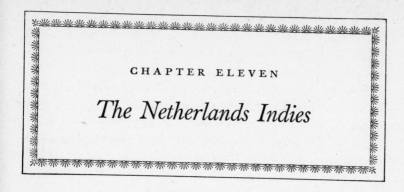

CHAPTER ELEVEN

The Netherlands Indies

SIZE AND POPULATION

FROM Darwin to Bali is eleven hundred miles, as K.N.I.L.M. flies. Bali and Lombok are almost at the centre of the southern arc of Nederlandsch-Oost-Indië, which swings through one-eighth of the earth's circumference, the three thousand miles from Poeloe Weh at the northern tip of Sumatra to middle New Guinea where the Dutch frontier marches with the Australian. From north to south, the islands scatter over seventeen degrees of longitude, six degrees north to eleven degrees south, roughly thirteen hundred miles. If you care to move Poeloe Weh to the Pacific coast of the United States, Sumatra will reach the neighbourhood of Phoenix, Arizona, and Java go on to Wichita Falls, Texas. Bali will be just above Austin (which should give the legislators a break), Timor will run northeast from Pensacola into Georgia, eastern New Guinea will lie across most of North Carolina and Virginia and continue far out into the Atlantic. Borneo will cover most of Kansas, Nebraska, and South Dakota and will stretch on into Wyoming and Colorado. The Celebes will curl round Lake Michigan from somewhere near Kalamazoo, go bang through the Palmer House and on into Iowa, Missouri, Arkansas, with a diversion through southern Illinois to Kentucky and Tennessee.

If you vary the scene (which is sometimes desirable) and put the north tip of Sumatra in Galway Bay, its southern extremity will be at Avignon, Java will reach from Arles to somewhere near Split on the Adriatic coast, New Guinea will plunge heavily into the Caspian, the Celebes will occupy most of the Ukraine and Borneo will cover what was Latvia, Poland, Czecho-Slovakia, Austria and much of south Germany on the maps of 1937.

The Netherlands Indies, in all, are about 700,000 square miles of land, fifty-eight times the size of the Netherlands themselves. They have a population of somewhere around 70,000,000, seventy per cent of it concentrated in Java and its little annex, Madoera, which might almost be considered a suburb. The rest of the Domain is known collectively as the Buitengewesten, the Outer Territories. Only in the last century and less have the Dutch been able to give the Buitengewesten (excepting the old Spice Islands of the Moluccas and Celebes) much attention.

POLITICAL GEOGRAPHY AND PEOPLE

The East Indies are a bridge between two continents, Asia and Australia; between two oceans, the Pacific and the Indian. They command the sea passages between Europe, Africa, Persia and India to the west, China, Japan and the Pacific countries to the east. They are incredibly wealthy and much of their wealth is still to be developed. They are the greatest colonial prize now in the world, as their little islands of spices towards the eastern edge were the first objectives of Europe's transoceanic adventure. The trading posts of Ternate and Ambon, with their old Dutch forts and Portuguese trenches, their handfuls of whites, their slow impoverishment, are much come down

in life, but it was for them and not for New York or
Buenos Aires that Columbus sailed.

Wave after wave of peoples (as we have seen) and of
cultures passed over Indonesia: Australians, Negritos,
Melanesians, Polynesians, each leaving pools of blood that
stagnated or merged in later streams. Behind the Melane-
sian-Papuans [1] came the Mongoloids whom we call Indonesians. They may have originated somewhere in Central
Asia: in Indo-China they seem to have mixed with a Caucasian strain. They have gone on mixing since, with Indians, Arabs, Chinese and now Europeans. You may lump
them generally as Indonesians.[2]

The Balinese have the typical physical characteristics.
They are browner than most Mongoloids, perhaps from
Indian strains and equatorial suns. They are slender but
wiry, the bones slight but the muscles strong. The women
have fine lines, straight shoulders and exquisite proportions. Dressed alike, the men would often be difficult to
distinguish from the women. Their strong black hair
seems to grow only from their tops. They seldom put on
fat, perhaps because of their diet or because they work
hard in the fields; though they do not develop the knotty
lumps of European labourers. The face is squarish with
high cheek-bones. Their carriage is smooth, quiet and

[1] Malay *puwa-puwa*, those with crinkled hair.
[2] The term Malay is better limited to the peoples of the
coasts and rivers who share a recognizably common culture
and familiarly use the Malay tongue. This rules out the majority of the Netherlands Indonesians. The degree of mixture
with Papuan, Arab, Indian, Chinese, or Negrito blood provides differences noticeable in character and way of life. The
Menangkabau, a highly developed people of Sumatra and the
Malay Peninsula, are widely believed to be the true proto-
Malay. The basic Indonesian stock is recognizable from
northern Sumatra to the Philippines: and so is a common
fundamental culture.

rather like a cat's. They talk softly, like our ladies who are ladies. Even youths, in their kampong clubhouse, are hardly heard ten yards away. The European sounds and looks a good deal of a lout beside them, especially when he walks about in shorts on hairy legs.

The Javanese are smaller and darker than those commonly called Malay: but in their own island the Soendanese are heavier and darker than the Javanese. The Balinese seem a trifle fleshier too and with a golden fleck in their bronze. They keep a peculiar suggestion of the exotic which Islam has obscured in Java.

Two thousand years ago the proto-Indonesians had occupied their lands all about the South China Seas and down to the Indian Ocean. Some had crossed it to Madagascar, and some were mingled with Polynesians and Melanesians of the Western Pacific. The dispersion, the lack of a written language, and the various alien intrusions gradually produced the differences now marked in language, custom and craft.

HINDU AND ISLAM

The first foreign influence was Hindu; though one can never wholly dismiss the Chinese from the scene. The sea passages from China are easy, and the Chinese settle and live so quietly amongst others that their impact is seldom dramatic enough for the sensation-monger, history. The Hindus were in regular contact with Sumatra, the Malaccan coasts and Java by the first or second centuries A.D.

The Chinese perhaps came and went with the sailing seasons. The Indians were further from home and, like the Europeans later, they founded trading posts, first along the Straits of Malacca, to protect their merchantmen from pirates and to gather from local trade the cargoes for fleets that went home on the wind from the East.

With the Indians or perhaps before them came the Arabs.

The little posts and forts, as such things do where territories are split into a crazy quilt of warring tribes, developed political power. Much as the Europeans later grew strong by playing off factions, now supporting this one, now that, so did the Indians. The strategy of "divide and rule" inevitably appears when the victims lack political unity. The Hindus organized large areas of Indonesia as the British later organized India itself.

The Indian settlements, again like the Europeans', followed the line of advance from the Straits and Sumatra to the distant Spice Islands, the object always of the alien drive. They moved into Java because Java was the great rice granary of all southeastern Asia, and with rice they bought the spices of the remote Moluccas.

For six or seven centuries the Indian tide flowed in, numerically stronger than the European to come, because India was already overcrowded and the islands very rich; but less important for its numbers than for what they brought.

The first Hindu epoch is marked by the Empire of Criwijaja which grew about Palembang in Sumatra (where Standard now sucks up oil). It spread across the Malayan Peninsula and Sumatra, and eastward influenced the principalities of Java to a Hindu shape. With Criwijaja or before it spread the culture which Sanscrit words were imported to describe, a vocabulary for the life of the mind and the sensibilities and for many crafts, as *agama* for religion, *tenggala* for plough. The Hindu régime of priests and princes was imposed upon the Indonesian village life. The first Hindu kingdoms in Java, Taroema and Kalinga, of about the fifth and seventh centuries A.D., were, like Criwijaja, probably Buddhist and Mhayanist. Taroema was south of Batavia, east of Buitenzorg: Kalinga about Magelang with a temple city on the Dijeng Plateau.

Against them rose, as Criwijaja declined, the Brahman power of Madjapahit centred southeast of Soerabaja, where the River Brantas divides into Mas and Porong, in the heart of the richest rice lands. By 1400 A.D. it was supreme from Timor to Siam, and under it the old Hindu and Indonesian elements fused in the culture characteristically Javanese. Eastward it strengthened existing Hindu elements in Bali which survived when Islam swept over Java. Bali then became a refuge for faithful Brahmans.

Islam first appeared in North Sumatra with Arab and Indian traders. By conquest and conversion it spread down the Straits and across them to establish a strong port and kingdom at Malacca. Thence it crept east to the Spice Islands and south to Java, eating away the realm of Madjapahit, until it splintered under pressure into scores of scrambling, struggling little kingdoms whose division made the way easier for the Portuguese, arriving almost on the heels of Islam. The first Portuguese found a Hindu régime at Bantam in Java, but by the early sixteenth century Bantam was Moslem. Madjapahit succumbed to another Moslem power, of Mataram, whose core was what are now the Native States of Soerakarta and Jogjakarta, into which the Dutch split its remnant during the eighteenth century. When the Dutch reached Java it was divided between the two Moslem Powers of Bantam and Mataram. Against Mataram, Bali stood. Its people still like to call themselves men of Madjapahit.

Roughly then, very roughly, the cultural strata of historic Indonesia are Animism, Hinduism (first Buddhism, then Brahmanism), Mahomedanism, Europeanism. Bali resisted the third and only now seems susceptible to the fourth. Where Islam failed, Greenwich Village makes a determined effort.

The Balinese worships as an Animist the spirits of the woods and waters, the rocks and rice fields: but he worships too Shiva the Destroyer, whose temples have eleven roofs; and Brahma the Creator who must do with nine, and Vishnu who Sustains though he has only seven. Shiva is enthroned on Gunung Anung, the highest mountain. His wife Durga discreetly removes herself to the foot of Mount Batur, where she lives, a Lady of the Lake: though, with considerable versatility, she also doubles as a virginal goddess of the fields and as Kali, the extremely rugged governess of Death, who also takes dramatic form as Rangda the witch and eats babies. Bali has multiplied and adapted gods with fervent zest, worshipping them all in its own inimitable synthesis and spirit; and from them were born its exquisite arts.

BALI

I suppose that most people are pretty bored by Bali. I was, until the first hour in which I saw it. How long it will remain as it is, how far it has already declined from what it was, you may variously guess. But it still has a rich creative life which raises query after query for our western values.

I have never quite discovered what our educators are doing unless to turn us all into clerks, stenographers, factory hands and readers of *Esquire*. But if it is a fair test that education should leave us with ideas and the capacity to express them, I do not know how we shall compare the Balinese peasant with the drab inhabitants of our suburban cots.

To the Balinese, life is packed with meanings. A primrose by the river's brim would never be a simple primrose and nothing more to him. With its spirit his own soul would dwell in whatever communications a man may have with a primrose. And so with the rice and earth, the mountains, fields and waters, even the familiar peg where the householder might hang his hat. He reveres and mingles with this life in all the round of the seasons. In the new leaf and old, at seedtime and at harvest, he shares and celebrates with fruits and flowers and feasts; and, that his thoughts and feelings may have more lasting representation, with his arts: the arts of music, of the dance, of architecture, of carving, of drawing, of metal-work.

He greets, on the whole, his gods joyously. His agriculture is itself an art and conducted according to the canons, for the spirits of the fields and plants have their own rights. The peasant co-operates with them: and so he tends his fields with the diligent care that makes all cultivated Bali and most of Java like a gentle garden. When his day in the fields is done, he turns, as the mediaeval European did, to give divinity a local habitation and a name. He works at his temples and shrines as the English villager worked at the parish church and roadside crucifix. Again like the mediaeval villager, he develops extraordinary dexterity, and as he carves creates, often with furious fancies whereof he is commander. Every Balinese is a carver, for he builds his little shrines in every corner of a field, by trees, on hillocks, above a running stream: and because the stone of Bali is soft he must be constantly renewing them, and endless practice perfects skill and provides for every play of idea and humour. He is quite capable of putting a god on a bicycle, and motor cars appear amongst saints. About the shrines, he plants gardens and builds altars, and makes festivals, for he can find as many holydays as the fourteenth century did to sing and dance and play through.

As in the mystical stones and glass of the Gothic, all forms and colours have meanings. That conventional bird is Garuda, the steed of Vishnu; the tortoise bears the earth; the elephant god is good fortune; Nandi the Bull is Shiva's mount; the swan is Brahma's bird. Red belongs

to Brahma, white to Shiva, black to Vishnu, yellow to
Baruna, god of the ocean. All these signs are a familiar
language of the Balinese, and in them they write their
poems of wood and stone. You can have a deal of fun in
trying to read them.

The arts grow in the worship of the gods, for religion
represents what men have most deeply thought and felt.
That is why an atheistic age so often seems arid and its
arts without grace. Old cities raised great churches like
our Lady of Salisbury, our Lady of Wells: but the modern
city is dominated by its insurance houses, banks and
cinemas, for these, I suppose, are the things we believe
worth celebrating. But I doubt whether even the Temper-
ance and General Assurance Company is likely to feed and
flower in the drama, the dance and the music which grew
round the Gothic churches and still flourish in the temples of Bali.

The drama both of shadow-plays and human actors is
drawn from Hindu cycles and local legends. Some themes
are ritual, some merely entertainment; and the theatre,
like the dance, is vigorous and alive. A deal of ribald and
topical stuff and local allusion finds its way into the play
through the "penasar," who comment on the doings of the
classic characters, like a Greek Chorus but much more
freely in every sense. The classic plays are usually in the
old literary and priestly tongue of Java which the people
seldom understand but running comment and improvised
dialogue provide the popular stuff and are apparently
rich and dirty.

Both plays and dances need the gamelan, the fascinating
orchestra which develops and immeasurably improves the
principles and range of the xylophone with percussion instruments of wood and metal, and bronze vessels rather
like soup tureens, gongs, drums, suspended tubes, flutes,
and rebab, the one- or two-stringed viol. The gamelan of

the play sets the characters to music, with recurrent motifs, and dramatic description. It has measures of yielding sweetness, and sharp, metallic effects that seem to etch a pattern on the air.

If you wander through the villages, you may hear the gamelan and see a play on most nights of the year. People make feasts and shows on the slightest provocation or none at all: for a marriage in the family, a birth, a meeting, a successful deal, a return from travel, the building of a house, the bringing in of rice, the birthdays of Queen Wilhemina or Princess Juliana or Princess Juliana's children, the arrival of a friend. When a gamelan is not performing publicly, it is probably rehearsing in some one's house, and as you hear it at evening through the scented trees, you should pursue it, and climb in under the low door and sit in the dusk amongst the men and boys and try your hand. The European has become a passive spectator at his mass entertainments, but the Balinese still makes his own pleasures with exquisite patience, love, and art. He is so much more a man.

One afternoon a few months ago, I fell into talk about Balinese art with the Director of an admirable museum at Jogjakarta in Java. We wandered into his office and he brought out portfolio after portfolio of drawings. He had something like five thousand of them. All were good and some superb in fancy, line and colour. They had been collected by a dealer in Bali who passed word amongst the villages that he would pay fifty or sixty cents for any drawing he liked; and when the Balinese found that he seriously meant it, hundreds of them cheerfully began to draw. Some used the themes of local carvers. Some represented traditional techniques of different villages. But these hundreds of peasants could outdraw any art school between Kiev and San Diego. Fifteen hundred of the

pieces were to go on exhibition in the United States. I
hope they set some local educationalists thinking.

Art, after all, is not just a pretty trick. Work of quality
requires ideas, intellectual discipline, patient skills, moral
qualities like perseverance and industry, all the benefits
we are supposed to have from education. But the village
boys in Bali draw better than the professors in our schools
and their art has more to say though they talk much less
about it.

When the Balinese die, they hope to go to heaven.
Heaven for them is to return to Bali. That, I suppose, is
as convincing a judgement as any people could pass upon
the lives they live.

The Balinese, like the rest of us, have some nasty superstitions and dirty tricks. They also have qualities of life
that we have lost. Allowing for the gulf between the Christian mind and theirs, you may recall the world reflected
in the bright mediaeval artists, in the Miracles and
Chaucer, with its feasts, holidays, pilgrimages and popular
theatre, its light, cheerfulness, piety, broad humour, lusti-
ness, earthiness, shrewdness and the air of well-being that
belongs to those who find many things to do and learn to
do them well. The man whose life is reduced to mechanical routines, crabbed offices and factories, who spends his
days adding up other people's profits and losses, is the dis-
contented, empty, angry man. Can you blame him?

The Javanese must once have been much like the
Balinese. They lost half their arts when Islam broke the
images. But Bali's peculiar misfortune was to be discovered not by fanatics and fierce adventurers but by dilettantes, art-dealers, and the tourist business.

Artists and some who pass as artists introduced the
Balinese to pretty Western forms. The Balinese have such
skill that they imitate with distressing fluency. Their imi-
tations sell for a few cents to the dealers who traffic in

souvenirs from Bali. The litter of cheap imitative stuff is now spread from here to Minneapolis, and endlessly repeated birds and fish and carved heads of dancing girls pour out of Bali as if the place were a mass-production factory. I just saw a fellow who is something in films buy five large wooden heads. You may see whole cases of identical heads being packed across the street for Sydney and New York. The Balinese have entered our money-economy, on the bottom rung. They have learnt what we will buy. And what we will buy is muck. So those who were goldsmiths, silversmiths, weavers, dancers, players, sculptors are now hands for hucksters.

Until the war, the place was becoming an international peepshow. The girls of Bali are delicate and their young breasts are bare. So they drew a Casino-de-Paris sort of audience. With normal smut came nastier stuff and some of it settled in comfortable bungalows. The Dutch a while back did some bungalow-cleaning, but the perverted dilettantes who cuss at missionaries and despise the patient officers of Empire have done immeasurable damage in a few years.

So a boy who can draw like an angel is carving suburban knickknacks, cheap, very cheap, sir; and he can take you where there are plenty girls, very hot, sir; for he has discovered what the customer wants.

Many influences work against European prestige in the East, but the most deadly is from moneyed and perverted idlers. They spread their corruption even where they are despised. Hearty, whoring planters and soldiers and sailors are one thing and taken much as a matter of course in the East: languid degenerates are another, and the one item of export we certainly cannot afford if we are to keep our place in the outer world. Let them stick to their own elegant metropolitan styles.

EVENING PIECE

I have been making these notes on the low terrace before the K.P.M. hotel, drinking a Bols before the late, leisurely Dutch dinner. The people drift endlessly up and down the road as they do throughout the East, with the gentle clip-clip of slippers, and quiet voices. A hundred people are walking within fifty yards but with less noise than the swish of bicycle tires, and somewhere very remotely a gamelan tuning, and night-birds in distant trees. Across the road, where the hotel has built a theatre in the Javanese mode, a broad platform and a roof and open court, a little group of dancers is preparing. They will presently do some bits and pieces from their repertory, a sort of brief anthology for the planeload of people who came in this evening. The gamelan is gathered, half to one side of the stage, half opposite. The girls have on their fantastic, lovely head-dresses and the heavy cloths of patterned gold and red and purple which they wind tightly about them. Their faces are startlingly white with rice powder. The comedians have their comic masks. The slim, half-naked man with the flower behind his ear is the greatest dancer I have ever seen. The whole party has just arrived in a bus.

This evening, before sunset, we drove and walked out amongst the flooded rice fields where the light falls redly across the channels and terraces and the standing stalks, turns the trees to bronze, the hills to violet, and the idols and temple gates to things seen in dreams. Processions of women walked leisurely with tall baskets of flowers to deck their gods: who, on festal evenings, are done up in blue-and-white-checked gingham. I do not know anything much more pleasant than Ganesha in a gingham vest. Boys came back from the fields guiding their ducks with long, flagged bamboo poles which, set all day in the wet sawah, will keep the ducks to their own puddle. Chaplets were hung at the crossroads where spirits gather; and there were offerings and tags of cloth for prayers on trees and shrines. Cooks and their customers sat together on haunches about roadside pots and ate off banana leaves and upturned boxes, and the sellers of sweets spread their pink stuff on a plank. Old women went chattering like birds, and old men gathered about the village gates, people being much the same everywhere. The young men, in their groups, were probably talking of fighting cocks or the arts of love. The girls were talking of the arts of love. They are inclined to giggle together at evening, and they roll their dark eyes.

You will always hear music at dusk, even away amongst the fields: some one singing in the brave voice of the lungs or the heavy voice of the liver or the light voice come from the gall or the high voice which lies in the dream of Semara, god of love; music in the villages of gambang, flute and rebab. A group of craftsmen came walking together, all fellows of their guild. A man came swinging after them quickly because his load was heavy. He had a shoulder-pole and at each end of it a basketed, suspended pig. I remembered a young American I once met at the airport here. He was shipping out eggs and turkeys. He had drifted into Bali and thought it an obvious place to grow eggs, as it is, so he sat down and grew them. Out of albino turkeys. Very good eggs too, for turkeys and albinos.

The light went abruptly, and the world was suddenly dark purple, with little yellow flames in the houses and laughter down the road and running children, and you caught the smell of wet fields and heavy flowers.

Suddenly, from the coast, there was the roar of engines. Odd lights flickered from somewhere towards Koeta. An old Balinese near by stopped and stared up at the sky, his mouth drooping. He must have remembered the day when a prince of Den Pasar burnt his palace and he and his relations and retainers, his wives, his children, his nobles and his servants, all in their richest things and jewelled, threw themselves against the Dutch bayonets near the place where the little museum and the K.P.M. hotel now are. The old man understood that war, and the piracy and looting which provoked it. But he did not understand this thing now that came out of the sky. He or his children will learn, no doubt, as they have learnt the tricks of the tourist. Civilization is over Bali, like the hot, foul dust of an eruption.

CHAPTER TWELVE

Batavia

DRAKE, DUCKS AND MOUNTAINS

"FROM whence continuing theire course still west, they came to the Ile of Java, where the contrey people were clothed in linen garments like smocks, of whom they had traffic vij or viij toon of rice, and also divers Java daggers, divers other things, as plantanes, cocus and great canes. . . ."

We had less rice than Francis Drake; but difficulties with ducks before we got out of Bali. At the airport they invaded the "vliegveld," taking the tarmac for a pleasant pond, where they sat, silly tails up, until a squad of anti-aircraft gunners, who should have been doing other things in the clear morning after reveille, removed them from the Douglas's track. The air sock may resemble their duck boy's fluttering rag and bamboo pole. But where was the duck boy?

At six A.M. we were over the Straits of Bali with the cape of Java already below us to the south. A twisting passage of blue and silver flecked with the white lateen sails of fishing boats, like gulls, approaches the swampy shore of Banjoewangi, the city of sweet-smelling waters, but not looking at all like it; where the cable comes in from Darwin. Then we were amongst the mountains; Merapi, Rante, Pendil, Soeket, Raoeng, eight, nine, ten thousand feet; mountains on both wingtips, in every window and damned near coming through the floor. We flew between mountains and over smoking volcanic lakes, tumbling craters, steam, cloud and the trees thrusting through them. We could have seen the birds in the trees and the eggs under the birds if any birds were foolish enough to be up in all those complications. Vegetation, unless the volcano is misbehaving, runs almost to the ragged crater lips, and red-roofed villages cling to the dizzy slopes as if they are roped there and all their inhabitants prehensile. The villages multiply as you break through that first terrific cluster of mountains, each village in its copse, a darker island in the lighter fields.

More mountains heave east and south as you strike off towards the Madoera Straits. Java has 125 volcanoes, many busy: one for each four and one-half miles of its length.

CITY BEHIND THE ISLAND

The Straits of Madoera are a funnel narrowing to the west, where Madoera lies just off the Java shore. Most of the natives you see about Soerabaja in Dutch naval uniform are Madoerese. They are a tough and enterprising people; and politically active. Soerabaja is half Madoerese. It is the second city of the Indies and by far the busiest. It spreads over alluvial flats at the mouth of the Kali Mas (River of Gold; the mud is yellow from the hills). The Dutch once had some plan of walling the town but it kept bursting out in long suburbs. Old Soerabaja is tightly packed by the river, with Chinese houses hanging over the water, and the Red Bridge crossing to the original European quarter, crowded with banks, department stores, cinemas, clubs, and insurance offices; where plump Dutchmen hurry even at midday. But Soendanese, Madoerese, Javanese, Malays, and Arabs keep their own quarters, more or less. Once they were ghettoed, when no native

might walk abroad at night unless in the clothes proper
to his sex and carrying a light, and none might cross a
bridge except at a slow walk. Soerabaja is a lesser Singapore, a medley and muddle of races. The Dutch keep a
firm hold on such places.

They have reason for fresh precautions at Soerabaja,
now the major naval and air base. The big new airport
is a training centre. Lines of grey seaplanes are anchored
in the bay, where Madoera cloaks for one hundred miles
the port and its approaches. The position is not unlike
Singapore though here the base is on the mainland.

A large part of the Dutch Navy was already stationed in
the Indies when war began. The whole fleet had 5 light
cruisers, 8 destroyers, 44 torpedo boats with 32 in reserve,
21 submarines, 12 minelayers, and 20 motor boats. It was
organized in fast squadrons about the cruiser nucleus,
designed to cover, skirmish, and delay. The strength in
light craft has been much increased. When I last flew into
Soerabaja the dockyard had 20,000 workmen busy on destroyers, sloops, and stainless-steel torpedo boats (an im-
provement on the Italian sea-sled) which were coming off
the stocks in great numbers. In force amongst the labyrin-
thine waterways, they would bother any battle fleet. The
Eastern Squadron is officered by Europeans but more than
half the personnel is from the seagoing coastal peoples: the
whole makes an unquestionably handy outfit.

BRITAIN AND THE NETHERLANDS

September, 1939, found the Dutch already braced for
trouble. They knew that Britain favoured their neutrality
if they could maintain it. Britain has long sought to
strengthen the Dutch in their Lowlands: a policy evident,
for instance, in the restoration to them of the rich Indies
in 1816. Friendly control of the Lowlands will always be

a vital British interest; so is friendly control of the Indies. A hostile power commanding the Archipelago could slice the British Empire into two, destroy the Indo-Chinese traffic, isolate Australia and New Zealand, and be comfortably based for attacks on British properties from Hong Kong to Suez, Fiji to Cape Town.[1] Strategically, the Indies have much the significance for the British Commonwealth that the Canal Zone has for the United States. The British have given hostages to Dutch fortune. Their dealings in the matter do no suggest ruthless power politicians.

The British in fact but not form were committed to the defence of the Netherlands and their possessions, but the Netherlands were not committed to Britain. Britain trusted to the general good sense and good will of the Dutch people. For a century no major difficulty has risen in British-Dutch relations. Holland accepted, in effect, the system of order and reasonable agreement which the British have been slowly building where and when they could. You may call it a good-neighbour programme, if you like.

But the Netherlands have one frontier where Britain could do little without thorough military and diplomatic preparations. These Holland would not join in or permit. So the German border of Holland proved the Achilles' heel of Anglo-French defence in western Europe, when on May 10, 1940, in the first hours of the morning, the air was suddenly filled with the roar of Goering's fleets and the frontier burst into flame.

News reached the Indies before noon. The Government moved ahead of rumour. Of eighteen German ships in the Indies' ports, the crews had time to scuttle only one. German seamen, arguing, found bayonets in their ribs, and behind the bayonets brown Ambonese, with an enthusi-

[1] Napoleon understood all this when he sent General Daendels to prepare from Batavia the downfall of Britain in the East.

astic glint in their eyes. The police work was brilliant.
Nearly two thousand arrests were made before dark. Both
the Germans and the N.S.B., the Dutch National Socialist
movement, were highly organized. The Germans were
the largest foreign group. Many were in government
services, or at key points in commerce and industry. With
Dutch Nazis,[2] they had coloured local opinion. They
were probably ready for a *coup d'état* or at least a *coup
de théâtre* if opportunity served. But they were swept up
without warning. Legend says that the warnings were
sent. But with the curious lack of imagination which
sometimes characterizes German officialdom the cables
were all couched in similar terms, which naturally provoked suspicion. So many grandmothers or whatever they
were could hardly have died at once.

Any rational man except, apparently, the Japanese, who
are simple souls, knew that the Indies would be one prize
of German victory. Here are raw materials the German
needs, and huge habitable areas of tropics whose wealth
is to be exploited but where the first difficult and expensive steps have already been taken. Java is overcrowded,
but Sumatra could carry many times its present population, and Sumatra has everything from oil to a mountain
climate on the equator where Europeans can work in comfort all the year round. Sumatra also had neatly planted
German groups and interests.

The personal anxieties of Dutch officials were considerable and worth our sympathy. Many Dutchmen have
German relatives, and until the massacre of Rotterdam

[2] The Indies had, in 1926-'27, serious Communist troubles,
with riots and shooting. (As a consequence some five hundred
people still live incommunicado up a hot greasy river in New
Guinea.) Communist agitation, as usual, provoked Fascist
tendencies, for as Marx would put it, thesis produces antithesis
(and sometimes the two produce a synthesis, but that is another headache).

on May 14, 1940, few Dutchmen hated Germans. The fire
the German bombers lit that day will not soon die. Every
Dutchman in the East had close relatives in occupied Holland: fathers, mothers, brothers, sisters as potential hostages. Most responsible officers were in their late thirties,
forties or early fifties, with their children gone home to
school. Their savings, capital, and life insurances were
largely in Holland. Men approaching retirement and old
age were faced with comparative poverty. These considerations must have weighted the private thoughts of many
in Buitenzorg and Batavia and Soerabaja. Their response
to the emergency then was both courageous and grim.

The German prisoners were truculent, at first, while
they were held on an island off Batavia. Then they were
shifted to Sumatra, and up country, up a lot of jungle
country with one tiger-haunted road to civilization. I
doubt whether any attempted to walk out.

On May 10 Batavia announced that as the Netherlands
were at war with Germany, all aid would be given to the
Allies, but that the existing authority was quite well able
to look after the colonies and would not welcome assistance "from whatever side it may be offered."

QUO ANTE AND QUO VADIS

Japan had already, before the invasion, declared somewhat ambiguously for the *status quo* in the East Indies.
So had Mr. Cordell Hull, and Britain. But on June 3 the
Japanese Foreign Minister delivered himself curiously:
"If there is a country which has a large population of
hard-working men bottled up in a small area not favoured
with natural resources and failing to secure economic stability on that account, and if beside this small country
there is a country having abundant resources, and if there
is no way between the two for ministering to the former's

wants, can true stability ever be possible at all?" Echo answered, "What's to do?" The official translation may not be elegant, but no one could say that he had not been tipped off.

The Netherlands Indies mobilized the Landstorm, announced new programmes for defences and for doubling the Air Force, and prepared to destroy instantly oil wells throughout the Archipelago if any strangers should come uninvited ashore.

On May 11 the Indies admitted to 100 fighters and 120 very recent bombers, mostly American. In 1941, I saw Dorniers on the sea patrols, Australian Tiger Moths, Curtiss Interceptors, Curtiss Hawk fighters, Martin and Lockheed bombers. Purchases in the United States during 1939 were heavy. During 1940 the United States shipped at least $5,000,000 worth of planes to the Indies. American civil instructors, who have been busy in the East these two years, joined the Dutch instructors to train pilots: and across one-eighth of the world's middle the big flying ships were patrolling daily every sea-approach, to guard against the surprise that comes sometimes by night.

Java lies in the second line of Dutch defence. Northward in Borneo, in the Celebes and Moluccas, are the advanced bases, mostly new, very hush-hush, and hidden in jungles that would cost any infantryman his hide for a ten-yards' advance. If there is to be jungle war it will be along the roads and dry fields, unless the troops can go where tigers do not.

Meanwhile, trade with the United States was up nearly 60 per cent each way in one year: rubber and tin for aircraft and machines. So Soerabaja was busy. We left it for the moment and went on to Batavia.

BATAVIA

New York and Java should be seen first from the air.
The pre-natal clinics may be able to do little about it, but
tourists should. Between Soerabaja and Semarang the
land slopes from high wooded hills to the sea, with swift

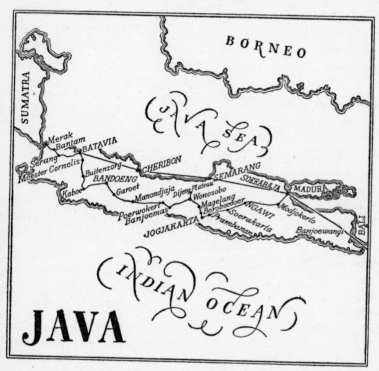

rivers knitted by networks of irrigation channels; terraced
hills, and a dazzling jigsaw of fields, bright reds, greens,
yellows, browns. One view may hold a hundred villages.
This is the most densely populated country in the world,
inhabited by 821 people to the square mile in the central
rice lands: twice as thickly settled as Japan, though Java
too has mountains and some waste. But Japan and Eng-

land are industrial countries. Java is almost entirely rural. It has 48,000,000 people but only twelve cities of more than 50,000.[3] Batavia, with half a million, is the largest.

Semarang is sugar, tobacco, and modern architecture; white bungalows in the pleasant hills above the port; and a gateway to the Native States southward. The coast dips and you ride across the coastal shallows of the Java Sea to Cheribon, Tji Ribon, the River of Crayfish (B.S.A.s do not go on, you may recall, from Natal to Cheribon), with the sea a green wash over yellow sands and coral reefs, and the coast rising to green hills and blue mountains. Cheribon to Batavia is another 150 miles over alluvial plains and plantations, but still with the mountains southward. I counted twenty-three rivers before we dropped to the new airport of Batavia, where, not so many years ago, Charles Kingsford-Smith, carrying the first Australia-England airmail, needed carpets and thatch stripped from cottages to make runways. Batavia Airport is not like that now.

Only the Dutch could have made Batavia; but they could have made it only in the East. Their first Batavia was a walled town at the mouth of the Tji Liwoeng, and they built it like Amsterdam and Rotterdam with a crisscross of canals, little arched bridges, and square Dutch houses. The Molenvliet Canal still runs for miles from the Old Town to Weltevreden, which grew in the eighteenth century. With its roadways beside it, Molenvliet remains the spine of the town.

Batavia is long, narrow, and (if you neglect Tandjong Priok, the modern port across the marshes) in three parts. Old Batavia is venerable Dutch houses become banks, insurance and government offices; a railway station, Chinese shops, native markets; fishing port, fishermen,

[3] Java is roughly 51,000 square miles; New York State is about 40,000.

fishy smell: the picturesque. Weltevreden (Well-Content) is Batavia Centrum, and official about the great park called Koningsplein. It has the hotels, corset shops, modistes, silk stockings, tourist bureaux, cinemas, book stores, drug stores and such. North from it the pleasant streets of the new suburbs reach to Meester Cornelis, whoever he was.

CABS, KOLYNOS AND CANNON

One takes a cab to the Old Town because the weather is hot, and probably wet, especially in the afternoons. It rains in the wet season of the west monsoon from October to April. It rains in the dry season of the east monsoon from April to October. When it does not rain you wish it would; and, anyhow, take a cab. You have no difficulty in that, for each cab has a spotter and his business is to spot. If you cross the grounds of the Hôtel des Indes, the cabs gather for your body at the gates. If you walk on the roadway (the sidewalks in Batavia are, when they exist, about eighteen inches wide and occupied by ladies with fowls, gentlemen with lamps on their heads, and parties eating ramboetans, a delicious but messy fruit) the taxis descend like market flies on a lemonade seller. Like flies, the taximen lead lean but exuberant lives. Sometimes they bump you, gently, to emphasize the dangers of pedestrianism. So you take a taxi. I have never discovered what Batavian taximen expect to be paid. They leave the sordid details to Allah, and when you find yourself the channel and vicar of Allah's beneficence, you hardly like to let Him down.

The Molenvliet displays the Javanese School of *plein air* washing. The Dutch meant Molenvliet as a canal, but the Javanese have immemorially adopted all streams and waterways as baths and public conveniences. The Molen-

vliet floats rafts of bamboo, dead animals, considerable
sewage and enough mud to be opaque; once in, the modest may wash naked and unashamed. Women go down
steps to the water swathed from breasts to ankles and
come up wrapped if wringing, and never seem to mis-
manage their sarongs, which are not at all like Miss La-
mour's. It is odd to notice some gentle brown girl emerging from the slush with her toothbrush and tube of Koly-
nos. Women and laundry-boys scrub and bang clothes on
the steps, and young bloods lather in scented soaps, and
beldames gossip. They are a very clean people, but like
their water dirty.[4] Municipal bathhouses have no popu-
larity. But I suppose the Molenvliet is not much worse
than many swimming pools.

The Molenvliet passes the Records Office, one of the
best bits of old Dutch in Batavia, which has little of the
aged, though Coen settled there before the *Mayflower*
sailed. The best early Dutch buildings in the East are
now on British ground, at Malacca: the British have a
weakness for old bits, pieces, and politicians.

The Records Office was the Governor-General's country seat when Batavia was wedged between its walls a mile
or two above. The old Batavians had a passion for profits
or duty, or a massive indifference to fevers and fret. In
1699 neighbouring Salak erupted, choked the river and
canals, and ruined the natural drainage; thus confirming
the insalubrity of the place. A million people died here
in a few years of the eighteenth century, when Batavia
was often five feet under water in the wets: though Da-
vidson, in 1824, remarked that five in six of the Europeans
dead were killed by gin and brandy. He thought Batavia
"a joyous place."

Under the modern Dutch régime Java's death rate

---

[4] I once saw a girl in Bali skin and wash a banana in a ditch
then occupied by several buffalo.

compares very well with that of many European countries. The population has grown from 13,000,000 in 1860
to 50,000,000 in 1941. The birth rate in 1939 was 29.4
per thousand. Much of it appears on Molenvliet: brown,
chubby, and chuckling or chubby, yellow, and solemn,
and in either case charming though not much accommodated with diapers.

You pass through babies and packed Chinese shops and
eating houses to the banks. You pick up the babies again
by the Amsterdam Gate, a surviving remnant of the ancient walls. Just within the gate is an antique cannon,
where native ladies pray (quite unnecessarily, one would
think) for fertility. A couple of fellows sell there paper
umbrellas and flowers, votive offerings for the barrel; and
prepare a mess of chopped green leaves to burn with incense. They will mutter the incantation too, if the sup-
pliant is shy. Results are remarkable.

The Indies have several "sacred" cannon, all apparently
progenitive. The Batavia piece has a wife at Bantam, and
a tradition that Dutch rule in Java will end when the two
meet. I suppose there is some old association with the
powers of Jacatra and Bantam whose division contributed
to the Dutch hegemony here. But someone has missed out
on a striking piece of propaganda.

At evening the fishing boats are in, and prahus from
down the coast, and from Sumatra and the Celebes.

They are lateen sailed, their home ports distinguishable by the colouring and carving at prow and stem, by
the long pennants, and by rig. The Madoerese riot in
colours, dramatized at evening when tall masts and furled
sails are against a pink sky and the pink sky itself is merged
in its reflection: then *Harry, Judith,* the *Saucey Jane,* and
Seabreaze (there seems some flair for English names but
not for English spelling) look like gondolas for rosy cheru-
bim. The harbour is now almost two miles from the sea,

for the land is growing, and a dredged channel leads to open water. From out along the built-up banks you can see the derricks of Tandjong Priok across the dark marsh. The narrow path is sometimes occupied by goats. I trust that yours will be amenable to reason or patience. When I last walked there at dusk I met a Bishop in white and purple, gold chain, jewelled cross, and that beaverish sort of hat that Bishops wear. I wish he would exorcise the goats. When the dusk snaps down, the waste and the swamp suggest Dante's approaches to Hell, a subject of meditation no doubt for Bishops.

FIRST ACRE OF EMPIRE

Out of this harbour went Abel Tasman to his circuit of the Indian Ocean and the West Pacific; and here came Cook in 1770, from Botany Bay. Here, in fact, came the first authentic news of Australia as the Dutchmen dropped anchor after the long easterly beat from Good Hope. The Australians might, one day, raise a memorial by the Quay.

On the east of the little harbour is a native market and beyond it a bridge and a watch tower: beyond the bridge an enormous long godown, with old black timbers, white-washed walls, and a tiled roof brown with age. Where it stands was the English factory in the year 1617, and near by the palace of the Sultan of Jacatra. Where you stand, looking across, was the fort of Jan Pieterszoon Coen, on the first plot of sovereign Dutch ground in Java. Somewhere hereabouts, his grave forgotten, lies Jan Pieterszoon. On these paths and waterways he fought the skirmishes that won for Holland her Dominion of the East. Not everywhere, even in London or in Rome, can you stand on the precise first acre of an Empire.

There are long grasses now and more goats in the yards of the godown, but still a fancied whiff of the old cargoes:

mace, cloves and nutmegs from Molucca, pepper, brown calicoes and checkered stuff, mallow girdles and painted cloths of batik, Java girdles and silver ewers. There, for two centuries, walked the Upper Merchants, the Merchants, the Junior Merchants, the Assistants, the boatswains and the gunners' mates; traded and took their wages in Spanish dollars, mas and cashes, perdawes and taels; weighed pepper by the bar of three hundred and three score pounds:

> *Goods in and out, which daily ships doe freight,*
> *By guesse, by tale, by measure, and by weight.*

There they composed their long reports and longer accounts for the Heeren XVII, the Seventeen Gentlemen of the Merchant Chambers of Amsterdam, Zeeland, Delft, Rotterdam, Hoorn, and Enkhuyzen, the supreme Collegium of the Vereenigde Oostindische Compagnie, the United East Indies Company of the Netherlands. It was, like many other things, the error of Philip II of Spain, who was always cutting off his nose to spite his face, poor man.

The thing began with the Lisbon traffic, when Portugal had all the gorgeous East in fee and sat upon it as a private nest-egg. For nearly a century Portugal kept the secrets of her routes, hoarding charts and sailing directions more closely than the emeralds and rubies.[5] They brought their cloves, silks, and white sandalwood to Lisbon where other Europeans came to market. The Dutch came first and most frequently: middlemen between the

[5] Father Stevens, late of New College, Oxford, a Jesuit and the first Englishman to step in India (his letters to his father, a London merchant, were much read by the promoters of the English East India Company), who went out with the "Portugales" in 1579, said that there was "not a fowl that appeareth or sign in the air or in the sea that they have not written down." But not for publication.

Tagus and the north of Europe. Their merchant cities grew upon the Lisbon trade.

But then the Dutch quarrelled with Spain, desperately and long. When Philip became lord of Portugal as well as half the world, he closed Lisbon to the rebel Lowlanders: William of Orange was provoked to commission his *gueux de mer,* the beggars of the sea, as privateers. The Dutch merchants invented their own Companies of the Indies. The sons of the sea beggars sailed the merchants' ships. News of the Eastern routes came from van Linschoten, who had somehow got to be writer to the Bishop of Goa and came home to Holland with his knowledge; and from one Ralph Fitch, an Englishman,[6] who in 1583, as Shakespeare noticed, was to Aleppo gone with the master of the *Tiger.*

Fitch and three others of the Levant Company, with a jeweller and a painter, crossed from Aleppo to the Euphrates on camels and went by boat down to Hit and Bagdad, to Basra and Ormuz, where the Portuguese Governor promptly shipped them off in custody to the Viceroy at Goa, who "for our better entertainment," as Fitch says, put them into a "fair strong prison." The Jesuits, at the instance of Father Stevens, had them freed, and John Story the painter turned monk a while and then took himself off with a native lady. Fitch, Newberry and Leeds the jeweller escaped across the Deccan to Hyderabad and went to visit the Great Mogul, where the jeweller took service at Court and whence Newberry disappeared. Fitch wandered up and down India, passed into Burma and Siam and to Malacca, and returned with astonishing adventures across India and Persia once more, by Mosul, and ultimately from Tripolis to England "where, by God's assistance, I safely arrived the 29th April 1591, having been eight years out of my native country"!

[6] And, of course, from Drake and Cavendish.

His voyage had consequences. In the Court Minutes of the English East India Company appears for October 2, 1600: "Ordere'd that Capitein Lancaster (and others) together with Mr R. ffitch, shall in the meetinge tomorrow morning conferre of the merchandize to be provided for the voyage": the first voyage of John Company. So he came to more estate than most travellers and set stones rolling to gather such moss for England as the Empire of India and the Dominion of the Seas.

The English Company was founded in 1599. In 1594 Cornelis de Houtman, who had been two years spying out what he could in Lisbon, commanded the first fleet eastward for the merchants of Amsterdam. He returned in 1597, and in the next five years 65 Dutch ships reached Asia and 54 returned safely home. In 1599, the Houtmans went again, taking as pilot John Davys of Stoke Gabriel in the County of Devon: the Davys of Greenland and Baffin Island and the Northwest Passage, author of *The Seaman's Secrets* and *The World's Hydrographical Description,* who served with Raleigh at Cadiz and the Azores, and later as Pilot-Major of the *Malice Scourge* with Lancaster, and as pilot in 1604 of the *Tiger* (Shakespeare's and Fitch's *Tiger,* probably) on which he was killed by Japanese pirates off Singapore in 1604.

The second Houtman voyage was sponsored by Balthazar de Moucheron of Veere in the Island of Walcheren: a type of the men who launched the merchant empires. He traded with Russia (his brother Melchior went as his agent to the Dwina and founded the city of Archangel) and all about northwestern Europe. His brother Pierre was grandfather to Frederick de Moucheron, the painter. The great merchants were men of culture and imagination. Their domestic architecture was the best in Europe: their patronage employed the Flemish artists. If the Dutch schools now became more concerned with domestic interiors, bricked walks, drinking parties and an overwhelming succession of red-faced merchants and ladies broad of bust and bottom instead of with the fields of heaven, the choirs of angels, and the hierarchy of saints, there were still great painters because there were still men who knew painting when they saw it. But the mood was unquestionably changed. Their empire was to be an affair of the City, not of Saints; and shareholders play a larger part than martyrs.

By 1602 ten Dutch Companies in the Eastern trade sensibly decided to amalgamate. Their troubles were many: shipwreck, scurvy, pirates, privateers, princes and the problem of finding cargoes for trade. Europe had little that Asia wanted. Europe was at first the poor partner in their commerce. Competition was obviously undesirable, and the States-General of the Netherlands gave Charter for a monopoly to the new united Company, which took the very characteristic motto: *Therefore Plough the Seas,* and for its device a sailing ship. You may still see the coat on a wall by the river in Malacca.

The object was the Spice Islands. To reach the Spice Islands safe ports were needed. Safe ports meant both diplomacy and armed force. The States-General gave the Company the powers in the Orient of a Sovereign State. The Company, not the nation, made treaties, raised troops, fought battles, acquired territories, appointed Governor-Generals. Dutch and English expansion eastward took much the same pattern, and while the Companies flourished, the Governments at home intervened little.

In 1605 the Dutch started their career of conquest by driving the Portuguese out of Ambon. The first Governor-General, Both, came in 1609 and brought clergymen, tradesmen and thirty or more women, for a colony. But Jan Pieterszoon Coen, already Director of the first factory, at Bantam, actually founded the Dutch dominion. Irritated by English competition at Bantam, he formed a second post at Jacatra along the coast, and in 1617 made it his chief factory, naming it for an old tribe of the Low Countries once bothersome to Julius Caesar: the Batavi. In 1619, with the politic aid of Bantam and with ships from the Moluccas, he ousted the English factors who had followed him to Jacatra. "Do not despair," he had written home to the Seventeen Heeren, in phrases that the Dutch remember now again, "nor be troubled for your enemies . . . something great can be done in India." His portrait is in the Museum at Batavia: a long face with drawn nose and cold, far-looking eyes above the starched ruff and the velvet.

EMPIRE IN THE EASTERN SEAS

In his Indies the Dutch had three times the English strength of ships; and in 1623, at Ambon they arrested English traders and executed ten, with their Japanese servants. The English Company, already involved in India proper, decided that the Spice Islands were not worth their trouble and gradually withdrew. The memory of Ambon was a remote cause of later English difficulties with the Dutch but at the moment it was a decisive stroke. Portugal, with too few people, was already defeated in the East and, as English energies turned to India, Holland had her way east of Sumatra. In 1638 she reached out to Ceylon, in 1641 wrested Malacca and command of its Straits from Portugal, in 1652 occupied Good Hope. Her stations thus ringed the Eastern seas. In 1669 the Company paid 40 per cent on its capital of 6,500,000 florins, maintained 150 trading ships, 40 ships of war, 10,000 soldiers, and the eight Governments of Ambon, Ternate, Java, Banda, Macassar, Malacca, Ceylon and Good Hope. The brains and digestive tract of the Empire were the Netherlands, but the Indies pumped its blood. They still do. Batavia's new port of Tandjong Priok normally docks 3000 steamers a year.

Coen's settlement gave command of Java from Batavia to Cheribon and across the island. The Dutch held in check the Sultan of Bantam to their west and the Susuhunan of Mataram to the east, by playing one against the other. In 1680 Bantam rose against them and was crushed. By repeated strokes of policy, Mataram was whittled away until its central territory was split between its Susuhunan at Soerakarta and a new Sultan promoted from his household at Jogjakarta.

The princes kept some independence but as subordinate allies of the Company. They governed, but the Company also governed through them and through native Regents, beside whom now appeared Dutch Residents and Controleurs. The method survives in the Indies. The small Dutch Service works with and through large Native Services. The device was ingenious and wise. It avoided sharp dislocations in the continuity of authority and muffled the shock of change. It preserved to complaisant rulers their dignities, to the people their traditional centres of loyalty and obedience. It made for stability.

So the Merchants became powers behind thrones, though profits remained their end and politics a means. But dominion changed the character of the Company; and when the spice trade and perhaps energies flagged, it sought its profits in what amounted to tribute from the native rulers and their peoples. Its officers encouraged crops useful to the Company's commerce, and presently began to enforce cultivation. Native princes were bound by treaty to deliver at market rates so much pepper, rice, cotton yarn, indigo: native peasants were compelled to grow them. The territories under Dutch control became a vast plantation with sugar, tea, camphor, coffee [7] rising in the bulk of ladings.

But prices fell as commerce developed and competition increased. Officials were badly paid and expected to make their fortunes on the side by extortion and squeeze. The traffic had to carry far more than it could bear in the long passage to the European markets. Illicit trade weakened the monopoly. Administration was poor and finances were confused. The Company was already near bankruptcy when the French Revolution descended upon Holland in 1795. General Dumouriez marched in with the Dutch Jacobite Daendels and a Batavian Legion in his train. (Fifth Columns are no new inventions.) The Stadhouder fled to England, the customary refuge. The States-General were upset, and the new Batavian Republic set up. On January 1, 1800, the Republic dissolved the Company, assumed its dominions, properties, and debts of 134,700,000 florins.

But in 1806 the Revolution went the way of most revolutions, and the Man on Horseback lent his brother Louis a Dutch saddle and crown. In 1808 Daendels arrived at Batavia as the Bonapartes' Governor-General. He was already known in the Napoleonic Armies as the Thundering Marshal. He proceeded to gild his own thorny thistle. But he properly belongs to Weltevreden at the other end of town.

[7] The Dutch first met coffee at Mocha, a bean which the natives "used to make black water which they drink warm": Klerk de Reus, quoted by J. S. Furnivall in his admirable *Netherlands India: a Study of Plural Economy*. Cambridge University Press, 1939.

DECLINE AND . . . ?

The Old Town is filled with memories and omens. There is the Portuguese Church, a curious mixture of Calvinist dankness, bare walls and austerity with Oriental or perhaps Catholic magnificence in the red and gold of pulpit and lectern. I have always felt vaguely uncomfortable in a church where more is made of the pulpit than of the altar-table; and so must many of its first parishioners, proselytized. Most were Portuguese-speaking natives and half-castes recruited for the Dutch service. In the seventeenth century a third of the Dutch chaplains here preached in Portuguese. It, before Malay, was the *lingua franca* of the Orient.

The Portuguese found the moral justification of Empire in the spread of the Christian gospel: the charge to the Church was to teach all nations, and they were part of the Church. When Portugal spread its religion it was sharing its intellectual and spiritual life with its subject peoples and consequently developing a measure of common understanding. The Dutch refused their culture to the natives, who were, until recently, discouraged from learning Dutch (one reason why you see many "English" schools, chiefly used by the commercially minded Chinese). Dutch civilization was to remain the mystery of the masters; which suggests a servile State but not a régime which seeks, as is now the case, collaboration.

Where Portugal christened the Indonesian, Christianity often stuck. The Dutch have practical benefits from Portuguese conversions in the Christian police and soldiers they recruit from Ambon and Ternate. But the Calvinists came to the Indies from the shadow of Alva, and seared by his fire and steel. They were more concerned to uproot the seedlings of Rome than to tackle the wildwood of Islam. Protestant ardour combined with shrewd

commercial sense; for doctrinal controversies might have
interfered with trade. The Susuhunan, Emperor of Java,
was a spiritual as well as a temporal power, and throughout the East the spiritual power is more formidable than
the merely political. So, while the Dutch slowly absorbed
the Susuhunan's temporals, they discreetly left his spiritual
reign unchallenged.

The times have changed. Christian missions in the Indies are very active, especially since the Protestant-Catholic
Coalitions at home. The majority of 500 hospitals and of
51 leper stations are conducted by missions, and they have
(Catholics especially) many schools; which make most
ground, curiously, in the Javan Native States, the centre
of the native tradition.[8]

The missions carry the moral and intellectual as well
as the religious values of the West to the natives. If white
and brown are to keep peace together, they must meet in
the province of ideas and values as well as over pickled
pork and rubber goods. Guns, cars, egg beaters, vaccines
and hard cash will not hold a respect which the Eastern
man reserves for mind, morals, and manners.

The handfuls of men who shaped and sustained the
European régimes in the East had qualities of moral and
intellectual courage, what the natives called the European
"strength," derived from a powerful and coherent culture.
The natives respected that. And as long as the European
believes in himself and his civilization, there is respect.
But now European dominion is threatened less by arms,
aircraft, and Japanese shipyards than by Asia's growing
suspicion that we become empty inside and blind mouths.

The Asiatic is still concerned for ideas, and the man
engrossed in material things is to him contemptible. The
European may have forgotten his God; but what remains

[8] Raffles may have been right when he thought that Catholi-
cism but not the austerer Calvinists could have won the Indies.

in us of mind, morals and manners has an essentially Christian bias. Mr. Wells, Mr. Shaw and Mr. Laski have not provided a satisfactory substitute. The Christian missions thus have a peculiar importance. Their place in international and interracial accord is illustrated by American-Chinese relations.

When the Dutch took Malacca, one said to a Portugal captain, mocking him: "When will you return to govern here again?" The Portuguese answered, "When your sins are greater than ours." The Asiatic would still understand that man. But would his own people?

NATIONALISM

If cultural divisions deepen, new political conflicts will follow; and the Asiatic becomes a politician. Islam is moving once more, and eighty-five of a hundred Javanese are Moslems with, for all their mildness, a fierce pride in the brotherhood. Religious and cultural influences promote Eastern nationalism. Nationalist movements brought Java near to revolution in the 1920s. The major organization was Sarikat Islam, a religio-socio-political movement of native workers. In 1918, it threatened to set up its own government. It became less violent as its Communists peeled away, but their dissident Red Sarikat Islam plunged into bloody riots in 1926, when there was a battle for the Telegraph Office down the street here.[9]

Nationalism has been also promoted, of course, by Eu-

[9] Near by the Portuguese Church is a reminder of an earlier nationalist, where a plastered-over skull transfixed by a spear surmounts a wall and plaque: *To perpetuate the cursed memory of the convicted traitor Pieter Elberfeld no one shall raise on this place house building or structure or plant any growing thing now or forever Batavia the 14th April, A 1722.* Elberfeld was a half-caste with notions, which did not work out, of making himself Tuan Gusti, High Lord of an independent Java.

ropean ideas and example; by the new sense of unity which has followed from the political organization imposed by Europeans themselves; and by the decline of European prestige.

The Russo-Japanese War contributed less to the decline than the fratricidal strife of Europe since. A civilization tearing itself to pieces is not commended to the intelligent observer. Again, Orientals of influence began to suffer our education when it had already lost its bearings. I know many Easterns educated in our schools, but few who will admit that our education is now more than a training in skills, without spiritual content or moral direction.

Old Hands argue that the influx of European women has helped to wreck what was perhaps a legend. But women commonly share the values of their men. The cinema, Communist propaganda, and tourists in search of honky-tonks have all contributed, but these are secondary causes.

Fortunately, native aspirations have the sympathy of the patient, conscientious, intelligent men who mostly staff the Eastern Civil Services, British and Dutch. Long aware that the old, unqualified supremacy must pass into a new order, they have worked for a peaceful passage, for old lion to lie down with lamb grown large. Within their range the Civil Servants of Malaya and the Netherlands Indies are still necessary to the orderly and peaceful progress of the peoples.

With the Indonesians, nationalism has a religious context. (The creed and culture of Islam is, in fact, the one considerable bond that the native peoples of the widespread Archipelago recognize.) It usually takes a separatist bent with "blijvers," the Europeans and Indo-Europeans locally born. They see autonomy as a route to domestic reform. Europeans settling permanently in the country, as many now do, and seeking education and opportunity

for their children want more political responsibility. Local
capital, for the most part, wants local autonomy. The balance and combination of these interests may well produce
something like "dominion status" for the Indies. The
process now is speeded by the enforced silence of the Netherlands Parliament and the war effort of the Indies themselves.

The situation resembles British India's, and native
movements are influenced by the Indian Congress. But
here a large European and Indo-European population and
a powerful Chinese interest are concerned. There are in
the Indies about 250,000 people of European status,
which embraces Japanese, Filipinos, Armenians, and Indonesians with some European blood, for the Dutch seek
to assimilate the Indo-European to what is usually his
father's people; and "European" is a legal rather than an
ethnic term. The European status of the 7000 Japanese
has long been a nettle in the flesh of the Chinese.

GENTLEMEN OF JAPAN

The Japanese were augmented in September, 1940, when
their Economic Mission arrived to talk to Mr. van Mook,
whose Bureau of Economic Affairs (on the right as you
return up Molenvliet) became the scene of the greatest
tussle for face between European and Asiatic since the
Russo-Japanese War. Mr. van Mook has a large and benev-
olent bearing; and, even to a Japanese skilled in the exercise, it must have seemed that he smiled and smiled and
smiled.

His career suggests the sort of Dutchmen now in high
places, eastward. He was born in Java in 1894, of peasant,
soldier, and school-teaching stock; began his education
there and went on to the University of Leiden. Most
Civil Servants for the Indies are educated at the schools of

Leiden or Utrecht. Van Mook had had five years in Java
with the Bureau of Agrarian Reform before returning to
Leiden for three years to study Indonesian Law and Custom.[10] The Dutch emphasize academic training as well as
field work and have notable benefits from it. Their civil
officers have a broad general culture. They know their
jobs, but they also know the human scene: which is perhaps part of the business of knowing such jobs as theirs.

Early in 1940 the Japanese suggested a review of their
economic relations with the Indies. These were already
considerable. Japan's exports to the Indies trebled between
1929 and 1934, and by 1939 were second only to Holland's.
The Japanese South Sea Development Company had lately
acquired 147,000 acres for cotton in Dutch New Guinea.
Japanese there were growing Indian corn, vegetables,
cattle. They had extensive shipping services. Japanese oil
interests missed a concession of 25,000,000 acres in 1934,
when Standard and Shell took a deep breath and dived
first. Japan was not amused. But she went heavily into
Borneo rubber and tin, and into propaganda.

She was frank enough. On January 5, 1939, Prince
Konoye declared that she had "the important task of eman-
cipating the Far Eastern States from the chains which it
was their misfortune to acquire before Japan had come to
play an important rôle in this part of the world." The
Navy encouraged Japan's economic march southward, and
talked of a cruising radius for the battle fleet to Borneo
and New Guinea. No illusions were present on September
12, 1940, when Mr. Kobayashi arrived at Batavia to talk

[10] Van Mook came back to administrative work until, in
1931, he was appointed to the Volksraad. He edited the economic monthly *Koloniale Studien*. Many people will remember him at the conference of the Institute of Pacific Relations
at Yosemite in 1936. In 1937, he became Director of Economic
Affairs, a Cabinet post. In 1940, he received the Japanese.

trade. He was accompanied by Army and Navy officers, who, he politely explained, were experts on supply. So Mr. van Mook turned out a guard for the guests. Dutchmen often are high, wide, but unhandsome if you are sensitive on the point of size. The Japanese delegation seemed rather lost in the tall timber.

Mr. Kobayashi and his officers were shown enough of local defence measures. Mr. Kobayashi had curiously little to say, and seemed rather ill prepared for talks on trade. But Mr. van Mook was emphatic that trade was his only subject. Politics . . . pouf! Commerce was Mr. van Mook's line. Oil? Well, oil perhaps was better left to oil people: a matter say for Mr. Mukai of the Mitsui Bussan Kaisha and for Bataafsche Petroleum Maatschappij (which, quietly, is Shell), and Nederlandsche Koloniale Petroleum (which happens to be Standard). Mr. Kobayashi probably knew that Standard and Shell deal in oil, and were always ready to consider custom. Unfortunately their commitments were rather heavy, but perhaps something could be done if Mr. Mukai would enquire.

The entertainment provided at Batavia was admirable. But Mr. Kobayashi, having said several times over all what he had to say, was presently needed at home to celebrate the 2,600th Anniversary of the foundation of the Empire. He shortly afterwards ceased to be Minister for Trade and Industry. Some of his officers remained at Batavia and saw a good deal of the countryside in very long week ends.

Holland is a small country with some grasping neighbours, and lives largely by its wits. On the whole, it normally lives better than anyone else in Europe. Diplomacy, as Japan was learning, is not a matter only of big sticks. But by December things looked black for Holland's friends. Japan had been tied into the Tripartite Pact: Mr. Matsuoka entered on his whirlwind career as Foreign Minister. The Dutch by now were surely more amenable. Mr.

Yoshizawa came to find out. He arrived in time for the
Christmas holidays and had leisure to admire the views. By
January 29, however, he was delivered of notions somewhat more developed than Mr. Kobayashi's. Japan wanted
to increase trade, and to share in the development of Indonesia. Mr. Yoshizawa suggested mines, Japanese colonists, artisans, farmers, doctors, dentists; some items of
fishing concessions; Japanese surveys of the lands between
Java, the Celebes, New Guinea and Australia; a development of Japanese air services. In brief, Japan proposed to
share the white man's burden in these difficult parts.

Mr. Matsuoka discovered that the world had changed
since the remote times of his predecessor, Mr. Arita. He
shook his head over it, but the *status quo* in the East Indies
belonged now to history, along with Magna Charta and the
Mings. "The change is so sudden that Japan has no intention of impeding it": a sentence which grows fondly upon
one the more one returns to it. Japan's heart was set upon
the Indies sharing in her Co-Prosperity Sphere, and if the
Indies did not care to co-prosper Japan must act firmly
for their good. The Dutchmen's response was terse and
blunt, their defences being now in strong shape. Their
Ambassador spoke in Tokyo: ". . . The Netherlands Government rejects any and every suggestion for the inclusion
of her territory in a New Order in East Asia under the
leadership of any Power whatsoever. Moreover, the Netherlands Government has no intention either by deed or
acquiescence, of contributing to the establishment of such
a New Order."

Batavia, putting a polish on the affair, announced that
with its basic position thus clarified, it was ready to renew
the economic chat. Mr. Yoshizawa feared that it set too
many obstacles in his way, regretted that Mr. Matsuoka
had been misunderstood. So hard, so hard not to be understood when you use words. He presented his final memo-

randum on May 14, and if it was not an ultimatum, it was what you might consider the opening remarks, preamble and prelude.

Mr. van Mook, the Governor-General, and Mr. Welter and Dr. van Kleffens, the Netherlands Ministers for the Colonies and for Foreign Affairs, then on a visit from London, studied it carefully until Japan was hopping with impatience. Their reply reached Tokyo on June 6. It repeated the Dutch case, a skilfully chosen one: that raw materials supplied by the Indies to Japan must not go to Germany, that the Indies were committed to priorities for Britain and America, and that the Japanese purchases of the last five years were a reasonable basis for further business. The Japanese had, they were reminded, obtained some additional oil supplies, though unfortunately all the high-octane plants in the Indies were already occupied with contracts for the Indies and her allies. The Indies could not make extraordinary concessions to Japan.

Tokyo went into its usual flutter of conferences. The newspapers roundly ground their teeth. Then Germany marched on Russia; and I trust that Mr. van Mook took a week end at his bungalow in the mountains, where he has neither radio nor telephone, and can play mashie shots, if he pleases, across the thin volcanic crusts.

END OF ROUND ONE

The affair is particularly interesting because it was the first considerable diplomatic check to the Tripartite Pact, and Japan's first major experience as a member. It illustrates the uses of diplomacy when your man is shrewd and tough. Holland, like France, was in enemy occupation. But the Dutchmen of the Indies cut quite another figure than the French in Indo-China. The Indo-China business might have been a fatal blow to white prestige in all the

Orient; but Japan will need large successes to counter Mr.
van Mook's effect.

Americans may not care to recognize it but a battle was
fought and won for the United States in van Mook's office
on the Koningsplein. American war industries would have
been sick in 1941 without the Indies' rubber and tungsten.
If the Indies had yielded, China and Malaya, India and the
whole world to Suez might have soon been shut to American traffic, and wheels presently have slowed and stopped
from San Diego to Maine. The raw materials of the Indies
are indispensable to America's war machines. I am sorry to
labour the point, but it sometimes seems to need a hammer.

The Japanese Mission used to sit about the Hôtel des
Indes during hot March politely sipping long drinks and
even risking rijsttafel. Perhaps they remembered William
Adams, the English Master Pilot of the first Dutch ship to
reach Japan, in 1600, who became master builder to the
Yedo Government, and an architect of Japanese sea power.
They must have remembered, in the Hôtel des Indes, an
earlier mission that once stayed here. In 1855, just after
Commodore Perry invoked the Open Door, the Dutch
presented to the Shogun a naval vessel called the *Kwan
Koo Maru*. She has had progeny. The Japanese Navy's
second steamship was built at Dordrecht in the Netherlands, "a war-steamer fully armed according to the latest
inventions," as the Japanese prescribed.

In 1862 nine Japanese officers arrived in Batavia en
route to Dordrecht. They stayed at the des Indes, and
"they were very willing to learn and paid many visits to
the Batavian bookshops." In Holland they studied naval
architecture, marine engineering, tactics, politics, all to
some purpose. The members of Mr. Yoshizawa's mission
also frequented the Batavian bookshops. But they no
longer needed to consult Dutch naval architects.

The 1862 mission had been a major turning-point in history. We all thought in Batavia that Mr. Yoshizawa's mission was another. I am sure that Mr. van Mook did. He knows his history and he does not seem to miss his turning-points.

Though apparently we have, downtown at the Portuguese Church.

NATIVE TOWN

I recommend a roundabout for the homeward trek, by the native kampongs which surround the town. Under the palms are rows of huts woven from fibres of bamboo and thatched, with fires flickering in the dusk by doors and roads. Beside the waterways are crowded high-pitched Chinese houses; street markets, crowded stalls, the smell of goats and honeysuckle, of frying food, and of stale sea-things drying on the banks. Fruit vendors go with piled baskets of mangosteens and mangoes, ramboetans (red and resembling a vegetable porcupine, but tasting like grapes crossed with sweet oranges), doekoes (dingy outside, in flavour reminiscent of a persimmon), and mildly rotten bananas. Coolies carry on their shoulder-poles (pikulans) huge loads of grass and hay for the deeleemen's jingle-belled ponies, or bundles of washing, or somebody's furniture. Chinese women sit quietly in the doors of shops, Chinese children play on the bolts of cloth. Drifting boat-men wear cone-shaped palm-leaf hats and ragged breech clouts, brown babies run naked, a contemplative gentleman smokes his long pipe in a doorway, his friends squirt betel juice.

Most of the Indonesians here are Soendanese or Batavian Malay. The Soendanese have their own language, but the Chinese, the Indian storekeepers, and the local mixture called Malay use the local mixture called Malay.

In Batavia East meets West in easy conjunction. The

Dutch canals become the baths and washtubs of the Oriental. The European's gun becomes a wishing place for childless women. The streets of modern Dutch architecture enter into the crowded Chinese markets. The Chinese merchant lives in bungalows with the doors flung wide so that all may admire his large floral lampshades. A saronged Indonesian mother dresses her child in European frocks from the sweatshops of Hongkong. Dutch soldiers wear bamboo hats, and Indonesian soldiers wear Dutch uniforms. Doves settle at dusk on the crocodile cages, feminine heads are uncovered in Roman churches, and ugly pulpits faced with cement appear in mosques. You stroll in a few minutes from wide parks and streets of cool houses behind trees to the Pasar [11] Senen, with its narrow streets and alleys of jammed shops and stalls, cooking stoves, eating tables, piled rice, maize, and fried cassava roots, sweet potatoes, onions, peanuts, soya beans, oranges, apples, melons, bananas, coconuts, dried fish, hens' eggs and green ducks' eggs, kerbao meat, chicken livers and bêche-de-mer, bolts of Manchester goods, and Shantung silk at 50¢ a metre, slippers, sandals, toothpaste, hairbrushes, and gentlemen's underwear, cellophane dolls, rattles, bicycle parts, carnations packed tightly in little bowls, Japanese hairnets, Japanese coiffeurs (but few Japanese acrobats or prostitutes since Japan grew great in the world). Babies (it is impossible not to mention them again, for they spill out everywhere), spread in the shops, on the counters, amongst the canned goods, in the gutter; all the combinations and permutations of babies from a hundred races: babies black as ink and brown as bears and yellow as old ivory and babies flaxen-haired and blue-eyed.

On Saturday afternoons youth groups stride through the town much as if they were wandervogeling across a Tirolean Alp. Legs range from large, mottled-pink and Dutch

[11] *Pasar:* market. Compare *Bazaar.*

to saffron, lean and supple, for in the Youth Movements we are very earnest about collaboration. There is a new world coming and it is doing at least four miles an hour on Molenvliet in the heat of the sun. It cleaves the loiterers like a driving phalanx.

DAENDELS AND RAFFLES

Some Sunday mornings you may hear superlative game-lan in the Museum (the Museum's Director, Dr. Van der Hoop, was the first airman to fly from Holland to the Indies): every Sunday afternoon you may see a soccer game, ten or a dozen soccer games, across the wide open spaces of the Koeningsplein. The Malayans take to games with gusto.[12] I recommend the Museum, where the human strata are in neat arrangements, from Java Man who did not know himself as *Pithecanthropus erectus*. You can contrast the earlier and chaste with the later and florid Hinduism, and contemplate the influence of burial customs on the development of trade: spices for embalming, linen for binding, small pots for ashes, Chinese jars for Celebean bones.

There are excellent ethnic, language, migration, and cultural maps for the attention of anyone seriously interested in the Archipelago; furniture of the seventeenth and eighteenth centuries, bookcases from the old law courts here and pieces from Coen's Castle of Batavia. One room has been brought whole from an early merchant's house, with a huge four-poster behind whose heavy curtains the heroic Dutchman and his wife once slept even in this cli-

[12] Rugby Union outdoes soccer in British Malaya, because, I suppose, R.U. is much more a public-school game than soccer, and British Malaya has the advantages of public-school connections. But soccer has spread until Australia plays China at it.

mate: and at its foot is the proper fruit of four-posters, a charming Dutch cradle.

The Koningsplein is the centre of Daendels' and Raffles' town of Weltevreden. Daendels moved his offices out here, where the land is higher and has sometimes a sea breeze. Raffles, with the sharp English nose for air (a proper English nose distinguishes the air of Brighton from the air of Hastings), continued his development. For Napoleon's general was followed by the English. Napoleon could blockade the English from the Continent, but they blockaded him from the world. Daendels and the English between them gave the Netherlands Indies a new start.

Daendels, like most of Napoleon's generals, was a strong-arm man. He used forced labour to restore the tottering economy, arrested or expelled scores of the old comfortable officials, and carried on in such absolutist fashion that Napoleon superseded him, and his successor could say that all the Indies yearned for the arrival of the English "not from any detestable Anglomania but to escape a terror that desolated all the world."[13] The English obligingly came in August, 1811: Lord Minto, the Governor-General of India with seven thousand of the Honorable East India Company's troops under General Auchtermuty (the Scots were always forward in John Company's service). Daendels' successor resisted and there was a brisk action here at Weltevreden. The French flag came down and the Union Jack went up. Thomas Stamford Raffles, thirty years of age and lately the English Company's secretary at Penang, became the local Governor. Old Jan Pieterszoon Coen's skeleton surely turned in its lost Batavian grave: and perhaps there was a rattle or two from distant Ambon.

Raffles was born in his father's brig at sea off Jamaica. His earliest ambition was to provide for his parents, a virtue since outmoded, and he went to work in his thirteenth

[13] Janssens, quoted by Furnivall, *Netherlands India*.

year as a sort of office boy at the East India Company's Offices in Leadenhall St. At eighteen he had given himself a candlelight education, strained his health, and was earning £100 a year. At twenty-four he was in Penang, married, and with £1500 a year. At twenty-six he knew Malay, wrote the Arabic script, was read in the native literature and in the native mind and heart, had made himself a geographer, a zoologist, a botanist, and could still work eighteen hours a day where two Governors, all the members of the local Council and most of the settlers had died of fever within a few years.

In 1808 Raffles went to Malacca. Malacca had been taken from the Dutch in 1795, when Napoleon was preparing his Army of the East for the advance on Egypt and India: the Army of the East which he called, being a man of large ideas and sounding phrases, a wing of the Army of England. The English then hurriedly collected Good Hope, Ceylon, and several points east as a precaution and at the invitation of William the Stadhouder and his refugee administration in London. Raffles, convalescent from a sickness, wrote at Malacca a *History of the Malays,* and a powerful report against the English Company's intention to demilitarize and abandon the town. He already saw that the key of the Orient was in the Malaccan Straits. A dozen years later his argument was to carry him to Singapore. Now it kept Malacca for the English and recommended him to the notice of his superiors. Lord Minto invited him to India; and to Lord Minto, Raffles suggested the interesting subject of Java. Minto had already considered it. A Governor-General of India could not be wholly oblivious to Napoleon and his Daendels. In 1810 Raffles was back at Malacca, preparing the way for General Auchtermuty; and a year later he was ruling at Batavia. His was one battle not won upon the playing fields of Eton.

Raffles did an extraordinary job in Java, though he had

more kicks than pence for it. He started with much in his
favour that a Dutchman would have lacked. England now
bought the colonies' produce, which she had previously
blockaded. An Englishman could cut knots of local tradition and privilege that a Dutchman must needs respect,
and build on the very real reforms of Daendels, which Raffles warmly acknowledged. But Raffles' merits contributed
more than any circumstances. He had the three great virtues of governors, seldom united: a lively sympathy with
human beings, the material of government; a passion for
information and the power to organize it as knowledge;
and a profound belief in and sense of order. To these he
added a fourth quality virtuous in their company: energy.

His range was startling. He collected butterflies, talked
to villagers in their mother tongues, wrote books, promoted sanitation, revised the laws and freed the slaves. He
established a new *modus vivendi* with the native princes
and to the peasants he "spoke in smiles." [14] He astonished
the countrysides and his officers by travelling at the unprecedented rate of twelve miles an hour, leaving many
gentlemen prostrate behind him: and as his horses gal-
loped, he composed his *History of Java*. He managed his
Sepoys and Englishmen so that Lord Minto wondered that
they "did not even kiss an old woman without her consent." Raffles made friends of the Dutch: the members of
the late Dutch Council "got most jovially tipsy at my
house in company with the new Councillors." [15] Dutch
officials served him. His economic, land, and administrative reforms produced their results only after he was recalled by an aggrieved and penny-wise authority at home,
but they had been deeply meditated and planned in a

[14] His secretary Abdulla bin Abdulkadar in the entertaining
biography which overflowed from him when Raffles was gone.
[15] Raffles to Minto in January 1812: quoted by R. Coupland
in *Raffles*, Oxford University Press, 1926.

personal investigation which had taken him from peasants' huts to the records of Mataram and Madjapahit.

Raffles had a vision of a great insular empire reaching north to Japan, east into the Pacific, south to the Australasian seas and centred in a majestic capital at Batavia: an empire of Insulinde uniting the best of native life with the best Europe had to give; a new reign of peace for the peoples that he loved, his own and those he served.

But in 1816, when he was gone, Britain restored the East Indies to the Dutch and the political unity his ambition had required was broken.

DUTCH RESTORATION

The Dutch accepted much of his work; and his influence persisted in both British and Dutch colonial administration. He put the good of the native as the prime end of colonial authority: and with him emerges the principle of responsibility and trusteeship. Slow to make way everywhere, it is now a major motive in the colonial services of Britain and of Holland. But the first years of Dutch restoration were reactionary, as those years were in Europe where the Holy Alliance and Metternich had reduced, they trusted, the revolutionary tiger to a hearthrug. Holland was almost penniless after the long wars, and to make good her losses the Government of the Indies returned to the "forced culture" system of crops profitable for trade. The natives were required to use two-fifths of their lands for prescribed crops or, if landless, to work one-fifth of their time for the Government. While the system lasted, until 1877, it produced 832,000,000 florins for the Dutch Treasury. More than half went to reduce the public debt and for public works and railways at home. The wages paid the natives and the time left for the cultivation of their own crops were utterly insufficient; and corruption

attached to the system, as one might expect.[16] It gave, however, an impetus to the tea, sugar, coffee, indigo, and tobacco industries.

The Dutch conscience was wakened by a novel from an
ex-official of the system, Dekker. This was the period also
of *Uncle Tom's Cabin* (novelists sometimes have their
effect in the world) and *Max Havelaar* produced a similar
public excitement. It won popular sympathies for the
"Ethical School" just born to Dutch politics. The first
consequences were a drastic reform of administration.
Indies' surpluses were reserved for the Indies. The Ethical
School became a party and in 1901 a Government, Kuy-
per's Coalition of the Anti-Revolutionary Party and the
Christian Historical Union. Its colonial policy was announced from the Throne: "As a Christian Power, the
Netherlands is obliged in East India to order better the
legal status of native Christians, to support firmly Christian missions, and to inform all the conduct of government with the knowledge that the Netherlands has a
moral obligation to the peoples of these regions." Wel-
fare investigations were launched. Loans owing by the
Indies were written off on the understanding that equivalent amounts should go to the economic betterment of the
people.

CONTROL AND DECENTRALIZATION

There have been two major administrative developments in the twentieth century: the pacification and organ-

[16] The Dutch have been much abused for the forced-culture
system, justly enough. But the actual annual profit was roughly
that which the United States had from Hawaii during the first
thirty years of occupation, when Washington spent $30,000,000
in the Territory and received in taxes about $171,000,000. See
Hawaii and its Race Problem, by William A. du Puy, U. S.
Government Printing Office, Washington, 1932.

ization of the Outer Provinces, and the increased decentralization of powers.

Until 1900 little was done to develop or police large areas of Borneo, Sumatra, the Celebes, and the outer islands generally. For instance, a jungle war with the Achinese of northern Sumatra dragged on through generations; and elsewhere the Dutch were content with their coastal towns and plantations. Under General van Heutsz, first as Commander-in-Chief and then as Governor-General (1904-'09), effective rule was established in the whole Archipelago. The Dutch were spurred by the rising ambitions of Japan. Uncontrolled and undeveloped territories were too large a temptation to leave about.

The extension of order coincided with a progressive decentralization. [17] In 1912 the Indies administration, finances, budget were separated at last from the Dutch. In 1922 a new Constitution created the Kingdom of the Netherlands comprising the Netherlands, Netherlands India, Surinam and Curaçao, with each part in large measure locally autonomous. The Governor-General is responsible for the administration, and, with the Volksraad, for legislation, subject to certain powers of veto, general control and supervision reserved to the Crown (and the Crown's Ministry) of the Netherlands, which appoints the Governor-General and several of his highest officials.

The Administration is represented throughout the Indies by Residents, Assistant Residents, and Controleurs. In some areas they govern directly. In others, as in Java, they act in concert with the Native Regents. The Regen-

---

[17] The rigid bureaucracy of Daendels had been continued through the nineteenth century, with both Dutch Residents and Native Regents as officers of the Indies Government, itself a department immediately subordinate to the Crown and (after 1848) to the Parliament of the Netherlands through its Ministry for the Colonies.

cies necessarily are still somewhat feudal in character (feudalism, after all, was one of the most stable and satisfactory forms of government ever evolved) but developing, much as Europe developed, organs of local responsibility: Regency, Regional and Urban Councils, with their own funds and spheres of administration. Java itself is now also divided into three principal provinces, and provincial organization is proposed for other parts of the Indies as political education progresses. A province has its own Governor and his Ministry elected from the Provincial Council, itself part elected, part nominated, with racial representation.

The general principle is to leave the Indonesians as much as possible under their own leaders. In Java, long occupied, only about seven per cent of the country remains to four Native States, but Native Regencies cover the island at large. In the Outer Provinces, more than half is preserved to 278 Native States. The new policies recognize the native juridical communities, institutions, customary law, and traditions as the frame of social order.

The constitutional problem now is whether the Indies will develop into a group of federated States or whether the decentralizing tendencies should be subdued in a unitary system. The Dutch would mostly prefer that the various regions and peoples should first develop their own governmental structures: local parliaments providing the political education necessary to a federal congress, which would in time follow. But the structure of Central Government is very strong. The Javanese nationalists wish to keep it so, for they would then, with popular government, be supreme in the Indies because of Java's preponderance of population. But the proud peoples of Sumatra, Borneo, Bali and the rest will be slow to accept a system subordinating them to the Javanese.

THE FUTURE

The Central Government is deeply involved in the economic life of the country and its tentacles will be difficult to untangle if its functions are reduced. It is a large entrepreneur, partly because it took over the old properties of the East India Company, partly because the Dutch have favoured State enterprises. It owns and operates railways, harbours, tramways, buses, mines, teak forests, cinchona, tea, and rubber plantations, and has something left of the old monopolistic character of the Company. Private enterprise was little encouraged in the Indies until about 1870, and Government still controls salt for fiscal purposes and opium because opium is not wisely left to private trade. It has its pawnshops to protect the natives from gross usury, its rural banks, and so on. Private enterprise, from the old-time administrators' viewpoint, is useful chiefly as a tax provider. It contributes about 40 per cent of public revenues, the population at large about 40 per cent, and the rest comes from State-owned industries. The economic power of the Central Government is thus a formidable factor in the evolution of the whole social economy.

So are the Civil Services, which have something like 18,000 European and Eurasian, nearly 90,000 Indonesian officers. The effective administration of the country is largely in their hands and their influence on its history will be great.

The central power rests with the Governor-General, his General Secretariat, his Council of the Indies and the partly nominated and partly elected Volksraad.[18] The Gov-

[18] The Volksraad has 60 members, 38 elected. The natives elect 20 and have 10 nominated members, the Dutch 15 and 10, other Asiatics 3 and 2. The assent of the Volksraad is required for the Budget and normal legislation; but the Governor-General and the Department Heads are not responsible to it for their acts.

ernor-General's functions are actually discharged more
and more by the General Secretariat. The G.-G. leads in
considerable state an ivory-tower sort of existence, a concession in large part to the Oriental wish to have the supreme ruler live somewhat hidden from the public; but
the crisis of 1940-'41 has thrown tremendous responsibilities back upon him.

Problems of political development in the Indies are
quite other than in a more homogeneous population at
approximately one general level of education and development. The suzerain must consider that some of the races
for which it has become responsible are barely emerging
from savagery or serfdom; that some belong still to the
primitive food-gathering levels of culture; that some were
yesterday cannibals and given to dark devilries that still
haunt their minds; that the conventions of Western democracy are as alien to their traditions and habits as the
life of the Esquimaux is to Tooting Bec or Brooklyn
Heights. In the depths of the jungles are strange, hidden
peoples who live eternally in a green shade where the deer
and the wild pig do not go for fear; far from the ballot
box. People talk glibly of European imperialism: but in
large areas of the Indies the retreat of the imperialists
would be followed immediately by fire and slaughter and
a renewal of the barbarous internecine wars that made
life poor and painful for countless generations. The Dutch
who know their job believe that its end is not in sight. The
best believe that in their Indies is the beginning of a new
relation between East and West of immeasurable value to
both. But the thing cannot be hurried; and those who
would hurry it do the masses little service. Time is not a
politician or a careerist, and you cannot design the course
of man from a blueprint.

CHAPTER THIRTEEN

More of Java

RIJSTTAFEL AND UP FOR AIR

WE LEFT Batavia after rijsttafel. It is an achievement to leave even the table after rijsttafel. The Hôtel des Indes, which overdoes the thing, in my opinion, uses a special squad of twenty-odd waiters to serve your rijsttafel: calculated, no doubt, to suggest the magnificence of the East. Rijsttafel was invented by the old merchants and should be eaten once in tribute to their heroism and as proof of your own. Its basic elements are a pile of rice, fried duck, fried chicken, eggs, sausages, various fish and meat balls, fried bananas, potatoes, vegetables, grated coconut, chutney, pickled cucumber, Bombay duck, and side dishes. Personally, I like the beer. The Dutch do amazing things on the combination. My last memory of the des Indes is of a hundred-odd Dutchmen singing old school songs after rijsttafel. The Dutch, of course, are a large people and mostly uncorseted in either gender. Before rijsttafel, Bols gin. Bols, beer and bed are the future, present and past of rijsttafel.

We dozed fitfully through the new suburbs and Meester Cornelis, where there was something of a housing boom. Since the Netherlands were invaded, people, upon retiring, have made their homes in the Indies; and there will be considerable economic effects from their capital remaining in the colonies. I was still worrying about Meester Cornelis. Opinion in the parish inclines to the view that he was a schoolteacher hereabouts. His little town is now a place of Chinese streets and old country houses where you begin to breathe the higher airs: where the streets are rather occupied by peasants walking in to market, perhaps from twenty or thirty miles away, with baskets and packs and bamboo hats. The walk to market is as cheerful an affair as a pilgrimage to Canterbury once was. As you go on between orange orchards and broad-spreading kapok trees, the country houses multiply, with white walls and columned porticoes under tiled roofs and set in deep gardens. Crotons come by the roadsides and on the road very small ponies and very large carts, painted and hooded.

Air-raid shelters were building in the villages. We had lately been exercised at Batavia in air raid precautions which here must be organized in racial and lingual divisions. Every public wall of the Indies was placarded for Prince Bernhard's Spitfire Fund. The communities of the Indies, apart from their own war effort and contributions by tax and loan, bought eighty fighters for the Royal Air Force by mid-1941. Early in the year a special fund was launched to provide a flight of bombers by May 14, 1941, the first anniversary of the merciless bombing of Rotterdam. Grimly, the Dutch named them Rotterdam I, Rotterdam II, Rotterdam III. By May 14 they had collected not for a flight but for thirty bombers. And on May 14, Rotterdam I, II, III, and the rest were over Germany. The Dutch, like the English, are a people slow to anger; but their hatred of Alva was not quenched in a hundred years.

TO THE HIGHLANDS

The road rises slowly to Buitenzorg. The volcanic soil is rich and red, with young peanut vines, and men and women in bright clothes hoeing in the orchards, and exact tidy farming. Rubber-wood goes on carts to Batavian cooking fires, and the native houses now are of bamboo frames and woven bamboo mats. A wall of woven mats costs about 75¢, and you may roll up most of your house and carry it on your head. Where there are convenient woods and brakes of bamboo a native's house may cost him nothing except for the tiles he buys in the market place. Government is discouraging the matting house, though it is cool, decent, and comfortable: but it harbours lice and their relatives, grisly to the European sense. Native incomes, in money terms, are extremely low, but most necessities of life are incredibly cheap, and the strong communal sense of the villagers provides a sufficient labour force for enterprises traditionally co-operative: building, sowing, harvesting, fishing.

The irrigation channels cross the hillsides, and naked bathers lie in the long grass, their bodies much the same red-brown as the waters'. Papayas droop heavily from slender stems under umbrellas of leaves. Salesmen sit by bamboo bridges to trade djeroeks, dryish and tight little oranges, and uncooked peanuts. The landscape is almost excessively domestic, with the family washing spread on banks and wrung by the ditch sides.

Buitenzorg is a place of trees, lawns, flowers, rain for five hours every afternoon, and spotted deer walking delicately in the Governor-General's park. The Governor-General and those who live about his Court have had their country places at Buitenzorg since the eighteenth century. It has the flavour as well as the name of the other Sans-Souci.

Its Botanical Gardens, now a century and a quarter old, are an index and tables of contents to the forests and jungles: with orchids flowering a hundred feet up in the tremendous reaches of the canary trees, whose nuts taste like green almonds. There is the lovely rose-trunked Alstonia of the Celebes; and pandanus starting from a flower pot to produce a family of trees from its air-roots; and Dysoxylum with buttresses strong and large as those that backed Norman walls; and the banyan, the great tree of Asia, which spreads across the countryside and becomes a tangled forest in itself with its hundreds of guests and parasites and, of course, its ghosts. Seven thousand men have taken shelter under one banyan. At Buitenzorg I met at last the cocacola tree, as yet without an American altar; and *Entada phaseoloides* which throws thick arms across other trees and wanders about the forest for several hundred yards in all directions, like an aerial and inoffensive octopus. At Buitenzorg also are tanked for observation the fish of the rice fields and domestic ponds. In this lavish country the sawahs, wet rice fields, are also fishing-grounds, with goerami, which is very eatable, and leleh that is soft flesh-pink and rather like a tubby madame with poisonous whiskers.

In the Gardens is a little memorial to Olivia Fancourt, Raffles' wife, who died here in 1814: "God has matched them," wrote Abdulla bin Abdulkadar, "as king and counsellor or as a ring with its jewels." Even Lord Minto remarked her dark eyes and her exquisite air. All her children too died of pest and fevers.

We went out of Buitenzorg through the Chinese quarter where yellow urchins played marbles under verandahs while it rained; and from the roofed tomb of a Chinese magnate stone cherubs swung suspended by wires in air. The peaks of Salak multiplied as we rose. This is the gate to the Preanger Highlands, the mountain complex which fills the skies of middle-west Java. Twenty miles of road from Buitenzorg climb five thousand feet to the Poentjak Pass: while the rivers from the hills speed to rapids, and bamboos grow gigantic, and the fields rise six or seven thousand feet in terraced steps, their banks like walls following the contours of the slopes.

SAWAH AND RICE

The terraced sawahs are the climax of man's art with the earth. Each field must be dammed and wet clay stamped and slapped into retaining walls. From streams or welling pools in the hills the water is run in mud channels or by bamboo pipes, hollowed and jointed, down the mountains. The bamboo systems may be articulated for miles, jumping roads and woodlands and crossing the hills by gulfs and passes. The pipes feed the higher terraces and the water drops by runlets, which may be plugged with a handful of clay, from field to field. On a steep mountainside rice at different levels may be at every stage of growth and you can walk up three thousand feet from harvest time to sowing. The whole mountainside has been shaped by the hand of man, through unnumbered generations kneading and slapping mud.

This husbandry is realistically illustrated in a drawing I found by a Bali village boy. On his mountain the peasants are planting at high levels, ploughing on another with their water buffalo, reaping with the curious small rice knives held between the fingers; [1] and at end they carry the harvest home, the sheaves hanging heads downward from the pikulans. The duck boy sets up his pole and flag to mark their pond for his faithful ducks. The water is too muddy to see the fish. The complaisant deities of the field observe proceedings from their walled shrine. The Bali-

[1] Rice must be taken gently, that its spirit may not be bruised or frightened; nothing will persuade the Indonesian to use a brutal sickle.

nese artist has the energy and eye of a mediaeval illum-
inator.

Rice is the staple food and crop for a third of the world.
Nearly three-fifths of Java is owned and cultivated by the
natives, and half the native lands are padi fields.[2] In most
places two, and in some places three rice crops are taken
in a year; even so, rice is imported. The Government is
extending and encouraging irrigation, for wet fields produce more than dry fields dependent on uncertain rains.
Dry rice fields, still frequent in the Outer Provinces, are
improvident farming, repugnant to both the industrious
Javanese and the careful Dutch. It was a shrewd stroke of
Providence to send to Java the Dutch, a people already
skilled in managing water. Dutch and Javanese paddle and
splash together and enjoy themselves immensely while
shaping the best irrigated landscape in the world. The
Javanese had, of course, the sawah from the immemorial
ages of India, but the Dutch irrigation engineers equip
ancient wisdom with new skills and tools.

Rice is first planted in nurseries usually identifiable by
brilliant young green where fields meet. It is transplanted
by hand and the fields flooded, drained and reflooded, the
water level rising with the rice until the harvest is ready,
usually in the fifth month. The whole dessa, all the villagers, turn out for planting, a back-breaking affair under
that sun, and for harvesting. They make both into festivals.
Quite literally, their bread is cast upon the waters. At
harvest the rice is gathered into the little bundles of the
Balinese drawing and carried off to the mills by pikulan.
One may entertain the congregation by trying to lift a
load which the peasant jogtrots under for miles. The principle of the pikulan is balance and a sort of staggering gait
which defeats its tendency to tip fore or aft. Rice, where

[2] Government forests cover a quarter, plantation estates
about one-thirteenth.

there is water enough, is now planted at almost any time
of the year, though Agrarian Bureaux encourage the peasants to vary it with root crops. The waters from volcanic
slopes bring in fresh soils which are all that is needed by
way of fertilizer in most of Java, though the stubble is
burnt and ploughed in and one often sees the blue smoke
curling up in the lucent evening air. An acre of sawah
normally yields about 1500 pounds of rice, which, in one
variety or another, grows from the tropical swamp of the
valley bottoms to the snow line.

The northern slopes of the Preangers are rich country
for root vegetables and for flowers, canna and wild roses.
Streams ripple over rocks shining in the sun and brown
girls unwind their sarongs and splash in the bright pools.
Crags and forests hang above domestic fields shaped by
slow art. The road winds up Goenoeng Mas, the Golden
Peak, at the east of the intricate Gedeh mountain mass, to
the saddleback of Poentjak, with tea plantations rising two
or three thousand feet from the road. Tea, like sugar, cinchona bark (for quinine) and tobacco, is almost wholly an
"estate" product. Maize, coconut, pepper, tapioca, rice are
peasant crops: and so is nearly half the Indies' rubber,
though one usually thinks of rubber in terms of the vast
plantations of Dunlop and Goodyear.

Tea is mostly handled by women who pick and sift and
sort it. The one shrub produces a whole variety of teas
from Orange Pekoe, the two delicate leaves at the end of
each twig, to Congo at the bottom. Green or black tea
is merely a matter of the drying. We sat amongst a group
of women and children on the floor of a little factory and
listened to their singing, dangling our legs and feeding
the children stickjaw which rather interrupted the sweet
course of song. Their work here, like so much else, is a
community affair, and varied with work in the fields. The
Soendanese are cheerful folk, and while we gossiped, our

driver Maheen, himself a Soendanese, told a story which the women approved as fair comment. Once there was an earthquake accompanied by such upheavals of volcanoes and uprisings of the sea that, by the mercy and justice of Allah, the whole earth was devastated and all mankind destroyed save two Soendanese. They met amongst the ruins of the world and in one voice cried out with enthusiasm: "Praise be, let us make a feast and dancing to celebrate this happy assembly."

Small girls balanced smaller brothers on their hips. With a virtue to be encouraged in women, they stuffed the first fruits of our paper bags into gaping male mouths.

MOUNTAIN CITADEL: BANDOENG

At the Pass, five thousand feet up, roses scramble on all the banks with begonias and cosmos, and a barber has his chair beneath a tree. The Pass carries into the heart of the mountains, a wall sheltering the lowlands of northern Java from the winds of the Indian Ocean, to which the south coast sharply shelves. Hundreds of rivers run northward, only two or three of importance to the south, and all reel and roll down the valleys and about the roots of mountains. Rivers rising in the same cup of hills and fed by neighbouring springs may end two hundred miles apart, though Java is seldom a hundred miles across; and here, near Bandoeng, the Tji Taroem dives into a mountain and comes up ten miles away considerably augmented.

The city of Bandoeng is in a gigantic bowl, 2300 feet above the sea, and circled by mountains: ten major peaks are in the view of suburban gardeners, from triple-cratered Tangkoeban Prahu, the Overturned Boat, in the north round to the great masses of the Kendong and Papandayan in the south.

The bottom of Bandoeng's bowl is flat like a plate; the

rims are fantastic, and constantly changing in a world of cloud and mountain and drifting smoke. Water lilies grow on midden ponds in the valleys and roadworkers crack stones under pink Japanese umbrellas. A water buffalo may be had for 25 or 30 guilders, and a hotel room costs daily about as much. There is a buffalo somewhere under your bed if justice has been done, for each new house or barn requires a buffalo head beneath its floor. The railroad people were once rather neglectful of buffalo for their bridges and had a run of minor accidents until the local spirits were placated with a buffalo's head and the local population with its meat.

The city is become a mountain metropolis and looks as if it was built yesterday from designs by tomorrow's architects. Much of it actually is new, its population having been increased by a third in ten years. Its streamlined and functional effects are presumably what London is in for after the bombing is done, and those of us who have a sentimental itch for old-world atmosphere will then retire to somewhere in the seventies off Fifth Avenue. But you cannot in Manhattan look between your toes at a crater fifteen hundred feet beneath or walk, as on Papandayan, amongst boiling mud and geysers.

Bandoeng is Army Headquarters. The thunderstorms roll about the hills all the afternoons, retired Dutch officers roll about the golf courses all the mornings, tanks and machine-gun carriers roll across the fields and dip in ditches and practise jungle war on the higher slopes.

The Indies' Army had in 1939 about 50,000 men. It grew to something like 150,000 by the third quarter of 1941. It has normally about 20 per cent of Europeans, 40 per cent Javanese, and 40 per cent from the Outer Possessions, mostly from Ambon, Ternate and Menado. Expansion is more a problem of material than of personnel. In June, 1941, at the insistence of native leaders, for the first time Indonesians came under the conscription laws. The Indies have much the same man power as the Japanese, and there is no reason to believe that the Indonesian is inferior fighting stuff. He is surprisingly handy with mechanical gadgets, takes fondly to motor cars, and is now employed by tens of thousands in munition plants, including the huge Artillery Works which occupy half a million square metres near Bandoeng (and date back to Daendels' "new weapon-shop" of 1808). The Dutch make their own field guns, anti-tank guns, machine guns, rifles, bombs, shells, and small ammunition. In 1940 they began to produce a light armoured car on a Chevrolet chassis which looks a useful job for the war they may need to fight, though it was first called, significantly, a "round-up" car and designed to deal with Fifth Columnists.

Normal infantry organization is four companies to the battalion: one "European," one Javanese, one from the drafts of the Outer Possessions, one a mixed machine-gun company also equipped with anti-tank guns and mortars. The European Companies are built up by the militia on the cadres of regular troops. Europeans are liable for one year's service at the age of 19 and then do a refresher every four years until they are 32, when they pass into the Landstorm for fifteen years. The Landstorm, Auxiliaries from the Native States, and the reorganized Town and Country Guards form the second line. The Town Guards revive the old city bands of the Dutch Merchant Guilds. The older Town Guards had to buy their own bows and arrows, helmets, breastplates and glaives. In a collectivist age, the State now hands out weapons, but the Indies' Town and Country Guards still look much like the burly burghers who once mounted the tall walls of Utrecht and Brabant.

The native soldier, until the recent conscription, was a volunteer vouched for by his village headman. Like the

European, who has been mostly recruited in Holland, he serves from 5 to 25 years.

In 1938 the Indies Government thought the islands wide open to a strong, sustained attack. Beach heads could still be established almost at will on most of the Outer Islands by a determined invader. But the air force is not housed on beaches there but in secret bases hidden in jungles. The Army's chief concern is to hold the jungle approaches to the outer ring of defences and the major base of Java. The general plan in Java is to defend the strong points of the coast with regular units supported by the main force, highly motorized, and operating on the extensive road system which can be powerfully defended at its innumerable mountain passes. The general body of the militia and the native regulars are being drawn into this mobile striking force. The cavalry, needed in the heavy, wet fields and narrow jungle paths, transports its horses by truck where a truck will go, and it also has light armoured cars of U. S. Army design.

The Dutch have great confidence in their Outer Possession drafts, but Javanese sections are usually given a European brigadier (corporal) to each fifteen or sixteen men. He serves under the native N.C.O., instructs in the new automatic weapons and stiffens the line. The Dutch Army, like its Navy, needs heavy stuff to back it: but in a campaign fought through jungles, across mountains and sploshing in the sawahs, it could probably handle in Java anything likely to come against it.

By July of 1941 the Dutch clearly had both their confidence and their dander up, for on the 28th they joined Britain and the United States in economic sanctions against Japan. Bang went Japan's oil agreement with B.P.M. and N.K.P.M., the one bit of business she had from all Mr. Kobayashi's and Mr. Yoshizawa's talk. Monetary and trade transactions and the shipment of rubber, tin,

quinine and fats were brought under rigid controls. The
Dutch, who have been a singularly peaceful people for
a century and more, are getting tough, and the results
may be unexpected. Netherlands India could be a considerable Power in the Asiatic world, and Netherlands
India is feeling its muscles. A new shape of things may
suddenly appear in the Pacific if Australia produces a
statesman of creative talents.

Bandoeng swims and plays tennis, grows flowers, dines
and dances. At the Savoy-Homann, an elegant Chinese
member of the Volksraad dances with a charming person
in the long slit Chinese skirt, and delicate Javanese ladies
flirt discreetly with young officers. One can usually find a
Resident or an Assistant from remote hinterlands of Borneo, Sumatra, the Celebes or New Guinea taking out some
leave in the cool mountain air; and hear in the lounge
admirable stories, amongst which one discriminates. The
plausible may be disbelieved: the incredible are almost
certainly true.

PLEASANT CORNER

The mountain valleys are endless and their variety infinite. I know a village named Tjandoengsari, Pleasant
Corner, where the ox carts cross a narrow mountain stream
and there is market twice a week. The peasants bring in
their mountain rice and sit about to gossip and eat, from
banana-leaf platters, swimming dishes of steamed rice and
native macaroni, boiled sugar palm and sweet potatoes,
djenkols (which, like an onion and the durian, are good
to eat but bad to smell) minced peanut mixed with chilis,
sliced cucumber, sprinkled heavily with long pepper and
salt. They drink pink lemonade and soft syrups from the
sugar or the sago palm, or from crushed tamarinds. They

shop, of course, in the Chinese store.[3] Tapioca is spread by the doors in thin wafers to dry, before cooking in coconut oil which has the uses here of olive oil in the Mediterranean countries. Poinsettias and marigolds scramble in the lanes, and where mountain torrents crash over into falls and the world stands on edge, the sawahs are majestic memorials of primitive irrigation engineers. You meet monkeys, some oddly like several of the more respectable spinsters amongst your acquaintance, and some with broad white shirt fronts who roll amongst the trees like bibulous clubmen.

The neighbourhood has tea, cocoa, coffee, tapioca and cinchona plantations. Bandoeng is the quinine centre. The local rubber lands are now mostly being resumed by the Government for native use. Golden mimosa spreads a gentle shadow above the delicate tea plants: and now there are barbed-wire entanglements crossing the hills and valleys, tank traps by the roads and details of troops at unexpected places.

CHINA IN INDONESIA

We left Bandoeng for Garoet (once a holy city forbidden to Europeans, now a hills resort), on a wet and dismal morning and immediately behind a hearse which housed six native gentlemen quite alive. The sawahs, as we climbed about Mount Malabar, were very small, but the

[3] The universal provider of pink, green and variegated sweets, face powder, felt hats, knitted booties, safety pins, nails, belts, lamps, studs, socks, sardines, sewing cotton, scent, slippers, canned salmon, garters, lace, pens, shirts, blankets, plates, cups, saucers, spoons, glasses, umbrellas, orange crush, sodawater, teapots, dolls, combs, spices, coconut oil, toothbrushes, kettles, tools, wire, singlets, sarongs, and badjoe (the little jacket that goes with sarongs), of turquoise, maroon, tomato red and peacock green.

SAWAH

"The Balinese artist has the energy and eye of a mediaeval illumi-
nator."—Page 254

MUNITIONS WORKER, BANDOENG

"He is surprisingly handy with mechanical gadgets."—Page 259

peasants presumably prosperous for they were ploughing with two buffalo each. Two buffalo in a small sawah are rather like two buffalo in a bath tub. We came across the Tji Taroem again, making desperate efforts to get out of the twisting valleys of the Malabar. Lower, you recall, it takes the shortest way by diving underneath Mount Pantjalikan (whose name satisfyingly means a place to sit in) which shows what a river will do when pressed.

At Tiparaj we went to see a little Chinese capitalist who has a weaving factory. His economics are interesting, and if you put him together with the universal provider at Tjandoengsari and with your Chinese tailor in Batavia you have a picture of what China is in the Malayan world. This fellow perhaps came in as a plantation coolie or a tailor's prentice. He worked and saved, saved, worked, saved, until he bought a pedlar's pack and stock and took to the roads. For perhaps two years he wandered and traded in the furthest parts of the countrysides, learning the country, the language, the habits of the people, and making enough money to open a little shop where no shop was before. Presently the shopkeeper was extending credit, putting out small loans, trading in local crops, building a little mill or establishing, as here, a sweatshop that absorbs the native craftsmen and undersells their own slow and patient product.

This weaver's fifty hand-machines cost perhaps twenty guilders each. The boys and young women of the village learn to use them and come in on piece-work rates when they have leisure from the sawahs. Each weaves one or, if the yarn does not much break and he is skilful, two pieces a day, for which he has 15 cents a piece. The Chinese entrepreneur tells me sadly that he now makes little profit, with yarn at 75 cents for a piece which finished fetches about 1.10 guilders, leaving only 20 cents for his interest and profits. But if forty of his fifty machines produce a piece a day, I think he is not doing badly.

The weaving plant is commonly behind the original shop, foundation of the family fortunes and where most of the family from gran'pap and grandmother's mother may sometimes be met: and the capitalist with three thousand guilders a year does not scorn to vend a tin of canned salmon or a bottle of eau de cologne. But I wonder about the tuberculosis rate in workshops filled with fine fluff.

The Chinese do not dominate the scene in Java as they do in Singapore, but they were at Batavia and Bantam and a hundred places in the Indies before the European and increasingly they outnumber him. In 1900 they were half a million. In 1930 they were a million and a quarter. Batavia is one-seventh Chinese, Medan in Sumatra nearly one-third.

They first came as traders, and in Java traders they mostly remain. In the Outer Provinces most are plantation labourers. They are the universal providers and, with the Arabs, moneylenders, pedlars of drugs, proprietors of gambling houses. They are clerks and craftsmen, and the essential middlemen, the buffer and the go-between of the Javanese and the European. The great Dutch companies are the main arteries of trade, but the Chinese are the veins which distribute it to every part. They are indispensable to the functioning of the economy, as both Dutch and Indonesian ruefully admit. The Chinese pedlar goes into the remotest villages, the Chinese shopkeeper sets up his stock where no European could see a cent. Patience, industry, frugality, long-suffering: the Chinese are terrible for their virtues.

They sometimes make trouble. Chinese Communism has been noisy in Malaya and the Indies in late years. In the eighteenth century, when the Dutch, plagued by their growth, shipped some Chinese as slaves to Ceylon, they rose in Batavia and were massacred for it. But as a body they bear the law patiently in the eyes of the world.

The Japanese strut and fume and make large mouths: but the Chinese already own the East. Theirs is the real power and it is growing. I do not know what could stop it if you wanted to stop it. When a man comes at you kicking, you can kick back. When he only wants to sell or to buy or to lend, you have little excuse for violent action, which anyhow would not succeed. A year or two after the slaughter at Batavia, the Chinese were there in the shops again, tailoring suits, making furniture, lending money. They move in like sand.

The Portuguese and the Dutch Company segregated them under their own headmen. Until this century their places of residence and licenses to travel and trade were strictly regulated. But their power reached out from those restricted areas. Because no one else would or could do it, the Dutch farmed out tolls and plantations to them. They controlled the sugar industry in the eighteenth century; and they dealt with the natives so harshly that the Dutch since forbid any non-Indonesian to buy native land. Chinese exploitation of native workers in the batik industry first provoked Sarikat Islam. They block native progress in the crafts and industry because their command of capital and their energy defeat the native efforts to compete. As they acquire the techniques of the higher business, they begin to oust the European. Yet, if you tried to rip the Chinese from the social economy of Netherlands India, the whole would collapse. They are an integral part of it. They are there, it seems, for keeps.

They are a great people. Who has suffered as they have suffered and who can work as they will work? A Chinese coolie may gamble away the earnings of a year with the magnificence of a Regency buck; and not all Chinese grow rich. But they have an enduring estate in their tireless labour, shrewdness, patience; and these, in the long run, are more than lands and bank accounts.

They remain Chinese. China, since the Republic, has remembered China Overseas. Once her emigrants were dead to her. Now she has discovered their resources. She gives them citizenship again. She encourages their Chinese education, Chinese culture, travel in China. China Overseas financed the Chinese Nationalists. It has made enormous contributions to the government and armies of Chiang Kai-shek. Some Chinese think of all these southward places as another province of the New China coming. History will probably agree with them. Nor will it need to impose a stupid trial of arms. The Chinese know a better way. When you have your tropical suits made (excellently made, of course, and cheap) at Mr. Tek Sik Sein's, you may note that he and his squatting workmen, his charming little wife, and his chubby serious babies are the germ of an empire: the Empire of tomorrow, perhaps, or of the year after or a century hence. Mr. Tek does not know and Mr. Tek does not care, probably; for Mr. Tek is already a little kingdom unto himself, already the successful imperialist. Mr. Tek has his nice little house, his nice little business, his nice little wife, his nice little children here in Batavia, while Sato San, poor stupid fellow, is getting himself killed with various people's guns in an effort to pick various people's chestnuts out of their various fires.

The Japanese were long ago admitted to European status and given access to the European law because they were few. The Chinese only now move towards full civil partnership with the European. But everything comes to those who wait. And no one can wait like the Chinamen.

THE FISHING, SOWING HIGHLANDERS

In the flat, rich plains between the mountains south and east of Bandoeng the sawahs are as broad as fields in Missouri; but each is peopled with two or three score of villagers stooping to plant rice, knee deep in the rich slush. The young women go to and fro with baskets, the old women sit at the sluices and catch fish in long hand nets, slung under bamboo rods. Presently the road climbs again through the twisting pass of Nagreg and amongst hedges of poinsettia, with grassy banks and green-and-brown hills which remind you of Devonshire about Ottery St. Mary until a sudden cluster of palms or the valley opening towards a tall volcano brings you East again: though there are grades here like the Old Road at Porlock. The fields are steps a few feet wide and a man stands in one to tend another like a shopman at his shelves. This road is one of the vital passes which command the land of Java; and we were in large notices verboden to fotografeeren or even to leave the highway.

Beyond Nagreg is the land of Leles with its lakes and wild canaries and great village fish ponds. Hereabouts, the fields become fisheries between harvests and sowings. Men with large baskets carry to spill in flooded field small fry, which in eight or ten weeks will fill and fatten. Most are varieties of carp, but there is betek, the climbing perch, which goes up ditch-side trees to feed on insects, and gabus, which the natives mostly eat dried, and goerami which will come to twenty or thirty pounds' weight if given time enough, though he should be eaten as a stripling of two or three.

Neither waters nor fishes have much life of their own in Java. Water is carefully conducted up hills and down dales, and from pool to pond. A proper fish pond is a se-

quence of pools linked by channels whose gratings grade
the fish for size from pool to pool. The full-grown golden
carp cannot squeeze back to eat his lesser brethren. At
the final gate sit the village grandmothers chuckling together over their large wicker baskets which finally receive
the pilgrims from the ponds. The old ladies sit on the
slithery banks and half in water. Each has her junior
granddaughter attached for aid and auxiliary, and they all
seem to enjoy themselves a great deal. They should be
talked to, for no one can tell you as much about a country and what goes on as old women who sit and crack and
tattle in the sun.

Our driver, Maheen, had a good deal of pleasure from
the crones by Tji Panas, the hot river, where the fish are
mildly parboiled already while they still feed amongst
the reeds. A pot is no novelty to a Tji Panas carp when
at last he comes to it. The crones ironically admired Maheen's uniform which was khaki with blue stripes, and
the neat black velvet koepia (which I take to be our *cap*)
of the Moslems.[4] Veterans of the childbed, they questioned
his paternal prowess, a popular theme everywhere with
the rustic satirist: but Maheen, with a delicious little wife
in Batavia and three plump children already, was armed
against their cackled shafts and had his own comments to
make on the generations of Tji Panas.

The warm waters of Tji Panas flow from the lava fields
of Mount Goentoer, and the air is languid. A man sits to

[4] The koepia is less worn hereabouts, as you come towards
the native states, than the cap of patterned batik, called ban-
doe by the Soendanese and blangkong by the Javanese; but it
is a matter of considerable dignity to own a fine velvet koepia,
which I have priced at a guilder and 1.50. But that was in a
market where we were offered ten fish for 35 cents, a gross instance of exploiting the innocent European, for they presently
went to a native at 8 cents the lot.

chop wood or to clean the head of a goat; but he may raise his eyes to any one of six volcanoes. Maheen had several stories for each. He speaks in anecdotes, as all Easterns do, who were once taught by parables. He has a shrewd view of the uses of the European. Thus, he told me that in some part of Sumatra, where he had acquaintance, the year's round of agriculture was determined until lately by the New Year when festivals required a harvest home. But the New Year was governed by the lunar months, so that in every few years seedtime and harvest would fall all out of season and the crops fail and people starve. After enormous efforts and desperate argument, the Dutch Controleur of the district persuaded the people to base their agricultural operations upon the sun instead of the moon; and now there is no drought in the growing time. Maheen considered it a ripe instance of the European common sense, which he admires: though I suspect he thinks less of our character and qualities at large.

At Trogong, which is a pleasant town in the valley of Garoet, we went to a wedding. The gamelan was on the verandah, pandopo, and it had a drum I still desire, one, I believe, of Cheribon, which once made such great drums and great gongs, Gong Ageng, Gong Sijem, and Kenong, that their echo still rolls in the hills after two hundred years.

The bridal bed was blue and white. Charms hung above it and about the doors, and all the village was gathered on the pandopo and in the inner room, omah, with cakes and fruits and syrups set, with flowers, upon the floor. The Javanese marry young and often, for Islam is casual about divorce. But the family life is intense, and nothing rouses the family to such largesse as a wedding. In the Indies, the women go unveiled and live a much more free and responsible life than Moslem women generally, perhaps because of the old matriarchal structure which still persists in places. The bridegroom's family pays handsomely for the bride, but the bridegroom goes rouged and resplendent to the mosque while the bride waits him at home, rouged and painted too, in rich sarong, her upper parts naked, as for solemn occasions, and rubbed with saffron and poppy oil.

One wife at a time is usual in Java. The poor cannot afford more and most others, publicly at least, follow the Christian custom. If a second wife is acquired, the first has primacy of place. Grandchildren are expected to provide for grandmama; though the old men must turn out to help young women with the rice.

The Soendanese have exalted manners which evoke good manners even in a European. An ancient man sitting on a platform to say his prayers acknowledges one's passing salute with the dignity and authority of a Pope giving benediction to the City and the World.

The Indonesians respect age and are passionately fond of children, whom they treat as adults, with an adult's claims to respect, from their first steps. At the death or divorce of their parents they usually stay with the mother's people or under the care of her brothers, in the matriarchal fashion. A man may obtain his divorce with little more trouble than the writing of the soerab lepas, a letter to inform the lady of his decision. Alimony is not provided, and as the mother and her family usually have the ultimate responsibility of the children, a woman's ambition is to achieve so many that she can look to a proper provision in old age. The kampong usually has a sort of community aid for homeless children. Inheritance goes to all the children and to the wife of the moment. The women, of course, get the worst of the deal, but less than in most Moslem countries, and the intense communal life of the dessa or kampong [5] is some substitute for the rather fluid character of the family.

Maheen went into the economics of housing about Garoet. He was moved to speech by a village where Government was actively discouraging the whitewashed woven huts with their thatch of sago palm or atap from the nipa leaf. The new wooden and tiled houses may cost a man 250 guilders, or about a year's income from a bouw [6] of sawah, and though they last much longer they cannot be repaired from the roadside copse. Moreover, your money goes to timber merchants and tradesmen not of your acquaintance, whereas you once assembled a party of friends to build your house and made a day and subsequently a night of it. Maheen dislikes the division of labour. Few young men, when they marry, can afford the expensive new houses, so they must go to live with their brides' parents. He recognized the good intentions of the housing and health authorities; but reforms should not be rushed. Maheen, like all the Easterns, is a Fabian. Colonial administrations need tremendous energy to get things done, as their critics might more often recognize.

Near Garoet we heard a cry in the hills which might have been the wild dog, adjak, though it is now rare except in the wastes of the south and west, where a few packs still hunt turtles on the beaches. About here too were some few Bengali Bulls, bred in Madoera for racing, and related to the bullock, sapi, whose habit and appearance is gentler than kerbao's. There are still a few tigers in the wilder Preangers and their whiskers are prized: while Chinese pay extravagant prices for the horn of a rhinoce-

[5] The dessa properly means the people of a village, the administrative and social community; kampong means the material village itself.

[6] One bouw equals about 1.7 acres.

ros. Fish hawks drift above the sawahs, but the familiar of the fields is the glatik or rice bird.

At Tasikmalaja they make umbrellas, which are spread like flowers along the road where the painters work patiently on linen starched with sago and stretched to the frame. With a proper regard for local art, everyone carries a sunshade about Tasikmalaja to brighten the roads and the fields, where women were gleaning. Perhaps Boaz first saw Ruth under a red-and-golden gamp. This is a soft and a kind country, with hillocks from some lava flow now green islands of trees, and flowers in the smooth fields.

EDUCATION VS. SEX

We went visiting schools near by. Most native children now have primary education. There are twenty thousand public elementary schools in the Indies, and nearly two thousand continuation schools: vernacular, Chinese, grammar, vocational, commercial, industrial schools, with fifty thousand teachers in all, though as yet literacy is low. But the education of seventy millions is quite a job where taxes are necessarily small. At the village school of Karangsamboeng, which we selected, so to speak, by chance, there were four classes and the children were mostly between six and one-half years and ten. There were 163 boys and 118 girls; the prejudice against instruction for girls is gradually being broken down. The teaching was in Soendanese and its emphasis upon their own and not the alien culture. The parents who can manage it pay from 5 to 25 cents a month for each child. A native teacher gets 20 or 25 guilders a month and is commonly valued at a bouw and a half of good sawah.

Education for the peasant child is designed to make better peasants. The Dutch do not encourage a rootless white-collar class of babus. But for the child of unusual talents the admirable Link Schools lead on from the vernacular to the secondary system with Western instruction, and to the higher education generally. The Javanese are not energetic but they are industrious, and education reveals much the same capacities as Europeans possess. But early adolescence and the love of women draws off their attention. From puberty to old age sex absorbs the Indonesian's energies: a pretty girl is of vastly more concern than sceptres and crowns and all the complications with which the European fills out his life. So, in lesser affairs, the Indonesian seeks the easy routine and most comfortable way. Even while he is reckoning accounts or typesetting or driving your car he is really thinking of what he will whisper in the dusk.

Hereabouts is the divide between the Preangers and central Java. A new strategic road under Mount Kempang has opened up areas of what were considered poor land, though there is splendid teak, coconut, and forest timber in the valley of the Tji Tandoe, which drains a whole family of volcanoes and is aptly a tempestuous river only now being reduced to order and use by the Dutch engineers. Settlers are moving in and growing magnificent rice. I tried one shoulder-load; it weighed considerably more than a picol, which as everybody knows equals 100 catty or 136.161 pounds. The little peasant had trotted four miles with it when we met him. Here you see the earth just beginning to feel the hand of man and take shape in the terraces that, twenty miles on, are two thousand years old.

MAIN STREET IN JAVA

The Oost Preangers are lumpish mountains thinly peopled, but where you cross the central marches is as good a place as any to linger at a Government Rest House and meet Main Street in Java.

It is a long and rather dusty street in a townlet which is centre for a group of kampongs and perhaps five thousand people. The family washing hangs beside the kitchen door, for the Rest House is kept by an Indonesian family; and you may see what they wear. Women have the sarong, of course; and kemben, a wide bandage of cloth which is wound tightly from under the arms to the middle and serves for corset (though nowadays one sometimes sees a brassière in the Western mode, and even Western panties); kelambi, a sort of camisole; and slendang, the long scarf worn like a bandolier and used for carrying babies, firewood and the groceries, and sometimes in the rain drawn over the head, though Javanese women go normally bareheaded save for flowers and gilded pins. The men wear sarongs too and cotton drawers and singlet vests, with a short jacket of cotton.

Across from the Rest House is the inevitable store of Sin Sin Joeng, and next door is the pawnshop, always a centre of local society in Java. You may walk to the pawnshop but you ride home in a pony cart, having money now in pocket, and every one who has something to sell gathers about the doors. The Javanese are not a provident people and between one harvest and another have all through history gone into debt. Marriages, births, deaths, betrothals and any of five-score excuses for junketing that will immediately occur to any Javanese, are strains on substance and on credit; and most natives were in a hopeless morass of debt to the Chinese and Arabs until Government set up its pawnshops which serve the people much as a bank. In 1939, 43,000,000 pawns were made in Java, and 80 per cent were for less than 25 cents, illustrating pathetically the poverty in liquid funds of the people, and the need for public protection in their borrowings.[7]

Indonesians may seem a thriftless folk. However, there was little encouragement to thrift through ages when they were grossly exploited by rapacious princes. The stability and order of the European dominion now gives incentive to the virtues esteemed in a commercial society.

Beyond the pawnshop is the aloun-aloun, the village green, which is balanced in the larger places by the European plein or town square. At one corner of the aloun-aloun is the Kliniek, centre of local health services.

Nearly six hundred doctors, European and Indonesian, are in public service in Java, with staffs of nurses, vaccinators, midwives, and analysts; and the death rate is below 19 per 1000, though the country is tropical, the most crowded in the world and was once constantly swept by fevers, famines, and plagues. The death rate in the countrysides is notably less than in the cities where all the East mixes: and less at higher levels than on the coastal plains. The medical services must work by patient education against traditional habits and superstitions and the native fatalism. Films are used now as well as talks, handbills and placards: *e.g.,* to demonstrate the dangers of intestinal infections from soil and water pollution. Something like 7,000,000 vaccinations are done each year. The housing measures of which Maheen complained are part of a campaign against plague, in which a million of Java's nine million dwellings have been rebuilt. Before the glib critic next assails European dominion in these parts, he may reflect that population increased five times over in Neth-

[7] With the pawnshops, looking after more pressing needs, go People's Credit Banks, which in 1939 lent on 650,000 bills averaging 46 guilders; and the Village Banks which lend both money and rice: 22,000,000 guilders and 110,000,000 kilogrammes in 1939. These people are only now entering a money economy, and Government agencies alone can educate them to it and prevent exploitation.

erlands India between 1860 and 1930 and added another
ten millions between 1930 and 1940. The Indonesian has
been given a reasonable expectation of life: and he, at
least, still believes that life is good.

Across the aloun-aloun, past the inevitable banyan where
children play amongst giant roots and fowls scout through
the long grass, is the school and, beyond it, the mosque.
The Javanese are earnest Moslems though not exactly
pietists. They carry Islam lightly; though in the last century and especially in the last decades there has been a
vigorous development of Islamic life and propaganda.
The Moslem Laymen's Associations are very active, especially in the Outer Provinces. Three in five of the ten
thousand Indonesian pilgrims to Mecca in 1938 were from
the Outer Possessions where the natives usually are more
prosperous. Islam gives a peculiar prestige to the local
Arabs, and especially to the hadjis and santris who come
to watch over orthodoxy and who are usually to be met
in kampongs of any size. The Arab, both hadji and
trader,[8] is active in promoting pan-Islamic sentiments.
Christendom and the West generally are indebted more
than they know to the British and Dutch régimes which
have established and sustained tolerable relations with the
great world of Islam.

But Islam is the garment of Indonesian society: the
way of life is still richly Animistic. It is not from Islam
that the rice mother is derived, who is represented by a
woman sent alone into the field: nor from Islam that the
growing rice is seen and honoured as a pregnant woman
who must have delicate care, so that one does not shout
in the fields while her seed is forming. At harvest, when

[8] He is often both, for the hadji is not a priest in our
anointed sense but one who has fulfilled the precept of the
pilgrimage and completed its studies and devotions.

the small knife is used hidden in the hand and a special language spoken so that the Saning Sari, the guardian spirit, shall not be frightened by what goes forward, the mosque has no part. Some scepticism grows amongst bright young men like Maheen. He still approves the small rice knife but because, or so he says, of its convenience, for as you cut with one hand you can conveniently gather with another. He has achieved some reputation with his wife as a fortune teller (a useful trick for any man) because he forecasts each month to her the day when she will have her housekeeping money. She has not caught on yet to the regularity of paydays, though I think that, in the way of women, she may be less guileless than she seems. And I doubt if Maheen is altogether indifferent to the uses of magic, white and black, to witchcraft and to love potions.

On the aloun-aloun is the fine house of the Native Regent if here happens to be the centre of a Regency. Java and Madoera have 19 Residencies with Dutch Residents, 79 Regencies with Indonesian Regents. The Resident is the "elder brother" of the Regent, but it is the Regent who directly governs his people according to their adat or customary law. He has his Regency Councils for which most of the male population is qualified to vote, though only a minute fraction cares to, this being a land where hereditary dignities are inestimably of more value than a ballot.[9]

[9] Residencies and Regencies are divided into districts where the native officer is the Wedono and the Dutch the Controleur. In such a town as I have here in mind it is probably the Wedono and Controleur you will find in authority, with their district and village Councils. Beneath the Wedonos are the Mantri, Assistants and Probationers, usually of Regency families, who are learning the business of government: and then the loerah, the chief or headman of the dessa. The mandoer may be anything from your head waiter to the foreman of a

The streets of the little town are lined with trees. Singing birds, usually the dove perkoetaote, are hoisted in cages to the top of tall bamboo masts beside the houses, for sun and air. Towards evening they are taken to the coffee house to sing competitively, each bird in turn as the veils of its cage are lifted, while the connoisseurs attend. A fluent bird, alive to its responsibilities, may win its man his coffee every evening.

Across the aloun-aloun and to and fro in the streets goes the endless, quiet motion of the people of Java. Brown gentlemen in pyjama coats and carrying satchels join the local bus. The village policeman in his green cotton at times considers the regulation of traffic. Goatskins are stretched to dry beside the road, with trays of pink macaroni. There are basket shops, pottery shops, shops of the blankong makers (though now, to see batik properly made, you must go to the Native States). There is probably a card or dice game going on. It is a world in which people always seem occupied, but never in a hurry.

CITY OF STRANGE GODS

Beyond Poerwakarta and towards Banjoemas, the Golden Water, you meet white herons on the trees, and the people go in for bamboo woven hats rather like inverted washbasins; and you come among the true Javanese, who are a slender people and more grave than those of Soenda, with ancient glories remembered in the peasant's gesture. We came to Wonosobo between tumbling green hills and tumbling brown streams. A pair of ridiculously dramatic mountains popped unexpectedly from the

gang of road coolies. He is usually a shrewd knowledgeable old boy, the non-commissioned officer of civil society, and to be cultivated by the worldly wise.

Publicity Dept. K.P.M., Batavia-Centrum (Java)

MAIN STREET, JAVA

". . . And slendang, the long scarf worn like a bandolier and used
for carrying babies."—Page 274

CHILDREN OF JAVA

Netherlands Indies Information Service

"The Indonesians ... are passionately fond of children, whom they treat as adults.

clouds while we had tea: Goenoeng Sendara and Goenoeng Soembing, each comfortably over 10,000 feet and occupying most of the sky above the hotel.

Wonosobo lies under the shelf of the Dijeng Plateau. The town is 2600 feet above the sea and you climb from it another 5000 feet in 12 miles by a narrow toll road which hangs above the canyons of the Tji Serajoe as it winds. It is rather a desperate sort of drive and traffic is one way: up until 11 A.M., down afterwards. The Serajoe flows southwards at the instance of a Prince who thought it unfair (so the Southerners say) that the notoriously Good People of the southern slopes should have so few streams while the Bad People northward were excessively accommodated as, alas, Bad People often are. Serajoe is, in fact, a lovely leaping sprite to whom the Prince made ambiguous love in the interests of his constituents: and she does flash amongst her forests like a silvered dancing girl.

The air is crisp like a European spring as you climb; and the mountaineers come down the paths to market with panniered ponies and shaggy donkeys. The hills grow wild and rocky, with high winds and huge boulders: but cultivation climbs the narrow clefts to six and seven thousand feet. Eucalyptus trees (brought from Australia but by whom and when?) droop long leaves over drops of three thousand feet, and the gigantic pyramid of Sendara closes in across the valley. Here the mountaineers scrape amongst the boulders to grow cabbages, and thin, poor sugar, and maize. The villages are built in tiers like fortress-towns of mediaeval Italy: and women squat to work in the fields because, I suppose, it is difficult to stand upright when the earth drops away at an angle of eighty degrees.

These mountain people are paler than those of the lower

lands: the women sometimes have pink cheeks. They have built terraces of stone by colossal labours wherever they had foothold; and they wear enormous hats woven of palm and quite twelve feet around. The source of the Serajoe is a few feet from the road, the legend illustrated in stone with cheerful bawdiness where it springs. This is in the very narrows of the Pass which leads to Dijeng, the hidden city of strange gods that was set amongst the clouds.

The Pass becomes a twisting passage through the hills, mossy, dank and shadowed even at midday: until it opens at a natural gate on a smooth plateau completely walled by mountains.

The plateau is a pear-shaped crater bottom. No one knows when men first came there or who built the city whose heroic fragments in stone are spread for miles across that place. To the primitive Javanese these heights were haunted by devils; but in time now remote from memory, the Hindu priests found their way up the cleft Serajoe cut, and made their shrines. A temple complex grew in the valley through centuries, and from one group to another paved walks crossed the marshy lands. Some hold that it became the centre of a Hindu civilization now utterly forgotten: others that it belongs to the age and empire which made the Boroboedoer and the Prambanan temples southward. It must long have been a centre of pilgrimage, for steps hewn of lava climb a dozen miles from the outer valleys; their stones worn by countless feet and the weathering of ages. No one knows when it began or when it ended, but after the city was deserted or all had died there the valley was forgotten to the race of men. Only after Europeans had seen it did the mountain people creep back: but even they, who keep their traditions with the tenacious memory of all primitives, know nothing of the city of the plateau save that it is a holy and a haunted place.

In the temple sculptures are traceable figures of Mahābhārata, one of the great primitive epic poems of India.[10] Early in the nineteenth century more than four hundred large buildings were counted on the Dijeng. Now thirty-six survive, excavated and preserved from the morass into which they were slowly sinking. The stones of many are dispersed amongst the houses and walls of the modern mountain kampongs. But most of the city perished perhaps in some volcanic holocaust; or it was swept by plague or ruined by red war. All the temple cities and their civilization in central Java end upon the question mark: their vast works were left unfinished as if catastrophe overwhelming fell suddenly on cities great as ancient Rome.

As we crossed the plateau there were whiffs of sulphur; and in the gullies boiling grey mud. The altars, now stained with volcanic soil and splashed with scarlet fungi, are broken to support houses of bamboo and to make paths across the sodden ground to cabbage patches.

The old man at the pasanggrahan [11] on Dijeng remembers the excavators. Watching them bring up the mighty stones of Krishna, he was chiefly impressed with their capacity for beer. They drank two barrels a week. Thus, at the end, is history resolved.

[10] Of which my friend Mr. R. S. Pullai has written: "The adventures, suspenses, sensations, and the thrills which it describes cast its readers to and fro choking sobs and bursting laughters; the manners, morals and wits converts the ignorants into wise and the vicious into virtuous. In eloquence it is marvellous, in plots unimaginable, in wisdom boundless, in effect exalts the minds. And, as a whole, it leads to peace in this distressfull-life, and to bliss in the after-life." That, he assures me, is putting it mildly.

[11] Pasanggrahan: a place to spread your bed, the Government Rest Houses.

THE MIND OF JAVA

I sat in Wonosobo talking to an old Dutchman of all this and being flippant about it. He shook a heavy head at me. "The peasants have forgotten it all," he said, "or so they say. I don't know. But sometimes here you catch a glimpse of a hidden life, of the memory of secret things, of a world that may be familiar to them as the sun and sky, though to us they deny all knowledge of it. Perhaps they take it for granted as one does the sun and sky. But there is a mystery in these people. A European may live here twenty years and never so much as lift a corner of the veil. But he grows aware that there is a veil. The people, as you know, speak in symbols. Their minds are oblique. Always they speak in references aside, in allegory, in metaphor. Consider even a matter comparatively simple, as the High Idiom with which they speak to their betters, the Low which they use for their inferiors; of Basa Kawi, the tongue of the poets, the true speech of Java. It is bedded in Sanscrit, Sanscrit words, Sanscrit ideas. What do we know of all that? The mind of Java is endlessly convoluted. It has passages where we shall never find the way. You notice the courtliness of a peasant to whom you speak at the corner of a field. Do you think his politeness only an empty and meaningless trick? Do men keep noble manners unless they also keep a noble tradition? And what people that has kept tradition ever forgot its history utterly as these say they forget the makers of the Boroboedoer and the shrines of the Dijeng?" He shook his head again. "I don't know. This is conjecture. But a conjecture that has formed through half my life. I have learnt that language may be a curtain drawn over meaning. I listen to the gamelan, and I have learnt to hear not a xylophone but doves, not rebab, the viol, but the humming of bees, not a flute but the nightingale, not the gongs but the tiger in the long grass. I hear the words of Kawi, and I can myself phrase a courteous turn of speech. But I only hear the viol, the flute and the gongs. I miss the doves and the nightingale and the tiger."

I looked across at Maheen washing the car. If he has the secret of the Boroboedoer he would cheerfully sell it, I am sure, for five bucks.

The old Dutchman followed my eyes and grinned. "Maheen is smart. He lives in the cities, he has been to school, he has heard of Chicago, he uses only the surface of his mind. I was thinking of old men who live here in the mountain villages, who remember what their fathers heard from their fathers and who know what is hidden underneath their fields. The peasant living, from generation to generation, in his own countryside and tilling age after age his fathers' field and transmitting from grandparent to grandchildren the accumulated experience of his people, is not a lost and solitary soul like your schooled city brat. His mind belongs to a continuum. It has the past and it is a bridge to the future. It is the mind not of a man alone and lonely but of a community persisting through time. It may not always be conscious of what it carries, but in its lore and its legend it has the history of a people and what they have learnt in their adventure with life. And if you scratch," he added, "the thin skin that is Maheen, I think you will find his father."

"I don't know about Maheen," I said, "but I am certain that his wife is quite familiar with Eve."

CHAPTER FOURTEEN

The Centre of the World

ON FROM THE NAIL OF JAVA

CENTRAL Java is a country of wide plains and of great isolated mountains. Rivers slash deeply into the brown plains: the volcanoes are blue pyramids, nine or ten or eleven thousand feet high. Toward Temanggoeng five or six are visible at a time; though in the middle hours of the day they are often lost in clouds and you might travel all about their flanks without knowing they were there. It is a strange country. Without the mountains it would seem as flat and clean of line as the country between Chateaudun and Chartres; its cultivated fields are green as East Devon, it suggests the wildness of a Cornish moor, it is more populated than Surrey. Curving bridges of bamboo cross the widest rivers, the smell of sulphur drifts down on the morning wind, smoke rises from the stubble, the fields are parcelled by neat irrigation channels, streams leap wildly amongst rocks, the graveyards are set along the hills, villages spawn new generations, rainbows rest upon the padi, and the rain it raineth most emphatically every day. Here the headgear is of joined mats rather like a boat which may be used as an enormous basket or inverted to cover one down to the rump in the sharp showers. Headgear varies astonishingly through the land, but one must always be careful to treat it with respect, for a man's hat counts more to his dignity than do his trousers.

It is cool after rain in the avenues of trees, but the rice fields steam in the sun. At Temanggoeng is a Chinese temple with its dragons, peacocks and faïence. A baby paddles eternally, I imagine, in a ditch while its father, in orange hat and scarlet sarong, eternally watches from the bamboo bridge; and the herons follow a timeless peasant as he ploughs his fields under the round hill that is the head of the Nail of Java driven precisely through the centre of the island at the centre of the world.

Southward from Malengang are the Native States and the heart of the ancient Hindu civilization which built the Boroboedoer and the temples of Prambanan. Soembing to the west, Merbaboe and Merapi to the east, brood menacingly at the gate. Merbaboe erupted in 1867 and killed a thousand people in Jogjakarta alone. Merapi in 1930 killed two thousand hereabouts. He trails his white plume in the sky, and is now watched by a staff of people wise in the ways of temperamental mountains. If you turn aside on the southward road at the village of Moentilan, you presently come upon the edge of the latest lava, a grey sheath thrusting down the valleys where the vegetation now creeps slowly back. I have walked there in the green hour when Merapi draws the night about him and darkness comes before sunset in the lanes between the bamboo brakes. Then the mountain seems to move up across the sky like a shape of life and men remember his dark heart of fire, the molten rock that coils within him, the breath that poisons his airs.

In 1930 people died of the gases at Moentilan. To the west he threw out scalding water and lava for twenty-five miles: but eastward he gave up a flow of water ice-cold and sand from some abysmal depths.

A small dessa of perhaps a hundred people stood high up there on the grey lava field. When Merapi moved and they saw the red wall of lava descending upon them faster than men or horses could flee, they flung themselves to the earth and cried to God. The stream divided and went about them to each side, though they were scorched with its heat.

No one now may settle in the immediate danger zones. But, as Maheen says, the people will return when time has churned the lava back with earth. Volcanoes make good soil.

Moentilan is west of the mountain, and five miles west of Moentilan is the Boroboedoer. The Buddhas look not out but in; and they brood upon the eternal lotus flower.

LOTUS FLOWER: BOROBOEDOER

The Boroboedoer is a Dhagoba, a place enshrining a relic of the Buddha. The relic was brought here perhaps in the days of the Emperor Asoka who, three centuries before Christ, sent out from India missionaries to teach the doctrine and to found such places. Its form is all symbolic of the teaching, as the stones of the Gothic are shaped to represent the articles of another Creed.

Boroboedoer is built about a hill. It has no interior sanctuary or chambers, for Buddhism is properly a philosophy and a way without mysteries. It has monuments and memorials such as this but not temples; places less of worship than for metaphysical meditation. The final form of Boroboedoer is probably from the eighth or the ninth century of the Christian reckoning, when hereabouts had grown a major civilization. It rises in nine terraces from a base 531 feet each way: the six lower terraces have thirty-two sides, the higher are circular: the lotus flower and its seed pod, the Buddha and the Order which grows from his teaching: while the Order is crowned by the great bells of stone which proclaim it to the world.

On the walls of the lower terraces are three thousand

tableaux of carved stone which tell the Buddha's story. On their parapets are three thousand cupolas, the opened petals, and between the arches more than 432 Buddhas are seated. On the circular terraces are 72 Buddhas more, and above each the stone petals have begun to open. The gateways are open to the four quarters of the earth. Four aspects represent the Four Truths of the Buddha, and eight staircases the Eightfold Way to Knowledge: Right Understanding, Right Purpose, Right Speech, Right Action, Right Memory, Right Judgment, Right Meditation and Right Profession.

If one is inclined to be diverted or to miss one's way on the lower terraces or to remain fascinated by their stone legends, so is one held from knowledge by Pride, Covetousness, Lust and all those devices of the world and flesh which also haunted Christian Everyman.

All the Buddhas contemplate Cause and Effect: the 72 above represent the 72 reincarnations when he was already freed for Nirvana but refused deliverance from the body of this flesh that he might teach the Way.

The Boroboedoer is as much a sermon as Amiens or Wells: but the Head of the Buddha is not raised to the mountains or to the skies. It looks downward and inward to an end that is Nihilist. I wonder how much of the history of two cultures is in those symbols of stone; the wisdom that seeks through the sad round of lives only a peace that is Nothing, and the Cross that leaps into the sky from the spire of Salisbury, the Sign of a terrible energy with which men have stormed the gates of God to claim citizenship in His City, and in this Sign have conquered.

The Lotus Flower rests upon green slopes. This was once a lake where its stone petals spread. It is infinitely moving; for there was one who saw all evil with candid eyes and knew no hope, but yet found within himself the courage, the wisdom, the tranquillity that his people here have renewed five hundred times in stone.

One crosses from the Boroboedoer to the Shrine of Mendoet, where are enthroned three great figures, the Buddha and his Disciples. They have the nobility and the pain of their great doctrine. Sorrow and death belong to existence: existence is the offspring of desire unconquered in the round of lives, which can end only in Nirvana: Nirvana must be sought in complete renunciation of the Self. The ultimate cause of desire and existence and birth and death is ignorance, for men attribute permanence and reality to a life which is illusion and whose proper end is annihilation in the Absolute: to be sought in charity, chastity, courage, knowledge, meditation, patience.

One may see it all written in the awful calm of the three figures of Tjandi Mendoet.

Men could not persist in that doctrine without corrupting it. Few could face with such austerity the dark. But a people who had once received it even for a moment must be marked: and to it belongs the dignity and the serenity of the people of Yawa.

Already, however, at the Dijeng and the Boroboedoer, the theme of the Mahāyāna appears. Buddhism in its first conception recognized no Supreme Being and the gods of the early literature are beings equally subject, with humanity, to life and rebirth. Often, indeed, they are abstractions, like the figures of a Morality. But the Mahāyāna is in some sense a synthesis of the Hindu religions and re-erects the hierarchies of gods. The Primordial Buddha becomes the source of all existence, and the aspects of his wisdom appear in five heavenly figures who are represented on earth in five vicars who find embodiments; of which the Buddha Gautama, our philosopher, was the fourth. The fifth is yet to come. To these the Mahāyānan adds agents and symbols of the whole range of human experience and draws on all the categories of the Indian gods, from the primitive projections of the jungle peoples to the trinity of Brahmanism. The Mahāyāna is a vast piece of eclecticism; and Mahāyānan Buddhism became the most latitudinarian of creeds. We have seen the same happen in other civilizations where tolerance was preferred to truth which has not peace but a sword.

THE TEMPLE CITIES

The Boroboedoer is at the frontier of the Native State of Jogjakarta and some twenty miles from its capital and the Kraton of its prince, the Sultan. Jogjakarta is one of the two States into which the remnant of the Moslem Empire of Mataram was divided in the eighteenth century; but it is also at the core of the earlier Mataram, the Hindu Empire of the seventh, eighth, ninth centuries which built the temple cities.

The greatest of these is a few miles eastward and still in the long view of Merapi: the temple complex of the Prambanan Plain. Walking perhaps two hours one way and an hour and a half the other, you pace the extent of the sacred city of the Prambanan; though as work proceeds and the peasant looks with new attention at the stones turned by his plough, the range of it still enlarges. But the major group of surviving temples is beside the road that goes to Soerakarta, the second succession-State of Mataram.

The temples were built of immense stone joined without mortar by tongue and groove, dowel joint and dovetails. They have been overthrown by earthquake, sucked into the soft earth, pillaged through a thousand years for peasants' floors and farmyard walls, princes' palaces and Dutch roads. But what can be pieced together is now being restored with infinite patience, and one can see again something of the majesty that once was here.

The first major survival as you go from Jogjakarta is the Tjandi Kalasan built probably a few years before the Boroboedoer. Enshrining Dhyanibuddhas, the heavenly expressions of the Primordial Buddha's wisdom, it is dedicated to the goddess Tārā, the female counterpart of Padmamani, the Lord of the Universe, who derives from one of the Earthly Vicars. She is a much more attractive goddess than most in the Mahāyāna's mixed pantheon; a mediator between earth and heaven who stoops to aid mankind.

A mile or two beyond is the great central group where worship and perhaps government was centred: the Vatican of a Hindu Rome. Tjandi Kalasan is a shrine of Buddhism, but a Buddhism already acquiring its pantheon. This larger group is Brahmanistic, though it was built in the same period and shared the same city. Buddhism was persecuted in India itself, but the Hindus here admitted all beliefs, it seems, which could be related in their large tolerant frame.

The group is properly the shrine of the Brahma, the primitive great neuter, the soul of the Universe; and of its three major emanations, Brahma the Creator, Vishnu who preserves, and Siva the Destroyer; and of their attendant divinities. The emphasis is on the worship of Siva here, and Prambanan thus belongs to the era of the Purânas, a comparatively late period of Hinduism, where the gentler worship of Brahma and of Vishnu was losing popular place to the grosser cult of Siva and his highly unpleasant wife Durgā, whose immense image is here enthroned in Siva's temple.

The local peasantry have their own version of the place and of that statue. There was once, they say, a princess whose father was Emperor in Mataram. She was called the Lady Loro Djonggrang and she was more beautiful than the moon, in the habit of princesses. There came, of course, a prince, and he fell in love with her, as the erudite reader will already have foreseen. But the lady was of that difficult sort who like to make bothers for their princes. She promised him her hand but only if he would raise a temple of a thousand statues in one single night.

The prince was up to her (it is pleasant to think that the princes usually were). He was favourably known to the local gnomes, djinns and afrites, as every prince with matrimonial intentions should be, and he set them to work. At dawn the thing was done or almost done, when the princess, by some legerdemain, made off with the last statue. The prince was so furious that he utterly forgot the code customarily provided for such cases: he turned the lady into stone, and there she sits, the thousandth image, and an example, one trusts, to all maidens still too coy. Presumably she has learnt wisdom and would do differently if she could, for Javanese girls pray to her now for husbands, and bring her unguents and chaplets.[1]

The shrine is an immense four-sided mound with a surrounding wall, and upon it are three large temples facing three smaller ones while the avenue between is closed at each end by a temple of the lesser sort. Siva's, at the centre of the western row, is the largest of all: to his north is Vishnu, to his south Brahma, and opposite are the temples of Nandi the Bull who is Siva's mount, of Garuda the Bird which is the mount of Vishnu, and of Ganesha the Elephant, distinctly one of the more attractive of our glorified acquaintance. He is an incredibly ancient god content with the roughest of stone altars and amiable to men, the god of good luck and of the primal earth, of villages and simple honest things; though, oddly, he gave writing and is responsible, I suppose, for authors, a dismal charge; and he patronizes merchants. In British India the merchant sadly

[1] The double rôle must be a trifle confusing to Durgā, who, it may be remembered from Bali, is also the Lady of the Lake, and Kali of Death, and Ragda the Witch who eats babies.

turns Ganesha upside down to declare bankruptcy. I take it that Ganesha prefers honourable merchants, while winking at some sharp practice of the heartier sort. (He probably understood the old Dutch factors, though I do not know what he would make of Wall Street and the Stock Exchange.) The Hindu Empires, like those that have succeeded, diffused a mercantile culture; and the shipmen and traders who first spread the seed of the Lotus teaching in these islands must have burnt too at evening under their sails a pinch of incense to Ganesha.

The temples are superbly carved, with heavenly nymphs, musicians, and gods. There Vishnu sits upon the world-snake and Rama bends the long bow of Janaka, troops of girls are dancing at a wedding, the monkey gods appear, and wrestlers, and Krishna smears himself with butter: all the legend and jest and horror of the Hindu myths and all the variety of Hindu life are worked in the stones.

There were once perhaps a hundred temples here, painted in gold and blue and red. Few inscriptions are left; Prambanan lay for centuries under the volcanic dusts of Merapi and was rediscovered only in the eighteenth century. About the main platform and beyond its walls are other concentric walls, as if the city were once built in rings: the inner circles have the tombs of priests and princes and, beyond, circle by circle, was a vast burial ground of castes and estates. Bronzes are sometimes turned up in the fields. On each burial urn is set the one word, *East.*

The archaeologists who are working there on a job begun in 1885 still walk in their leisure through the villages for twenty miles about looking for pieces, and the restoration has been a stupendous jigsaw puzzle. Some of the items have been recovered from collectors in Europe and the United States.

By the first wall of the city when last I stood there and

in the shadow of the tombs of kings was a billboard adver-
tising Jack Benny. The world does march. Near by at
Tjandi Sari (which was a convent of Buddhist monks and
not a temple proper), Maheen was puzzled at large niches
in the wall where once presumably the Dhyanibuddhas
sat. He thought that they may have been intended to
house gold and silver cups: "You know, Tuan, for sporting
events."

Some vast catastrophe in the tenth century fell upon
Prambanan, suddenly. Tombs were left unroofed, sculptors dropped their tools with figures half cut, and the great
city, which must have seemed like a cloak of many colours
spread for miles across the plains, was suddenly emptied of
life. Men fled far into eastern Java from whatever evil
came upon Prambanan; but perhaps only a few escaped,
for the Hindu culture never recovered elsewhere these
splendours. Most of the priests and the craftsmen they inspired must have died here in the ruin of scholarship, of
sculpture, and of books. Madjapahit, the last Brahman Empire of Indonesia, was to grow great and flourish until the
fourteenth century, but it was a Javan civilization which
only remembered Hinduism as Bali does. Mataram lay
beneath its ashes. When the name recurs in history it belongs to the new rude Moslem power which proclaimed
One God and struck down the images.

Yet Hinduism persists in the arts and life of Java, in the
Shadow Play of Marionettes and Wayang Wong, the Human Play (which are best seen here in the Native States), [2]

[2] Wayang is drama. Wayang Purwa is the ancient shadow
play with themes from Sanscrit classics, narrative and effects
from Dalang, the storyteller. W-Gedog uses leather dolls to
cast the shadows and uses native legends. W-Kelitik produces
the dolls of painted wood and not merely their shadows on a
screen. W-Golek has marionettes with moveable heads and
arms, and characters ranging from the Hindu Gods to local
Dutch officials. W-Topeng introduces the human actor,

in the ronggengs of public dancing girls with their delicate plastic miming, and in bedayas, which are danced by royal daughters. Drama and dance were used, much as our own mediaeval Mysteries and Moralities, to propagate sound doctrine.

JOGJA

But Jogjakarta now is but a humble descendant of the glory.

Jogja is a city surrounding a city, the Kraton of the Sultan, which houses twenty-five or thirty thousand of his relatives, retainers, women, guards, servants, craftsmen and those who are for one hereditary reason or another entitled to live within his walls. About the Kraton are public places, wide aloun-alouns with sacred banyan trees trimmed to the shape of pajongs or umbrellas; in Java the symbol of dignity and power, indicating rank by size, colour and ornament. Mr. Chamberlain's notorious gamp would have been approved but its drabness would have been thought ill-omened.

It is well to get up on hats and umbrellas before one visits the Native States. Kuluk, the hat of dignitaries, is an elevated fez but black and shining like a topper and decorated according to its wearer's station. Blue appropriately is for the blood royal, white and gold for Regents, black for the Mantri, yellow for lesser Officers; though in Malaya I recall white as the colour of a royal parasol and yellow for the heir apparent.

On certain occasions of ceremony the Sultan appears on the Sitinggil, the wide dais which fronts the aloun-aloun; and there his people bow to the dust before him. Public displays are held there, and the Sultan's companies of

masked. W-Beber unrolls the story on a cloth to the Dalang's recitative. Wayang Wong has human actors in traditional costumes and accompanied by the gamelan.

players sometimes perform before the subjects squatting for a quarter of a mile around. But popular drama and gamelan are now chiefly supported by the Chinese, those eternal conservators. The natives cannot afford them.

One should poke about Jogja in the cool of the day. There is an admirable little Museum to serve as an academy of the native life and arts (it actually is so, for art and craft schools are attached to it). There is the Water Palace built in the eighteenth century in the further grounds of the Kraton, at once a fortress with dark dripping passages and a pleasure palace with marble pools for the harem. Its moat was once kept by a squad of alligators. Beyond the city are the tombs of the Sultans of Moslem Mataram where four hundred princes lie; and in stone ponds the sacred turtle swim amongst the sacred carp. [3]

The tombs are at Kotta Gedeh, four miles from the Kraton, and perhaps the parent city; and at Kotta Gedeh are the streets of the craftsmen in silver, in tortoise shell, and in buffalo horn who beat their silver with rythmic hammers and heat and bend their horn to song. When they grow a little tired of singing, they turn on the radio.

At Kotta Gedeh I met an old man of Islam whom I shall always remember. He was a silversmith of great skill and his house was loud with the singing of his workmen and with children; for, like Job, he had been blessed in his labours and his substance and with many sons and daughters. There is light in Islam. It was shining out of his face. He and his wife and daughter were gathered in the chief room of his house and the women were weaving baskets

[3] Oddly, the sacred turtle are albino and no common man has learnt how they come to their pond amongst the tombs; one, at least, is incredibly ancient even for a tortoise, and there is some suspicion that he is an early Sultan returned, though one would have expected a Sultan of Jogja to prefer the bathing places of the Water Palace.

of the leaf of the useful banana: and as they finished their baskets he filled and piled and heaped them with food and gifts of tortoise shell, which he also works. The baskets were spread all about the floors of his house. To-morrow was his birthday, and to-morrow he was to entertain the poor; so he made such preparations for the beggars of Kotta Gedeh as a man might make for the wedding of his son.

It is sugar country hereabouts, for the Native States were more tolerant of large plantations than the Dutch administration beyond the borders. Sugar sweeps up to the suburbs of the cities and laps the ruins of Prambanan: though Javan sugar has fallen on evil times and from eleven per cent of the world's production in 1929 to five and one-half per cent ten years later. Sugar is a delicate subject in Java. Men who used to gamble in the club at Jogja for a picol a point when sugar sold at six guilders a picol have now long been clerks and warehousemen at Soerabaja: and along the roads, mills gather dust and rust and bats and clambering vines.

In Jogja and at Soerakarta the best batik is now woven and printed, or better, hand written, as the Javanese say. Batik is a method peculiar to Java, and though now the sarong and blankong, the native headdress, are mostly cheap manufactured prints, the traditional designs usually hold. The batik maker draws on cotton cloth patterns of wax: when the cloth is dipped in dye the waxed parts do not take the colour, and a design appears. By rewaxing and redyeing, with varieties of colour and slow careful skill, cloths of intricate patterns are produced. Batik has many hundreds of traditional designs. Some colours and patterns are reserved to girls, some to married women, some to the Sultan, some to the Susuhunan, to the Princes of the Blood, officers of the court, headmen of villages. Against batik the Old School Tie seems but a poor vestigial remnant. A native can read a good deal from the sarongs he meets upon the road, as a man of the Middle Ages could read the liveries and emblems of the crafts and guilds. It is a depressing feature of modern egalitarianism that we neglect the distinctions that might appear, for instance, in pants. The suburban scene would be considerably cheered if butchers came in red with stylized chops, greengrocer's boys in the vividness of spring with vegetable motifs. Reluctant ladies might be reconciled to an emblazoned autumn, and secretaries be carboned *en règle*.

THE KRATON AND ITS POLITICS

The Kraton is a world of its own, behind its yards-thick walls. The throne room has two thrones: one for the Sultan, one for the Governor who represents the Crown of Holland. But the Dutch intervene little in the life that is led within the great palace. It belongs to the royal family and all its collaterals and consanguinities, the forty sons, their uncles, aunts, cousins, cousins german and cousins conventional, from generations now remote; to the women and their people, the players, artists, clowns; and to the queer murk of politics that invests such places, the factions of the blood and the ruthless jealousies of the harems.

Palace and harem politics have always been a canker at the heart of Oriental despotism. It was a quarrel between the Susuhunan of Mataram and his brothers which led to the division of the remnant of his Empire in the eighteenth century. The Dutch, called to arbitrate, set up the Susuhunan's uncle in this western part of the domain as an independent Sultan: not quite independent, perhaps, because both recognized then the supremacy of Holland, and the Sultan bowed to the spiritual authority of the Susuhunan and long did him homage at prescribed intervals. But Jogja was centre of the last royal resistance to the

Dutch, when in 1825 Dipo Negoro raised central Java and hell for five years in a war which cost fifteen thousand Dutch lives. Dipo Negoro was deported to Macassar, where Mr. Bruce Lockhart once went looking for his grave but found all memory of him lost or at any rate unuttered. Dipo Negoro threatened for a time to become a sort of recurrent Mahdi, and the Dutch are very firm with that brand of fanaticism, The Dutch then set up, one beside the Susuhunanate, one beside the Sultanate, great vassals with their own estates and semi-independence. Their kratons are beside the royal kratons, symbols of a system of balances: but the beam is really controlled in the palaces of the Governors, which both at Jogjakarta and at Soerakarta face the royal gates. Near by the kraton at Jogja is the Club, as much a symbol of European dominion as Governors or guns.

But the Princely Lands remain the core of Java; and there the ancient loyalties and crafts, traditions and way of life are still best realized. It is difficult to estimate what allegiance Susuhunan and Sultan still have in the hearts of the people. The Dutch, however, know it is necessary not only to treat the princes with all the honours of their stations but also to set up the second throne: signal that, like English judges, Susuhunan and Sultan hold office *quamdiu se bene gesserint,* during good behaviour.

Soerakarta, the seat of the Susuhunan, is thirty-six miles from Jogjakarta and, with 170,000 people, a rather larger city. As is proper; for the Susuhunan is not only the head of Islam in Java, but also the Nail of the World.

INDOS

I happened to travel that way with a man who remembered the wars with the Achinese of northern Sumatra. He complained that the sort of European coming out nowa-

days was not the stuff of his fathers; and indeed this is a
pretty general theme in the East, upon which one is entitled to play one's own variations after the first leave
home. But along the roadside my companion of the moment cited Johansa Batoe, who was a soldier of the old
school and lived hereabouts in his retirement after forty
years of corporaldom. It was "Brigadier" Batoe who once
turned out a guard to give a general's salute to a barrel of
gin. He did very well in the war in Achin after the Dutch
gave up their practice of sending out slow masses of
heavily equipped troops and used instead small flying
columns of such people as Batoe; but when he was congratulated by the Commander-in-Chief, he sniffed and
took the liberty to remind Excellency that Corporal Batoe
had known the Indies since Merapi was a hillock under
his hand.

The Corporal Batoes commonly married native wives,
and now you meet their Eurasian progeny in office
throughout Java. They have some advantages that the
European lacks: they understand the native mind and
often share the native sensibilities, sometimes excessively.
They have a strong community sense amongst themselves.

The Dutch now deliberately aim at making the half-
breed a bridge between the races, and when he is born of
an honest and faithful marriage he may reasonably expect
to draw on the best of both his worlds. There is a much
higher proportion of Europeans in the Indies than in
British India, and the Dutch have always been more inclined to intermarriage than the British. Many of the
greatest Dutch families have had Indonesian blood, and
Indo-Europeans have held the highest offices here. The
child of a chance liaison, left to its mother's people, often
has a thin time and becomes a festering little sore on the
body social. But the Indo-European who comes of decent
stock and is decently reared may be history's solution to

the problems set both white and brown man now at their meeting.

Most of the older Dutchmen who have stuck out the colonies believe in some such answer. The colonies for centuries drained the best blood of Holland: and until this century and its hygienic progress there was little prospect of rearing healthy European families here. In the first century or so, white women did come in some numbers, especially with the Portuguese; but the experiment was sad and bitter and not much renewed until malaria was brought pretty well to heel from 1910 onwards. Even now the majority of white women are reluctant to make the Indies permanently their home and the home of their children.

Yet, obviously, whatever the political future of the Indies, the white strain is here to stay, as the Hindu strain and influence remained. The Dutch are aware of the problem and eager to resolve it in whatever synthesis will best preserve the values of all parties. The Indo-European is bound to play an increasing part: and it is good to know that the son of Corporal Batoe is quite likely to be Dr. Batoe and a thoroughly sensible and able fellow.

TOWARDS SOERABAJA

Beyond Prambanan you cross into the Susuhunanate. The common people, where convention still lies heavy, wear batik of dull and unpatterned blue, though one may run into a troop of Boy Scouts underneath walls and arches of stone that hint at some distant Chinese influence. The carts, drawn by Bengali cattle, are very fine, with carvings and scroll work and woven bamboo covers painted in lively fashion.

Soerakarta, as the Guide Book says, is a city that offers no difficulties for the visitor. You ride about in bicycle taxis. The Susuhunanate has a population of something over twelve hundred to the square mile, and quite a respectable proportion seems to have acquired the flowerpot hats and umbrellas of office.

Soerakarta has two Kratons and is the capital of two reigns, for beside the Susuhunan is his great vassal, the Mangkoe Negoro, who has his own little army. The Kraton of the Susuhunan is a tremendous affair: a tangle of courtyards, streets, and quarters within the walls, the houses of the women (the Susuhunan's person is attended only by women), the streets of the craftsmen, the great mosque and its schools. A recent Susuhunan is said to have maintained three thousand ladies of the harem. His parasol is of gold; he wears an enormous diamond in the crown of his kuluk; many of his people still look upon him as the immediate viceregent of heaven and almost indistinguishable from God; his guests have beer from tankards of gold; he shows himself to the people several times a year and always in the company of the Governor.

For a century he had lived a dim life amongst his splendours. In the present reign he has become a more active figure. As the new order has developed in Netherlands India collaboration grows between the traditional centres of Javan authority and the Dutch Administration. The Native States are the focus of much nationalist sentiment, but it is a conservative nationalism. The royal interest is clearly in social stability, and Susuhunan and Sultan now disturb the Government less than agitators in the kampongs of Soerabaja.

Beyond Soerakarta, travelling north of the mass of Mount Lawoe towards Soerabaja, the country opens out. When we passed in June, the fields were in stubble, the drained earth caked to hard grey clods, the rivers low, and a heat haze hung above the teak woods. In the middle of the day the peasants come out from their fields to sleep on grass beneath the tamarinds or to gather at wayside stalls. This became, before the slump, sugar country, and the natives still suffer for it. The large plantations hired the land for their sugar, restoring it after harvest; and the peasant went to work as a coolie. He could not resist the immediate temptation of 50 or 60 guilders down, hard cash; when he had it, he commonly went on a buying spree. At the end of the year's cycle he found himself miserably poor. He had perhaps 100 guilders a year for his labour. If he could not live and keep his family on the income of 150 or 160 guilders, he would sell his water buffalo. Then he could only rent out his land again and become dependent upon the fluctuations of markets abroad, which had seldom troubled him as a subsistence farmer.

As the native began to understand the process in which he had involved himself, there was trouble. Hereabouts in the early 1930s there were riots on the sugar estates, and mills were burnt. The Government will not permit the European to buy out native land; but without an almost totalitarian control which the Dutch are reluctant to impose, it is difficult to prevent the native renting it. The only alternative is education.[4]

The landscape renews its dampness. Little bamboo bridges cross ditches to the houses; and hats become conical and green or red, though one may also wear a tin

---

[4] One is reminded of the Controleur who objected to a Sumatran ritual method of killing beasts for meat. After careful instruction and explanation, he killed an animal himself to demonstrate the hygienic process. The natives refused to touch it. He mixed his meat with meat ritually killed. They threw it all to the dogs. The same officer (he was an earnest young man and filled with good intentions) once persuaded his people to grow two peanut crops a year in place of the traditional one; but when the harvest was in, the traditionalist merchants refused to attend an untraditional market.

washbasin or a fishing net. A little further on they approach the style of a poke-bonnet or an inverted bucket; the ditches grow to streams, and the Brantas River, defeated by the mountains southward in an attempt to reach the Indian Ocean, turns north and east to feed the irrigation of the rich Soerabajan lands. Beyond Madjaagoeng is a small roadside museum, marking the centre of the mediaeval Hindu Empire of Madjapahit which succeeded Mataram and fell before Islam. The fragments are curiously interesting for the Chinese influence they reveal. Soerabaja, in the days when it was the port of Madjapahit, must have been in regular commerce with the China of the Mings. To-day, of course, it opens to the world; even the cab-drivers of eastern Java go about in sailors' jackets, and the peasant has turned huckster. Soerabaja is the Indies' gateway to the future. I feel some gratitude that I have seen it before the stable, static life of ages wholly succumbs to the queer flux and formlessness of the twentieth century.

THE GHOST TOWN OF BANTAM

The Province of Bantam is the northwest corner of Java with a Regent and Resident at Serang; and the port which was for a century the most famous of the Eastern trade is now a fishing village between two muddy creeks. At Calicut, Goa, Malacca and Bantam, the West met the East, and here began modern times: the merchant fortunes and the trade in cotton goods, from which came Industrialism in the West, Imperialism in the East, the impact of cultures, the flux of people, the dynamics of the new world, and much still in the womb of ages.

The country from Batavia is exceedingly lush with hills rising to the heights of Salak. Naked boys occupy the backs of buffaloes (which are amenable to small brown boys but truculent to Europeans), the buffaloes occupy the ditches, and flies occupy the boys and buffaloes. We passed by Tangerang which has made straw hats for a thousand years and, though we deployed all the resources of our Malayan vocabulary, failed to get gin tonics at Serang; and towards dusk dropped through marshy flats to a muddy river and the small shabby village that is Bantam.[5] The people sat listlessly beside the water or lay sprawled on their boats. A few were mending fishing nets without enthusiasm. The women were cooking in red clay pots. Advertisements for cigarettes and for Lifebuoy Soap (B.O. is still B.O., apparently, in Bantam) peeled from the walls. We found the Bantam gun, wife to the Batavia piece, in a shed and heaped with dead flowers; and half the village gathered surlily about while we stared at it.

We walked up a muddy lane where once the Dutch merchants and the English walked in lace and velvet; and we found their burial place, stone tombs slowly sinking into the quaggy ground.

You look through the mangroves towards the sea and think of the ships: the English *Helen* and the *Susan;* the *Nieuw Vrieslandt* of Hoorn, *Het Wapen van Amsterdam:* "From the frontiers of Coromandel is dailie expected the vessel Tergoes . . . there sailed this year for home Den Swartern *Beer,* laden with indigo, for Japon there sailed Den Swartern *Leeuw."* One looks at the tombs and remembers Master Gabriel Towerson and Master Robert Browne who were left "by me, Henrie Middleton, at Bantam, beginning their pay the first day of October, 1605." Master Towerson had £6 a month, George Woodnoth and John Sayers £3.6.8, Matthew Price and James More £1.4.0, and some but twenty-two shillings. They were to attend to the business of John Company: pepper, cloves: and "I

---

[5] Bantam is the Anglo-Dutch version of the native Banten.

do ordain that every merchant left here by me do keep an account of his own business, for the better satisfying of the Company, and his friends to whom he shall bequeath his goods, if it please God to call him out of this life." That was the second voyage of the English Company.

Thomas Cavendish was at Bantam in 1587 where on the 13th of March "after the breake of day there came to the number of 9 or 10 of the Kings canoas so deeply laden with victuals as they could swim, with two great live oxen, halfe a skore of wonderfull great and fat hogges, a number of hennes which were alive, drakes, geese, eggs, plantans, sugar canes, sugar in plates, cocos, sweet oranges and sowre, lymes, great store of wine and aquavitae, salt to season victuals withall, and almost all manner of victuals else."

Amongst the King's Officers came "two Portugales, which were of middle stature, and men of marveilous proper personage; they were each of them in a loose jerkin, and hose, which came downe from the waste to the ancle, because of the use of the Countrey, and partly because it was Lent, and a time for doing of their penance, (for they accompt it as a thing of great dislike among these heathens to weare either hose or shoes on their feete:) they had on ech of them a very faire and a white lawne shirt, with falling bands on the same, very decently, onely theire bare legs excepted."

The Portugales amiably described to Cavendish the state of the country and its prospects for trade, and introduced him to the King: "A man of great yeeres, and hath an hundred wives." [6]

[6] His son, who already had fifty wives, later corresponded with James I, and congratulated him on his accession, though perhaps Middleton found the English phrases: "I did heare that your Majestie was come to the Crowne of England, which doth greatlie rejoyce my harte now England and Bantam are

The Portuguese had come first in 1522, a party sent by great Albuquerque from Malacca, and their advent coincided with another great change. In 1522 they met a Hindu Prince of Bantam. When they returned in 1527 Islam and a Moslem Sultan had overthrown the ancient realm. Now the marble is gone from the brick walls and the Chambers of the Sultan are open to the winds, and the grass grows across their graves; and only some few natives come to pray between the broken gates to those who were Lords in Islam.

Bantam declined when the English turned to India Proper and Coen made Batavia his town: but Bantam is the Birthplace.

On down the muddy lane one comes into the ruins of the Dutch fort with its wide walls and weeds and lizards sunning on the pavements. It is now unroofed and untenanted except for the dark storehouses underground which house the generation of bats. One lonely sentry box stands above a bastion: the place is loud all day with cicadas and it has a damp and churchyard smell and the stench of the bats.

The Dutch broke the régime of the Sultans in the eighteenth century, but it was Daendels who finished with them. The Sultan was restive at the General's reformations, so Daendels went down to Bantam and personally pitched His Highness neck and crop off the throne and planted thereon his own broad Jacobite bottom. The heavens did not fall and the earth did not split asunder and the Dutch have sat there since. Unthroning kings was a pleasure to Napoleon's revolutionaries, and one can only think that the Sultan was very ill instructed.

both as one," which sounds suspiciously like a plug for the Company at Court. You may see back along the road the ruined palace from which the letter was written and the tomb of its writer amongst the other dead of his dynasty.

Beyond the fort again is the creek which once led to the sea, where the Indian cottons came out of the holds to be transhipped to the Moluccas; whose spices were gathered to the godowns here with the raw silk of Japan. The Dutch, seeking stuffs to trade for spice, developed the secondary traffic for calicoes of Calicut. The English were provided for trade with lead, tin, iron, pieces-of-eight, powder, rapiers and English cloth, headpieces studded with a vent to set a feather in behind, Hamburg pistols plated, cloths and scarfs of Venice red, scarlet wool and popinjay green, Devonshire kirtles in mulberry colour, yellow and green, and blue Watchett stuff.[7]

At the mouth of the creek Middleton beached his flagship of the Sixth Voyage, *Trades Increase*, for she was worn out and leaking (in her, he was held at Mocha and had blockaded the Turkish ports), and himself died like his ship, "hartesore." Here, by the quay, William Mettiwold wrote a couplet and set it up:

> *The English and Dutch were here,*
> *And drank toddy for want of beer.*

An older thing than any of theirs survives them: a little temple of the Chinese Buddha across the bridge, with lovely hanging lanterns and rich cloths of Canton and votive lights and flowers. The local Moslems, who in these matters are not bigoted, say their own prayers within the gates.

ABOARD FOR SUMATRA

We came back to Serang in the dusk past the old pleasure-house of the Sultans on an island in a lake: the watery

[7] Watchett is a small, amiable village on the Bristol Sea, where I have often waded after the muddy tide to take winkles: the wools woven in its cottages were once famous to Surat and the Celebes.

landscape at sunset was rose and silver, but the mountains were like indigo in skies of amber.

I remember breakfast at Serang because we had some difficulty in collecting it, in spite of what we now considered our fluency in Malay up to sentences of three words. Perhaps Malay was the wrong tongue, for many in Java consider it an inferior speech to which no man of reputation will admit. Breakfast, as at last put together but mostly uneaten, was composed of slabs of fish, raw ham and cooked ham, gingerbread and cheeses, brawn, thick slabs of moist white bread, rye bread, jars of hundreds-and-thousands which we presumably were meant to scatter on the butter, cold coffee, and Australian apricot jam. We were being introduced to the diet of the Dutchmen when the Dutchmen have their way. I recalled another breakfast in a more fashionable hotel, when I had succeeded in working my way, on a torrid morning, through one small glass of orange juice, a cup of weak tea, and a piece of dry toast. The Dutchman with me opened with fruit juices and wedges of ham and cheese between thick slabs of brown bread. Then he had a steak with fried potatoes. Then he had three boiled eggs and a pound or so of uncooked ham, with toast and coffee. He idled away the last twenty minutes of his meal with a bowl of strawberries and cream while he told me that he, as a Continental, could never understand the English liking for large breakfasts.

Northwest of Serang and by country roads is St. Nicolas Punt, the northmost head of Java, which the pilots knew: and offshore, just visible, in the mouth of the Straits of Soenda the islands Dwars in den Weg, Right in the Way, at which the pilots swore. It is a thinly peopled country towards the Point, with some primary forest: many varieties of ficus; waringin, the banyan, spreading each over its private countryside; nippa palm; teak, a great wood

in Indian affairs and human history. Along the coast are
curving soft bays with hedgerows and ditchrows of red and
golden lantana, and coconuts leaning over the waters of
the sea. This is something of a coconut economy: it provides fuel and food and thatch and occupation for small
boys and skipping monkeys. Bananas grow well hereabouts, a score of the fifty varieties. Women gather wood,
and the fishermen sit at their nets or on the fallen coconut
trunks and gaze in meditation on the sea. Fishermen the
world over are men much of a kind.

At Merak we took ship for Sumatra. The ship stood at
a little pier which jutted from a railway station and a
hill of palms. Oddly, there was a customs examination
before we boarded and another across the way in Sumatra,
as if travelling between the islands were an international
passage. The Dutch watch carefully for opium and for
firearms. The control of firearms is tactfully embraced
by the regulations on big-game hunting, but one recalls
that there are parts of Sumatra only lately reduced to order. I suspect too that there were yet more topical reasons
for the scrutinies at Merak and Oosthaven, but I, like Mr.
Yoshizawa, have found the Dutch tight-lipped on their
occasions.

People of all the races of the Indies came on board and
spread across the ship like a brown tide. They were followed by a herd of cattle which mingled placidly with
the other passengers. For a time we suspected a herd of
goats would join us: brown, white, black, blue, grey, skew-
bald, piebald goats and every cross and combination of
these. But they were too busy eating down the railway
station.

The Stoomschip *Duymaer van Twist* was painted wartime grey and prepared for blackouts in her night passages of the Straits of Soenda.

She carries six or seven hundred passengers with their

baskets and suitcases of Japanese cardboard mostly crowded on the forward hatch; and she sails where wooded knolls rise from the water and mountains and palm trees shadow the sea. Her passage of the Straits takes five hours. Half is under the Sumatran coast northward, with islands scattered on the sea like leaves blown by October winds. Southward, through most of the crossing, is visible Krakatau.

KRAKATAU

Krakatau's performance in 1883 was, I suppose, the most distinguished upheaval on record. The volcano belongs to the chain which comes down through Sumatra (90 volcanoes, 12 active) and continues eastward to New Guinea. Krakatau is usually three islands, as he is just now, though he is given to blowing their heads off and plunging again into the seas. The principal crater in 1883 was on Rakata, which the old men say, exaggerating perhaps, then rose ten thousand feet. The sailors remembered his history. He had risen violently in 1680, and he continued to quiver, as he still does, at frequent intervals. But no one was prepared for the sustained exhibition which began in May, 1883, and reached its climax in August, the 26th to 28th, when two submarine craters exploded with a noise which was heard in Australia and Japan and, faintly, in Europe; and half the Peak of Rakata was blown to dust that filled the skies of the world and gave a year of fantastic sunsets to places as far removed as Spitzbergen and Brazil. Molten rocks and ashes were thrown up to seventeen miles and descended on the Cocos Islands, away in the Indian Ocean, like a pall. Batavia was darkened at midday. Where half the mountain had risen there was now a gulf one thousand feet deep. A tidal wave 140 feet high swept the Straits of Soenda and the towns on either shore. At least forty thousand

Publicity Dept. K.P.M., Batavia-Centrum (Java)

THE HELMET, MOUNT SERILLO

"It was obviously designed by the architect of the Chrysler Building."

HARVEST HOME—JAVANESE COLONISTS, SUMATRA
"They can employ others, who now follow from their home village."

DRY RICE FIELD, LAMPONG
"Repugnant to both the industrious Javanese and the careful Dutch."

Publicity Dept. K.P.M., Batavia-Centrum (Jav

people died in that hour. Only a lighthouse keeper on the immediate Java shore was saved; but the wave put out his light and went on about the world, casting pumice on Madagascar and washing twice past Cape Horn. The ocean boiled. Three hundred miles away it rose 10.5° Centigrade above normal. The shores of the Soenda Sea were twisted to new shapes as you might mould putty.

In October, 1883, scientists went ashore. They found no vestige of any growing thing. A year later there was grass. Winds, birds, bats and currents brought seed. Now Rakata is entirely clothed with vegetation. No animal could possibly have survived. But in 1884 Cotteau found a spider there busily spinning his web. The eggs of lizards came with driftwood. Pythons and crocodiles swam out. Krakatau is now made a reserve of natural life. For my part the pythons, crocodiles and spiders are welcome to the place. It has been building up new submarine craters, with belches and heaving since 1927. A new crater popped up in 1928 and then went below again to consider more mischief. In 1929 there were eruptions to 3500 feet and a new island appeared, Anak Krakatau, "Child of the Terrible One."

Krakatau is now constantly under observation from volcanologists and a station on the Java shore. Krakatau often smokes quietly during the day and the reflection of its fires may sometimes be seen at night. It is not usually as spectacular as Stromboli, but has annual turns that give the neighbouring peoples jitters.

The Straits of Soenda are a funnel between the vasts of the Indian Ocean and the East Indian Seas. Strong airs blow up it and monsoonal clouds. Between the monsoons, in what the Dutch call the kentering, the sea is like white metal, and haze hangs over the islands. But in clear weather the many islands are glad and the mountains rejoice. Radjabassa, the Wet King, rises 4200 feet at the very tip of Sumatra: and the surf breaks under the boughs of forest trees. Sharks cruise the beaches and there are alligators in the estuarial waters. On the *Duymaer van Twist* beer costs 45 cents and a bottle of Bommel 4 guilders 50.

The seamen spread their mats upon the forecastle and turn to Mecca. Palm branches swim by the ship, and sodden baskets, and coconut shells. Outriggers fish in the island channels and off the wide shoals of Oosthaven, the Eastern Harbour of Sumatra; from the ship it is visibly another scene than Java's. Here the hills are wilder and the primaeval forest comes down to the narrow shore.

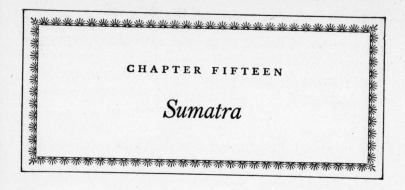

COUNTRY OF THE LAMPONGS

OOSTHAVEN, like Merak, is chiefly a wharf, a long railway shed, and humid heat that rises against you in beating waves. Two other K.P.M. ships were lying under the hills, for through the place goes all the export of southern Sumatra.

Sumatra runs northwestward from Oosthaven for 1090 miles. It has a population of eight and one-quarter millions, which is jumping rapidly by natural increase in the new dispensations of health and social order and by immigration from Java.

Parts of it are still little travelled. When we proposed in Batavia to go from south to north by car, many of our acquaintance flatly declared that it could not be done. Actually, we came through with one puncture. A fortnight earlier we might have been held by late rains in the south and centre which swept away bridges and would have delayed the passage by ferries of turbulent rivers; and we should probably have spent a good deal of time digging the car out of mud. As it happened, we jaunted in comparative comfort.

We had much amiable help from Dutch officers. The Outer Possessions are now three Governments, of Sumatra, Borneo, and the Eastern Islands. Sumatra is sub-divided into ten Residencies, the Residencies into Divisions and

Sub-Divisions. In most places of any size, you find a Dutch official.

At Oosthaven, the Assistant Resident of the Lampongs came on board to carry us through the Customs and to Telok Betong, the capital of the Residency. Mr. Yselstijn remains for me a representative figure. The heat was unbelievable, but he came up the gangway in a white uniform tight at the neck, heavily braided with gold, and completely bandbox. He had been six years in Sumatra without long leave, but he looked as fresh and pink and trim as if he had just walked out of the Kalverstraat in Amsterdam.

This is the country of the Lampongs, a people who may represent the primaeval stock of Sumatra, who are much crossed with the Soendanese and were long vassal to Bantam until Daendels ended that. Since a fierce insurrection in 1850, the Lampongers have lived quietly enough. They have been very prosperous for most years of the Dutch régime. As we drove up to Telok Betong we noticed Buick cars tucked away under native houses. Buick had a peculiar success with the Lampongers, who bought cars not to ride in but because a car became the symbol of dignity, much like umbrellas in Java. The Lampongers often live in river villages reached only by water; where you still find cars beneath the houses, slowly rotting into the mud. Since they were fetched upstream, their wheels have never turned. But, after all, who wants to go anywhere anyhow?

Pepper bought the Buicks. Sumatra produces 80 per cent of the world's pepper. It is almost entirely a native crop and has been grown in the Lampongs since the Sultans of Bantam required it as a tribute. In 1929 pepper fetched about 100 guilders a picol. In 1940 it was down to 8 guilders. The natives would be grateful if some one would explain.

PEPPER AND PROTOCOL

Pepper suits their style. It is an easy crop, and the Lampongers are much taken up with protocol and etiquette. The descendants of chiefs are in high honour, and almost every one succeeds in being descended from a chief. One is reminded often of Back Bay in Boston. Life largely turns about the problems of precedence: and most Lampongers now bear high titles once granted by Bantam to the greatest chiefs. As in other societies which attach importance to them, hereditary honours may be bought. Between the cost of motor cars, honours, and wives, the Lamponger is usually in aristocratic debt. The unmarried girls wear dowries in silver ornaments about them as an incitement (sometimes, I am told, they have notes and bills pinned to their underwear), but a handsome dowry also means a high marriage price. The Lamponger, as one might expect, has the worried look and sour manners of Mayfair and Park Avenue; and a profound contempt for people like the Javanese, who work.

We drove up to dine with the Resident and his Lady at Telok Betong, which grew into the hills after Krakatau drowned forty thousand people in the lower town, and washed a light-buoy from the Straits to the gates of the Resident's house on high, where it still stands, *memento mori.*

De Heer en Mevrouw Meindersma (to whom, these presents) will not object, I trust, if I describe the circumstances of a great Dutch official. He rules, in the Lampongs, half a million people, 900 Europeans, 10,000 Chinese, 220,000 Lampongers, 40,000 Bantammers (Coast-Malay and Soendanese mixed) and 220,000 Javanese, mostly colonists in the new lands now being cleared and opened. The Resident conducts his government with 12

European and Indo-European Civil Officers and about 20 Indonesians. He is responsible for law and order, education, roads, posts, forestry, public health, and the colonizations, and, of course, has his specialist staffs.

He has had over twenty years in the Indies and so comes to his great responsibilities in the prime of life. He was educated, like most of his fellows, at Leiden. His wife is the daughter of an earlier Resident, and his son has followed him into the Indies Civil Service. Many Dutch families have a continuous tradition of service in the East.[1]

The Resident has served in the Celebes, in Borneo, and in different parts of Sumatra, for the Dutch officials are moved about a good deal in order that they shall keep the whole scene in mind and not become absorbed in any one people and its special problems. The Resident knows well at least half a dozen languages spoken in the Archipelago, and is necessarily expert in the customary law and social and religious traditions of all the peoples with whom he has been concerned.

He has worked, for a quarter of a century, about ten times as hard as the average man of business: he has lived, in his younger days, in queer places, feverish and distant outposts and amongst tribes who still rather yearn for the good old days when they might hunt a man's head or his heart as an habitual entertainment.

The Resident now lives in a fine house, of the old Dutch colonial mode, admirably suited to its climate; but he has slept up trees and passed months in tumble-down pasang-grahans. When his wife had her babies, he probably lived

[1] For example, Louis Couperus the novelist (his books remain the best studies of the merchant and service families) was great-grandson of a Governor of Malacca, grandson of a Governor-General, son of an Indies Civil Servant. His brother became an Assistant-Resident, his brother-in-law a Resident, and he was distantly related to another Governor-General.

in some primitive bungalow on the outskirts of a native kampong with perhaps a dozen Europeans in a hundred miles about.

THE LONG DRINK AND THE SHORT

We sat out on the enormous stoep, partly enclosed, and designed as a lounge in the old Dutch houses: there you drink the long drink and the short drink which are the preprandial custom of the Dutch. In looser moments you might make bets on the tchitchaks, the little semi-transparent lizards (they look rather like X-ray photographs) which haunt the ceilings and keep down the insect vermin. "Tchitchak" is the hunting cry and the most familiar note in the quiet Indonesian nights. Beyond the stoep is a huge middle room, perhaps fifty feet by forty feet and twenty-five or thirty high. Old Dutch built in single storeys to get height to the rooms, and these central chambers are cool and dark all day behind the massive walls. You dine there: hors d'œuvres and soup, fish if the local fish is good, neats' tongues perhaps as the *pièce,* and on any sufficient occasion (the Dutch have many sufficient occasions) champagne.

A few years ago, within the house, the master would have worn pyjama pants, a cotton jacket, and sandals: the mistress a sarong and camisole. Nowadays, the Dutch customarily stick to European clothes.

A man who has served twenty years in the Indies has collected lovely stuff: fabrics and furniture, silver and lacquer. He has also collected good stories.

I remember once, on such a stoep, a high official talking of his time as a young Controleur in a district of the deep hinterland then newly brought under administration; a country of wild hill and jungle. He was the only European in his district and filled with enthusiasm, as young officers are, for their new reign of order and enlightenment. He himself, at the end of his first six months, was very proud of his district and perhaps of himself. Both his district and his information must have been well organized, for he was an organizing sort of man; but there are some items of information which the best of native intelligence services are slow to transmit: items, for instance, which concern deaths unexplainable and graveyard horrors.

So he was disturbed when he noticed in one group of kampongs a queer change of temper in the inhabitants. They had been a busy and active people. Now they drooped into a grey listlessness. They gathered within their bamboo walls while the sun was still above the horizon. They forgot to sing. They grew sullen. He recognized the symptoms. They were afraid. But he could not make them talk.

The native will not speak directly of the things he fears. A tiger becomes the Striped One, the Lord in the Jungle, He of the Whiskers. But this was a fear greater than the fear of tigers. They will talk of tigers, though they take precautions of address. This was a fear that chilled speech.

Then the Controleur noticed that men he might expect to meet did not appear when he came. Some were gone away; some, he discovered, were dead.

It took him weeks and Heaven knows what persuasions and threats to break through the silence. But at last he got the story.

Between the kampongs ran a path usually much frequented, until suddenly a series of horrible assaults happened on it. Men gone that way at dusk were found at morning thrown down, some bound and some strangled with cords of woman's hair. Those who survived were in the depths of terror and had no coherent explanations.

There was other queer stuff; and the natives had re-

membered that the way went through some old burial
place, long lost amongst the grass.

The Controleur was not and is not (for explanation,
he shrugs his shoulders, which serves as well as any elaborated conclusion) persuaded of the supernatural. His
first guess was a gang of ingenious bandits, and bandits
were his meat. So he compelled the district radjah to
gather men and to accompany him at evening on a patrol
of the path and a sweep of its adjacent thickets.

He and the radjah headed the rest. They saw nothing
of ghosts or gangsters. But the Controleur had a curious
experience. He walked into a morass; or what he first
thought a morass. It was as if his feet and legs were caught
in stuff that clung to him, held him, dragged at his every
step. With terrific effort he forced his way through. In a
dozen strides he was pouring with sweat. The strain was
appalling. Oddly, none of the natives seemed to feel it.
None even seemed to notice his difficulty. Then he saw
that it was not a morass at all. The path was not even wet.
He was struggling not with mud but with a mesh. He
struck down with rifle-butt and then with clawing hands
to tear it aside. There was nothing to tear. Yet his legs
were so entangled that every muscle of his body was strain-
ing. Never before or since, he says, has he known a physical effort like it. Then suddenly he was clear of it and
walking freely in the moonlight. The radjah said: "The
burial place is about here somewhere, Tuan."

They went back over the ground. They traversed it,
crossing through fields and copse. There was nothing
more. There never was anything more, he said, sitting on
his stoep and drinking beer.

We canvassed pretty thoroughly our hearsay of grave-
yard ghosts; but the Controleur knew no coherent tradition or myth which would fill the facts of his case.

Some weeks later I was poking amongst the ancient

stones of Criwijaja, and met the leering image of a she
devil of the cemeteries, Parnacabari; unbelievably foul,
incredibly ancient, and from the darkest distances of
Hindu demon worship. You can draw what conclusions
you will or, like the Controleur, shrug your shoulders.

MIDNIGHT STUFF

Ghosts are most often met in drizzling rain. I was once
carefully instructed never to speak to one who walks
through the rain with a pot of fire upon his head. I pass
on the caution.

Meeting Pontianak, the banshee (cat's face on an owl's
body), you say firmly: "Your hoot is near, your grave is
far, and you are sprung from the lid of a cooking-pot in
a deserted house": which is calculated to fix him. Bajang,
a malignant forest sprite convertible into a familiar, may
be taken at night from the grave of a still-born child unless
you have the fortune to inherit him: once acquired, he
becomes a sort of family heirloom. But he must be kept
in a stoppered bamboo container and fed with eggs and
milk. Djinns sometimes spring from coconut monkeys;
though the green djinn is from the leaf of the mangrove
blown into the green sky, and the black djinn from a leaf
gone to dark rot in the gates of the forest, while the white
djinn is from the leaf fallen on the sea.

To make sure that you will see your ghosts, anoint your
eyes with tears of the slow loris, the lemur which lives his
nocturnal life in the tall trees of the jungle.[2]

Here and there one hears of a European ghost. Thus,
in a small post of the Celebes, a Dutch sentinel has made
his nightly round for fifty years; since, dozing, he was cut
down by native murderers, and so betrayed his comrades

[2] For this and items of similar entertainment, see *Shaiman,
Saiva and Sufi,* by R. O. Winstedt, Constable, 1925.

to the knives. He clumps up and down the passages in his heavy ammunition boots. I knew a man who four times accosted him, but had no answer.

In Sumatra, Islamic and Christian influences are still at war with ancient horrors, and amongst the secret peoples of the jungles much must remain of murderous and lecherous cults that reek of the authentic brimstone. In the country of our next few days were once the Bhairawas, the Terrible Ones, who worshipped their gods in graveyards with flaming pyres of corpses. Their inscriptions record the sensations of the dreadful orgies and of the stenches, which are compared to the smell of flowers and of generation.

This is midnight stuff. Now there is light in the Lampongs, and they are become the scene of one of the great creative enterprises of the Dutch: next day we started out with the Resident and the Assistant to look at the colonizations.

THE HABIT OF HOME

Java, as we noted en route, has had in the last century a fantastic multiplication of population, especially remarkable because it was not accompanied, as in England and Japan, by extensive industrialization. It was owing partly to the influx of Western capital which enormously increased the productivity of the island, partly to the new personal and social security and improvements in public health and hygiene under the reformed Dutch régimes of the nineteenth and twentieth centuries. The rising birthrate coincided with a decline in deaths from endemic diseases and internecine wars. During the last two generations, the Dutch have lifted the standards of living, well-being and education; but fast as they worked the population always outran them, and every increase in the resources of Java was more than counterbalanced by the increase of population which, by 1930, was 600,000 a year.

The Dutch pushed industrialization to the degree they believed wise in the circumstances of the Indies. They encouraged native home industries and the better use of land and resources. But early in the twentieth century they already saw crisis coming, and in 1905 they launched Javanese colonizations in the Lampongs. For a time the colonists were financed by the Lampong Credit Banks and each group was led by the bank manager (a characteristically Dutch touch), who advanced his colonists loans for transport, stock, seed, sustenance and so on. But this method ultimately cost close to 600 guilders a family, which prohibited extensive settlement. Moreover, the easy credits often attracted peasants who, unaccustomed to such resources, were inclined to sit on their haunches and chew betel like any gentlemen of leisure.

Some thousands, however, were satisfactorily established. They began to bring members of their families and fellow-villagers to Sumatra, who worked first as harvest hands and then settled on new clearings. The Javanese have strong local loyalties. They like their own people about them. They like a place to be "ramay," to have the habit of home, of their village, their own adat and custom.

The Dutch have made this amiable character the principle of their colonizations. Now a group goes, whenever possible, from a particular kampong in Java and under its own headman or one approved by him. It forms the nucleus of a new kampong, clears land, plants its crops. The first stage is expensive, for Government must then provide for irrigation, roads, clinics, schools and the skeleton of the economy; but when the new settlers are established they can employ others who now follow from their home village. These help at harvest and have their share of it; and then, with the aid of the established settlers, clear their own ground and sow their own first seed.

Government helps with food supplies, tools and housing materials. It joins in the general co-operative enterprise, encourages the sense of membership one in another
which makes the whole thing possible: the character which
St. Paul recommended to Christians but which seems of
more effect amongst these unbaptized.[3]

The colonists are carefully selected. Young married people are preferred with one or two children out of in-
fancy. The colonists, curiously, often do not have more
children until they have eaten the rice of their own land,
and feel the place "ramay." It seems less a matter of birth
control than of some profound accord between the rhythm
of the peasant's life and of the earth that nurtures him.

Between 1935 and 1940, Javanese were settled in the
Lampongs to the total of 116,000: a steadily increasing
number each year. Ultimately, the Residency may provide
for a million. With colonizations elsewhere, the aim is
an annual emigration from Java of 120,000 families. As
these are mostly people of child-bearing ages, their emigration should stabilize the remaining population at somewhere near its present level.

The whole affair has an exquisite economy and proportion in its detail; and it is remarkable evidence of the ca-
pacites of the Dutch colonial service.

We travelled first to the Soekadana area which has been
wholly developed under the new method. It began in 1932
with 300 families. It is now absorbing 12,000 people a

[3] Once the nucleus is established, later colonists are settled
for little more than the cost of transportation: and even this
they now repay after the fourth year. The percentage of fail-
ures is very low—far below, for example, the proportion in the
settlement-schemes of Australia and New Zealand—perhaps
because the Javanese now does not begin under a load of debt,
and because he is encouraged to make the sustenance of his
family and not the production of particular market crops the
first object of his farming.

year, and it will continue to grow while good land is available and where Government can carry its irrigation channels. Its capital is Metro. The first officer who went into the wilderness there ironically headed his letters from "The Metropolis," meaning his tent. Within a decade the irony is rounded off: Metro [4] has become a little metropolis and may soon be a large one.

LITTLE YEOMEN OF A NEW WORLD

About Metro, as the original nucleus of the Soekadana area, live the earlier colonists; after eight or nine years, mostly in brick bungalows with tiled roofs, gardens, paved walks. Their standard of living is far higher than in Java. As taxpayers, they have probably now returned to the Government more than the original cost of their settlement. They have become propagandists for the colonies amongst their friends and relations in Java; they help the newcomers. We met one plump burgher who wanted the Controleur to take films of his family for propaganda in their native place. He had seventy relations living and working about him. Some were already self-supporting. Within a few years most will be independent farmers, little yeomen of a new world opening to the poor men of Java. Under the hands of the Dutch officers is growing a new province for humanity, a new life for tens of thousands of families and for the generations to come.

Let us sit about on the floor and pass resolutions on the subject of imperialism.

We worked out from Metro, and the great weirs and channels which are the arteries of irrigation, to the frontiers of the forest. We bounced in the Controleur's battered Chevrolet across roads still to be made and cordu-

[4] In Javanese the word "mitro" means a very close friend: so the title has happily stuck.

roys of bamboo spread on oozy mud. In thirty miles appears the whole pattern of the colonization. At the edge of the jungle the latest immigrants are clearing, hacking at the undergrowth, sawing giant trees, clawing stumps, and burning. The thick humus of centuries of fallen leaves and rotted growth is ploughed into the soil now opened to the sun.

The settlers here had come from Java for the last harvest. Now they were on their own land. Government supplies, for the harvest workers, "beddings" or dormitories for twelve families; then, as land is cleared, palm leaf for the family hut and whatever additional rations are needed. Each family has a quarter of a bouw of land for its house and dry garden, and a bouw for sawah, the wet rice field. The extension of sawah is one of the great merits of the whole scheme.

The Lampongers and most of the peoples of the Outer Provinces customarily grow their rice in ladangs, dry fields. After a few years the fields are exhausted, and the farmer moves on to burn out areas of valuable forest for new ladang. The impoverished fields go under alang-alang, a useless grass, and secondary jungle. Both soils and forests are wasted. But the Lampongers are learning from the Javanese the lasting uses of irrigated fields. Nuts and soya beans, tapioca and maize are the first crops. When the sun and cultivation have drawn the sourness off these rich new soils with their forest mulch, two and three varied harvests may be taken in a year.

Parties of new colonists are advised by a predecessor known as kamitoewa, the old boy. He may rise to become a loerah, a village headman, whose rank and estate is the pinnacle of the Javanese peasant's earthly ambitions. We called on a loerah and his wife in their fine new house with its broad stage where he meets his people, and where his clerk was busily typing on a soapbox. When the kampong is established with its loerah and its gamelan (usually a gift and reward for virtue from the Dutch Government) then a Javanese truly feels that his settlement is "ramay." [5]

Malaria is always troublesome in opened jungle-country, but the health services have it in hand; though malaria is the principal reason for discouraging settlers with infant children. But elephants have been almost as bothersome as mosquitoes in the Soekadana area. They have a sweet tooth for fresh young crops; and when a herd of elephants wanders about a settlement they do not always look where they are treading. Sometimes they walk down the mosque or knock over the club. They were on the move at this season when we saw Soekadana. While we drank lemonade with the headman news came that a herd had spent the morning trampling over a neighbouring village. The Resident believed that they were making for the mountains. They move to and fro across the country according to their own mysterious purposes and the degree of dampness underfoot. Often along the roads you see trampled growth and uprooted trees where they have passed.

I remember once in Natal a series of automobile accidents when a hippopotamus formed the habit of going to sleep on a rural road. Elephants are an anxiety to the Sumatran motorist; while across the water, in British Malaya, is a monument erected by the State Railways to an elephant which once charged the local express: a rather

[5] Each colonization-area has also its system of clinics and hospitals. Soekadana, for instance, has a general medical supervisor, fourteen male nurses (mantri), a number of quinine-distributors, two jungle-hospitals for immediate treatments and for minor cases, and a general hospital conducted by a Catholic Sisterhood. The settlers have prophylactic treatment against hookworm, and injections against smallpox, cholera, typhus, and dysentery.

Publicity Dept. K.P.M., Batavia-Centrum (Java)

BHAIRAWAS, THE TERRIBLE ONES

". . . Who worshipped their gods in graveyards with flaming pyres
of corpses."—Page 321

THE MOESI AT PALEMBANG

Publicity Dept. K.P.M., Batavia-Centrum (Java)

surprising tribute from the authorities, when you come
to think of it.

The elephant is a curious cuss. All Malayan peoples
believe that he gathers with his tribes to dance in the
jungle. He also produces lightning, though the savants
dispute regarding the manner of this: the Bataks say that
he throws it with his trunk, but the erudite of Palembang
hold that he strikes out lightning when he sharpens his
teeth. He carries souls to heaven upon his broad back, as
you may see in the primitive stone carvings of Palembang.
He is followed in his forest marches by companies of lesser animals, wild fowl that scratch amongst his droppings,
and the monkey people, deer, and pigs who feed on the
creepers, young leaf and shoots that he pulls from the
high trees. After pig and deer prowls too the tiger. Tigers
haunt the outskirts of new settlements which have invaded their familiar hunting grounds. The colonists build
their first jungle huts high on piles, and ascend to sleep,
drawing up their ladders after them.

IN THE FORESTS OF THE NIGHT

We were instructed in the habits of big game before
we left Soekadana. We wanted to push on for the night
to Martapoera on the River Komering, a matter of something over a hundred kilometres. The afternoon grew late
and the Resident suggested that we should halt at Kota
Boemi, a place halfway, with a pasanggrahan sufficient for
our comfort and cheer. We argued to and fro. The roads
admittedly were poor. We had an excellent native driver,
but we were unarmed and ignorant of the country. It
ended in a compromise: if we could reach Kota Boemi
with an hour of daylight left and if our driver was willing
to go on, we were to try it. But if we had a breakdown
after dark we were not to leave the car.

We rather suspected that our legs were being pulled; for the innocent abroad is always fair game. We knew all about tigers. People may live in the Indies for twenty years and never meet one outside a zoo. Nor, to be brief, did we. But at Martapoera the local Controleur told us that he had shot three man-eaters within a month.

If you leave a car at night to change a tyre or something of the sort, you should flash a torch and fire a warning shot or two; and keep your torch turning on the roadside brush and a gun to hand.

With a herd of elephants, of course, there is no debate. We heard, further on, of a party that left its car beside the road. An elephant came to inspect, and presumably his trunk touched the radiator, run hot. The elephant roared, rolled the car over and trampled it to scrap. That night, on the road, we consoled ourselves with the legend of the man in Kenya who met a herd of elephants while he was cycling on a bush track; and rang his bell.

Without elephant or tiger, it was an exciting ride enough to Martapoera, for the road declined to a jungle track and the sunset came in red and black as a prelude to a terrific thunderstorm which turned the forest to a world of blue fire and rolled with appalling echoes through the trees. In the weird light we were aware of the tunnel in which we travelled. The boughs tangled a hundred feet above us, the sky was utterly lost, the sides of the roads were suddenly watercourses, and giant lizards came up in our lights.

Martapoera lies under the Barisan Ranges. The east of the island is low marshy country, the west and west-centre is a spine of giant mountains; and on such nights as these the jungle of the foothills is loud with rushing waters and the crash of rapids.

Our driver was rather pale when we pulled into Martapoera: so, no doubt, were we beneath the sploshes of mud.

I shall remember that storm. The rest house hangs two hundred feet above a river and all night the blue light quivered even beneath closed eyelids. For minutes at a time you could be heard only by shouting against the thunder. The frame walls shook. The drains and runlets swept across the yard and under the wooden floor. Until we finally got to sleep, we were reasonably convinced, on the available evidence, that the rest house and ourselves were destined to slide into the upsurgent river before the night was out; and only that we felt ashamed of stepping over the native asleep at our door, we should certainly have removed ourselves to other ground.

In the morning, the fresh, washed and unexpected morning, the local Controleur came to breakfast. We remarked, with what we thought praiseworthy steadiness and restraint, on the terrors of the night. "Oh," he said, "was it pretty bad last night? I didn't notice actually. We get it most nights here, and you just don't distinguish."

Humbled, we ate our eggs. But I swear that the storm had addled them.

LAND OF RIVERS

From Martapoera, on the addled eggs, we made for Batoe Radja, and in the morning the air was surprisingly noisy with cicadas and with monkeys. There were yellow flowers that looked like buttercups errant from an English field; and the local peasantry walked abroad with waste-paper baskets on their heads, a trick to which I propose to train my secretary. The people hereabouts are prosperous. While the poor fishermen of Bantam cook in clay pots, here they afford tin pans and kettles, and the children wear slops from village stores which are stocked up with canned fruit from Mr. Libby. In a few miles, however, we ran into alang-alang country, and immedi-

ately the effects of dry-rice cultivation were visible not
only in the wastes of thin grass but in the declining populations by the roads and the rundown habit of the villages.

Beyond, there was native rubber, like groves of young
larches, with delicate grey-green leaves. Kapok is grown
in avenues to Batoe Radja, where one can go to the "Special Bioscope" for five cents or purchase pink and purple
lampshades from Eng Hin, the Official Ford Dealer, or
have one's teeth extracted in open shops upon the street.
The prospective customer can thus compare techniques.[6]
Bamboo houseboats are tied by the river banks and bamboo rafts drift by the red villages. The houses here are
built high, with bird-cages, broken bicycles, cats, goats,
piled wood, gourds, coconuts and roosting fowls beneath.
Porcelain plates are set in the walls; and sheep, geese,
babies, ducks and dogs plash in the middle of the road.

We turned northeast in the valley of the Ogan and ran
all day beside the twisting river as it made for the Moesi
at Palembang. This is the great alluvial plain of eastern
Sumatra watered by countless streams from the mountains. A whole river system converges to form the Moesi,
navigable for ocean vessels as far as Palembang, Sumatra's
major city, and the centre of an antique civilization from
which the Javan Hindu cultures were derived—or were
they?

There is extraordinary confusion in the memories of
Palembang. It was unquestionably the heart of a great
Buddhist power, Criwijaja, which grew perhaps from the
conversion of an older Indonesian civilization known as
Malayu. Criwijaja was great by the seventh century, and
had flung out colonies and missionaries to Java and the

[6] The dentists' shops are something of social centres, like
barbers' and blacksmiths' establishments in other worlds. The
dentists themselves fill their own teeth with gold, as advertisement for the trade and perhaps as storehouses.

Peninsula of Malaya where its strong place was the first Singapore: in Sanscrit, Singa Pura, the City of the Lion, a title still most apt. For centuries the kings of Cambodia bowed prayerfully each morning to the west as tribute to the Lords of Criwijaja.

The Chinese, who in their records speak of Criwijaja as Che-li Fo-che, were of the general opinion that its rulers were sprung from the spawn of serpents: which may represent some early propaganda, pro or contra. The Sumatrese more conservatively held that their empire was founded by a descendant of Alexander the Great; a young man who first appeared to them upon a mountain top and seated upon a white buffalo amidst considerable fire and fury. The dullest account suggests that its founder came from the sea with twenty thousand men and, after the customary preliminaries, begot upon a local princess his heir and dynasty. One might feel happier about the Alexander version if it were not that so many families of royal pretensions in the Orient claim origin from Alexander; which suggests the impact of the great Macedonian on the world but does not much assist the Higher Criticism.

We know that a great imperial civilization grew here amongst the rivers one crosses to Palembang; but we know only enough to recognize one of the most tantalizing of all historic mysteries.

Criwijaja flourished for six or seven centuries. In 1017, when its ambassadors travelled to China with treasures of cloth and ivory and Sanscrit texts and slaves, the Chinese chroniclers first use the word Sumatra: perhaps the Sanscrit, "Samudra," meaning the land of the sea. In the eighth and ninth centuries there must have been great temple cities about Palembang, with thousands of Buddhist monks. Surprisingly little survives, perhaps because this is a spongy country still being raised by the silt of

its rivers. In 1251 Criwijaja was still strong enough to
send a murderous expedition against Ceylon; but within
seventy-five years its great colony at Singapore had been
destroyed by the Javanese in a catastrophe so complete

and horrible that the island was avoided as a haunted place
until Raffles and his English arrived. The Sumatran kingdom itself was breaking into little principalities as Islam
advanced and converted and conquered piece by piece.

Marco Polo was probably in time to see the end of Criwijaja, though he did not know it. But he found Moslem
kingdoms growing in Perlak and Sumatra.

On the Peninsula the refugees of Singapore fled to found

Malacca. On the island of Sumatra appeared a score of minor states: notably a Sultanate here at Palembang and, in the mountain country to the northwestward, the Kingdom of the Menangkabau.

Sumatra is an almost hopeless confusion of cultures and bloods. The early European visitors thought it Ptolemy's Golden Chersonese; and certainly, from the remotest times, it knew the crossroads traffic of the Orient world.

The names of kings upon inscriptions appear in Sanscrit from the third and fourth centuries; but there are titles before them from elder languages. Sanscrit became the tongue of princes, priests and poets, but ancient Tamil words represent the traders of South India, and through them too came terms for merchandise from Arabia and Persia. Arab words are still flowing in with the pilgrims from Mecca and the Moslem literatures; and one meets an astonishing number of derivations from Portuguese. The Padris, the holy men of Islam who gave the Dutch trouble here a hundred years ago, had their title from the Portuguese padres. In Menangkabau, the Dutch Controleur is the Tuan Kumandur, which is English "commander."

If any coherent story is yet made of the strange histories of the Sumatran races, it may come from the philologists rather than from the chroniclers: and some Jespersen yet unborn has a fascinating career awaiting him.

We came down to the main Moesi system at Indralaja, where the Kleker joins the Ogan and they head together for Palembang and the major channel. People were wading and presumably working neck-high in the watery fields and their conical bamboo hats moved across the surface in the oddest way. Half the population seems to live in gondolas; and lotus spreads broadly amongst the reeds. So do ducks in the highways. With so much water about, you might reasonably expect them to keep off Main Street; but I despair of proper dispositions in Sumatran ducks.

MOSTLY IN OIL

We met the Moesi itself at Kertapati and crossed by ferry to the city of Palembang. The Moesi at Palembang is about half a mile wide where it gathers its tributaries to it before dividing again in the network of its delta. The city lies on each bank and right across the river, for a considerable part of the population lives in houseboats; while a great many houses, especially of the richer Chinese and Arab traders, are built on piles and have their shopfronts to the stream; so you go by boat to your shopping. The houseboats may be just an old custom of the Chinese, though it is likely that they took to water when they were forbidden by the Sultan to own houses ashore. However it happened, the whole effect is distinctly picturesque; and the population gets a great deal of healthy exercise from pulling against the powerful current.

Palembang has about 110,000 people, of whom 1900 are Europeans and perhaps 16,000 Chinese. The Europeans are mostly in oil. Downstream are the refineries of B.P.M. and N.K.P.M., the Standard affiliate, with tanks, wharfs, compounds, bungalows spread for miles along the bank; and a very pleasant club house which may help to make some moments of life tolerable for the Companies' people.

The Indies export normally over six million metric tons of petroleum products a year: in 1938 the largest export, in 1939 second to rubber. Oil, coal, the agricultural potential, and geographic situation make Sumatra obviously a fulcrum for the coming industrial and commercial organization of southeastern Asia.

In 1890, when Mr. Rockefeller's first series of amalgamations was a quarter of a century old and his Standard ruled the oil markets of the world, a company was formed with Dutch capital to consolidate the several little oil shows already developing in the Indies. It called itself the Royal Dutch. In 1896, it took into its employ a young man lately an accountant in northern Sumatra (at Medan and Deli) for the venerable Netherlands Trading Company. His name was Henri Deterding.

A few years earlier another young man had built an interesting business in the East. He sold sea shells, and with their profits bought into Borneo oil. In 1897 he was able to unite several interests in a company registered in London. Faithful to his beginnings, he called it the Shell Company. His name was Marcus Samuel, though most people remember him better as Lord Bearsted.

Shell acquired oil tankers and depots. Royal Dutch stayed chiefly in production. When it met difficulties with distribution, Mr. Deterding and Mr. Samuel got together. In 1902 appeared Royal Dutch-Shell. In 1910 Royal Dutch-Shell produced bouncing children: Bataafsche Petroleum Maatschappij (the Batavia Petroleum Company) whose business was production and which was for years to pay dividends approaching half its capital; and Anglo-Saxon Petroleum, whose affair was transport and sales. Presently, Asiatic Petroleum appeared as the sales organization, leaving storage and transport to Anglo-Saxon. Royal Dutch and Shell became holding concerns. They soon held half the oil of the world, with subsidiaries in Ceylon, Egypt, India, China, Siam, the Philippines, the Straits, Australia, New Zealand, South Africa, Italy, the Indies East and West, Germany, Britain, Russia, Louisiana, Panama, California, Oklahoma, Canada, Mexico, Venezuela, Turkey, Virginia, Austria, Hungary, Poland, Jugoslavia and the Ozarks: all by way of what you might call a serious beginning for Mr. Deterding and

Mr. Samuel. They fought Standard in China. Then they moved in on the States and fought Standard at home. They represented what was, in effect, a new sort of empire.

Deterding unquestionably was one of the builders of a world economy. The mighty Shell structure shadowed out the shape of things to come, whether they came from private or from public enterprise. With it, the economic pattern had already outgrown the nationalist State. There is a special and peculiar irony in Deterding's long tussle with the Soviets. He, more than any agent of the Comintern, was a mechanic of the new internationalism. Shell and the like are building the machinery of the world economy. The great political debate of our times is to decide how and by whom the machinery will be controlled.

The economic organization of the world has long outrun the political, but a political order and control must follow if the affairs of the world are to be reasonably ordered. Hitler, Stalin, Trotsky, and Cordell Hull, each from his own position, have understood this well enough. Hitler and Stalin have sought to capture the world economy from the strong-point of a national State. The nationalism of both was an expedient. Their real end was world control. Trotsky believed that the world economy was already developed beyond the point at which it could be captured by a nationalist State, however strong: only international revolution, he believed, could now master the growing world economy. Mr. Cordell Hull has believed that the thing can be done by reasonable agreement. He proposes the most difficult task of all, because his method requires the education of men and their governments throughout the world; and not least in the United States where, for instance, the Smoot-Hawley Tariff Act of 1930 was symptom of a sharp reactionism which provoked reaction elsewhere.

Whether the development of a world economy is in itself good or ill, the fact remains that it is with us, and the conditions it creates must now be met. A world economy requires a world polity, just as a national economy requires a national polity to control and direct it for the general good. But our tribes at large have been singularly slow to discover what was happening: and our troubles now, in large measure, follow from that failure.

There can be no lasting peace in the world until the problem is recognized, and political and moral developments sufficiently correspond to the economic developments in being. But politicians and moralists have, for the most part, been distressingly slow to understand what was happening.

The one considerable effort to establish some sort of political order and moral authority was at the very beginning of this new world in 1494, with the Treaty of Tordesillas, so much misunderstood. But Tordesillas did not provide for the rise of new world Powers which would refuse the moral authority Rome then exercised. When the moral unity of Christendom was broken there was no power sufficient to organize and control the rival interests. The great problem of modern politics is to create such a power. One can only trust (and pray) that it appears as Mr. Hull would have it appear; by the moral education of mankind. . . .

Standard and Shell long ago came to terms in the Indies and elsewhere. Nederlandsche Koloniale Petroleum, a daughter of Standard Oil, makes most of the noise down the river here at Palembang. Koloniale derives from Standard of New Jersey and produces and refines here for the Vacuum and Standard of New York amalgamation, Socony-Vacuum, which transports and sells. People who

take pleasure from genealogical trees might have fun
working out the permutations and combinations of the
oil companies. North, in Djambi, the fields are worked
by the recent Nederlandsche Indische Aardolie, a joint
promotion of the Indies Government and Royal Dutch.

Palembang ships out oil, rubber, and rattan from the
jungles. Ulu the Kite hangs over the river and clotted
masses of water lilies, like flowery islets, go down to the
sea amongst the flotsam of the port. Secretary birds and
speckled deer walk quietly in the little parks; young
eucalypts droop by the peacock trees, and a Chinese merchant in his river house does twenty thousand guilders
a month of business in kretek, the palm leaf used for native cigarettes. Beyond the Ogan the Ramasan comes in
to join the Moesi: paddle steamers go upstream from here
five days to the foothills of the Barisan Mountains. Barges
come in laden with green bananas and the boats are
painted like birds. In the centre of the city the vast for-
tress-palace of the old Sultans is now an Army barracks.
A little outside the city is the tomb of the Sultans who
reigned here after the fall of Criwijaja. Each Sultan lies
attended by his senior wife, his eldest son and his gurra,
his teacher.

The coastal Malays, both of the Peninsula opposite and
of Sumatra's east coast, are a people of the waters; they
rarely move off the rivers which are at once their high-
roads and fishing grounds. Even their towns, when they
can manage it, are built over water. At Palembang half
the ways of the old town are canals and creeks. The Chinese houses have ornaments of porcelain on roof and
beam-ends: a galvanized-iron roof may be a mark of distinction and wealth. At night the glow from the oil refineries fills the eastern skies. By day, with the tempera-
ture high in the nineties and humidity almost intoler-

able, the magnificent Dutchmen can eat a lunch of brown-
bean soup, calf's liver, bacon, sausages, apple sauce, and
semolina pudding.

MEN OF THE GOOD OLD TIMES

We left Palembang in an early hour when the river
was a Whistlerish brown and silver under a monsoonal
sky and the air like thin crystal. Across the river again we
followed the river flats, where the rain trees spread, and
the fan palms, and flame-of-the-forest with its delicate leaf;
and memjaivak the long lizard scuttles along the roads. A
railway went with us, making for the Government's coal
fields at Moeara Enim. Road and rail track have been
slashed through heavy jungle to which we presently rose,
where the elephant hunters still take a useful haul of
ivory and the rattan-getters watch fearfully for tigers and
the unpleasant Sumatran bear; a long, lean, muscular
beast for whom there is little to say in any circumstances.

Moeara Enim lies amongst the first hills and between
the River Enim and the Lematang. It is a fairly typical
example of State enterprise: a wide-spread coal field,
chiefly of open cuts, which employs three thousand Javanese. The local inhabitants are not much inclined to hard
work of any sort. The indigenous Koeboes of the neighbourhood are primitives, rarely seen by other men, living in the hidden depths of the forest, seldom visiting
the sun. They go stark naked. Sometimes one bolder than
the others creeps out to the roads or settlements. They
give a queer account of themselves, oddly circumstantial.
They are all descended, they say, from a brother and
sister cast ashore by pirates (pirates have been an immemorial feature of the Malaysian scene) before any other
humans came to Sumatra. The first descendants of this in-

cestuous union lived a long Golden Age and are remembered as Orang Bari, Men of the Good Old Times.

The Dutch officers and a missionary or two have established an intermittent contact with the Koeboes and some effort is being made to study their lives and habits; but it is difficult to follow them into the hidden jungle unless they lead. You can, with a sufficient labour force, hack your way into the jungle beyond Moeara Enim, and may make a mile a day. But a fellow by the road, who bet that he could reach a tree we had hit with a stone, spent an hour and a half on the first twenty feet and then came out to cover himself with sticking plaster and to find some clothes. The Koeboes and the hunters have their own paths in the fringes of the forest; but a mile or two in, the jungle is already a perpetual twilight. None of the great beasts penetrate there; only birds and whatever may lead arboreal lives a hundred feet above the floor of sodden humus and the terrible tangle of vine and thorn.

It is an odd experience to turn from the primaeval world by a twist of road into the suburban avenues of Moeara Enim, where the mine officials live in pleasant bungalows along paved streets and have their clubs and schools and swimming pools.

The Javanese miners are admirably housed too. The old dormitory "beddings" are now replaced by little houses for one or two families, with tidy cottage gardens. The Javanese are fond of flowers and train convolvulus and climbing roses across their porches.

The mine workings spread for two or three miles along the valley and the dumps are largely inhabited by goats. They graze through the machine shops and apparently thrive on dynamos. One party was busily eating the galvanized-iron recreation hall when we passed. In Cornwall and Malta goats are tolerated for their milk; but the Indonesians do not use either goat or cow milk, though sometimes they will buy condensed milk for the babies. Goats are here chiefly for their meat and because they are an irrepressible sort of beast anyhow.

They attract tigers when pig and deer are scarce and tigers are old. No sensible tiger eats a man while it can catch a pig, a deer or a goat: a fact which might lead us to chastening reflections. A man-eating tiger is thought very little of by his acquaintance. A tiger will not attack a man from the front, because on the forehead of every man is written that text from the Koran which proclaims man supreme amongst the creatures of Allah.

A tiger family (father, mother, and perhaps two cubs) keeps pretty much to its own territory and respects the beat of its neighbours. In central Sumatra an Assistant Resident estimated the family territory at about 600 square kilometres. A grown tiger may run 30 or 40 kilometres a night. He will return to feed upon a kill. He is a stupid beast. Several officers whose business it is occasionally to shoot a killer have told me that when they wait for the tiger to return they hang a light above his meat to shoot by. He is apparently not disturbed by a stationary light.

Beyond Moeara Enim, road and rail rise to Lahat where the rail ends. The country grows rugged, the trees enormous, the rivers churn over rocks: and the curious mountain called Serillo, the Helmet, by the Portuguese, rises between the rivers. It was obviously designed by the architect of the Chrysler Building. It thrusts a fantastic long pinnacle high in the air from its main mass.

I do not know when the Portuguese found and named Serillo, but here as everywhere in the East they were the first-come of Europeans. In 1514 a Portuguese expedition sailed up the Siak River, which opens opposite Singapore, and established relations with the Menangkabau Kingdom. In the seventeenth century Thomas Dias made an incredible journey up the Siak and into the mountains to the heart of Menangkabau; and he seems to have gone again as an agent for the Dutch and to have had great success with the Menangkabau King, who sent his sons and four thousand men to meet him, with innumerable umbrellas of gold; while the King mounted him on a horse, Goenoeng Lajang, the Flying Mountain, and offered him betel nut from a great silver salver. [7]

It is more than possible that the Portuguese made many journeys into Sumatra that are now forgotten. Their official policy of secrecy deprived them of much renown; though perhaps they felt they had enough to spare.

The English and Dutch were mostly content, in the "earlies," to coast about Sumatra, trading here and there. John Davys has left a formidable portrait of a King of Acheen, in the northern parts, whom he met in the year 1599:

His Court is from the citie halfe a mile upon the River, having three Guards before any can come to him, and a great greene betweene each Guard; his house is built as the rest are, but much higher, hee sitteth where hee can see all that come to any of his Guards, but none can see him. The Wals and covering of his house are Mats, which sometime is hanged with cloth of Gold, sometime with Velvet, and sometime with Damaske. Hee sitteth upon the ground crosse-legged like a Taylor, and so must all those doe that be in his presence. He always weareth foure Cresis, two before and two behind, exceeding rich with Diamonds and Rubies; and hath a sword lying upon his lap. He hath attending upon him fortie women at the least, some with Fannes to coole him, some with Clothes to dry his sweat, some give him Aquavitae, others water: the rest sing pleasant Songs. He doth nothing all the day but eate and drinke, from morning to night there is no end of

[7] There is some account of Dias in *Forgotten Kingdoms of Sumatra*, by F. H. Schnitger. E. J. Brill, Leiden, 1939.

banquetting: and When his belly is readie to breake, then he eateth Arecca Betula,[8] which is a fruit like a nutmeg, wrapped in a kind of leafe like Tabacco, with sharpe chalke made of Pearl Oystershels: chawing this, it maketh the spittle red, draweth the Rhume exceedingly, and procureth a mighty stomacke: this maketh the teeth very blacke, and they be the bravest that have the blackest teeth. By this meanes getting again his stomacke, he goeth with a fresh courage to eating. And for a Change with a Cracking Gorge, hee goeth into the River, where he hath a place made of purpose, there getting a stomacke by being in the water. Hee, his great men and women doe nothing but eate, drinke, and talke of Venerie. If the Poet's Fables have any show of truth, then undoubtedly this king is the great Bacchus. For he holdeth all the Ceremonies of Gluttonie.[9]

The English East India Company made only one sustained effort to establish itself in Sumatra. From 1685 until they exchanged it for Dutch Malacca in 1825, the English held Bencoolen (Dutch, Benkoelen), on the west coast and across the mountains from Moeara Enim and Lahat. Both English and Dutch dreamed awhile of making it the great mart of the Indian seas, but it is a shabby place now and

[8] Arecca Betula is the betel nut, of Arecca Catechu the Pinang palm, a slender, delicate tree forty or fifty feet high in full growth. The nut is rolled in pepper leaf and chewed with lime; and exquisite craft is devoted to the silver boxes in which nuts, leaf, and lime are carried. Betel is rather more to the Indonesian than meat or drink. It blackens his teeth, but it scents his breath, and if the drooling red mouths of girls are something of a shock to Europeans, their lovers think of mouths red like pomegranates. The betel is apparently harmless enough to use. The slightly elevating effects are probably from the pepper leaf more than the nut; and the local poets can make something even of black teeth.

[9] From *The Voyages and Works of John Davys the Navigator.* Edited by Markham, Hakluyt Society, First Series, Volume 59. London, 1878.

was when Raffles came there as Lieutenant-Governor in
the years after his Javan adventure. The indefatigable man
for a moment galvanized it into life. He abolished slavery
and the forced cultivation of pepper which the English
Company here, in a desultory fashion, had imposed. With
his second wife, he made astonishing journeys across the
mountains into the heart of old Menangkabau and contemplated restoring that kingdom as the central instrument of a British protectorate for all Sumatra. He and his
contemporary Marsden wrote the first serious works upon
Sumatra. Raffles and his wife learnt languages and nursed
the sick and climbed mountains and walked thirty miles
a day and came down rivers on bamboo rafts and discovered the giant flower three feet across, *Rafflesia-
Arnoldi.* He imported two French naturalists; and his
children shared their apartments with two small tigers, a
baby bear, a blue parrot and a favourite cat. He kept a
pet elephant and had an orang-outang which was dressed
in a "surtout of fine white linen" and which Raffles expected would "soon become a great favourite in Park
Lane." He had difficulties with the Dutch and with the
Court of the Company at home and with the Foreign
Office, for officialdom was not in the least sympathetic
with his efforts to create a new eastern British Empire.
But it was as Lieutenant-Governor of Bencoolen that he at
last went to Singapore.

There is little left at Bencoolen now to remind one of
the English, except the curious high stone graves which
are distinguishable throughout the Indies as the graves of
Englishmen. Amongst the tombs of Bencoolen is Parr's,
Raffles' predecessor. He was murdered by natives in his
bed though his wife covered him, wounded, with her own
body and fought his murderers until they flung her away.

ELEPHANTINE WAYS

We had been joined at Palembang by a Dutchman who probably would not much care to be identified with a book of this trifling sort, and whom we shall consequently call T. He was once a planter in the rubber country behind Medan, but long ago he turned orchidist. He has an estate in the Toba country where he grows seven or eight hundred varieties of orchids (a good proportion of the orchids at places like Philadelphia and Kew came from his cultivations); and he spends most of his time now travelling the country. He has an astonishing acquaintance amongst the natives from one end of Sumatra to another; and he handles a car in bad country better than any man I have met in much travelling that was rough and tough. We ran into a stretch beyond Lahat, where the road becomes a twisting track amongst the bouncing foothills and the jungle is overhung with cloudy mountains. T. slowed to fifty miles an hour, and said, "We must be careful, isn't it?" To which we, watching women washing amongst the rocks of the ravine two hundred feet beneath the offside wheels, agreed.

Ficus, of which there must be hundreds of varieties in the Indies, dominates the scene as you go north; with the original indiarubber (guttapercha) trees, and boengoer, whose flowers resemble the lilac's. Tgitgirawa's warbling note sounds in the glades: "He is so nice, he is so friendly," says T. But beyond, when we rose to brown bracken country, we met the lalang bird, bronze, and black tailed, and with red beady eye: a fever carrier, the natives believe, and altogether of evil omen. Settlers are gradually moving into the jungles here and making lonely sawahs. They come out to the roads and build platforms where they may in their leisure sit to see whatever of the world goes by. Women in the little villages beat out the marrow of the sago palm. The trunk must be beaten seven days before it is split for its heart. The men sit circlewise and regard the village scene: the slush under the houses, the tailor in his shop, the rusty tin advertisements for Sunlight Soap (I suppose no one has such faith in advertisement as the soap makers), the vast mass of the Dempo which erupted violently in 1930. The villages seem part of the jungle itself, in all but those curling tin advertisements. The life of the people belongs to the earth: they are rooted in it, weave their houses from its growth, are eternally attached to it by plough and hands moiling in the slush of sawahs.

Stream after stream runs down the hills, headwaters of the Moesi system, turning by bamboo brakes and clumps of tall sword ferns in the secondary jungle. Beyond Tebing Tinggi there is primary forest again. The forest is eternally in leaf. In these tropics it has at once its spring, its summer, and its autumn: across its hillsides one may see young leaf and old, the full green of summer and the sere and yellow; for the trees vary in their seasons. But it has colour only where it reaches the light. In the wet, cold darkness below, the leaves are limp and white and eddy quietly down in the windless places to the humus, the fungus, and the mould. Trees, creepers, lianas, rattans struggle up towards the air. Each great tree is host to countless guests and parasites that coil like ropes about the boughs and trunks to seek the sun. Beneath are silence and shadows and dripping moisture and mildew spread like a silver web across the darkness of decay.

But at night there is light, of phosphorescence and fireflies; and the forest is loud with cicadas.

The monkeys walk in the tree-tops and suck eggs. The natives shop in the forests for fruits and rattan and bamboo and thatch. They go in paths beaten by the heavier animals. Elephants carefully pick the easier grades and

firmer footholds. And in these parts, before the main-
roads survey comes through, the roadmaker usually follows
where the elephant led. Where the track gives out in slush,
the industrious Roads Department spreads what the Dutch
call a knuppel weg, the bamboo corduroy which survives
all but the wettest wet but makes damned rough going.

T. kept an eye out for Koeboe in this neighbourhood.
He has several times seen them here crouching beside the
road; and has talked with them. They live well enough, he
says, on pig and deer, young palms, fruit, and fish. They
watch you with their heads oddly cocked to one side, like
a dog listening and looking. T. considers them a happy
people. No tax gatherer has yet caught up with them.
They have only one weapon, a long piece of wood sharp
enough to gut a tiger. Their more civilized neighbours
build houses very high, for this is tiger country, and a tall
clean pile also discourages the green scorpion which is
even more of a pest. T. remarked that as he came this way
to meet us he heard of a woman who was lately cutting
grass in a roadside field. She cut right up to a dozing tiger
before she saw it. She died of fright.

ANIMAL OF DISTINGUISHED MAGIC

We came at evening by Bangko, a high promontory between rivers. It looks west to Soembing, Raja, Patahtiga,
and Korintji, 12,540 feet above the Indian Ocean, the land
of Indrapoera, the City of the Gods, the Sumatran Olym-
pus. The women of Korintji sing sacred songs in a strange
language about neolithic monuments of stone, survivals
of old phallic worship: and all the Archipelago knows that
the men of Korintji are tiger people who are transformed
in season.

Paddle steamers come up from Djambi to the markets
of Moeara Tebo. The people trade mats of crude native

rubber to Chinese middlemen. Fishermen paddle their dugouts. Caladium spreads leaves six feet across. They make useful umbrellas. The banana palms grow gigantic. The rivers, brown and turgid, swirl under high banks, and toss matted vines and clotted lilies and sometimes the wreck of bridges. We crossed the Hari at Poelau Moesang, named for an island of polecats now happily gone with the stream.

Ferry crossings are rather disturbing affairs where a slippery track drops sharply to what looks like a primitive raft of planks, mostly loose. All the population of the ferry-side turns out when a car appears, for there is always the exciting possibility that it will bump across and off the raft. The river is very deep and was running down at fifteen miles an hour. The week before it had carried away a car and a Chinese family.

The ferry has an outboard motor, satisfactory enough if it continues to function; but outboard motors sometimes stop in midstream. Then you go on the current while the crew does what it can with poles and sweeps. So you employ half the men of the village for the crossing, which costs in all 75 cents.

Another ferry followed at Tandjoeng. On some roads you may do a dozen ferries in a day; the rivers are intolerant of bridges. The Tandjoeng ferry is a wooden platform across three dugouts. The motor developed in midstream a distressing asthma. T. was reassuring. The current would, he said, bring us ashore within six or eight miles, if the engine failed. So we sat on the boards and talked to a travelling tinker. He had two large boxes filled with Japanese thermos flasks and electric torches, mugs and kettles and cooking pots and braziers. Business, he said, was good in the jungle kampongs. But he disliked the peoples of the rivers. They do, indeed, look a dark and surly sort, and it is advisable to conform to their own code of manners. The

tinker told us that a pig-eating python had been killed
that morning back along our road. The pythons of these
parts manage anything from the mice of the rice fields to
a tough old boar. We heard in the mountains of a python
which entered a cage and ate a stud boar of the domestic
breed. Boar eaten, however, python could not get out
again between the bars: and so was taken and dispatched.
I now never eat my bacon in a cage.

The conversation turned to crocodiles, as we watched
the grey trunks go downstream. The crocodile is an
animal of distinguished magic who looks into the future
and the past and governs rain and wind. Every man has
his own crocodile and may ride upon his back wherever
he will, if he can find his affinity. The first crocodile, of
course, was made of betel-nut palm and the joints of the
sugar cane by the nurse of Siti Fatima, the daughter of the
Prophet, as a plaything for the lucky child. But the crocodile misbehaved, and Siti Fatima cursed it: "Thou shalt
be the crocodile of the sea, no enjoyment shall be thine,
no lust or desire." She deprived it of its teeth and tongue
and drove nails into its jaws, as you may see at a glance.
But the crocodile is still kramat, sacred: though you may
sometimes hunt him, if with proper invocations and apol-
ogies. Thus, in Perak, when the line is set with a white
fowl, the crocodile is properly addressed: "O Dangsari,
lotus flower, receive what is sent thee by the Lady Princess
Padang Gerinsing. If thou receivest it not, may thine eyes
be torn out." A crocodile may be trapped if he takes a
member of one's family; and nowadays, of course, his
leather is profitable and an economic twist has been given
to the old relationship.

On these roads we put up at the Government's pasang-
grahans. The degree of comfort depends mostly on the
mandoers and their families who usually conduct such
places, and upon the attention which the local Control-

eurs are able to give them. The conveniences are limited, though there are bathrooms where one sluices oneself, on the Dutch dipper system; and the septic tanks commonly function. There may be beer and Bols and Australian sherry to drink. The food is mostly out of cans, though one can always depend upon bananas. Surprisingly often there is ice, sent out from the sub-district centre. The company is usually small officials, foresters, road engineers, and commercial travellers, and loud over its beer. The decorations are invariably portraits of the Dutch Royal Family during several generations. Top-score in any pasanggrahan of my acquaintance is nine Queen Wilhelminas. Spiders and scorpions may appear, but you squash them for the ants to clean up.

LAND OF MENANGKABAU

Beyond that day's third ferry (this worked on a cable against the stream) at Kota Baroe begins one of the loveliest countries of the world: the land of Menangkabau, of mountains, lakes and flowery meadows, where the peasant's house is wrought with intricate art and the craftsmen remember skills learnt in the courts of empires that are now half myth, half legend.

You begin to climb immediately from the river bank, through ficus and the tall red hardwood, moranti, and wild kapok which spreads beside the road and above the delicate russet leaves of cinnamon. The road twists and turns at acute angles and sharp elbows. You have seldom fifty feet of it visible ahead. It winds twenty miles up the passes; then suddenly you are out on a long plateau between new and utterly unexpected mountains which march across the whole horizon, a succession shaped like Assyrian helmets or the Sugar Loaf at Rio, each suggesting a gigantic mono-

VILLAGE UNDER THE HILL
"Tucked in plantations of coffee, bananas and cinnamon."—Page 356

MENANGKABAU COUNTRY
"West, above the Indian Ocean, is Lake Manindjau."—Page 355

Publicity Dept. K.P.M., Batavia-Centrum (Java)

MENANGKABAU FARMSTEAD

"Six rice barns . . . the roofs thatched, the walls of carved panels:
but all worm-eaten and harbour now for rats."—Page 356

HEADMAN'S DWELLING-HOUSE

"One central room perhaps fifty feet in length and many small
chambers."—Page 356

Publicity Dept. K.P.M., Batavia-Centrum (Java)

lith. The passage broadens to a plain and narrows to a pass. It opens to wide pastures of green and gold where the shepherds sit beneath their Japanese umbrellas: the peaks close above you and you swim in their blue haze. And in that incredible dale, you meet the first Menangkabau houses.

The Menangkabau house is of carved wood and brightly painted. Its roof should be thatched. It is shaped like a ship, long and with its ends rising as if to prow and stern. It rests on piles and seems to float upon its meadows. Its legend goes back to an ancient prince of this ancient people who travelled once to Java in a Chinese junk, and was so taken with the cut of it that he turned it to domestic use.

The style is in decline, of course. Galvanized-iron is replacing the soft thatch, and new generations build in the fashion, which has overtaken all the world's domestic architecture, of making a house to resemble a box. There is still enough of the old stuff left to state again the case for peasant cultures; but soon the traditional arts will be as remote from the common men of Menangkabau as they are from the modern clerks and garage hands in Chartres and Canterbury.

So that it was apt enough that we came out of the dales to Sawah Loento and the coal fields of the Oembilin.

The Menangkabaus occupy most of the mountain country of central Sumatra. They regard themselves as the pure fount of Malay life and culture. Their colonies in the Malayan Peninsula, surviving from their old empire, preserve with the fidelity of these Sumatran mountaineers the adat and traditions of Menangkabau.

> *What in the beginning are covenants*
> *Grow into customs:*
> *Custom is lord over covenants.*
> *Water proceeds along waterways,*

Sanction proceeds from covenant;
A country grows with its customs.[10]

The Menangkabaus still work in glass, in filigree, in the precious metals, in copper and in wood. They are potters and boat builders. The women weave in silks and cloth of gold. They are all shrewd traders, and the Chinese make little headway in Menangkabau. Nowadays, the young men scatter and find employment as clerks in Batavia and Soerabaja, Singapore and Medan. There is an amiable tradition that their literacy is partly from an old custom of conducting courtships with love letters. Every young woman expected a pretty turn of phrase from her young man, and the sort of leisurely dalliance usual to societies where women strongly influence social habits. Menangkabau is a matriarchal society.

Inheritance is in the female line: names, property, and privileges descend through the mothers. A wife continues to live at home with her mother's people, and her brothers are the guardians of her children. The husband continues in his mother's house and governs the property and the children of his sisters. Whatever property he may acquire on his own account passes not to his but to his sisters' children, while his children inherit from their maternal uncles. It is all very complicated, but it gives the women a social significance almost unparalleled in Eastern countries.

When holding was dovetailed into holding,
When our stretches of rice field were made,
When the shoots of our plants swayed in the breeze,
When our betel palms grew up in rows,
Then were established our custom and system of entail.

. . . .

[10] Quoted from *Jelebu Customary Songs and Sayings.* Journal 78 of the Royal Asiatic Society (Straits Branch).

Warden of the wife is the husband,
Warden of the husband his wife's family,
Warden of the family its elders,
Warden of the shire the chieftain,
Warden of the world the king.[11]

The structure is hierarchical; and though the Menang-kabau have been Moslem for centuries, their matriarchal *adat* has survived the pressure of Islam.

Each village has its Council House, and each old house its rice barns worked with all the ornament and carved beam ends and arabesques of the family dwellings. The adult men of the village meet in the Council House with their headman to discuss their local government. But they are mostly now old men; and the rice barns are falling into ruin. In the villages between the River Oembilin and the Lake of Singkarak, you hear all day the clatter of looms, but now in little factories, not in private houses. The Industrial Revolution is beginning.

We talked with a group of elders. They said that there are still master carvers to be met. But now you must pay for all things not in rice but money. A fine house in the great style might cost four thousand guilders. There are no rich men any more since wealth was counted in paper and silver. Once a man's wealth was stored in his barn. Now the crops go to the middlemen for whatever price they will fetch. The young men work for wages in the coal fields and the shops, and many leave their own country. Some return to marry with their people, but not enough. It is hard on the girls. There are fewer labourers in the fields, fewer children in the houses.

So Menangkabau meets modern times and a social revolution apparently quite inevitable unless the country could be sealed against the world. Even the old men do

[11] *Ibid.*

not think that possible. The fever is already in the young men's blood.

The problems are understood by the Administration, and the Dutch do what they can to ease the course of change. But, whatever Menangkabau is to be to-morrow, it remains now in my mind a sunset land. I remember Singkarak in the evening, the wide waters turned to rose and silver, the fields gently going to the shores, the women in white santri at prayer upon the rocks.

CHAPTER SIXTEEN

Dominions of the Sunset

LAKE MANINDJAU

FORT DE KOCK, 3000 feet above the sea, is now the centre of Menangkabau. It has its name from the Dutch commander in the Padri War, and his Redoubt crowns a sharp hill in the middle of the town. West, above the Indian Ocean, is Lake Manindjau, clearly designed to the specifications of a tourist bureau. You go by lanes and villages where poinsettias droop over mossy walls, giant marigolds mount the slopes amongst palms, sugar cane grows to violet feathery tufts, and pomegranates are in fruit and flower. Cinnamon bark, stacked, sweetens the roadside airs; orchids grow with spears of flame amongst the bracken. Buffalo carts, highly decorated, come to market. The buffalo wears shoes cut from old tyres. Each house has its long fish pond which also serves the sanitary needs of the household. Sometimes the house is built across the pond; the householder bathes under his bedroom and catches his breakfast through the kitchen floor.

In the mornings people fill the roads to fields and markets. The Menangkabau businessman carries his dispatch case and his umbrella neatly balanced on his head, a thing which I have never seen in the City. Chickens defy your automobile until the last desperate moment and then, remembering that they are birds, take to the air. Each village with its mosque looks in the distance like a little port of ships.

You climb the hill called Poentjak, and Manindjau lies three thousand feet below, a dark pearl, a moonstone in its setting of jagged hills. It is smaller than Singkarak, perhaps ten miles long and six or seven wide, but it has great depth of water. Under its hills and about the shores are wooded promontories and little islands: through the gap which is a river gate, where the Antokan goes out, the Indian Ocean shines across twenty miles of coastal plains. Poentjak drops almost perpendicularly through a tangled scrub of bronze and green to the shoreside sawahs and the villages. Birds plummet past into the deep. You hear doves cooing a thousand feet below.

In a dip along the hilltop we found a man and his daughter and their wooden sugar mill; the immemorial mill that men and oxen worked in Egypt and Chaldea, the beginning of all our mechanics. The kerbao walks in his wooden yoke endlessly circling. The wooden cogs grind and crush, the juice flows out to wooden pans. Small girls appeared out of the brush and picked us orchids. We ladled melted juice before the fire and poured it into cups to crystallize.

In a village under the hill, we came upon the finest group of Menangkabau houses we anywhere saw, tucked in plantations of coffee, bananas and cinnamon. One headman's house had six rice barns, each twenty feet high and balanced by carved legs on broad flat stones, the roofs thatched, the walls of carved panels: but all worm-eaten and harbour now for rats. The families of his sisters and their daughters occupied the enormous dwelling-house, which had one central room perhaps fifty feet in length and many small chambers. At one end and raised like a dais was a curtained bedchamber done in dirty blue satin and lace, where the betrothed daughters of the house re-

ceive their acquaintances before marriage and presumably
their husbands for the honeymoon. I never discovered, to
my complete satisfaction, how the husband and wife manage. I suppose he calls at intervals. Queen Wilhelmina
presided over the blue-satin covers, so all is done, presumably, in good order.

The headman complained, like the elders, of the money
system. Once he paid his people with coffee, corn, cane and
rice. Now he must sell his crops for money to pay wages.
Middlemen have the most of his harvests. Every one nowadays wants money and what money buys. The headman's
own house was a litter of cheap chairs and oil lamps and
brummagem stuff. Chairs are chic. The family usually
squats on the floors, but when we arrived, chairs were
drawn out and every one sat awkwardly on them. The
headman delivered himself, perhaps for the family's benefit. Once a man was happy for days if he had but a new cap
or a new sarong, going about from one neighbour's house
to another to show himself off. Now there must be teacups
and tin kettles; and a day's wages go on bus rides in and
out to Fort de Kock. So the rice barns empty and the fields
are pawned away.

They think such things in Menangkabau and there may
yet be consequences. They have taken to repainting on
their houses the kerbao horns, symbol of the old power of
their kingdom.

The Javanese once came against Menangkabau with
great force. The armies were ranged when a chief of
Menangkabau proposed that instead of a human slaughter,
arbitrament should be by battle between two buffaloes.
The Javanese agreed, and the day of trial was appointed.
The Javanese chose a hefty cow. The Menangkabau, with
their native shrewdness, took an unweaned calf from its
mother until it was frantic for milk, and, on the day of
battle, fixed bamboo shafts to its budding horns. Led into

the arena, it saw the Javanese cow and charged the milk-supply with such enthusiasm that it transfixed the enemy. So, at least, they tell the story to innocent strangers.

THE PASSIONATE MOUNTAIN

We came back in the evening by the mosque of Sarek whose sacred pools are fed by living springs, and between the twin mountains which are south of Fort de Kock: Singgalang, whose name means Singing Birds, and Marapi, King of Fire, both volcanic cones rivalling the Javan Merapi. Northward is Ophir. Once Marapi's summit was lost in heaven. Snow was brought from his slopes to cool the wine at the wedding of princesses. But Ophir had a lovely daughter, with whom Marapi fell in love. To demonstrate his affection, and doubtless to impress the lady with his peculiar talents, he blew and he blew upon his heart of fire, until he blew off his head. Now he is a mere ten thousand feet and still a bachelor, though said to have some arrangement with Singgalang across the valley.

But his volcanic passion has enriched the earth, and the best rice I ever saw grows about his feet. At evening over Marapi hangs a rainbow, the sign of the Radjah, its one end leading to the Radjah's gold and the other to the bathing-places of his royal daughters.

By Sarek are antique tombs in Hindu styles. Women winnow rice in the wind; and when one halts, the children gather about to talk, the boys with their pet chickens and followed by the ducks and geese. We met a man by the mosque who had seen us at Palembang. He was curious to hear of our country and our people and our purposes. The Menangkabau travel about much and they like to discuss one's comings and goings and the state of the roads in Afghanistan, so to speak.

At Fort de Kock we were tempted for the first time in

Publicity Dept. K.P.M., Batavia-Centrum (Java)

MARKET PLACE, FORT DE KOCK

"All Menangkabau comes to be barbered, doctored, dentisted . . . above all to gossip."—Page 359

Publicity Dept. K.P.M., Batavia-Centrum (Jav

MODERN DUTCH
ARCHITECTURE
SUMATRA

" 'It is easy to becom
more Menangkaba
than the Menangka
bau.' "—Page 360

years by golf, but resisted. The course lies in a tremendous canyon on the edge of town, a gigantic rift in the earth four hundred feet sheer down except by winding paths, and thirty miles long. It has a violent tropical growth along its walls and there I recklessly clutched at a bamboo and felt its hairs in my skin for three days. Scraped from the cane and added to food, they make a nasty instrument of murder.

At Fort de Kock we met a huge red orang-outang still mourning, after months, for his dead mate. There too we at last had a fair chance at the gamelan and played, to the dismay of the neighbourhood, on drums and gongs and, to our own peculiar delight, on the viol en rebab.

We went much to market. The market is an enormous affair on four levels, each nearer Babel than the last. I suppose that it occupies in all a square mile, with its terraces and slopes. All Menangkabau comes to be barbered, doctored, dentisted, and tailored, to buy, to sell, to be entertained, and above all to gossip. There are ducks, geese, wicks, flints, steels, slippers, shoes, sarongs of Padang, axes, leather, tobacco in long rolls and in sheets, knives and grinding-stones, straw hats and portraits of Queen Wilhelmina, copies of the Koran, French novels done into Arabic, margarine, Oat Flakes, Mobiloil, old keys, orange-ade from Hong Kong, jam from Chicago, umbrellas, chalk, baskets, praying-mats, brooms, fishnets, cordage, bird cages and photographs of Deanna Durbin.

I itemize because the standard of living represented is much higher than in the markets of Java. For instance, you can have Mickey Mouse in rubber and the Seven Dwarfs in coloured prints, stained-glass windows, watches, babies' comforters, moneybelts, and goldfish, which you carry home gasping in wet sacks on your head. There is all the customary stuff: collar-studs in a world where no one wears collars, old tyres, chillis, soda, beeswax, alum, feather-dusters, glass bracelets, garlic, papayas, and djoe-roek toetji kapula (a little green citrus for washing your hair), incense, cakes of Government salt, bowls of tea to be blended to the customer's taste, spools of cotton, marrow-bones, and packets of flower petals to scatter in the bath, fishballs, cakes, eggs, and the hundred varieties of rice, dried fish in uncountable stinking heaps, baskets of pigeons, peanuts, sewing machines and unmentionable meats. The biggest single markets are for fish, meat, coconuts, rice the spices: the basis of the native economy. The show is like a mediaeval fair, even to the tumblers and jugglers. It functions three days a week, which indicates the strength of the economy and the Menangkabau passion for trading. We bought in the market tictacs, ticlacs, or whatever they are called: the wooden sandals that go tic-tac-lic-lac along the roads of Asia. The transaction spread over four stalls and fifty-five minutes.

In the market we met an old man with a champion singing bird. He was properly proud of it and had adorned its cage with electric-light bulbs clothed in red wool.

The Dutch officers usually develop a strong attachment to Menangkabau. The Assistant-Resident, whose seat is at Fort de Kock, grinned: "It is easy to become more Menangkabau than the Menangkabau." Menangkabau has its own People's Council for the Residency of Sumatra's West Coast whose capital is Padang. The Council has nominated representatives, some elected by taxpayers whose income is above 120 guilders a year, some elected indirectly from the villages. Its meetings are distinguished for their debates; in Menangkabau the sovereign power is not in Sultan or radjahs but in palaver, and interpretation of the customs. Immemorially, the people have governed themselves by communal, clan, village and family councils. In a village council, one man's sustained objection may defeat a proposal, for people have a vast respect for considered opinion. A newly come official sighs over them. The consensus of opinion is sovereign, with custom. The Menangkabaus are earnest Moslems (much more so than the Javanese, for example) and have their mosque in every kampong: but even the mosque cannot resist the adat. The Menangkabaus are a proud and independent people; all, by the way, descended from Alexander the Great; and their lords of the Gold Land, "fragrant with strong drink."

THE FACTOR OF ISLAM

Padang is southward, on the ocean coast and by a road which winds through Anai-kloof, a gorge reputed to send painters crazy. This country is tough on writers too. There is, after all, a limited vocabulary for mountains, lakes and forests. I leave it to the Guide Book: "Constantly scenery which is never dreamt of, is placed before the astonished eye and be it that no multi-coloured meadows like in Europe are seen, in its stead the various forms of trees and the different shades of green, noticed on all sides, are a perpetual feast to the eye." We and our eyes came out, slightly intoxicated, at a fishing village where the Indian Ocean was crisping mildly on the beach, and the fishermen were working from the sands and from prahus offshore with seines woven from the sugar palm, and eight or nine hundred feet long. The boats are bright affairs, green and white and blue and black, beaked like a bird and with a painted branch in place of a mast. On its trimmed twigs, the fishermen hang their hats and lunch and lights. The familiar "eye" design of the Eastern seamen, from Sicily to China, is painted at the bow. The fishermen, burnt through ages on equatorial beaches, are much darker than the mountaineers, and much poorer.

The old port of Padang, where the Dutch established a factory in 1684 as counter to English Bencoolen, lies at

the mouth of the Harau and under the Apenberg, but the
river is still filled with prahus, some careened, which are
much the size, when one remembers, of the little tubs that
came and went by Good Hope. There are English graves
at the mouth of the river, relics perhaps of some forgotten
foray. Along the river are fine old Dutch houses (one
now houses the Council of the Menangkabau), and great
godowns still in use. The Chinese quarter may outdate the
Dutch. It has a temple worth attention. There is a lovely
Chinese house in the heart of the town, with wide gardens
and seven delicate pavilions, built for the seven daughters
of the house that each might there receive her lover in the
moon time. At the turn by the bridge are the graves of
Arabian merchants who grew to great estate long before
Dutch or English sails appeared on Indian seas. But Marco
Polo may have known some who lie here.

"A nice and refreshing seat," says the Guide Book,
"offers the verandah of the clubhouse"; but somehow we
missed it.

The Resident's House is an admirable example of colonial Dutch. Across from it is an interesting Catholic church
in the latest manner, which the Dutch invented. We talked
to missionaries at points along the way. They make, the
Catholics especially, considerable headway amongst the
Chinese, but little with the Sumatran Moslems. We saw
the reason, at the large mosque across the river. Islam is
getting organized. From the mosque were coming long
processions of the Congress Perti: Moslem Boy Scouts in
blue and khaki, girls in blue with white veils. Islam is
building up youth movements, and making extensive
propaganda with newspapers and pamphlets and through
its powerful Laymen's Associations.

There is unquestionably new life in Islam. The instructed Moslems of my acquaintance all see Christendom
as in decay. Its wars are symptoms, in their eyes, of moral

and social collapse. They are men whose whole history attests the power of religious ideas. Islam is an empire which transcends races and leaps frontiers and passes deserts and oceans. The power of the Prophet and the swords that leapt to his bidding once organized half the world. To such men, it is clear that the end of Europe's faith is the end of Europe's power. A man is strong while he believes. For a thousand years, the two great Internationals stood over against one another. Now it seems that strength oozes from the Christian Thing. But Islam remains immeasurably strong. It waits the return of its time; which, it believes, is almost come.

Islam as a factor in the modern situation has been strangely neglected by most Western commentators, perhaps because they have forgotten the power of great dogmas. The men who really understand seldom talk to the Radio Audience. Their reports are tucked in the files of British and Dutch Colonial Offices.

Nearly 3500 pilgrims went to Mecca from Sumatra in 1938. The journey cost them six or seven hundred guilders apiece. Each returns as hadji (wearing the white cap of virtue) and probably a propagandist of Pan-Islam. Many establish schools. One meets hadji schools here and there about Sumatra: little villages in themselves. The courses may last four or five years. The instruction is usually in religion, Arabic letters and literature, and bookkeeping, for Islam is a hard-headed creed.[1]

[1] At graduation, the student makes the pilgrimage to Mecca and returns either to teach or to trade. The mosque people, the teachers, and the merchants are the nervous system of Islam, and transmit intelligence. The British Ministry for Information in Asia distributes in the remotest villages news of Britain's supporters amongst the great of Islam, and the peasants of jungle villages are quite familiar with the names and politics of the leaders of Islam in Egypt, Arabia, and all that world. The Dutch colonial services have produced great

THE MONKEY KEEPS COUNT

Beyond Padang is the modern port of Emmahaven, which ships out pilgrims and the coal of Oembilin. "Nothing can exceed the tranquil loveliness of this small bay," says the Guide Book, "only disturbed by the constant arrival of trucks loaded with coal." So we kept on southwards to the superlative Boengoes Bay, a Riviera to end all Rivieras, with forest-clad mountains dropping to the beaches, freshwater springs and streams, long shoals alive with bright fish, wooded coral islands, turtles . . . the obvious locale for pirates and buccaneers, Long John Silver and all.

The fishermen of these parts wear the only thoroughly sensible hats I have ever seen. Hats in the rest of the world are so much waste of space; but about Boengoes they are enormous flat bamboo affairs, raised at the sides, and lined with banana leaf made waterproof by pitch. The top of the hat may then be filled with water, like a bowl, and fish carried in it home alive.

We met a great many monkeys under the hills. They came and sat on the car and complained politely but firmly of our lack of bananas. There was something of a squabble on the front seat over a baby, but a tribal Solomon gave judgment and cuffed the illegal claimant off. Then he cuffed the obviously authentic mother. Women do need to be kept in order.

That afternoon we walked with two men and their monkeys to get coconuts. Here, if you want coconuts, you

Arabic scholars, and the Indies' Administration maintains diplomatic contacts with the rulers of Islam's Holy Places. Some thousands of students from the Indies are studying at the great schools of Arabia and Egypt; and the health and safety of the pilgrims are obvious concerns of the Dutch authorities.

first catch your monkey. This is the sort of thing which slows the tempo of Eastern life, no doubt. Monkeys are trained for coconut picking by fixing a coconut to a chain dropped through the worn hole of an old rice mortar. The man twists the coconut as he might twist it from its stem. When he has done this several hundred times, the monkey becomes interested and experiments himself. When he has the idea, he is tried out on trees. A graduate monkey can go up a palm, twist his nut and fetch it back to earth in about 32 seconds flat. Monkey and man then hire themselves out. They receive one coconut in every ten they pick. The monkey keeps count. At evening, going home, he clutches his chosen coconut. He does not really like coconuts, but he has an acquisitive instinct, like some of his relations.

On this day we slew our first kampong hen. We were to score heavily later, but no kill is like the first. Nor did other poultry make such a mess on the wheels. During negotiations that followed, we learned a good deal about the care of hens. This hen was the only hen of its owner, which made it a hen of great price and not only in the sentimental view. If a man has only one hen, it is his affectionate friend. He strokes and caresses it and feeds it with the titbits of his table. He squirts mouthfuls of water over it in the heat of the day, he washes it with scented soap, he carries it to bed with him. The hen responds, to lay a steady egg a day, taking hardly more than a few weeks' holiday each year. But if a man owns two hens, he cannot give each such attention. Total output falls to an average of about an egg and a half per diem. If a man owns a hundred hens, he would hardly be bothered at all at the death of one. But as it was, his heart was broken and his breakfast uncertain. We paid up.

But we asked anxiously about ducks, whose tendencies are even more suicidal than kampong hens'. It seems that a duck, with loving-kindness, may push its production up to 350 eggs a year. We were very careful about ducks from thenceforward.

LAND OF OPHIR

North from Fort de Kock we travelled by canyons and the rounds of hills into the land of Ophir, a great fair mountain visible far out in the Indian Ocean.

The Exegetes, disappointingly, insist that the Biblical Ophir was in Arabia or Africa. John Davys had other views. The Rumos, he said, by whom he meant the Turks (the Commentator asserts that "the reason of that name is their Metropolitan and Imperial citie of Constantinople, called New Rome"), sail out of a port in the Red Sea, "the place from whence Salomon sent his ships to Ophir for Gold, which is now called Achien, as by tradition they doe affirme. And the Rumos people from Salomons time to this day have followed the same trade." Achien, of course, is Sumatra, and the people here have traditions of men who came through distant ages from the West, seeking gold. Gold, as Raffles discovered, is found in caves on Ophir, vestiges of primitive workings. There is said to be an ocean drift from the Abyssinian coast to this where the style of craft in the seashore villages of Sasak and Pariaman suggests Arabian and even Egyptian influences; and there are always those queer Arabian stories of marsupials.

Did the navies of Tarshish and Hiram take three years to go and come from Africa? And where in Africa did they find peacocks or almug, which is the Indian sandalwood? Fortunately for the Exegetes, whom otherwise we should have on the hip, the Portuguese were excessively enthusiastic in these matters and named another Ophir on the Malayan Peninsula to confuse the issue; unless Solomon knew several Ophirs. He probably needed them, what with the many strange women, the daughter of Pharaoh, women of the Moabites, Ammonites, Edomites, Zidonians, *and* (as the Testament emphasizes) Hittites.

In an elbow of the River Masang is a school of carp, thousands in a few yards of stream, and especially blessed by Allah. The native will eat fish from fifty yards up or down the river, but if he ate one of these huge carp he believes that his belly would swell (which seems likely) to exploding point (which seems less credible).

Near by is a rice mill of a sort older, I imagine, than any other water mill. At one end of a beam is a pestle. At the other end is a tub. Water runs into the tub from a bamboo shoot. The bucket fills and empties. As it empties, the pestle at the opposite end descends upon a mortar filled with rice. Man is an ingenious beast.

We had left heavy rain behind us and we wished to know the state of the roads ahead. We asked if there had been rain here. The question was considered carefully. The issue was not whether there had been rain but whether we would care to hear about it if there had been. The Indonesian is very polite. He prefers to give an answer that is pleasing rather than one that is merely true. T. joined the conclave, which some time later settled that there had been showers.

The native vocabularies are rich in local usuages. Thus "topi" is a general word for hat, but each village or even each family may use its own peculiar word for its own peculiar sort of hat. Ordinary speech uses words sparely. If a dog is described in his absence, he may be called the white dog of Mahomet Oelong. In his presence he is merely "Whitey," and you use your intelligence. Formal speech is often confusingly oblique. Women are seldom called by name. They are the mother of my friend Ismail, or the elder sister or the wife. Mother and father are often addressed as the parents of their first-born: thus Mak

Awang or Pak Awang, the mother or the father of Awang. There are forms for those older than one's father; and for the various grades of social superiors and inferiors. It seems a world designed for or by Mrs. Emily Post.

We passed the relics of a village which was swept away in flood with most of its people three years back. T. had known the place and mourned over it, until we found pigeon orchids by the road which distracted him.

EQUATORIAL

This day we crossed the Equator north of Ophir, in heavy forest. The roadside runlets were appropriately steaming from sulphur springs. I remember the forest about Panti chiefly for its butterflies of yellow, purple and ebony, and its scarlet dragonflies; and our lonely pasang-grahan for its files of Punch. Here we fell into talk about the mouse deer, which we thought we had seen in the forest. The mouse deer, as you are aware, is a time server, and an Eastern counterpart of Renard the Fox. We heard a tale.

Once a mouse deer was sitting eating terong rimbang, which are ants, when he heard a tiger approaching. He was terrified, and all his bones seemed to melt; but he made a great noise as he chawed up the ants and cried out: "Ah, my friend, how delicious are these tigers' eyes." Then he ate another and answered in a still louder voice, "Especially pickled." The tiger, naturally, was startled, and he went off through the forest thinking heavily, until he met a bear to whom he said, "Hiya, Sang Bernang, has Your Bearship knowledge of a vast animal that lives in the ant-heaps yonder and eats tigers' eyes?" The bear had not the pleasure and answered truthfully, "Thy slave knoweth him not." The tiger then said, "Let us go together and see, and in case one of us be more alarmed than the other, let us tie our tails together, so that each shall be, so to speak, the other's rearguard." The bear (foolishly, I have always thought) agreed.

They approached the mouse deer and his bones were now turned to nothing better than streams of water, but his intellectuality still functioned. "Ho yo," he shouted, "look at this misbegotten tiger. His unmentionable father was indebted to us for a white bear, and now he comes dragging a miserable, shabby, and moth-eaten black. Is this the way Sang Haramau pays his debts?"

The bear naturally cast a cold eye upon Haramau the Tiger. "So that's your game is it?" he grunted, and began to pull and to heave. The tiger too tugged, for there was funny business hereabouts and he thought it well to leave. They tugged and they tugged, until suddenly the bear's tail tore right off. And that, of course, is why bears have no tails.

Beyond the forest, we passed into the Residency of Tapanoeli, and the country of the Mandalings. The great hills of the borderland have been burnt off and it is a lonely and a haunted land, the Hills of Ghosts. These marches between Menangkabau and Mandaling knew long ages of war, and Bataks from the north came raiding in the days of their cannibalism. The sulphur pools add to the effect, and doubtless shrewd border strategists encouraged nasty stories. But the land beyond is beautiful, with wide green valleys between the mountains and an air both domestic and wild, like Italian mediaeval landscapes. Beside the roads grows ironwood, a timber so heavy that a man can hardly lift an ordinary chair made of it. It keeps a hundred years in water and the Dutch have used it for bridges and telegraph poles and, in the old days, for stockades as they pushed this road northward in the pacification of the country.

We were soon to enter country where men now middle-aged have been cannibals. Their sons may live under a democratic order if Dutch ambitions are fulfilled. From Padangsidempoean we struck towards the Indian Ocean again at Sibolga, a bay of islands and coral reef and charcoal burners, which trades with the strange islands of Nias, and is famous from of old for its export of gumbenjamin. From Sibolga, the highroad makes a return literally dizzying into the mountains: a sign in Sibolga warns of 1300 corners in the 64 kilometres to Taroetoeng, while Taroetoeng announces that it was 1400 corners in 66 kilometres. I do not in the least blame the locals for their confusion. As T. says, the road is a snake with a very bad stomach-ache. It tunnels through rocks, runs under waterfalls, slashes the red hillsides, and its banks are drifts of flowers. It climbs into the Batak country.

BATAKS

The Bataks occupy all the hill country of north-central Sumatra. Little was known of them until the third quarter of the nineteenth century, when the Dutch gradually imposed their peace. The Bataks had a remarkably unsavoury reputation for cannibalism; and it is pretty well established that cannibalism persisted in out-of-the-way villages until recently. The Bataks are sensitive on the subject. We passed a monument in the hills to Munson and Lyman, American missionaries killed and supposedly eaten there: but the word "eaten" is said to have been erased from the original inscription out of respect for the rude forefathers of the neighbouring hamlets. The Bataks have for centuries held grimly their mountain passes. Islam made little progress amongst them until the nineteenth century, when the Mandalings were won over by the Padris. Now the Mandalings dispute that they are Bataks; perhaps because the word Batak means pig eater and is a Moslem term of abuse. There are now more Christian than Moslem Bataks; but many remain heathens. Their High God seems to be an anthropomorphic figure married to a Blue Chicken. Creation was hatched out. The evil divinity is Naga Padoha, the World Serpent. In spite of their long isolation and much that is barbarous in their social habit, they retain from an antique civilization (presumably Hindu), the wet-rice culture, the plough, the horse, chess, cotton, the spinning wheel, divination. Their religion seems to have a Brahmanistic background, though it is a materialistic creed and chiefly concerned with their temporal prosperity. They are shrewd, hard, and mercenary. T. always called them "the Prussians"; curiously, German Lutheran missionaries have had more success amongst them than propagandists of other creeds. They have a written literature preserved on palm leaves and bamboo. Their alphabet was once thought indigenous, but it seems to be of Hindu origin. Women and thieves and sorcerers are said to have each their private dialects, and the "language of the leaves" is for lovers. There are considerable differences in dialect amongst the seven or eight major groups of Bataks. They are eager for education. One already meets Batak doctors and teachers, lawyers and (of course) politicians. Smiths are specially honoured amongst them. They have copper gongs and clarionets and a small violin. They smoke copper tobacco pipes and they eat anything from dogs and cats to frogs, ants, snakes, and elephants.[2]

They are notoriously warlike; many villages are heavily fortified and unapproached by paths. But their rules of war respected growing crops, chiefs, women and children. Wars were formally declared and the lands of the con-

[2] The most adequate account that I have met in English of the Bataks is in E. M. Loeb's *Sumatra,* published by the University of Vienna Press.

quered could not be annexed. On the other hand, when
feeling ran high, prisoners were frequently eaten. The
Bataks probably encouraged their grim reputation as a
weapon of psychological warfare. Before they ate a man,
however, they declared him a blackguard and possessed
by an evil spirit. To dispose of him became a public duty.
It is said that slices off the living body were roasted and
eaten before the victim's eyes: but the facts are now difficult to get, and customs probably varied from place to
place.

From the barren frontier hills, three and four thousand
feet high, open the dales of Taroetoeng of the Christian
Bataks: smiling meadows, soft curling streams, rustic lanes
and village churches, as it might be in the Tirol. But
roofs, we noticed with a little shock, were painted in
camouflage. We were within range of bombers based on
Indo-China. There are thermal springs in the plain and
terraces of calcium sulphate building below steaming
pools.

Efforts have been made to establish European colonists
in this hill country. The ideal elevation for Europeans
is between 1500 and 2500 feet, and a good farmer could
make a living according to Western standards on 15 or
20 acres but for native competition. The Europeans tried
various crops unfamiliar to the natives; but when they
were profitable, the peasant switched to them and under-
cut the European. Unquestionably, however, these up-
lands are a potential ground for European colonization.
Sumatra is still much of a wide open space, as the Germans know. It has had its rôle in their scheme of geo-
politics.

Under these hills is the great lake of Toba. It is sixty
miles long, thirty wide: but half its area is occupied by
the thickly populated island of Samosir. Slaves were
traded on Samosir until 1914. From the southern heights

and three thousand feet above, Toba Meer is lapis-lazuli and all the colours of black opal. The lake has a special and persisting blue, perhaps from its sulphur content. Samosir and the lake itself were long sacred and their secrets guarded. A party of French and American explorers were murdered in an attempt to reach it during 1835. Van der Tuuk saw it in 1863, and got away with his life.

On the southeastern shores of Toba the villages are walled by clay mounds in which planted thorns and bamboos make a most formidable defence. A well-grown thicket of bamboo is practically impenetrable. The villages here rise like green islands in a sea of rice. It is a country of wide fields and golden palms, of cliffs torn by seismic shocks, ravines, and terraced sawahs. Every prospect pleases, but man is fairly vile. Behind the green walls of bamboo, the people live in an accepted squalor. The beautiful houses survive culture long declined. The great banyan, the ghost tree that presides in every village, may remember old glories but is better acquainted with centuries of misery. Beneath it, locked in wooden stocks, the prisoners were kept, and there were slaughtered.

Within, the painted houses are dark as a pit. Each, in tiny cubby-holes, houses eight or ten families, with one rickety open space of floor amongst them. The family pots and possessions are heaped before each cell: its bamboo water pipes, knives, baskets and pandanus mats, its piles of yams, potatoes, coffee, tobacco, coconuts and sugar cane. In the roof hang baskets of rice and corn. Shadows in the corner are babies, old women or just sacks. The light is from cracks in the floor and dim torches of banana wood, which emphasize the prevailing darkness and add to the variety of stinks. The cooking is done beneath the houses, which are raised on piles. I went poking in the villages with a medical officer. He says that the houses are probably aseptic from the reeking smoke of the fires. But the morning fug must be terrific.

A family sleeps in its cubicle, except for its unmarried men and adolescent boys, who are turned out to the sopo, the village council house. The precaution is necessary, for Batak morals are distinctly loose. They grin over a pretty girl. "There is no dainty cake on which a fly fails to settle," they say, and the shrewd, dirty imagery is characteristic. Lean and vicious pigs scavenge through the village and serve the same sanitary functions as the fish of Menangkabau. The filth is unbelievable.

Their society is patriarchal. A woman is the property of her father or her husband. The Toba Batak speaks of his wife as "that which I bought." The women wear large silver ornaments, ear-rings, bracelets, necklets. Their teeth are filed at puberty. Once the incisors were knocked out. Teeth filed to fangs and blackened with betel are not attractive. The filed teeth rot.

The Bataks, even where prosperous as they now often are, seem still shadowed by ages of cruelty and oppression. When faiths and cultures die, dark things rise from the depths of men's souls to possess them. The devil, too, abhors a vacuum. In a living culture, man's personal life is sustained by the beliefs he inherits, the traditions of his tribe, the social complex in which he is bred, the ethos of his people. When these fail, he is a naked prey to evil and not least to the evil within himself; prides, lusts, and cruelties that were called Original Sin. And when religion dies, it is succeeded by the abominations of superstition crawling up like slimy things.

This perhaps is what we see beginning in the West. It happened to the Bataks and a hundred other peoples. European imperialism at least did them this service. It let in light and air upon their stagnant, twilight world.

The squalor of the villages is not only a physical squalor.

BATAK HOUSE

"Each, in tiny cubby-holes, houses eight or ten families."—Page 373

Publicity Dept. K.P.M., Batavia-Centrum (Jav

BATAK HOUSEWIFE

"The Toba Batak speaks of his wife as 'that which I bought.'"
—Page 374

It is a strange and maybe a frightening thing to recall, but the only village I saw in the Batak country where men seemed *clean* and at peace with themselves was a leper colony. I do not know how to make this understood, for we too now forget the things that are to our peace.

This affair of Empire is something more than the ships, the armed men, the great plantations, new security, exploitation; it is also the medical services, the schools. The whole story is not in the economics of imperialism. There are also the hospital at Kabandjahe and the lazar houses of Laoe-si-Momo.

In the hill stations of the Toba country, at Prapat and Brastagi, you may see the planters at play in resort hotels which have the customary manners of such places. We preferred to watch them at their jobs and went down to Pematang Siantar.

BIG RUBBER SHOW: SIANTAR

Siantar is in the heart of the Residency of Sumatra's East Coast, which includes the Sultanate of Deli, and adjoins Acheen. Until late in the nineteenth century all northern Sumatra was left much to itself. Tobacco planters appeared in Deli during the sixties. Acheen remained recalcitrant and a nest of pirates who worked the northern waters of the Straits of Malacca, which has been, since the opening of the Suez Canal, the main route east to China. In 1871 the Powers gave Holland a free hand to bring Acheen to order. The job took nearly a generation. Recurrent and stubborn jungle fighting continued until 1908. The interior is still tough. Perhaps that is why the Dutch put their German internees in Acheen.

There are still 127 native principalities in Sumatra, most in these northern parts. The Dutch govern with and through them under terms prescribed by treaties and what is commonly called the "Korte Verklaring," the Short Declaration, which defines the principles and privileges of the arrangement.

This was a country both rich and sparsely peopled in comparison with Java: with untenanted lands sufficient for large plantations. It has consequently become the principal centre of European activity in Sumatra. Medan, the capital of the East Coast, has a higher proportion of Europeans and of Chinese than any other city of the Indies. The Residency is Sumatra's chief producer of rubber, tobacco, tea, oil palms, and fibres.

Siantar is in the middle of vast estates. It is a bright, modern little town with long clean Chinese shopping quarters, clubs, swimming pools, and schools, including a special academy for the sons of Batak headmen, who are being educated for responsibilities still hereditary.

The Goodyear Estates, occupying many square miles east from Siantar, are a good example of a big rubber show. They have their own estates, roads and rail tracks, coolie lines and villages with shops and native markets, schools, hospitals, maternity homes (one, I recall, mounts a stork: which probably makes little sense to the natives who are familiar with all the facts of life at six years of age). The coolie lines are long wooden buildings partitioned off for families, with bathrooms and cooking-places. The European managers and sub-managers and sub-sub-managers live in bungalows across the terrain, and in little townships.[3]

Rubber estates are a vast monotony of tidy grey-green trees whose neat rows run for miles unbroken. The

[3] Rubber was first grown seriously in British Malaya and the Indies in the eighties. *Hevea Braziliensis* is native, of course, to the Amazon; but Brazil produces about only 1½ per cent of the world's supply, British Malaya more than 50 per cent, the Indies something over 25 per cent. Of the

planters have every excuse, in my opinion, for behaving like the characters of Mr. Somerset Maugham, if they do.

The estates are commonly policed by huge bearded Sikhs and Punjabis, warriors from British India. The Sikhs also seem to have a corner in cow milk at Siantar and Medan, where the enormous men in flowing white ride bicycles about with cans of milk suspended from the bars.

Some of the great Dutch estates about Siantar combine rubber with oil palm and sisal. We travelled, on one estate, through twenty miles of sisal and manila hemp.

The largest estates may employ thirty Europeans and up to 20,000 coolies. The Sumatran will seldom work as a coolie and these labourers are mostly Javanese; though in the Outer Possessions as a whole, half the plantation labour is Chinese.

The Javanese worker on a Sumatran estate earns much more, in cash, than he could earn on the cramped lands at home. But he is a rather dismal figure. Shades of the prison house begin to close about the employee. When a man only cuts sisal or only taps rubber all day long he has become an industrial worker. He loses the varied skills of the peasant. In the alien coolie lines he is lonely for the life of his village; until he forgets. He becomes a rootless man, a man desocialized: a number in what is no longer a community but an aggregate of toiling individuals. He becomes a modern man. And that, I suppose, is the heaviest charge against the plantation system. It reduces the social and cultivated men of Java to an industrial proletariat.

Indies' contribution, roughly half is grown by the estates, half by the peasantry. The restrictions by agreement of 1934 and the years following reduced production drastically. By 1939, however, it was up again beyond the figures of 1933.

SHAPE OF THINGS TO COME

We turned west again, climbing amongst the tea estates, on rising country between 1500 and 6000 feet. The bright-green shrubs are shaded by *Grevillia robusta,* the Australian silky oak, here called the Shadow Tree. Tea is picked in the green leaf, dried a little, crushed in red copper, fermented, dried again. By the roads were hedges of blue verbena, alive with yellow butterflies, drifting in millions like leaves on the wind.

T. has his estate on the eastern slopes of the mountains, and a long rambling house which he built himself. His Dutch ancestors hang upon the walls and are rather surprised, I imagine, to find themselves in the Toba Highlands. He has bronzes from Herculaneum and Tanagra figurines, and a long gallery of the Sumatran crafts; progressing from Acheen in the north to the Lomboks of the south: the textiles, silver work, horn and copper, the variety of creeses and scabbards, of drinking trays, betel boxes, and models of houses and ships. The creese (kris) is the characteristic weapon of all these peoples: a waved, serpentine, two-sided dagger, eleven to fourteen inches long: the blade of watered or of damask steel. Dip in poison before using. T. has gathered gold and silver from the ancient mines and amethyst from a cave he once discovered where, he says, the stuff is in lumps as big as cart-wheels, more or less. He refuses to prospect further. "One is caught up again in the machine, isn't it?"

Several hundreds of varieties of orchids were in bloom in their houses. The lady with us came dripping with orchids and gardenias and demanding to be taken to the opera at once. T. grows his own tapioca, rice, maize, pine-apples, fruits and vegetables of various sorts. He has his own strip of forest and his own tumbling mountain stream.

He lives very well, and there seems no reason, as he says, why other Europeans should not settle on the country.

We returned to Toba, climbing the stiff hill of Oerong Pani to a little pasanggrahan and an eighty-mile view in all directions. The lake is far below. Mountains leap about it, most volcanoes. The lake is probably a result of seismic disturbances and subsidence. If volcanoes insist on belching out the innards of the earth, ground must give somewhere. In the hills behind Prapat are strange valleys filled with moss of such perilous consistency that a man walking would be immediately engulfed. Perhaps the elephants go there to die; the old African puzzle is also a question here. We came by Seriboedolok, the land of a Thousand Hills (it seems a serious under-estimate) and saw, far to the south, how Samosir was made an island by a Dutch canal across its neck. The Bataks were much perturbed when the job was done. Samosir, they said, would fall like a severed head to the bottom of the lake. The Dutch established a Resident on the island to reassure them.

The women of the Karo Bataks, north of Toba, wear their sleeping cloaks drooping upon their heads. Their clothes are indigo-dyed, blue, black and purple; so often are their hands. The old crones' tortured mouths are fallen in on toothless gums. The country is too cold for regular bathing in the open, and the Karo Bataks just stay dirty. They have much tuberculosis, dysentery, and endemic typhoid. Every woman between fifteen and forty (estimates are difficult with a people so wizened and wrinkled) has a baby present or to come. Each in a market group, amongst the chickens, potatoes, twist-tobacco and the foul-smelling doerians, suckles a naked child. Silversmiths in the markets melt down old coins, long used as amulets: thalers and Spanish dollars, guilders and English crowns. I imagine that you might find a tester there if you hunted long enough.

They seem a poor, dirty, and unhappy people: yet great natural virtues appear now as the centuries of oppression are lifting. The doctors at the mission hospital at Kabandjahe speak well of them and a doctor has opportunities to judge. Kabandjahe is training Batak girls as nurses and midwives. They are intelligent and teachable.

These hospitals are admirable. Kabandjahe has a good operating theatre, laboratories, specialized clinics, and accommodation in the wards for hundreds of bed cases. The mission has a Government subsidy, and the patients are expected, properly, to pay some small fee if they can. The maternity wards are for normal as well as abnormal cases; a woman who has been through normal childbirth in the hospital will instruct other women in the villages, where the native Sairey Gamps have been an abomination.

VILLAGE OF HAPPINESS

From the hospital we turned back into the hills, to the leper station of Laoe-si-Momo, the Murmuring Waters, though the natives call it, and not ironically, Koeta Keriaken, the Village of Happiness. We went up with the young doctor who directs both the hospital and the lazar village. He and his wife were six years from Haarlem. They have three flaxen-haired, pink children, with Dutch cheeks still in the upland climate. I have thought of them often since.

Leprosy is very frequent amongst the Toba and the Karo Bataks, but oddly distributed. Scores of cases may come from one narrow area while the neighbours seem almost immune, though all live much the same life, eat the same diet, mingle in the markets. The causes of leprosy are still obscure. Under the microscope, the bacillus resembles tuberculosis: and lepers give a Wassermann reaction, though there is little venereal disease in these parts. A man may live with a leprous wife and not take the disease. Babies are born clean to leprous mothers. When we left the place, we washed, and were made to wipe our shoes on mats drenched with Lysol. No one knows whether these precautions are of any consequence, but they are comforting. The horrors of the disease have not been exaggerated: the rotting fingers and toes, the decay that creeps on to eat hands and feet, the blinded eyes, the nose receding into the face, the terribly dropped lobes of the ears, the ulcerous flesh. In its nervous form, leprosy twists the hands and feet like arthritis.

Yet the lepers are strangely patient. They joked with the doctor. An old man fumbled with what was left of shrunken thumbs and fingers to show that he could still roll his cigarette.

The Chinese seem especially susceptible to leprosy. The face of a young Chinese woman, who must once have been beautiful, was an eyeless blank. We talked a long time with a Chinese boy. He was markedly intelligent, curious about the affairs of the world he will not see again: and resigned. The disease sometimes is checked, and the leper goes back to his village. But these returns to the world are not much approved either by staff or lepers, for the last state then may be in misery and neglect. Once the round, white, insensitive blot appears upon the skin, the leper belongs no more to the world outside. When they enter here their relatives may come to see them, two or three or four times. But gradually they are forgotten. The leper is still an outcast. Once, they were driven into small houses of thatch and burned alive.

Most lepers are happier amongst their kind. They live here in four beautiful Batak villages which they themselves have built. Each village has its headman and councillors, like villages outside. They farm their own land, grow their own rice, fruits, and vegetables, and are partly self-supporting. The missionaries, we noticed, paid them for any work they did or for materials, so the leper has a small money-income. Leper is trained to help leper and himself. In such a place as Laoe-si-Momo, a leper may live twenty years with the disease, though each year since its foundation has added a long line of crosses to the grave-yard of the Village of Happiness. Crosses, because, without persuasion, the lepers almost all become Christians. In their darkness, the Christian Thing shines; and whence else have they had succour?

Laoe-si-Momo is a sad and terrible place, but beauti-ful with more than a mere loveliness of woods and streams. I can even understand why the lepers call it the Village of Happiness. In a queer way, it made me happy. There is still pity and mercy and heroic virtue: there are still Christian men.

We came down through the mountains, by the smoking mountain of Sibajak, the Exalted One: between the ave-nues of teak to the tobacco fields of Deli and the planters' town of Medan. But we were not thinking of these things.

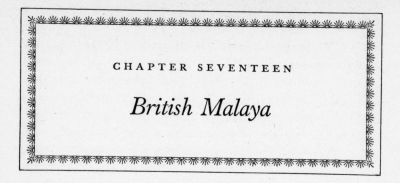

THE STRAITS

A PASSAGE of the Straits of Malacca, when the sun is northward, is a slow process of stewing. The sky is blanketed in grey-white cloud, piling to solid cumuli about the horizons. The sea is much the colour and texture of elephant skin, and sluggish. You lie on the bunk under a fan and read the stale detective stories which must represent the major part of English literature to Dutch travellers; or you drink liverish Dutch lager; or you sit spread-eagled to such breeze as may be, in the long Dutch chairs. You sweat, not fully and freely but with a slow greasy ooze.

The sun is seldom seen in its passage across the sky. The fin of a flying fish draws a pin scratch across the water. Distant islands are blue pencil strokes. A flotsam palm or some broken frame of basket or bamboo is visible two miles away in the flat sea. The torrid day draws up all colour. One conceives that even the fish below are sucked of energy and roll listlessly in their luke element.

But the stars are brilliant at night: and the dawn over Malaya might serve as dust cover for such a title.

The Straits are little more than water lapping over mud, seldom more than 100 or 150 feet deep, and shoaled and islanded. Sumatra is shadowy to the west, the long penin-

383

sula of Malaya to the east. There may be ground for the ancient tradition which Camoens knew:

> *From this Peninsula, they say, the sea*
> *Parted with puissant waves, and entering tore*
> *Samatra's noble island, wont to be*
> *Joined to the Main as seen by men of yore*
> *'Twas called Chersonese . . .*[1]

Men have always lived an amphibian existence in the Straits. With huts on mudbanks or coral islets or in the mangroves of the coasts, they have fished and traded, sacked and sunk and slaughtered.

These Orang-Laut and all Malays are men of the waters. Inland they keep to the rivers, fishing and irrigating; and the sea still murmurs in their blood. At sunrise in the Straits, the boats spread from horizon to horizon: painted canoes (kolek pulau) in the estuaries; koleh sa-hari pulan (called for the crescent moon) drifting with four-sided sails across the fishing grounds; and the two-masted payangs and prahus which lump cargoes between the ports and bowl along very well in a breeze, as the ships of His Majesty's Navy learnt when any coasting trader might turn pirate on occasion.

Malayan piracy has a long and distinguished tradition. The Straits have always been a great trade route, and along these coasts villages grew to empires on the profits of trade and toll and murder. Criwijaja was an empire of seamen. As Empire declined, the pirates rose again much as the robber barons succeeded the imperial police and law of Rome. The seas and islands and coastal swamps are a labyrinth for swift escapes, hideouts, and secret docks and depots.

Piracy always appears in a dissolving order, and when

[1] From Richard Burton's archly archaic translation of the *Lusiad,* Canto X, Stanza 124.

those who should police begin to plunder. The little pirate risks his neck. The princeling founds his gangster state. Civilization goes down in grab and graft.

Grab and graft were already established habits of the Orient régimes when the European first came East. The European often joined in the local game, but his superior discipline in the long run pulled things back to some shape of order. The factories at Malacca, Bantam, and Batavia became safe ports of trade. Native shipping and commerce revived. But peaceful traffic was always an encouragement to pirates until European sea power came to dominate these seas. The flag was often slow to follow trade. In the early nineteenth century, piracy was at its peak. From the Philippines to Timor, from Burma to New Guinea, cutthroats scoured for slaves and spoil; and most of the native princes up and down the Peninsula and Archipelago were partners in the business. The British East India Company's port of Penang was regularly skirmished, and pirates lay up in Singapore to watch the departure of honest junks and prahus which they promptly followed to sea. They raided into the harbours. Singapore was often under what amounted to blockade. In the 1830s the administration was gloomily forecasting the end of the settlement, for the cost of suppressing piracy seemed more than the town and its trade were worth. News of the bonanza spread to China and new fleets of pirate junks appeared.

Britain was slow to act the brutal imperialist and kick the pirates heartily in the pants. Not until the late thirties were sufficient ships of the Royal Navy sent to Eastern stations, and pressure put upon the native princelings. I suppose that those who object to British imperialism will still object: but the alternative east of the Bay of Bengal was chaos. No other Power in Asia could have policed the seas; and peace upon the seas was a first condition of progress for the Easterns themselves. Peace was a British interest and it was the British interest that the Navy served: but it also made possible the reorganization and renaissance of the Indonesian world which then began.

With a strengthened China Squadron and the work of Brooke of Sarawak, and with the aid of a reformed administration in Johore, the Straits Government brought the Malayan pirates to heel: though in 1855 indignation meetings at Singapore were still viewing "with deep concern the ravages committed by pirates, Chinese particularly, in the immediate vicinity of the port, to the great destruction of human life and detriment to trade."

At any weakening of European prestige and power in the East piracy has recurred, as in the years since 1914-'18. In the 1920s many ships out of Singapore were pirated by Chinese gangs, who usually embarked as passengers; eight in 1926, six in 1927, for example. Hundreds of attacks were made on prahus and junks each year until the pirates were smoked out of Bias Bay.

Piracy helped to break the Roman Empire; for a thousand years after, it clogged the whole world's progress. The point is worth re-emphasis: Hong Kong, Cavite, Singapore are not only forts and markets of economic imperialists, but police stations on the waterways. All who benefit from peaceful commerce and the intercourse of nations are their debtors.

We met no pirates in the Straits of Malacca. I wonder how it may be ten years hence.

THE GATE OF HISTORY

You pass the Straits and think of the history that has preceded you: the dugouts creeping from primaeval homes beyond Burma, Akyab or Hanoi, to people the Indies and the islands of the Pacific; the great junks and

Chinese embassies, kings travelling with parrots, gold and pearls to receive a silken robe and seal from an Emperor in Nanking; prahus from the Spice Islands whose cargoes were traded and reshipped and traded until they reached the furthest markets of the world and stirred ambition in Lisbon and Genoa, London and Amsterdam. Here began the trade routes to China and India and the Persian Gulf, to the Euphrates and Oxus and the Mediterranean cities. Here were the ultimate riches of the East for which Columbus sailed. Here Albuquerque, dreaming a fantastic dream of Empire, made it real in ten years. Here came Xavier, with Goa and its difficulties behind him, Japan and death and the altars of the Church ahead.

I was reading Dampier, who always noticed carefully marks for seamen: ". . . Several islands lying S.E. by E. Easterly from Pulo Verero . . . when they bear S.E. at 3 or 4 Leagues Distance, you may steer away E. by S. for the Malacca Coast; which standing by its self amidst a low Country, it appears an Island, though I know not whether it is really one. . . . It is a very remarkable Hill."

It is indeed. It has guided the seamen and the great enterprise of Europe in the Far East. Here and at Goa are the beginnings and the symbols; Malacca, where Albuquerque conquered and Francis raised the Cross; fort, mart, and mission. There is no city in the world where you may better catch the image of an age when one small shipload of men might sail to make an empire and two poor priests go out to convert the kingdoms of the East.

Malacca has been, these hundred years, a quiet little town with the Union Jack drooping lazily above its ancient stones and the historic sea. It is a period piece, almost a museum piece. But now it enters history again, for in the shadows of walls that were Portuguese and then Dutch walk Australian infantrymen. Where Albuquerque and Xavier once dreamed of an Imperial and Christian civilization, they are followed by men of their European sort but from a continent of which they had heard no more than a wild rumour (else Xavier would certainly have set out to convert it): who now hold the road and gate which Albuquerque and Xavier opened for Europe to the furthest East.

Malacca is a European town, Portuguese, Dutch and English; a Malay town, a Chinese town, and an outpost of India. It has known the meeting and the clash of men and cultures, and has had for generations now the quiet air of an English village. It may be a sign for the future as well as a memory of the past, if order is extended and prevails. Brahman, Buddhist, Confucian, Moslem, and Christian have made Malacca; and learnt to live in peace.[2]

It was a fishing village when the first Singapore fell to the swords of Madjapahit in the fourteenth century. A handful of survivors fled north: and Permicuri, their Prince, "fortified himself on the crest of the hill, in a strong position where he was free from the fear of the enemy." He enlarged his territory by conquest and his city by commerce. Presently, the Chelis or Klings of Coromandel came to trade their stuffs for the gold and spices

[2] Malacca is one of the Straits Settlements. Eastward is Negri Sembilan, a member of the Federated Malay States: southeast is Johore, an Unfederated State. British Malaya consists of the Federated Malay States of Perak, Selangor, Negri Sembilan and Pahang, the central bloc of the Peninsula; of the State of Johore which lies between them and the island of Singapore; of the Unfederated States of Kedah, Kelantan, Trengganu, and Perlis to the north, which were ancient dependencies of Siam and were brought under British protection only in 1909; and of the Colony of the Straits Settlements, which means the islands of Penang and Singapore and the small enclaves on the mainland of Malacca and Province Wellesley, with Labuan, Christmas and Cocos Islands. The Colony, in all 1351 square miles, is British territory: the States, with 52,000 square miles, are Protectorates.

of the Peninsula and Archipelago. By the fifteenth century Malacca was a great market, in regular diplomatic relations with the Emperors in China: from Nanking came gifts of silk with golden flowers and curtains of gold and recognizances, and to Nanking travelled the King of Malacca to pay tribute.

The city grew behind its wooden stockades. Its prince turned Moslem and presently began to call himself an Emperor and the Shadow of God upon Earth. He too discovered that he was descended from Alexander the Great, King of Rome (the local historians were a trifle confused), from Darius the Persian, Artaxerxes and even (as Malacca grew great) from Kaiomerz, the son of Adam. Most of the present princes of Malaya share his distinguished descent. I too, I trust, am a child of Adam.

In 1509, five Portuguese ships arrived off Malacca, seeking peaceful trade. They found the régime debauched, the Sultan sodden in his harem, the city become a centre of notorious racketeers. A party put ashore, under Ruy de Aranjo, to negotiate a treaty, was treacherously seized. The rest, too few to recover their comrades or even to hold their ships in face of the assault that threatened, put to sea. Their news, in time, reached Goa.

At Goa that year Affonso de Albuquerque had become the second Viceroy of the Indies. It was twelve years since da Gama had turned Good Hope. The energy and speed of the Portuguese expansion is almost incredible. Albuquerque in 1509 was already an old man for his times: in his late fifties or early sixties. He was to die in 1515. At his death, Portugal was suzerain of a maritime empire which extended in the Orient from the Red Sea to the Spice Islands above Australia: and she had broken the power of Islam.

The Portuguese, unlike the Spaniards, were a trading people; but they were also a crusading people. Their little kingdom had been hammered out in the defence of the Christian frontier; their men had been steeled in those long wars. When they came East they sought spices. But their prime object was to turn the flank of Mahomet's vast dominion and to cut the lines of supply which fed the Moslem powers of the Mediterranean littoral.

Constantinople had passed to the Turks within a year of Albuquerque's birth.[3] All his life was lived in the shadow of the peril. He died two generations before Lepanto. But at Lepanto his great ghost must have stood with Don John in the galleys. For he had made Lepanto possible when he slashed the main commercial artery of Islam.

The Portuguese were, amongst Europeans, the first world strategists; and Albuquerque was their master strategist. The plan was executed with superlative mastery of the arts of war and of diplomacy. It was at once simple and gigantic: to take command of the Indian Seas; to cut the traffic at its junctions in the Red Sea; and to control its sources in the merchant cities of the Indies. Ormuz at the gate of the Red Sea was one point of control. Malacca, the market of the Spice Islands, was the other. Between was needed a base. In 1510 Albuquerque seized Goa. In 1511 he postponed his expedition against Ormuz and moved on Malacca. Ruy de Aranjo was his friend; and Albuquerque did not leave his people prisoners of the Infidel.

Albuquerque was a great soldier turned great sailor. He understood the nature of sea power. He sought territorial dominion only for the bases of sea power. With an old soldier's touch of sentiment, he liked to call his seamen cavaliers. But he held them to the ships. He had the supreme virtue of conquerors, without which they are destroyed in the end. In arms he had the ruthless energy of

[3] He was born probably in 1452, at Lisbon.

MALAY

"Better a rain of spears in one's own place . . ."—Page 410

Dept. of Information, Malaya

MALAYAN TYPES: A TAMIL, A MALAY BOY

"The Malay himself has contributed little   ." —Page 195

the masters of war; but he knew that it is wiser to make
friends than slaves, and that victories are better won by
negotiations than battles. He made Portugal the first of
trading nations, for he diverted the Eastern traffic from
the Arabs to his ships. But the control of that traffic was
always only a means to the security of Christendom.

His dominion grew more by treaty than by force. Kings
sought his friendship, and he made the Indian Ocean the
most peaceful of all seas. Albuquerque knew that the interest of a merchant people is peace; that peace is the first
purpose of sea power.

In the last year of his life he came, an old man tired
and dying, to Ormuz. Princes, chiefs, and tribesmen travelled from the interior of Arabia and Persia to look once
at him. The Shah sent painters to make a portrait of the
greatest man of his time. Albuquerque turned his ship
eastward again, hoping to die in the Goa that he had conquered and loved. His flagship reached the bar of the
harbour as he lay dying on the deck. He ordered his pilot
to anchor. He recited with his friars the Passion according to St. John. He commanded them to dress him in the
habit of the Order of Sanctiago whereof he was Com-
mendador. On the Sunday, one hour before the morning,
he rendered up his soul to God, and there finished all
his troubles without seeing any satisfaction of them. . . .

"He was a man of the strictest veracity, and so pure in
the justice he administered that the Hindoos and Moors
after his death, whenever they received any affront from
the governors of India used to go to Goa to his tomb, and
make offerings of choice flowers, praying him to do them
justice." [4]

Not every conqueror has such a requiem. He was a great

[4] Commentaries of Afonso Dalboquerque, second Viceroy
of India. Vol. IV. Translated from the Portuguese by Walter
De Gray Birch. The Hakluyt Society, London, 1875.

man and an image of much that is gone from our civilization.

He came to Malacca in February of 1511. As was his custom, he sought to settle the differences and to recover his countrymen by negotiation. The talks dragged on through weeks and months, while the Sultan's ministers strengthened the defences and brought in alien mercenaries. Albuquerque held his hand as long as he dared. But on July 25, the feast day of St. James, Patron of Portugal and the Order, he struck; and after a desperate and bloody action by the bridge he took the town.

He built a fort which was called A Famosa, the Famous, on the site of the burnt wooden palace of the Sultan. He paid the natives the equivalent of $20 for a hundred stones, and 2½ cents each for eggs used in the mortar, and 50 cents for a day's labour.

Portuguese Malacca was a city containing a fortress and surrounded by a wall twenty feet high, with bastions, parapets, breastworks, and 41 pieces of bronze artillery. About the city lived the married Europeans, perhaps three or four hundred families. Christian Malays lived in surrounding kampongs and were trained to arms. The colonists had gardens, orchards, and farms for many miles up the river.[5]

The five-storeyed fort was provisioned against siege. But for most of their time, the Portuguese lived at peace with their neighbour, the Sultan of Johore and Pahang; which perhaps was as well, for he could put 12,000 men in the field, with artillery, muskets, spears, swords, bows and

[5] The city proper was chiefly occupied by the Convents of St. Paul, St. Dominic, and St. Augustine. St. Paul's stood (and still stands, in ruin) at the top of the hill. It was Albuquerque's first church, and when Xavier came, the Jesuits there built a school. The Cathedral of the Misericordia stood at the foot of the hill. The Bishop reigned over thirteen churches, three hermitages, and two hospitals.

blowpipes (the poisoned darts are called "anak sumpitan," the blowpipe's child).

The place was plagued by crocodiles and by jungle people in the shape of tigers, who walked the roads and ate the local ladies until the good Bishop Dom Georges de Santa Lucia (whose merits, as the Chronicler says, should always be exalted) excommunicated them by bell, book, and candle, to the admiration and subsequent conversion of many Malays and Indian Klings.

From the interior Malacca drew eaglewood, and japanwood for dyes, porcupine quills and betel nuts. It traded with Patane, a land long governed by women, selling stuffs of Cambay and Coromandel for gold, rice, meat, melons, sugar, oils, and fowl. From Cambodia the ships brought angely wood, resins, and oil-benjamin. In Champa they traded the black cattle of China and gold thread for blackwood rarer than that of Mozambique. Malacca was, as Camoens said, "a market grand and opulent." Its ships went to Japan and Timor, to the Persian Gulf, to Brazil, and home to Lisbon.

PATHS OF GLORY

Malacca, the Cape, and Goa were the hinges of the Empire of the East: and by the Cape and Goa there came to Malacca, in 1545, the second supreme figure of the Portuguese years. He was a man burning with an ambition that would not let him rest, a passion that sent him out to the ends of the earth, to run, like St. Paul, with good tidings.

Francis Xavier was a young professor of the University of Paris and the *beau monde* when he met the strange, intense Ignatius Loyola, the soldier turned saint, and with him founded the Society of Jesus. Loyola sent him, in 1540, to Goa, for the conversion of the Indies. Xavier preached and taught, but his asceticism was the best sermon in an India which understood poverty and to rulers wrapt in Babylonian luxuries. Xavier hammered at his own people. He built schools, he founded a college and a seminary for an Indian clergy, he taught the peasants and the fishermen, fought the avarice of local officers, and made enemies, as saints commonly do, whose protest is against the world. He grappled with whirlwinds. His life was haunted by a sense of defeat; but defeat he never accepted. He drove always on into new efforts and to prodigious campaigns. In 1545 he was at Malacca, nursing at the Fever Hospital and teaching in Portuguese and Malay. He went to found the missions in the distant Moluccas. In 1547, back in Malacca, he met a Japanese student earnestly (as one would expect) taking notes of his teachings; and in 1549 he was in Japan. He lived and worked there two years, learning the language, writing a Catechism in Japanese, and reluctantly going in silks, to meet the local proprieties. He introduced the Japanese to clocks and eyeglasses, and he made converts who were to stand steadfast in the persecutions to come. And there he heard constantly of the cultural life of China, to which Japan long looked as Europe looked to Greece and Rome. Xavier resolved on the conversion of China.

He returned to the Indies to order the affairs of the Indian Province of the Society; and in July, 1552, he sailed again from Malacca for the conquest of China. His one companion was a Chinese boy. He landed in the delta lands by Canton; and there, waiting in a miserable hut beside the shore for some opportunity to enter the Forbidden Kingdom, he took fever and died.

His Chinese boy dressed him in his sacerdotal vestments. A Portuguese sailor helped to shape a rough coffin, and they buried their Saint under quicklime in the land of Sancian.

The body was recovered, and in March of 1553 it was brought again to Malacca. It is said that as the coffin was carried ashore a plague which had threatened to devastate the city ceased; and when the coffin was opened, the body was found incorrupt, only a little flushed, as if asleep. So it is said still to appear in Goa where it is sometimes exposed. It lay nine months in the Church of St. Paul of Malacca before it was again removed. The tablet now above the empty tomb was set there by an English Governor of Malaya, Weld, who himself had martyr ancestors.

If Europe had sent only Xaviers into Asia, preaching, teaching, with their hospitals and schools, we should have known another world. But there are few Xaviers; and our world must be much what we are ourselves, a strange mixture of good and evil. Your merely pious and humane man hopes too much of others; and the humanitarian often ends as the cynic. But the saint, who knows men better, expects of them less, and continues to work his good until the end. The saint, struggling with his own heart and conscience, knows the confusion and the struggle of all humanity. He strives in humility. The man who believes the world perfectible is a man who believes himself perfectible; and such a man has not yet met himself.

The course of history is not all black or white any more than the course of one man's life and conscience. With imperialism, Portuguese and Dutch and English, came great evil but also great good. The societies of the East were gone to cruel confusion. They left myriads in a dulled, darkened life of ignorance and want. On the thrones of the East there were tyrants. In the depths were savagery and blighting superstition. The impact of the West was violent and sometimes cruel. But it opened Forbidden Kingdoms of the mind and spirit and brought new possibilities of life to multitudes in Asia. There is something to be said for the European. But nowhere more than by the empty tomb on the hill of Malacca.

About those broken walls are other graves and stones: there is Peter of the Society of Jesus, the second Bishop of Japan, who died in the Straits of Singapore in February, 1598; and Dom Miguel de Castro, son of a great Viceroy; Antonio Pinto de Fonseca, Commander of the Order of St. James, Captain-General of the Sea and Land in the Parts of the South; and the beloved wife of the noble Heer Pieter Rooselaar, Councillor-Extraordinary of India, Governor of the Town and Fort of Malacca. There lies Theodorus van de Kerckhoven, "in his life his father's and his mother's joy and loved his brother dearly; one year less three days was this sweet plant when God took soul from body; and often after his burial people asked for him." And about him lie the Doms, the merchants, the factors, the shipmasters, freemen, and Governors, their wives and children, Portuguese, Dutch, English: the trumpets silent, the banners dust.

The Dutch, who had been long whittling at the declining realm of Portugal, laid (after some vain attempts) successful siege to Malacca in 1640. With their own fleet and 40 sail of the Sultan of Johore they blockaded it for seven months; but no assault succeeded until the population was reduced from 20,000 to 3000 and most of the city was in ruin.

Malacca remained Dutch until the nineteenth century and slowly declined; for the roadstead was silting, and the Dutch wanted the place less for its own sake than to cripple the Portuguese and to reduce a competitor of their own established ports. But it has more of the flavour of the old Dutch times than any place in the Indies. You can walk there, as you no longer can in Batavia or Bantam, through streets of old Dutch houses. The Stadthuys still stands, built of Portuguese materials and perhaps by

Portuguese workmen immediately after the capture; and
the Gatehouse is from 1678. The Dutch built massively
their fort and harbour works, mounting their demi-can-
nons, culverins, clocksgewijs, grenades, and the great gun
they called "The Dog": and there they lived, the Governor, the Chief Merchant, the Preacher, Surgeons, Junior Merchants, Captains and Ensigns, Gunners, Clerks,
Master Coopers, Gunpowder Makers, Journeymen, Bookbinders, Executioner, Midwife, Quartermasters, Provosts,
Trumpeters, Sailmakers, Gaolers, and the Governor's Life
Guard, Cooks, Chamberlains, Gatekeepers, Beadles, Sex-
tons, Schoolmasters, Customsmen; horse soldiers, sailors,
craftsmen. Their Malacca squadron watched the northern
approach to the Indies. A few score burghers lived and
traded there. Life must been strange enough for the young
wives from Delft and Rotterdam and Utrecht.

Malacca shipped out, as Dampier noticed, Malacca
walking-canes; and it had its troubles with the neighbouring States. Most of the hills about are crowned with forts
or watch-houses. But its tide ran more and more slowly
until 1795, when the British occupied the town as part of
their precautions against Napoleon, then planning an advance on Egypt and India.

In 1807, the English East India Company, bored with
the place, proposed to demolish its defences and leave it
to the Dutch. They had actually blown out the fortress
walls when young Mr. Stamford Raffles made protest and
persuaded the Government of India to retain the post. In
1811 it served as base for the expedition to Java. Minto
and Auchtermuty assembled their army and stores on the
levels north of the town. Abdulla, Raffles' Malay secretary, was very taken by the tiger skins of the British cavalry
and by the feathers dyed red, white, and black of the Staff
Officers: but he thought less of some Indian regiments

who "tied three strands of thread around their bellies before they ate nor did they stop eating till the thread was broken." [6]

SURVIVORS

In Malacca, one evening when the sunset was spread like a royal umbrella, we climbed the eastward hill to the outer fort of St. John. Up those sharp slopes toiled for centuries the armoured men to watch the land approaches for raiding Bugis and the forces of Johore. There, by what Dampier called "the Backsides of the Town," came the Dutch attack in 1640. There too, through the century before, all Malaccans used to come to Mass for the Patronal Feast of St. John: all those multi-coloured Christians, men of Lisbon, Canton, Coimbre, Goa, Calicut. Changkow and Java, coiling in slow processions from their various parishes, with bells and banners and candles. The whole countryside and the kampongs of the races who traded there were Christian when Gardinho de Eredia saw the place early in the seventeenth century. The Dutch put an end to the candles and the banners and to St. Thomas's in Kampong Kling and to Our Lady of Pity beyond the Guardhouse and to St. Francis in Bukit China. But they could not put an end to the Portuguese, who ironically survive them here.

We went down from St. John's Hill through palms where cooking fires burnt brightly: and the moon came up from behind the Malayan Ophir to light the gravelled

[6] In 1818 Britain re-delivered Malacca to the Dutch with the rest of their possessions in the East; but in 1824 it was exchanged again for Bencoolen in Sumatra, and the Peninsula was recognized as the British sphere of influence while Britain withdrew all claims in the Archipelago. In the century since, Malacca, for all its exotic background, has become astonishingly reminiscent of Lyme Regis or of Budleigh Salterton.

ways to a village by the sea, a place of neat little cottages
that Government lately built for the fishing people who
live there, the descendants of the Doms.

The dark men and the women in white dresses sit at
their doors in the evening or in their little parlours (where
there are coloured prints and plaster statues of saints as
recent as Teresa of Lisieux), and they bear the great names
of Portugal. There you might find a de Brito and Gon-
calvez, Ferreira and de Souza, perhaps even a da Gama
or a João de Castro: the names of the Governors and the
Captains that once clanged through the world.

The Portuguese of Malacca must be the oldest single
European community in the East. They have retained
their identity, their language, their religion: although
their blood is mixed and their language influenced by
Malay. Some have played considerable parts in the later
history of Malaya. You meet them now at Singapore in
the professions and in business.

The Malacca Chinese also are such an enduring community. They were there before the Portuguese, before
the Hindu Klings, before the Malay Sultans. From their
kampong by the river they have succeeded to the neighbouring Dutch houses as they succeed to so much else
that the European has made.

In the Street of the Heeren and the Jonkers Street hang
long Chinese lanterns and Chinese signs in red and gold
and black. Chinese children play solemnly on the Dutchmen's steps, and in wide rooms behind the colonial verandahs are fine Chinese drawings, lacquered furniture
and tapestries. The Chinese living here are mostly rich
Chinese: the Baba Chinese of the Straits. Some came perhaps when the ships of the T'ang Dynasty were finding
their way to Persia in the seventh century; some came
with the Ambassadors of the Mings bearing decrees and
poems on the Imperial tablets; or in years when the junks

from India gathered here to await, for the homeward voyage, the south wind which blows from the middle of the fifth month.

Their old village of Bukit China is now a vast burial ground. In its temples Chinese Malacca still remembers its dead. Dampier knew those of his day: "Some of them keep Tea-Houses, where for a Stiver, a man has near a Pint of Tea, and a little Porrenger of Sugar-candy. Others of them are Butchers . . . they will cut a Piece at one Place, and the like at another, either fat or lean as you would have it." They were always an accommodating people; and now some Baba Chinese are millionaires in Singapore, for it was they who opened and worked the tin mines. But however great a Malaccan Chinese grows, he still belongs to Malacca; and men in palaces still come home to the old Dutch houses of the Jonkers and the Heeren Streets.

The Baba looks upon Malaya as his native place, much as a descendant of the *Mayflower* now may properly regard himself as an American. They speak their own tongue, Baba Malay, which has become the business language of British Malaya. It includes many Chinese words and its idiom is Chinese, but it is mixed with a Malay vocabulary pronounced in Chinese fashion.

The Baba Chinese are the aristocracy of the huge Chinese colony in Malaya. They are faithful British subjects and have played a great part in the history of British Malaya: but they are conscious too of their cultural relations with China. They have created a Sino-Malayan culture with European affiliations; a new synthesis of great importance if the Malay, the Chinese and the European are here to live at peace.

Other colonial Powers may have done better than the British in matters of plumbing and prophylactics. But the great British merit in places like Malaya is the British sense that progress slowly broadens down. They know that Chinese, Malay, Tamil, and Englishmen must find the balance of a common social order by trial and error, by experience, and in slow passages of time. Such a society with its infinite variety of susceptibilities and traditions cannot risk the rude grasp of an enthusiastic planner. It must grow and the peoples merge by minute subtle changes, adaptations, adjustments of personal values, personal beliefs, racial habits. Government may train the sensitive plant but it cannot chop and change the stuff of a living society. The mixture of races and beliefs sets a tremendous problem in government. Yet the peace of British Malaya, sustained by a handful of Civil Servants, has been like the peace of our grandfathers' Sunday afternoons.

It is so yet in Malacca, or was until war again made this a great garrison town. When I think of Malacca, I think first, ridiculously, of something that I never saw: of great-aunts and grandmothers sitting at their bobbins weaving lace, as it might be in Honiton, and of Malay dandies strolling in the sun with lace collars and frills on their pants. I think too of Xavier and the Franciscans; of the Harbour Masters; of Johanna, wife to Heer Balthasar Bort, who died here at the pitiful sweet age of two months less than twenty-three years; of Cheng Hoon, Bright Clouds; and of an Australian soldier, long and lean like a young tree, the other day by the old stones of the river walk. And they seem to be all of one community; though so different, citizens of one imperial city. That is the thing that England has made; and the meaning of England in the Outer Marches.

F . M . S .

Singapore is the capital of the Straits Settlements. Its Governor is also High Commissioner of the Federated

States whose capital is at Kuala Lumpur. The Supreme Authority in each State is the Sultan or Ruler in State Council. The State Councils include the British Resident, Malay Chiefs and Officials, and Unofficial members who represent the racial groups: Malay, Chinese, Indian, and European.

The central States were federated in 1896. The general purpose was to improve the administration in backward States and to strengthen their resources. It was an astonishing success. The population of the F.M.S. was, before Federation, about 380,000. By 1938, it had passed 2,000,000. Federation was, in fact, almost too successful. Responsibility and power flowed into the hands of a brilliant Federal administration under the British Secretary. Government in recent years has reversed the process in some measure and by a programme of decentralization thrust responsibilities back upon the Native States: the Malays are being encouraged to preserve and strengthen their own political institutions. The principle has been constantly emphasized that Malaya is the country of the Malays, and that the first task of administration is to prepare the Malay for the new responsibilities of history.[7]

The general picture of Government may seem confused, but a uniform structure would have overridden the traditional native institutions, rights, and privileges.

[7] The British Advisers and Assistant Advisers, the Residents and the District Officers work with the traditional native authorities: the Ruler, his Council, the District and the Village Headmen and the Elders. All Malaya then, with the exception of the tiny Colony, remains under native régime; although the Malays are now actually outnumbered by the Chinese who in 1938 provided 2,220,244 of a population of 5,278,866. The Malays were 2,210,367; the Indians 743,555; the Europeans 28,211. The Straits Settlements had 1,357,854 people: a population which chiefly instances the human uses of the great entrepôt of Singapore.

As it is, the thing works; and it exemplifies the British sense that political systems should be designed for the human situation rather than to the specifications of some tidy social planner. I might reduce my acquaintance to what I think a proper symmetry with my chopper, if they did not obstinately perish in the process.

From Malacca you may head for Singapore by the coastal road with its estuaries and ferries, or work first north and east to Kuala Lumpur or Seremban and then down the main trunk road. The second gives a broad view of the country.

Negri Sembilan is peopled by Sakai, who are commonly taken to be the primitive forest dwellers, and by Menangkabaus, colonists from Sumatra in the days of their greatness. It is itself a federation of nine tribes established in 1773 under a Prince of Menangkabau recruited from the Sumatran royal line: a curious instance of the loyalty of Menangkabau to its blood and customs. The little Federation has a British Resident as Adviser to the Chiefs, who instal their prince, the Yam Tuan Besar, and are pretty much autonomous in their internal governments.

The Sakai, of course, are the little people whose weapon is the blowpipe and darts poisoned from the upas tree. They adopted the Australian Army during jungle manœuvres, and the Australians, who are of a curious and enquiring mind, picked up their tricks of the jungle. Six feet of sunbaked Australian and four feet of brown Sakai trotting by him make quite a spectacle.

We met, in the neighbourhood of Port Dickson, an Australian brigade largely composed of enormous young farmers from the Riverina districts of New South Wales. The Australian soldier has a reputation for toughness. In point of fact, he usually gets along extraordinarily well with the peoples amongst whom he serves. The Australian soldier is a citizen volunteer. He is well educated, usually with a good home behind him. His chief trouble, even in the tropics, is energy. He is always pushing his nose into things. The troops we met had two urgent demands: they wanted fruit cakes, like those that mother makes down in the Murray country, and lectures. The lectures startled us a bit. The troops wanted to know about the forest timbers, the agricultural possibilities, the history and habits of the Malays and of the Chinese. "After all," said one private, "if we're going to live amongst these people, we ought to know what makes them tick. And if we've got to fight in the jungles, the more we know about jungles the better." His particular unit had not a serious crime on its sheets, after months of heavy training in torrid country.

The citizen volunteer has not the parade-ground discipline of the regular [8] who serves through years of peace, which have their own problems of morale. The soldier in war needs battle discipline: that the Australian imposes on himself, grimly.

His Armies are educating the Australian. His influence upon imperial policies in the Eastern world should and must increase. He is meeting his neighbours and learning his geography; serving beside the Sikh, the Pathan, the Punjabi, and the Ghurka in Africa, the Near East, and the Far East: to the growth of a hefty mutual respect. The friendship and stability of India is a vital Australian interest; as the young men will know when they come home from the wars. Or so we took their meaning as

[8] The Australians began to arrive in Malaya early in 1941. As the first ships came alongside at Singapore, the troops tossed pennies to the native boys. Presently they began to toss them to the Governor of the Straits Settlements and the Commander-in-Chief, waiting to welcome them. Grinning, Sir Shenton Thomas and Air Chief Marshal Brooke-Popham picked them up. . . . Momentarily this episode, having been passed by the censor, is *ipso facto* "old stuff." It is here recorded for the benefit of posterity.

we talked under Gundong Ledang, the Malayan Ophir.

On this Ophir, behind Malacca, lives Queen Purti, the most beautiful of women. She is dressed in silk and cloth of gold, and she rests upon a bed of men's bones. Her caves are loud with music. She is guarded by tigers and the forest-dwelling Benuas, to whom she has taught all the virtues of herbs and those curious arts by which they change themselves into tigers, crocodiles, and lizards; though, since the good Bishop Dom Georges de Santa Lucia found it necessary to deal with them, no Benua turned tiger has harmed man, woman, or child. Nevertheless, Malays are reluctant to climb Purti's mountain (though she admits Englishmen to her domain, not expecting them to stay). She was once wooed by an enterprising Sultan of Malacca, but she required as a marriage settlement a golden bridge and a silver bridge from Malacca to her mountain top, a tub of tears, a basin of royal blood, and seven trays piled with the livers of mosquitoes: conditions which defeated His Highness.

"BETTER A RAIN OF SPEARS . . ."

We came into the F.M.S. at Lubok China, where there is a Customs House, which chickens were busily undermining. The Malay official is almost as polite as the Malay peasant, who is as polite as the Malay raja. When people who know the Malay have finished swearing at their faults, chiefly of omission, they invariably add: "But, after all, the Malay is a gentleman." Even his vices are aristocratic. The Malay himself has contributed little to the development of Modern Malaya. Britain has provided peace, order, and technical skills; the Chinese and the Tamils brought labour, energy, and their commercial talents. The Malay seems to have been originally a naked man of the beaches and riverways. Everything that he has, weapons, utensils, clothes, are of Chinese, Indian, Arab or European origin. Even the creese (which Government now forbids him to carry) is probably from South India.

At Seremban, in the park before the Rest House, tulip trees droop over little lakes that were once tin mines. Tin has been worked here immemorially, but the Chinese of Malacca began extensive mining in the eighteenth century. Tin has been the foundation of the great Chinese fortunes. The Chinese own most of the tin mines and a great many of the rubber estates.

The Chinese are actors, artists, musicians, clerks, chemists, cashiers, architects, doctors, surveyors, butchers, hawkers, keepers of eating houses and lodging houses, ferrymen, merchants, pawnbrokers, servants, planters, bricklayers, market gardeners, chandlers, shopkeepers, tailors, coopers, engineers, basket makers, miners, soap boilers, undertakers, fortune tellers, smiths, painters, printers, water carriers, ricksha boys, wood carvers, gangsters, carpenters, cabinet makers, boatmen, bookbinders, trades-union secretaries, millionaires.

Apart from the Chinese established in Malaya, there has been an enormous flow in and out of Chinese labour. Between 1929 and 1938, 465,000 arrived and 434,000 went home. The migrants are mostly employed in tin or rubber and retire to their native villages with their savings. The great Chinese expansion in Malaya followed the extension of British order to the Native States. Malaya gave the immigrant opportunities he could not know at home and he has made the most of them.

The Chinese strength, besides their capacity for work, is in their genius for combination. The Chinese family and clan amount to a co-operative enterprise, and the social structure is endlessly developed in guilds and associations, public and secret: agricultural, trading, benefit, burial societies, pirates' leagues and pickpockets' unions. Organ-

BRITISH, AUSTRALIANS, CHINESE

"The Army of the Far East is the Commonwealth itself."—Page 421

Dept. of Information, Malaya

SIKH AND MALAY AT SINGAPORE

"Who serve where they have eaten salt, who keep their allegiance and are soldiers. . . ." — Page 422

izations survive through centuries, The Triad (Thian Tai
Hué), long active in Malaya and with a ritual symbolically
represented in the Willow Pattern, goes back two thousand
years. Its objective was long the overthrow of the Manchus.
Under the Republic it became again chiefly a Benefit
Society; but some of its Lodges were perverted by gangsters
and racketeers, as secret societies often are. In Malaya,
lodges fought one another and, on occasion, the Kongsis,
the traditional Benefit Societies of the Chinese Provinces.
If a man belonged to both the Triad and his Provincial
Society, he often found himself at war with himself: presumably he fought for one on Monday, the other on Tues-
day. For decades, street battles were frequent in Singapore,
though they were politely interrupted when a European
passed.

Cavanagh, who was Governor of the Straits in the
middle of the last century, used to swear in lodge masters
as special constables whenever trouble broke. After a few
hours of trudging the streets, these plump Chinese gentlemen usually called the riot off. The Societies had a powerful political influence. When they objected to some public
measure, they sometimes made protest by closing up their
shops and assaulting one another *pro bono publico;* a technique difficult for the police to tackle. During the nineteenth century, however, both Dutch and British officials
were learning more and more about the organization and
traditions of the Chinese groups. In 1877 a Chinese Protector, W. H. Pickering, was appointed in Singapore. He
spoke the dialects and understood the people and the problems, and he made it his affair to explain and interpret
Government policy and regulation. He often attended
meetings of the Lodges, and he acquired such credit
amongst the Chinese that they still call the Protector's
Office in Singapore Pek-ki-lin, which is as close as a Chinese tongue can get to Pickering.

Singapore had troubles prompted by political agitators during the years of civil disorder in China, when refugees poured south and many brawlers, political and otherwise, came with them. But, taken over all, the Chinese of the Straits are admirable citizens and faithful to the British connection. Their ties with China have been strengthened in the travail of the Japanese Incident. The Republic now looks out to the Chinese overseas. It draws resources from them and renews the bonds. China is being hammered into a national community; the Chinese have a new political and national consciousness. The future of the Far East probably belongs to China; and the Straits Chinese may have a great rôle to play as a bridge between two worlds.

More than three-fifths of Malaya is still forest country. There has been more than enough room for both planters and peasants: there still is room for great developments. But Government believes that these must now largely wait on the Malays and the long-term programme of strengthening native institutions and morale. If the country were thrown open to unrestricted immigration, the Malay would be swamped. The British prefer, in the Malay interest, to keep something like the present balance of population: although Malaya might have been a great outlet for masses of the Indian peasantry.[9]

The Government must make itself understood in sixty or seventy tongues and to every variety of religious and moral persuasion, and at every level of culture from the naked jungle primitives to Chinese, Hindu, and Arabian scholars. The armed forces normally maintained are very

---

[9] There are three-quarters of a million Indians now in Malaya. The women's bright saris seem everywhere in the Rubber Lines and along the country roads. The labourers are chiefly Southern Indians, who are here called Klings (from the old kingdom of Kalinga on the Coromandel Coast) : Tamils and Telugus. The Tamil labourer seldom stays more than a few

small and rarely used to support the Civil Power, and then much in the rôle of the National Guard in the United States. The police forces consist of a handful of Europeans, Chinese, Indians and Malays. Government rests, in fact, upon moral prestige and popular assents.

The Malay is a traditionalist. He accepts with little question still the hierarchic order of society: rayat, penghulu, raja: peasant, headman, and the Blood. He does not lack courage, but he has accepted centuries of privation and tyranny with a fatalistic sense that such was the order of things. Yet he is intelligent, quick, and curious. He is extraordinarily sensitive to suggestion: the curious phenomenon known as "latah," a sort of trance which seems peculiar to the Malays, is induced by suggestion. A Malay amok, too, is commonly one whose finer sensibilities and self-respect have been affronted.

He has a reputation for thriftlessness and none for industry (if a Malay has land which might bring him, by his own labour, 500 Straits dollars a year, he will cheerfully rent it to a Chinese for 300 dollars, and go sit in the shade). But through his history his goods and his crops and his women have been at the mercy of little local tyrants. In his new security, he begins to develop the pedestrian virtues. Passing into territories which have been for a generation or more under British direction, you immediately notice the rising prosperity of the countryside. The Malay will work, like the rest of us, for to-morrow, when he is reasonably sure that to-morrow will not bring pillage and rapine.

years in Malaya, unless he turns shopkeeper or moneylender. The moneylending "chetty" was gradually acquiring the Malayan peasants' lands until Government declared wide territories in which only the Malay may own the soil. From northern India come a smaller proportion of Punjabis, Bengalis, Afghans, Pathans. Sikhs and Moslem Jats came to join the old Malay States Guides, and with the garrison regiments. They are now mostly policemen, watchmen, bullock drivers.

But, even in the teeth of oppression, he clings to his native earth. "Better a rain of spears in one's own place than a shower of gold abroad."

SINGAPORE

On January 31, 1819, Thomas Stamford Raffles addressed a letter. "Here I am," he wrote, "at Singapore, true to my word and in the enjoyment of all the pleasure which a footing on such classic ground must inspire." He had won his way at last: Britain was in command of a route to China which would not depend upon the favour of the Dutchmen, and which she could adequately police. All through Raffles' service he had argued for such a post: from Penang, Malacca, Batavia, and Bencoolen. Now, at the end, he had the grudging assent of the Honourable East India Company to found a fort and port.

His eye had been on the islands of Rhio south of Singapore. The Dutch moved in ahead of him. He turned to Johore. The succession there was in dispute. Raffles gave aid and comfort to the elder son of the late Sultan; and at his accession the new Sultan leased, by treaty, the little island of Singapore for a yearly rental to the British.

The Dutch protested powerfully. They insisted that Singapore and the Straits generally were within their sphere of influence and that Raffles was intruding. The British Government at home almost gave way, but left the final decision to the Governor-General in India. He had heard Raffles. He listened again. The Dutch were not and never had been in occupation. The affair concerned the Company and Johore. Raffles dug in his heels; and the English stayed.

If the Dutch had agreed, Raffles would have preferred the Rhio (Riow) Archipelago whose first islands are visible from Singapore where the Dutch Line comes almost into the great harbour. But Singapore remains, as Raffles said, "his child": and the selection of the site reveals astonishing prescience. The Suez Canal was to divert almost all east-bound shipping through the Straits. Singapore opens to the China Seas. The little island itself has a wide sheltered roadstead and, between it and Johore, the narrow water-way which now contains the Base. Raffles knew very well what he was about. In June, 1819, he observed: "What Malta is in the West, that may Singapore become in the East." Already 5000 people had gathered at the new post, amongst the mounds and earthworks of the ancient colony of Criwijaja. [10]

Singapore was essential to the expansion of world com-merce: it was essential also to the opening and develop-ment of Malaya. It represented free trade and traffic with all peoples; is a representative city of the new world econ-omy which it was created to serve. Its normal export to the United States, for instance, is roughly double its export to Great Britain. The United States, in effect, shares the economic dominion of the British and Dutch in the Far East. Economic empire does not always carry the burden of political responsibility; but every great modern State is an economic imperialist, and every automobile on tyres is a subscriber to the structure.

The island is 25 miles long and up to 14 miles across. The city is on its south coast, facing the Roadstead and the main Strait. If you come in from the west by the Straits of Malacca you approach through a maze of islands behind which is tucked Keppel Harbour. Once, flying out of Sing-apore, I began to count islands: but I was utterly defeated.

The Base is on the opposite side of the island, tucked in the water alley of the Straits of Johore. You might spend

[10] Five years later the population was 10,000. In 1840 it was 39,000; in 1850, 59,000; in 1941, 750,000. In 1824, 35,000 tons of shipping used the port; in 1938, 15,000,000.

years in Singapore and see nothing of the Base except, on rural jaunts, the new roads and rails that lead to it through the tangled scrub.

In 1824 the British and Dutch reached a comprehensive agreement; the British bought Singapore from Johore for a lump sum down and an annual payment to the Sultan; and Raffles went home. [11]

The great entrepôt lies about the curve of a slow bay from Kalan Basin and the new magnificent Civil Airport to the South Mile and the Yatch Club. Singapore is all things to all men. When the cricketers are at the nets in the green fields by St. Andrew's, it might be some quiet Wiltshire town on a baking July day. The cricketers are all in white, with various blazers, like the mixed bag of a village eleven: and you wonder whether you might wander round to the tent and find the familiar keg of beer. But the cricketers are probably Chinese and Malays. And the pleasant nineteenth-century Gothic of the Cathedral was built by Indian and Chinese convicts. The Chinese convicts were at first rather disturbed: they heard it rumoured that the Lord Bishop intended to bury thirty Chinese heads beneath the corner stone. A larger experience of the Anglican clergy reassured them. Much of the Government building, including Government House in its wide sweeps of lawns, was convict work. There was some competition for the draft amongst the Indian Thugs, for the convicts were allowed a good deal of freedom in those spacious days and most had married and settled down in Singapore before their time was up.

The business centre of the city is Raffles' Place, with the banks and their Sikh Guards, the bookshops, the insurance

[11] To meet less than little gratitude from the Honourable Company: and to found, with Humphry Davy, the Royal Zoological Society, and the Zoo at Regent's Park. Raffles died in 1826.

houses and cool arcades leading out to the Esplanade. Behind it begins the fantastic Chinese town, with its temples
and its tailors, carpenters and eating houses, and all the
tribes and clans of Fo-kien, Kuan-tung, Kuang-si, Hainan,
and Teo-chiu: Hokkiens, Cantonese, Khehs, Hailams. The
streets here take Chinese names: Anson Road becomes Old
Idol Street, and Bain Court the Water Fairy Gate Stables
Lane Within (North Bridge Road being the Water Fairy
Gate and Bain Court a cul-de-sac). The Police Office is
Chief Big Dog's Office; as a policeman is a dog, an impor-
tant policeman must politely be, of course, a big dog.
Alexander Road is Within the Water Rice Mill, and the
Railway Station is Fire-Carriage Head.

You can, with a little trouble, make acquaintance with
almost all varieties of mankind in Singapore: monks from
Tibet, desert Arabs, negro seamen, English curates, White
Russians, Mongols, Japanese acrobats, and lecturers gather-
ing material for the circuit of the Women's Clubs. These
are commonly to be met in coveys at the Raffles or Seaview.
They compare notes over stengahs. They go to the New
World and the Happy World and the Great World: those
curious amusement parks where you may take pots at a
coconut shy or watch interminable Chinese plays or hear
Hamlet done in Malay or, if you are feeling especially
gloomy, dance at 10 cents a time with the taxi dancers,
who are quite the most wooden variety of dolls now mobile. There apparently was a day when Singapore was
giddy, and I suppose there is still the usual provision of
seaports for those who come in from the ships with a
month's wages to spend; but European society seems always
to have been staid and sober. It usually is in both the
Dutch and British East. Government has a cold eye for
flightiness where Government is much a matter of prestige.
In the old days the European ladies of Singapore had a
reputation for prudishness: it was once complained of

them that they would waltz and polka only with one another. But as the garrison officers were then turned out in tight red uniforms, gold braid, wiry whiskers and Macassar oil, the ladies were probably well advised, the climate being what it is, distinctly sticky.

The old bawdy days, if they ever were, are now gone with the snows of yesteryear and San Francisco's Gold Coast. But they live in the imaginations of the Older Inhabitants: and Things Are Not What They Were. The Chinese clerks go to night school and occasionally to the New, the Happy, or the Great. The general population usually prefers the talkies.

The structure of British defence in the Far East swings on three small islands: Penang, the old post of the East India Company at the top of the Malacca Straits and covering the eastern seaboard of Malaya; Singapore; and Hong Kong. That triangle covers the eastern approaches to India and Malaya, the northern approaches to the Netherlands Indies, Australia and New Zealand, the western approaches to the whole Pacific basin, including the Philippines and everything east to Hawaii, and the southern flank of China. Much more than the commercial interest of Britain is involved in the fate of that central strong position: with it goes, ultimately, the destiny of two-thirds of the world.

Until lately Hong Kong was the most formidable of the three bases and it remains a great fortress. The Singapore Base is, indirectly and in some part, the creation of American public opinion; for it was in deference to American opinion that Britain did not renew the alliance with Japan which had covered her Pacific and Eastern interests in 1914. Singapore became an elementary precaution in the absence of a close and certain friendship with Japan. But Singapore was not conceived only as a bulwark against Nippon. British strategists have never forgotten that Napo-

leon came close to command of the Middle East, and that
the British axis might one day be severed at Suez: when
Singapore would become the backstop of naval and air
forces designed to hold the Indian Seas and the communications of the Indian Ocean, with Colombo, the Indian
ports, and perhaps the western Australian coast as its
advanced positions. Singapore, for example, at present
covers the long line of communications that feeds supply
from San Francisco to Suez, and the Burma Road. The
whole range of American policy and commerce in Asia as
well as the supply of essential strategic materials is dependent now upon the fate of Singapore.

THE BASE

Singapore was one point the importance of which the
British recognized. The naval base was scheduled for
completion in 1939, but, in spite of a slowing off during
Mr. Ramsay Macdonald's first administration, the original
scheme was in being by 1935 and a further programme of
development was advanced. Singapore was designed pri-
marily as a naval and air base. The core of the naval programme is the great graving dock, 1000 feet long and 135
feet wide, with its yards, its adjacent quays, and its defences: all set in the marshy southern shore at about the
middle of the Straits of Johore. The narrow, winding
channel is netted, boomed, and mined. The coastal forts
with their great guns are miles advanced. It is inconceivable that the base could be reduced from the sea until the
outer works were silenced. That is going to be quite a job
for any man's navy. Companion to the King George
Graving Dock is an enormous floating dock which can lift
a ship of 50,000 tons. The docks are the heart and meaning of the naval base.

But a naval base, it must be remembered, is nothing

without ships. Singapore cannot steam about and join
battle. It makes possible the operation of a battle fleet in
Eastern seas, when a battle fleet is available. Without its
ships it can physically influence events only within the
range of its batteries: though the moral effects of Singapore have clearly been very great.

The air base is another matter. The Royal Air Force
has a huge establishment a little to the east of the Dock-
yards, and there has been continuous development of the
air defences since they were first projected as auxiliary to
the naval base. The original scheme was an £11,500,000
job. But in 1935 thousands of extra labourers were added
to the pay roll. The first appointment as Commander-in-
Chief, Far East, went not to a sailor or a soldier but to an
airman. The range of effective air operations is obviously
wide. The ring of outer fields extends northwestward to
Burma, southeastward to British Borneo and interlocks
with the system which the Dutch have developed from
Sumatra in the west through Borneo and the Celebes to
the Australian frontiers in the Timor Sea and in New
Guinea.

The British have much strengthened the line running
from Penang through Burma, as a counter to the Japanese
moves towards Thailand; and behind that potential front
the Dutch have been busy about Medan and in Acheen. [12]

The third phase of development at Singapore belongs to
the Army. The original scheme provided only for a suffi-

[12] Singapore is thus become the centre of a system whose
circumference reaches to the Philippines. But into the vital
northeastern arc a wedge has been driven by the Japanese
occupation of Indo-China with its air stations and the naval
position at Camranh. Camranh is a superb natural position,
almost equidistant from Hong Kong, Manila, and Singapore.
The French began to develop it in 1936-'37. Progress was
slow before the fall of France; but even with improvised equipment it is an advanced post of great potential importance.

cient covering force of garrison troops. But, as the purposes
and methods of Japan in Asia became more and more apparent, the problems of the land frontiers acquired new
weight.

In the north the Peninsula is pinched to the Isthmus of
Kra, and Malaya meets Thailand: and north again the
Thai frontier marches with Burma for hundreds of miles.
Burma is the southern gate to China; and beyond Burma
is India. British strategists have had to contemplate the
possibility of a drive from Indo-China across Thailand
against Burma and its Road, with a secondary offensive
designed to contain the British forces in Malaya. The
northern neck of Malaya, with its jungles and waterways,
is considered highly defensible, but the British in Malaya
could not be content with defensive action if Burma was
seriously threatened. It would make every effort to produce a counter-stroke, taking the enemy in the flank of
his westward march.

Until the last few years British and French influence
was dominant in Thailand. The old Siam had use for
something like thirty British and twenty French advisers.
British officers served the Siamese Government as Residents in Siam's Malay States for many years. American
influence was also strong from the beginning of this century. But in 1935 the King, who had strongly favoured
the traditional associations with the three democratic
Powers, abdicated; and Japanese diplomacy moved on
Bangkok in force. Japanese officials were attached to every
Government Department of consequence: War, Transport, Education, and so on. Cultural and commercial programmes and what is pleasantly known as "co-operation"
were pushed. Thailand was the one member-State of the
League of Nations which refused to approve the Lytton
Report on the Manchurian affair. And there was a lively
renewal of rumours about the Kra Canal.

A canal across Kra would link the Indian Seas directly with the South China Sea and save the trudge down the Straits and about by Singapore. Its cost would be enormous: economically, hardly worth the candle. But it would reduce Singapore, commercially, to a third-rate port.

The talk about Kra was probably promoted by Japan chiefly as a matter of "face," as counter-propaganda to the prestige-value of the new works at Singapore. But it emphasized Japan's increasing concern with the southeastern corner, and stimulated British thinking. Considerable preparations that have not been widely publicized were projected; and from Singapore spread a complex of military defences which extend throughout Malaya.

When the hour ripened, the garrison battalions proved the cadre of an Imperial Army; the expansion had been prepared.

FAR-EAST COMMAND

The Army of the Far East introduces a new passage in British history. No great force has ever before been maintained east of India. The mere fact that it is in being has had notable consequences. The first contingent of Australians which arrived in Malaya was the largest single force of white troops ever put ashore in the Far East, unless in the Spanish-American War. In regions where a few hundred Europeans, armed usually with walking sticks, have shaped and ordered and governed great dominions, the simultaneous arrival of many thousands of white soldiers made a decided impact on the Eastern imagination. At a distance it is difficult to convey the effect; but the news ran through Asia, and its sound was thunder. The notorious old Lion was baring its teeth and showing its claws.

For years there has been in Asia (as, indeed, elsewhere) a strong and sustained anti-British propaganda. It went, froth and dregs, down the drain on that day when the long Australian columns began to move up through Malaya.

The Army of the Far East is something more than a fighting force. It is a symbol; and Asia reads in symbols. It is a clear declaration that Britain still stands to her mission in the East; that she does not abandon what she has slowly wrought; that while the trusteeship is hers, she will keep trust. She has imposed an imperial order: but her order brought peace. She has made her profits; but she has brought prosperity unprecedented here in all the passages of time.

Singapore represents new life in Asia. Like all life, it bears the sins of men; but, like all life too, the promise of redemption. One can regret much that is gone: one can deplore much that has come. But this is the march of life. Singapore is a melting pot of custom and convention as well as of tongues and races. It is also a growing-point of consciousness in the Asia to be. It is a door knocked in an ancient and stale room; and through it blows the strong wind of change, to the remotest jungle villages. A long twilight of the mind and spirit lifts. The things to come will ripen both to good and evil; but there will be growth again.

Like all the great cities of commerce, Alexandria and Venice, it will sublimate old cultures. This was a frontier. It is now a centre. It is a solvent. It will produce new syntheses. It already presents both the problems and the promise of to-morrow.

This is the real significance of the imperial order. In long experience, the British and the Dutch have learnt to ease the inevitable strains and tensions of societies in transition. There has been, if you like, a period of exploitation, but it has passed into a period, inevitable, of tutelage. Through it a new era steadily emerges: an era in which the native peoples achieve political and economic maturity, responsibility, adulthood.

In British Malaya now the governing power provides for health and education: it has provided for minimum wages and minimum ages in industry, for workmen's compensation, for labour codes and factory laws. It has encouraged trade unionism, it is creating a native class of professional workers: doctors, lawyers, engineers. These are the symptoms of the new thing and its needs. One can regret that some are needs; but one cannot regret the evils that have been swept away.

The adventure requires of the subject peoples exercise of their minds and wills; and with the exercise, their subject-status is inevitably shed.

Within the British Commonwealth the progress may be seen at every stage, from the autonomy of the Dominions now politically mature to the paternalism still necessary for the protection of the primitives. It is concerned with people at every level of development. Those are stupid and unfair who expect that the Commonwealth should immediately and everywhere present the level of democratic responsibility achieved in Jersey City. Justly, it should be seen as a system of order in which the various peoples have first the protection of the law, [13] and in which

[13] The phase defined by Raffles in his Proclamation of 1823:
"Let the principles of British law be applied not only with mildness, but with a patriarchal kindness and indulgent consideration for the prejudices of each tribe as far as natural justice will allow, but also with reference to their reasoning powers, however weak, and that moral principle which, however often disregarded, still exists in the consciences of all men.

"Let all the native institutions, as far as regards religious ceremonies, marriage, and inheritances, be respected when they may not be inconsistent with justice and humanity and injurious to the peace and morals of society.

"Let all men be considered equal in the eye of the law."

they may find their way to political and social responsibility.

Amongst the advanced peoples of India, unity and a broad liberal order became possible as the divisions of races, castes, and creeds are subdued to the common interest. In the flux which followed the meeting of the East and West ideas and values new to India spread. She seeks to integrate them with her own great traditions, They must work through the mind and will of India, modifying cultures and social structures. India, Burma, Malaya can hardly be democratic in the sense of Omaha until Indians, Burmese, and Malays are themselves informed and moved by the democratic idea. In spite of all the advances of modern science, no one has yet made an omelette without eggs.

Democracy is not a piece of mechanism, but a philosophy which works first in the mind and through the will of men to its visible expression in a way of life and institutions. It needs time. It needs opportunity. It needs order. Whatever may be said against the British system, it has given opportunity and order. Of time, no man is master.

"BOUNDS OF THEIR HABITATION"

The British Armies of the East are a symbol, also, of that order. To the Army of the Nile came representatives of all peoples who would be free: Poles, French, Greeks, Slavs, Dutch, Czechs, Belgians. The Army of the Far East is the Commonwealth itself. Never before have armies so various been gathered. Even Rome, which gave law and laid the foundations of the Western world, which civilized to the Danube and the Irish Sea, lacked what is to me the splendour of these legions. Paul, who was a Jew, saw the evils of Rome and flinched to the Roman whip and died by a Roman axe: but Paul could still cry proudly in appeal that he was a citizen of Rome. He knew that there must be law, and the security of the frontiers, and the peace of little houses. He knew that there must be room under the law for men to work out their destinies according to the conscience and the talents that are theirs. Caesar might be capricious, but over all was the reign of law. Paul resisted with all his soul the tyranny of the world; but he accepted the *imperium*.

And, though it killed him, it gave opportunity to his mission. The Christian gospel sped on the ships and roads of Rome.

In Singapore, I talked long with a Hindu officer. He had all this in mind. He had volunteered a year before to serve the British Raj: "Not," he said, "to keep a couple of thousand Civil Servants in their jobs in India, but to save for India the opportunity to be India." He used the words that have so often recurred to me in the passage of this book. "We've worked out an order, a kind of frame, which gives the chance to move and to grow. That's why I find myself, to my own astonishment, with a commission from King George VI. I guess," he said (he had been talking all the afternoon with American correspondents), "I guess you might call it a commission of the peace. Our peace as well as yours."

The Army of the Far East is an army of volunteers, a muster of peoples who have lived under the law. It has Sikhs, Pathans, Punjabis, fighting peoples who serve where they have eaten salt, who keep their allegiance and are soldiers because they have been free. It has Chinese of the Straits, and Malays whose loyalty to soil and custom is now enlarged in a great membership. It has regiments from English Counties that gave crews to Lancaster and Middleton, and yeomen to Massachusetts, Virginia, and New Zealand; Scots and Irish who have stood at odds with

England but whose Empire this is also, with its merits and its faults; and Australians, who are bred of all three.

Look back over the course that this book has taken: back to the first phase of English Empire on the Atlantic coasts, and to the American Empire which spread across a continent while this went overseas. The expansion has been more than an affair of trade and traffic and the clang of arms; it has belonged also to the moral intelligence. From New York to Sydney and from Sydney to Singapore, there is now one common character. It is in the American, the Dutch, and the British, it appears in the Indian, the Chinese, the Malay: it is that which struck off the ancient shackles and gives his final dignity to man. Some have bought freedom with a great sum; but these are now free born.

Acknowledging . . .

IN THE course of this book I have incurred many happy obligations; its merit, to me, is the range of acquaintance of which it was occasion.

For photographs I am grateful to His Highness the Tungko Temenggong Ahmad of Johore, to the Australian Department of Information and the New Zealand Government, to the Regeeringspubliciteitsdienst and to the K.P.M. at Batavia, to the Department of Information, Malaya, and to Qantas-Empire Airways.

I have special debts to the Australian Minister for Information; to the Director of Information at Singapore; to T. Elink Schuurman, the Netherlands Minister to Australia; to J. H. Ritman of the Regeeringspubliciteitsdienst at Batavia; to J. H. Admiraal of Batavia, to Mr. and Mrs. Meindersma, Mr. and Mrs. Kruys-Kolkmeyer, and Th. O. Thyssen of Sumatra; to F. H. Chasen, of the Raffles Library and Museum at Singapore; to David Waite of the *Singapore Free Press;* to David W. Bailey, Director of the Australian News and Information Bureau, New York City; to Dr. N. A. C. Slotemaker de Bruine, Director of the Netherlands Information Bureau, New York City; and to many Officers, Australian, Dutch, and British, who have been patient beyond all reasonable expectations and unfailingly kind to one who must often have been a considerable darned nuisance.

426   *Acknowledging . . .*

I salute, too, Maheen and Ahmad, Adok and Ismail:

Betty Arnott, who unscrambled the script and drew me maps:

And my wife, who with indescribable fortitude has read the whole thing through.

P. M.

Index

427

Index

Index 431